Authors & Artists for Young Adults

ISSN 1040-5682

Authors & Artists for Young Adults

VOLUME 63

THOMSON

GALE

Detroit • New York • San Francisco • San Diego • New Haven, Conn. • Waterville, Maine • London • Munich

Authors and Artists for Young Adults, Volume 63

Project Editor
Dwayne D. Hayes

Editorial
Katy Balcer, Jennifer Greve, Joshua Kondek

Permissions
Margaret Chamberlain-Gaston

Imaging and Multimedia
Dean Dauphinais, Leitha Etheridge-Sims, Lezlie Light, Michael Logusz, Dan Newell, Christine O'Bryan, Kelly A. Quin, Denay Wilding, Robyn Young

Composition and Electronic Capture
Carolyn Roney

Manufacturing
Rhonda Williams

LIBRARY OF CONGRESS CATALOG CARD NUMBER 89-641100

ISBN 0-7876-6651-3
ISSN 1040-5682

Contents

Introduction

Authors and Artists for Young Adults is a reference series designed to serve the needs of middle school, junior high, and high school students interested in creative artists. Originally inspired by the need to bridge the gap between Gale's *Something about the Author,* created for children, and *Contemporary Authors,* intended for older students and adults, *Authors and Artists for Young Adults* has been expanded to cover not only an international scope of authors, but also a wide variety of other artists.

Although the emphasis of the series remains on the writer for young adults, we recognize that these readers have diverse interests covering a wide range of reading levels. The series therefore contains not only those creative artists who are of high interest to young adults, including cartoonists, photographers, music composers, bestselling authors of adult novels, media directors, producers, and performers, but also literary and artistic figures studied in academic curricula, such as influential novelists, playwrights, poets, and painters. The goal of *Authors and Artists for Young Adults* is to present this great diversity of creative artists in a format that is entertaining, informative, and understandable to the young adult reader.

Entry Format

Each volume of *Authors and Artists for Young Adults* will furnish in-depth coverage of approximately twenty-five authors and artists. The typical entry consists of:

—A detailed biographical section that includes date of birth, marriage, children, education, and addresses.

—A comprehensive bibliography or filmography including publishers, producers, and years.

—Adaptations into other media forms.

—Works in progress.

—A distinctive essay featuring comments on an artist's life, career, artistic intentions, world views, and controversies.

—References for further reading.

—Extensive illustrations, photographs, movie stills, cartoons, book covers, and other relevant visual material.

A cumulative index to featured authors and artists appears in each volume.

Compilation Methods

The editors of *Authors and Artists for Young Adults* make every effort to secure information directly from the authors and artists through personal correspondence and interviews. Sketches on living authors and artists are sent to the biographee for review prior to publication. Any sketches not personally reviewed by biographees or their representatives are marked with an asterisk (*).

Highlights of Forthcoming Volumes

Among the authors and artists planned for future volumes are:

Monica Ali	Howard Hawks	Sam Raimi
Stephen Baxter	A.E. Houseman	Alberto Rios
Hieronymous Bosch	June Jordan	Philip Roth
Tim Burton	Bel Kaufman	Jane Smiley
Joseph Campbell	Henry Kiyama	Stephen Sondheim
Robert Capa	Peter Kuper	Oliver Stone
Jonathan Demme	Yann Martel	Bruce Timm
John Donne	Steve Meretzky	Diego Velazquez
Hilda Doolittle	John Milton	Keenen Ivory Wayans
Peter Fernandez	Michael Ondaatje	Billy Wilder
Robert Frank	Susan Orlean	Simon Winchester
Jorie Graham	Connie Porter	Thomas Wolfe

Contact the Editor

We encourage our readers to examine the entire *AAYA* series. Please write and tell us if we can make *AAYA* even more helpful to you. Give your comments and suggestions to the editor:

BY MAIL: The Editor, *Authors and Artists for Young Adults,* 27500 Drake Rd., Farmington Hills, MI 48331-3535.

BY TELEPHONE: (800) 347-GALE

Authors and Artists for Young Adults
Product Advisory Board

The editors of *Authors and Artists for Young Adults* are dedicated to maintaining a high standard of excellence by publishing comprehensive, accurate, and highly readable entries on writers, artists, and filmmakers of interest to middle and high school students. In addition to the quality of the entries, the editors take pride in the graphic design of the series, which is intended to be orderly yet appealing, allowing readers to utilize the pages of *AAYA* easily, enjoyably, and with efficiency. Despite the success of the *AAYA* print series, we are mindful that the vitality of a literary reference product is dependent on its ability to serve its readers over time. As critical attitudes about literature, art, and media constantly evolve, so do the reference needs of students and teachers. To be certain that we continue to keep pace with the expectations of our readers, the editors of *AAYA* listen carefully to their comments regarding the value, utility, and quality of the series. Librarians, who have firsthand knowledge of the needs of library users, are a valuable resource for us. The *Authors and Artists for Young Adults* Product Advisory Board, made up of school, public, and academic librarians, is a forum to promote focused feedback about *AAYA* on a regular basis, as well as to help steer our coverage of new authors and artists. The advisory board includes the following individuals, whom the editors wish to thank for sharing their expertise:

- **Eva M. Davis,** Youth Department Manager, Ann Arbor District Library, Ann Arbor, Michigan

- **Joan B. Eisenberg,** Lower School Librarian, Milton Academy, Milton, Massachusetts

- **Susan Dove Lempke,** Children's Services Supervisor, Niles Public Library District, Niles, Illinois

- **Robyn Lupa,** Head of Children's Services, Jefferson County Public Library, Lakewood, Colorado

- **Caryn Sipos,** Community Librarian, Three Creeks Community Library, Vancouver, Washington

- **Stephen Weiner,** Director, Maynard Public Library, Maynard, Massachusetts

Acknowledgments

Grateful acknowledgment is made to the following publishers, authors, and artists for their kind permission to reproduce copyrighted material.

BARAKA, AMIRI: From a cover of *Dutchman and the Slave,* by LeRoi Jones/Amiri Baraka. Perennial, 1964. Copyright © 1964 by LeRoi Jones. Reprinted by permission of HarperCollins Publishers, Inc./ From a cover of *Blues People,* by LeRoi Jones/Amiri Baraka. Perennial, 2002. Copyright © 1963 by LeRoi Jones. Reprinted by permission of HarperCollins Publishers Inc./ Baraka, Amiri, formerly LeRoi Jones, leads a protest against the New Jersey Senate, photograph. © Bettman/Corbis. Reproduced by permission./ Baraka, Imamu Amiri, leaning on door jam, 1977, photograph. AP/Wide World Photos, Inc. Reproduced by permission.

BROWNING, ELIZABETH BARRETT: Browning, Elizabeth Barrett, 1848, illustration. © Corbis-Bettmann./ Title page of *Aurora Leigh,* written by Elizabeth Barrett Browning. C.S. Francis and Co., 1857. Courtesy of the Special Collections Library, University of Michigan. Reproduced by permission./ Alinari, photograph. From a cover of *Aurora Leigh and Other Poems,* by Elizabeth Barrett Browning. Edited by John Robert Glorney Bolton and Julia Bolton Holloway. Penguin Classics, 1995. Selection, Preface and Notes copyright © Julia Bolton Holloway, 1995. Reproduced by permission of Penguin Books, Ltd./ From a cover of *Sonnets from the Portuguese and Other Poems,* by Elizabeth Barrett Browning. Dover Publications, Inc., 1992. Reproduced by permission.

CARTIER-BRESSON, HENRI: Faulkner, William, 1947, gelatin silver print of photograph by Henri Cartier-Bresson (1908-2004). © Magnum Photos. National Portrait Gallery, Smithsonian Institution/Art Resource, NY. Reproduced by permission of Magnum Photos and Art Resource, NY./ Cartier-Bresson, Henri, photograph. Photo by Arnold Newman/Getty Images./ Cartier-Bresson, Henri, photographing three men under a "Jesus Saves," sign in Brooklyn, photograph. © Genevieve Naylor/Corbis./ Cartier-Bresson, Henri, looks through the viewfinder of a movie camera on the set of the made-for-television film "California Impressions by Henri Cartier-Bresson," photograph. Photo by CBS Photo Archive/Getty Images./ Cartier-Bresson, Henri, holding graduation cap, photograph. AP/Wide World Photos, Inc.

CASH, JOHNNY: Wynette, Tammy with Johnny Cash, photograph. © Bettmann/Corbis./ Cash, Johnny, playing acoustic guitar on an outdoor stage, dressed in all black and looking away from the camera, photograph. Copyright © Jack Vartoogian/FrontRowPhotos. Reproduced by permission./ Cash, Johnny, sits on his patio with a guitar, photograph. John Chiasson/Getty Images./ Album cover art for "Ring of Fire: The Best of Johnny Cash," photograph. Blank Archives/Getty Images./ Douglas, Kirk, and Johnny Cash fight in a scene from the film "A Gunfight." © Bettmann/Corbis./ Cash, Johnny, singing for the inmates at the Cummins Prison Farm. © Bettmann/Corbis.

COOK, MONTE: Zug, Mark illustrator. From a cover of *Children of the Rune,* by Monte Cook. Malhavoc Press, 2004. © 2004 Monte J. Cook. Reproduced by permission.

EGOYAN, ATOM: Pastko, Earl, as Hartley Otto, comforts Arsinee Khanjian as Wanda Otto, in a scene from 1997 film version of Russell Banks' "The Sweet Hereafter," directed by Atom Egoyan. Kobal Collection/Speaking Parts Ltd./Alliance Comms. Reproduced by permission./ Hoskins, Bob (L) as Joseph Ambrose Hilditch, and Elaine Cassidy as Felicia, in "Felicia's Journey," the 1999 film version of the novel by William Trevor Cox, directed by Atom Egoyan, photograph. The Kobal Collection / Artisan Pics / Sophie Baker. Reproduced by permission./ Egoyan, Atom, receives the order of Canada medal from Governor General Romeo LeBlanc, photograph. © Reuters/Corbis./ Egoyan, Atom, talking to an actor during the filming of "Ararat," photograph. The Kobal Collection./ Egoyan, Atom, Cannes, France, 1997, photo by Lionel Cironneay. AP/Wide World Photos, Inc.

FORMAN, MILOS: Poster of the Milos Forman movie, "The Fireman's Ball." Photo by Giulio Marcocchi/Getty Images./ Nicholson, Jack, in a still from the film "One Flew Over the Cuckoo's Nest," directed by Milos Forman. Photograph by Republic Pictures/Republic Pictures/Getty Image./ Actor John

Turturro and Director Milos Forman, photograph. Evan Agostini/Getty Images./ Forman, Milos looking into a movie camera during the filming of "Taking Off," photograph. © Bettmann/Corbis./ Forman, Milos, directing the film "Valmont," 1989, photograph. The Kobal Collection./ Forman, Milos, speaks to reporters after receiving the "Legion dHonour," during the 57th International Cannes Film Festival in 2004, photograph. Photo by Carlo Allegri/Getty Images.

HALL, DONALD: From the cover of *Life Work,* by Donald Hall. Beacon Press, 2003. Copyright © 1993 by Donald Hall. Reproduced by permission of Beacon Press, Boston./ Barnes, Pat, photographer. From a cover of *The Painted Bed,* by Donald Hall. Mariner Books, 2002. Cover photograph © Pat Barnes. Reproduced by permission of Houghton Mifflin Company./ Wolff, Stephanie, photographer. From a cover of *Without,* by Donald Hall. Mariner Books, 1998. Cover photograph © Stephanie Wolff. Reproduced by permission of Houghton Mifflin Company./ Hall, Donald, photograph. Reproduced by permission.

HARTLEY, MARSDEN: "Indian Composition," painting by Marsden Hartley. Frances Lehman Loeb Art Center, Vassar College, Poughkeepsie, New York. Gift of Paul Rosenfeld. 1950.1.5. Reproduced by permission./ From a cover of *Seeking the Spiritual: The Paintings of Marsden Hartley,* by Townsend Ludington. Cornell University Press, 1998. Copyright © 1998 by Cornell University. Used by permission of the publisher, Cornell University Press./ "Maine Seascape," by Marsden Hartley. © Peter Harholdt/Corbis./ Hartley, Marsden, portrait. © Corbis./ Hartley, Marsden, next to unfinished portrait of girl, photograph. © Bradley/Corbis. Reproduced by permission.

JOHNS, JASPER: "Target," painting by Jasper Johns, c. 1955, photograph. Photograph © Geoffrey Clements/Corbis. Art © Jasper Johns/Licensed by VAGA, New York, NY. Reproduced by permission./ Johns, Japper, leaning over back of chair, photograph. © Christopher Felver/Corbis./ Artist Jasper Johns stands beside his mixed-media painting "Target." Photograph by Ben Martin/Time Life Pictures/Getty Images./ Artist Jasper Johns speaks with American art dealer Leo Castelli and his wife in New York City in 1966. Photo by Sam Falk/New York Times Co./Getty Images.

JOHNSTON, LYNN: From cartoon strip, "For Better Or For Worse," in *What, Me Pregnant?,* by Lynn Johnston. Andrews and McMeel, 1991. For Better or for Worse © 1991 Lynn Johnston Productions. Dist. By Universal Press Syndicate. Reprinted with permission. All rights reserved./ Panels from the comic strip, "For Better or For Worse," by Lynn Johnston. For Better Or For Worse (c) 2004 Lynn Johnston Productions. Dist. By Universal Press Syndicate. Reprinted with permission. All rights reserved./ Johnston, Lynn, photograph. Reproduced by permission.

KENYON, JANE: From a cover of *The Boat of Quiet Hours,* by Jane Kenyon. Graywolf Press, 1986. Cover art is "The Boat," by Claude Monet, reproduced courtesy of Musee Marmottan. Book cover reproduced by permission of Graywolf Press./ From a cover of *Constance,* by Jane Kenyon. Graywolf Press, 1993. Cover art is "Constance," Albert Pinkham Ryder, 1896, oil on canvas. Courtesy, Museum of Fine Arts, Boston. Book cover reproduced by permission of the publisher.

KIMMEL, HAVEN: Cozza, Marc, photographer. From a cover of *The Solace of Leaving Early,* by Haven Kimmel, copyright. Anchor Books, 2002. Cover photograph © Marc Cozza. All rights reserved. Reprinted by permission of Anchor Books, A Division of Random House, Inc./ From a cover of *A Girl Named Zippy,* by Haven Kimmel. Broadway Books, 2001. Copyright © 2001 by Haven Kimmel. All rights reserved. Used by permission of Doubleday, a division of Random House, Inc./ From a cover of *Something Rising (Light and Swift),* by Haven Kimmel. Free Press, 2004. Jacket copyright © 2003 by Simon & Schuster, Inc. Reproduced by permission of the publisher. All rights reserved.

LAIRD, ELIZABETH: Velasquez, Eric, illustrator. From a dust jacket of *Secret Friends,* by Elizabeth Laird. G.P. Putnam's Sons, 1999. Jacket art copyright © 1999 by Eric Velasquez. Reproduced by permission of G.P. Putnam's Sons, a Division of Penguin Young Readers Group, A Member of Penguin Group (USA) Inc., 345 Hudson Street, New York, NY 10014. All rights reserved./ Zelvin, Diana, photographer. From a cover of *Kiss the Dust,* by Elizabeth Laird. Puffin Books, 1994. Cover illustration copyright © Diana Zelvin, 1994. All rights reserved. Reproduced by permission of Puffin Books, A Division of Penguin Young Readers Group, A Member of Penguin Group (USA) Inc., 345 Hudson Street, New York, NY 10014./ From a cover of *Jake's Tower,* by Elizabeth Laird. Barron's, 2001. Copyright © 2001 Elizabeth Laird. All rights reserved. Reprinted by permission of Barron's Educational Series, Inc., Hauppauge, NY 11788./ Author photographs reproduced by permission of the author.

Amiri Baraka

■ Personal

Born Everett LeRoi Jones, October 7, 1934, in Newark, NJ; name changed to Imamu ("spiritual leader") Ameer ("blessed") Baraka ("prince"); later modified to Amiri Baraka; son of Coyette Leroy (a postal worker and elevator operator) and Anna Lois (Russ) Jones; married Hettie Roberta Cohen, October 13, 1958 (divorced, August, 1965); married Sylvia Robinson (Bibi Amina Baraka), 1966; children: (first marriage) Kellie Elisabeth, Lisa Victoria Chapman; (second marriage) Obalaji Malik Ali, Ras Jua al Aziz, Shani Isis, Amiri Seku, Ahi Mwenge. *Education:* Attended Rutgers University, 1951-52; Howard University, B.A., 1954; Columbia University, M.A. (philosophy); New School for Social Research, M.A. (German literature).

■ Addresses

Office—Department of Africana Studies, State University of New York, Long Island, NY 11794-4340. *Agent*—Joan Brandt, Sterling Lord Literistic, 660 Madison Ave., New York, NY 10021.

■ Career

State University of New York at Stony Brook, assistant professor, 1980-83, associate professor, 1983-85, professor of African studies, 1985—. Instructor, New School for Social Research (now New School University), New York, NY, 1962-64; visiting professor, University of Buffalo, summer, 1964, Columbia University, fall, 1964, and 1966-67, San Francisco State University, 1967, Yale University, 1977-78, George Washington University, 1978-79, and Rutgers University, 1988. Founded *Yugen* magazine and Totem Press, 1958; co-editor and founder of *Floating Bar* magazine, 1961-63; editor of *Black Nation.* Founder and director, Black Arts Repertory Theatre, 1964-66; director of Spirit House (black community theater; also known as Heckalu Community Center), 1965-75, and head of advisory group at Treat Elementary School, both in Newark; Kimako Blues People (community arts space), co-director. Founder, Congress of African People, 1970-76. Member, Political Prisoners Relief Fund, and African Liberation Day Commission. Candidate, Newark community council, 1968. National Black Political Assembly, former secretary general and co-governor; National Black United Front, member; Congress of African People, co-founder and chair; League of Revolutionary Struggle, member. *Military service:* U.S. Air Force, 1954-57; weather-gunner; stationed for two and a half years in Puerto Rico with intervening trips to Europe, Africa, and the Middle East.

■ Member

All-African Games, Pan African Federation, Black Academy of Arts and Letters, Black Writers' Union, United Brothers (Newark), Newark Writers Collective.

■ Awards, Honors

Longview Best Essay of the Year award, 1961, for "Cuba Libre"; John Whitney Foundation fellowship for poetry and fiction, 1962; *Village Voice* Best American Off-Broadway Play ("Obie" award, 1964, for *Dutchman*; Guggenheim fellowship, 1965-66; Yoruba Academy fellow, 1965; second prize, International Art Festival (Dakar), 1966, for *The Slave*; National Endowment for the Arts grant, 1966; D.H.L. from Malcolm X College, 1972; Rockefeller Foundation fellow (drama), 1981; Poetry Award, National Endowment for the Arts, 1981; New Jersey Council for the Arts award, 1982; American Book Award, Before Columbus Foundation, 1984, for *Confirmation: An Anthology of African-American Women*; Drama Award, 1985; PEN-Faulkner Award, 1989; Langston Hughes Medal, 1989, for outstanding contribution to literature; Ferroni award (Italy), and Foreign Poet Award, 1993; Playwright's Award, Winston-Salem Black Drama Festival, 1997; appointed poet laureate of State of New Jersey (position abolished, 2003).

■ Writings

PLAYS

(Under name Leroi Jones) *A Good Girl Is Hard to Find*, produced in Montclair, NJ, 1958.

(Under name Leroi Jones) *Dante* (one act; excerpted from novel *The System of Dante's Hell*; also see below), produced in New York, NY, 1961, produced as *The Eighth Ditch*, 1964.

(Under name Leroi Jones) *Dutchman*, (also see below; produced Off-Broadway, 1964; produced in London, England, 1967), Faber & Faber (London, England), 1967.

(Under name Leroi Jones) *The Baptism: A Comedy in One Act* (also see below; produced Off-Broadway, 1964, produced in London, England, 1970-71), Sterling Lord, 1966.

(Under name Leroi Jones) *The Toilet* (also see below; produced with *The Slave: A Fable* Off-Broadway, 1964), Sterling Lord, 1964.

Dutchman [and] The Slave: A Fable, Morrow (New York, NY), 1964.

(Under name Leroi Jones) *J-E-L-L-O* (one act comedy; also see below; produced in New York, NY, by Black Arts Repertory Theatre, 1965), Third World Press, 1970.

(Under name Leroi Jones) *Experimental Death Unit #1* (one act; also see below), produced Off-Broadway, 1965.

(Under name Leroi Jones) *The Death of Malcolm X* (one act; produced in Newark, NJ, 1965), published in *New Plays from the Black Theatre*, edited by Ed Bullins, Bantam (New York, NY), 1969.

(Under name Leroi Jones) *A Black Mass* (also see below), produced in Newark. NJ, 1966.

Slave Ship (also see below; produced as *Slave Ship: A Historical Pageant* at Spirit House, 1967; produced in New York, NY, 1969), Jihad, 1967.

Madheart: Morality Drama (one act; also see below), produced at San Francisco State College, 1967.

Arm Yourself, or Harm Yourself, A One-Act Play (also see below; produced at Spirit House, 1967), Jihad, 1967.

Great Goodness of Life (A Coon Show) (one act; also see below), produced at Spirit House, 1967; produced Off-Broadway at Tambellini's Gate Theater, 1969.

The Baptism [and] The Toilet, Grove (New York, NY), 1967.

Home on the Range (one act comedy; also see below), produced at Spirit House, 1968; produced in New York, NY, 1968.

Junkies Are Full of SHHH . . . , produced at Spirit House, 1968; produced with *Bloodrites* (also see below) Off-Broadway, 1970.

Board of Education (children's play), produced at Spirit House, 1968.

Resurrection in Life (one-act pantomime), produced as *Insurrection* in Harlem, NY, 1969.

Four Black Revolutionary Plays: All Praises to the Black Man (contains *Experimental Death Unit #1*, *A Black Mass*, *Great Goodness of Life (A Coon Show)*, and *Madheart*), Bobbs-Merrill (New York, NY), 1969.

Black Dada Nihilism (one act), produced Off-Broadway, 1971.

A Recent Killing (three acts), produced Off-Broadway, 1973.

Columbia the Gem of the Ocean, produced in Washington, DC, 1973.

The New Ark's A-Moverin, produced in Newark, NJ, 1974.

The Sidnee Poet Heroical, in Twenty-nine Scenes (one act comedy; also see below; produced Off-Broadway, 1975), Reed & Cannon, 1979.

S-1: A Play with Music (also see below), produced in New York, NY, 1976.

(With Frank Chin and Leslie Siko) *America More or Less* (musical), produced in San Francisco, CA, 1976.

The Motion of History (four-act; also see below), produced in New York, NY, 1977.

The Motion of History and Other Plays (contains *Slave Ship* and *S-1*), Morrow (New York, NY), 1978.

What Was the Relationship of the Lone Ranger to the Means of Production? (one-act; also see below; produced in New York, NY, 1979), Anti-Imperialist Cultural Union, 1978.

Dim Cracker Party Convention, produced in New York, NY, 1980.

Boy and Tarzan Appear in a Clearing, produced Off-Broadway, 1981.

Money: Jazz Opera, produced Off-Broadway, 1982.

Song: A One-Act Play about the Relationship of Art to Real Life, produced in Jamaica, NY, 1983.

General Hag's Skeezag, 1992.

Also author of plays *Police*, published in *Drama Review*, summer, 1968; *Rockgroup*, published in *Cricket*, December, 1969; *Vomit and the Jungle Bunnies*, 1969; *Revolt of the Moonflowers*, 1969; *The Coronation of the Black Queen*, published in *Black Scholar*, June, 1970; *Black Power Chant*, published in *Drama Review*, December, 1972; *Primitive World*, 1991; *Jackpot Melting*, 1996; *Election Machine Warehouse*, 1996; *Meeting Lillie*, 1997; *Biko*, 1997; and *Black Renaissance in Harlem*, 1998.

Plays included in anthologies, including Woodie King and Ron Milner, editors, *Black Drama Anthology* (includes *Bloodrites* and *Junkies Are Full of SHHH . . .*), New American Library, 1971; and Rochelle Owens, editor, *Spontaneous Combustion: Eight New American Plays* (includes *Ba-Ra-Ka*), Winter House, 1972.

SCREENPLAYS

Dutchman, Gene Persson Enterprises, Ltd., 1967.

Black Spring, Jihad Productions, 1968.

A Fable (based on *The Slave: A Fable*), MFR Productions, 1971.

Supercoon, Gene Persson Enterprises, Ltd., 1971.

POETRY

April 13 (broadside), Penny Poems (New Haven, CT), 1959.

Spring and So Forth (broadside), Penny Poems (New Haven, CT), 1960.

Preface to a Twenty-Volume Suicide Note, Totem/Corinth, 1961.

The Disguise (broadside), [New Haven, CT], 1961.

The Dead Lecturer (also see below), Grove (New York, NY), 1964.

Black Art (also see below), Jihad, 1966.

Black Magic (also see below), Morrow (New York, NY), 1967.

A Poem for Black Hearts, Broadside Press, 1967.

Black Magic: Sabotage; Target Study; Black Art; Collected Poetry, 1961-1967, Bobbs-Merrill (New York, NY), 1969.

It's Nation Time, Third World Press, 1970.

Spirit Reach, Jihad, 1972.

Afrikan Revolution, Jihad, 1973.

Hard Facts: Excerpts, People's War, 1975, 2nd edition, Revolutionary Communist League, 1975.

Spring Song, Baraka, 1979.

AM/TRAK, Phoenix Bookshop, 1979.

Selected Poetry of Amiri Baraka/Leroi Jones, Morrow (New York, NY), 1979.

In the Tradition: For Black Arthur Blythe, Jihad, 1980.

Reggae or Not!, Contact Two, 1982.

Transbluency: The Selected Poems of Amiri Baraka/LeRoi Jones (1961-1995), Marsilio, 1995.

Funk Lore: New Poems, 1984-1995, Sun & Moon Press, 1996.

Beginnings and Other Poems, House of Nehesi (Fredericksburg, VA), 2003.

ESSAYS

Cuba Libre, Fair Play for Cuba Committee (New York, NY), 1961.

Blues People: Negro Music in White America, Morrow (New York, NY), 1963, reprinted, Greenwood Press (Westport, CT), 1980, published as *Negro Music in White America*, MacGibbon & Kee (London, England), 1965.

Home: Social Essays (contains "Cuba Libre," "The Myth of a 'Negro Literature,'" "Expressive Language," "The Legacy of Malcolm X, and the Coming of the Black Nation," and "State/meant"), Morrow (New York, NY), 1966, Ecco Press (Hopewell, NJ), 1998.

Black Music, Morrow (New York, NY), 1968.

Raise, Race, Rays, Raze: Essays since 1965, Random House (New York, NY), 1971.

Strategy and Tactics of a Pan-African Nationalist Party, Jihad, 1971.

Kawaida Studies: The New Nationalism, Third World Press, 1972.

Crisis in Boston!, Vita Wa Watu People's War, 1974.

Daggers and Javelins: Essays, 1974-1979, Morrow (New York, NY), 1984.

(With wife, Amina Baraka) *The Music: Reflections on Jazz and Blues*, Morrow (New York, NY), 1987.

Jesse Jackson and Black People, 1996.

The Essence of Reparation, House of Nehesi (Fredericksburg, VA), 2003.

Contributor of essays to *Lorraine Hansberry, A Raisin in the Sun*; and *The Sign in Sidney Brustein's Window*, Vintage Books (New York, NY), 1995.

EDITOR

January 1st 1959: Fidel Castro, Totem, 1959.

Four Young Lady Poets, Corinth, 1962.

(And author of introduction) *The Moderns: An Anthology of New Writing in America,* 1963, published as *The Moderns: New Fiction in America,* 1964.

(And co-author) *In-formation,* Totem, 1965.

Gilbert Sorrentino, *Black & White,* Corinth, 1965.

Edward Dorn, *Hands Up!,* Corinth, 1965.

(And contributor) *Afro-American Festival of the Arts Magazine,* Jihad, 1966, published as *Anthology of Our Black Selves,* 1969.

(With Larry Neal and A. B. Spellman) *The Cricket: Black Music in Evolution,* Jihad, 1968, published as *Trippin': A Need for Change,* New Ark, 1969.

(And contributor, with Larry Neal) *Black Fire: An Anthology of Afro-American Writing,* Morrow (New York, NY), 1968.

A Black Value System, Jihad, 1970.

(With Billy Abernathy under pseudonym Fundi) *In Our Terribleness (Some Elements of Meaning in Black Style),* Bobbs-Merrill (New York, NY), 1970.

(And author of introduction) *African Congress: A Documentary of the First Modern Pan-African Congress,* Morrow (New York, NY), 1972.

(With Diane Di Prima) *The Floating Bear, A Newsletter, Nos. 1-37, 1961-1969,* McGilvery, 1974.

(With Amina Baraka) *Confirmation: An Anthology of African-American Women,* Morrow (New York, NY), 1983.

OTHER

The System of Dante's Hell (novel; includes the play *Dante*), Grove (New York, NY), 1965.

(Author of introduction) David Henderson, *Felix of the Silent Forest,* Poets Press, 1967.

Striptease, Parallax, 1967.

Tales (short stories), Grove (New York, NY), 1967.

(Author of preface) *Black Boogaloo (Notes on Black Liberation),* Journal of Black Poetry Press, 1969.

Focus on Amiri Baraka: Playwright LeRoi Jones Analyzes the 1st National Black Political Convention (sound recording), Center for Cassette Studies, 1973.

Three Books by Imamu Amiri Baraka (LeRoi Jones) (contains *The System of Dante's Hell, Tales,* and *The Dead Lecturer*), Grove (New York, NY), 1975.

Selected Plays and Prose of Amiri Baraka/LeRoi Jones, Morrow (New York, NY), 1979.

The Autobiography of LeRoi Jones/Amiri Baraka, Freundlich, 1984, Lawrence Hill Books (Chicago, IL), 1997.

(Author of introduction) Martin Espada, *Rebellion is the Circle of a Lover's Hand,* Curbstone Press, 1990.

(Author of introduction) *Eliot Katz, Space, and Other Poems,* Northern Lights, 1990.

LeRoi Jones/Amiri Baraka Reader, Thunder's Mouth Press, 1991.

Thornton Dial: Images of the Tiger, Harry N. Abrams (New York, NY), 1993.

Jesse Jackson and Black People, Third World Press, 1994.

Shy's Wise, Y's: The Griot's Tale, Third World Press, 1994.

(With Charlie Reilly) *Conversations with Amiri Baraka,* University Press of Mississippi (Jackson, MS), 1994.

Eulogies, Marsilio Publishers (New York, NY), 1996.

The Fiction of Leroi Jones/Amiri Baraka, foreword by Greg Tate, Lawrence Hill, 2000.

Works represented in anthologies, including *A Broadside Treasury, For Malcolm, The New Black Poetry, Nommo,* and *The Trembling Lamb.* Contributor to *Black Men in Their Own Words,* 2002; contributor to periodicals, including *Evergreen Review, Poetry, Downbeat, Metronome, Nation, Negro Digest,* and *Saturday Review.*

Baraka's works have been translated into Japanese, Norwegian, Italian, German, French, and Spanish.

■ Sidelights

Amiri Baraka, who published under his birth name LeRoi Jones until 1967, is known for his strident social criticism and an incendiary style that has made it difficult for some audiences and critics to respond with objectivity to his works. Baraka's art stems from his African-American heritage. Throughout his career his method in poetry, drama, fiction, and essays has been confrontational, calculated to shock and awaken audiences to the political concerns of black Americans during the second half of the twentieth century. Baraka's own political stance has changed several times, thus dividing his oeuvre into periods; a member of the avant garde during the 1950s, Baraka became a black nationalist, and more recently a Marxist with socialist ideals. In the wake of the September 11, 2001, bombings of the World Trade Center, Baraka was accused of adding anti-Semitism to his political outlook when in his poem "Somebody Blew up America" he suggested that New York's Jews had been warned in advance not to enter the doomed buildings on that fateful day; public outcry became so great that the State of New

This 1963 work, written under the name Leroi Jones, chronicles the evolution of Black music in the United States and examines social and cultural issues.

Jersey took action to abolish the position of poet laureate Baraka then held. Baraka, for his part, threatened legal action.

Throughout his career Baraka has stirred controversy, some praising him for speaking out against oppression and others arguing that he fosters hate. Critical opinion has been sharply divided between those who feel that Baraka's race and political stance have created his celebrity, and those who feel that Baraka stands among the most important writers of the twentieth century. In *American Book Review,* Arnold Rampersad counted Baraka with Phyllis Wheatley, Frederick Douglass, Paul Laurence Dunbar, Langston Hughes, Zora Neale Hurston, Richard Wright, and Ralph Ellison "as one of the eight figures . . . who have significantly affected the course of African-American literary culture."

Conventional Middle-Class Upbringing

Baraka did not always identify with radical politics, nor did he always channel his writing into use as their tool. He was born in Newark, New Jersey, and enjoyed a middle-class education. During the 1950s he attended Rutgers University and Howard University. Then he spent two years in the U.S. Air Force, where he was stationed for most of that time in Puerto Rico. When he returned to New York City, he attended Columbia University and the New School for Social Research. Baraka lived in Greenwich Village's lower east side, where he made friends with Beat poets Allen Ginsberg, Frank O'Hara, and Gilbert Sorrentino. The white avant garde—primarily Ginsberg, O'Hara, and leader of the Black Mountain poets, Charles Olson—and Baraka believed that writing poetry is a process of discovery rather than an exercise in fulfilling traditional expectations of what poems should be. Baraka, like the projectivist poets, believed that a poem's form should follow the shape determined by the poet's own breath and intensity of feeling. In 1958 Baraka founded *Yugen* magazine and Totem Press, important forums for new verse. His first play, *A Good Girl Is Hard to Find,* was produced at Sterington House in Montclair, New Jersey, that same year.

Preface to a Twenty-Volume Suicide Note, Baraka's first published collection of poems, appeared in 1961. M. L. Rosenthal wrote in *The New Poets: American and British Poetry* that these poems show Baraka's "natural gift for quick, vivid imagery and spontaneous humor." The reviewer also praised the "sardonic or sensuous or slangily knowledgeable passages" that fill the early poems. While the cadence of blues and many allusions to black culture are found in the poems, the subject of blackness does not predominate. Throughout, rather, the poet shows his integrated, Bohemian social roots. For example, the poem "Notes for a Speech" states, "African blues/ does not know me . . . Does/ not feel/ what I am," and the book's last line is "You are/ as any other sad man here/ american."

With the rise of the civil rights movement Baraka's works took on a more militant tone, and he began a reluctant separation from his newly adopted bohemian milieu. His trip to Castro's Cuba in July of 1959 marked an important turning point in his life. His view of his role as a writer, the purpose of art, and the degree to which ethnic awareness deserved to be his subject changed dramatically. In Cuba he met writers and artists from Third-World countries whose political concerns included the fight against poverty, famine, and oppressive governments. They felt he was merely being self-indulgent, "cultivating his soul" in poetry, while there were social problems to solve in America. In *Home: Social Essays,* Baraka explains how he tried to defend himself against these accusations, and was further challenged by Jaime Shelley, a Mexican poet, who had said, "'In that ugliness you live in, you want to cultivate your soul? Well, we've got millions of starving people to feed, and that moves me enough to make poems out of.'" Soon Baraka began to identify with Third-World writers and to write poems and plays with strong ethnic and political messages.

Sets New Course with *Dutchman*

Dutchman, a play of entrapment in which a white woman and a middle-class black man both express their murderous hatred on a subway, was first performed Off-Broadway in 1964. The one-act play makes many references to sex and violence and ends in the black man's murder. While other dramatists of the time were using the techniques of naturalism, Baraka used symbolism and other experimental techniques to enhance the play's emotional impact. Lula, the white woman, represents the white state, and Clay, the black man in the play, represents ethnic identity and non-white manhood. *Dutchman* is an emotionally charged and highly symbolic version of the Adam and Eve story, wherein a naive bourgeois black man is murdered by an insane and calculating white seductress, who is coldly preparing for her next victim as the curtain comes down. Baraka's play is one of mythical proportions, a ritual drama that has a sociological purpose: to galvanize his audience into revolutionary action. The play's major characters force the audience to examine their prejudices through the violence of the dramatic action. Baraka makes the audience face and confront the violent reality of the subconscious hatred buried in its psyche. He clearly challenges the audience to recognize that it makes the moral standards by which it chooses to live. Certainly, Baraka wants his viewers to see Clay and Lula as real people; at the same time, however, these characters must be understood to be character types. *Dutchman* is set in a New York City subway car in which Clay and Lula are riding beneath the city. The action of the play thus takes place in the heart, the very infrastructure, of the city; the setting thus seems emblematic of the sociopolitical structure of the United States. As the dramatic action evolves, it is possible to see the "true" feelings of the characters as demonstrated by their language and gestures. It seems obvious the action is intended to represent the class struggle going on in society. Clay wants to be a man, but Lula hatefully attacks his attempts toward manhood; she asks him, accusingly, "What right do you have to be wearing a three-button suit and striped

tie? Your grandfather was a slave, he didn't go to Harvard." Racial stereotypes are revealed in the play's dialogue; Lula, for example, remarks on the black male's supposed sexual ability. *Dutchman* proved to be an important element in the black drama of the 1960's, both mirroring and fostering the black militancy of the time. The play established Baraka's reputation as a playwright and has been often anthologized and performed. Considered by many to be the best play of the year, it won the *Village Voice* Off-Broadway Award in 1964. Later, Anthony Harvey adapted it for a film made in Britain, and in the 1990s it was revived for several productions in New York City. Darryl Pinckney commented in the *New York Times Book Review* that *Dutchman* survived the test of time better than other protest plays of the 1960s due to its economic use of vivid language, its surprise ending, and its quick pacing.

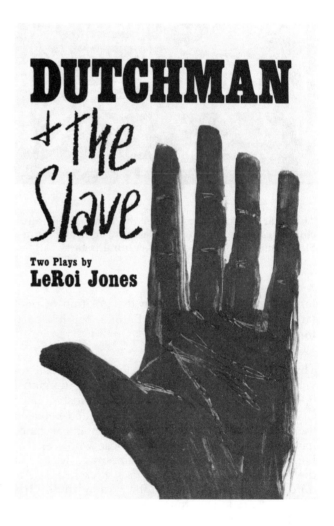

In *Dutchman,* a 1964 drama that received an Obie Award for the best American off-Broadway play, and *The Slave,* Baraka addresses racial conflicts.

The plays and poems following *Dutchman* expressed Baraka's increasing disappointment with white America and his growing need to separate from it. He wrote in *Cuba Libre* that the Beat generation had become a counterculture of drop-outs who did not generate very meaningful politics. Baraka felt there had to be a more effective alternative to disengagement from the political, legal, and moral morass the country had become. In *The Dead Lecturer* Baraka explored the alternatives, finding no room for compromise: if he identified with an ethnic cause, he would find hope of meaningful action and change; but if he remained in his comfortable assimilated position, writing "quiet" poems, he would remain "a dead lecturer." The voice in *Cuba Libre* is more sure of itself, led by a "moral earnestness" that is wedded to action, Baraka wrote in a 1961 letter to Edward Dorn. Critics observed that as Baraka's poems became more politically intense, they left behind some of the flawless technique of the earlier poems. *Nation* review contributor Richard Howard wrote: "These are the agonized poems of a man writing to save his skin, or at least to settle in it, and so urgent is their purpose that not one of them can trouble to be perfect."

To make a clean break with the Beat influence, Baraka turned to writing fiction in the mid-1960s, penning *The System of Dante's Hell*, a novel, and *Tales*, a collection of short stories. The novel echoes the themes and structures found in his earlier poems and plays. The stories, like the poems in *Black Magic*, also published in 1967, are "'fugitive narratives' that describe the harried flight of an intensely self-conscious Afro-American artist/intellectual from neo-slavery of blinding, neutralizing whiteness, where the area of struggle is basically within the mind," Robert Eliot Fox wrote in *Conscientious Sorcerers: The Black Post-Modernist Fiction of LeRoi Jones/Baraka, Ishmael Reed, and Samuel R. Delany*. The role of violent action in achieving political change is more prominent in these stories. Unlike Shakespeare's Hamlet, who deliberates at length before taking violent action, Baraka sought to stand with "the straight ahead people, who think when that's called for, who don't when they don't have to," as he explained in *Tales*. The role of music in black life is seen more often in these books, also. In the story "Screamers," the screams from a jazz saxophone galvanize the people into a powerful uprising.

Chronicles Black Social History

Baraka's classic history *Blues People: Negro Music in White America*, published in 1963, traces black music from slavery to contemporary jazz. The blues, a staple of black American music, grew out of the encounter between African and American cultures in the South to become an art form uniquely connected to both the African past and the American soil. Finding indigenous black art forms was important to Baraka at this time, as he was searching for a more authentic ethnic voice for his own poetry. From this important study Baraka became known as an articulate jazz critic and a perceptive observer of social change. As Clyde Taylor stated in *Amiri Baraka: The Kaleidoscopic Torch*, "The connection he nailed down between the many faces of black music, the sociological sets that nurtured them, and their symbolic evolutions through socio-economic changes, in *Blues People*, is his most durable conception, as well as probably the one most indispensable thing said about black music."

Baraka will also be long remembered for his other important studies, *Black Music*, which expresses black nationalist ideals, and *The Music: Reflections on Jazz and Blues*, which details his Marxist views. In *Black Music* John Coltrane emerges as the patron saint of the black arts movement after replacing "weak Western forms" of music with more fluid forms learned from a global vision of black culture. Though some critics have maintained that Baraka's essay writing is not all of the same quality, Lloyd W. Brown commented in *Amiri Baraka* that Baraka's essays on music are flawless: "As historian, musicological analyst, or as a journalist covering a particular performance Baraka always commands attention because of his obvious knowledge of the subject and because of a style that is engaging and persuasive even when the sentiments are questionable and controversial."

Shifting Political Philosophies

After Black Muslim leader Malcolm X was killed in 1965, Baraka moved to Harlem and became a black nationalist. He founded the Black Arts Repertory Theatre School in Harlem and published the collection *Black Magic*. Poems in *Black Magic* chronicle Baraka's divorce from white culture and values and also display his mastery of poetic techniques. As Taylor observed, "There are enough brilliant poems of such variety in *Black Magic* and *In Our Terribleness* to establish the unique identity and claim for respect of several poets. But it is beside the point that Baraka is probably the finest poet, black or white, writing in this country these days." There was no doubt that Baraka's political concerns superseded his just claims to literary excellence, and the challenge to critics was to respond to the political content of the works. Some critics who felt the best art must be apolitical, dismissed Baraka's

Baraka leads a protest against the New Jersey Senate after officials failed to enact a tax plan to fund New Jersey's public schools.

newer work as "a loss to literature." Kenneth Rexroth wrote in *With Eye and Ear* that Baraka "has succumbed to the temptation to become a professional Race Man of the most irresponsible sort. . . . His loss to literature is more serious than any literary casualty of the Second War." In 1966 Baraka moved back to Newark, New Jersey, and a year later changed his name to the Bantuized Muslim appellation Imamu ("spiritual leader," later dropped) Ameer (later Amiri, "blessed") Baraka ("prince").

A new aesthetic for black art was being developed in Harlem and Baraka was its primary theorist. Black American artists should follow "black," not "white" standards of beauty and value, he maintained, and should stop looking to white culture for validation. The black artist's role, he wrote in *Home: Social Essays,* is to "aid in the destruction of America as he knows it." Foremost in this endeavor was the

imperative to portray society and its ills faithfully so that the portrayal would move people to take necessary corrective action.

By the early 1970s Baraka was recognized as an influential African-American writer. Randall noted in *Black World* that younger black poets Nikki Giovanni and Don. L. Lee (later Haki R. Madhubuti) were "learning from LeRoi Jones, a man versed in German philosophy, conscious of literary tradition . . . who uses the structure of Dante's *Divine Comedy* in his *System of Dante's Hell* and the punctuation, spelling and line divisions of sophisticated contemporary poets." More importantly, Rampersad wrote in the *American Book Review,* "More than any other black poet . . . he taught younger black poets of the generation past how to respond poetically to their lived experience, rather than to depend as artists on embalmed reputations and outmoded rhetorical strategies derived from a culture often substantially different from their own."

After coming to see black nationalism as a destructive form of racism, Baraka denounced it in 1974 and became a Third World socialist. Hatred of nonwhites, he declared in the *New York Times*, "is sickness or criminality, in fact, a form of fascism." Beginning in 1974 he produced a number of Marxist poetry collections and plays, his newly adopted political goal the formation of socialist communities and a socialist state. *Daggers and Javelins* and the other books produced during this period lack the emotional power of the works from the black nationalist period, contended many critics. However, some reviewers agreed with his new politics. Exiled Filipino leftist intellectual E. San Juan, praising Baraka's work of the late 1970s, wrote in *Amiri Baraka: The Kaleidoscopic Torch* that Baraka's 1978 play *Lone Ranger* was "the most significant theatrical achievement of 1978 in the Western hemisphere." Joe Weixlmann responded in the same book to the tendency to categorize the radical Baraka instead of analyze him: "At the very least, dismissing someone with a label does not make for very satisfactory scholarship. Initially, Baraka's reputation as a writer and thinker derived from a recognition of the talents with which he is so obviously endowed. The subsequent assaults on that reputation have, too frequently, derived from concerns which should be extrinsic to informed criticism."

If you enjoy the works of Amiri Baraka, you may also want to check out the following books:

James Baldwin, *Notes of a Native Son*, 1955.
Eldridge Cleaver, *Soul on Ice*, 1968.
Nikki Giovanni, *Racism 101*, 1993.

Recognition of Baraka's impact on late twentieth-century American culture have resulted in the publication of several anthologies of his literary oeuvre. *The LeRoi Jones/Amiri Baraka Reader* presents a thorough overview of the writer's development, covering the period from 1957 to 1983. The volume presents Baraka's work from four different periods and emphasizes lesser-known works rather than the author's most-famous writings. Although criticizing the anthology for offering little in the way of original poetry, *Sulfur* reviewer Andrew Schelling termed the collection "a sweeping account of Baraka's development." A *Choice* contributor also praised the volume, calling it "a landmark volume in African American literature." *Transbluency: The Selected Poems of Amiri Baraka/LeRoi Jones (1961-1995)*, published in 1995, was hailed by Daniel L. Guillory in *Library Journal* as "critically important," and Donna Seaman, writing in *Booklist,* commended the "lyric boldness of this passionate collection."

While Baraka's legacy as a major poet of the second half of the twentieth century, as well as his importance as a cultural and political leader, remained widely acknowledged, the changing political climate during the late 1990s and into the next century found the iconoclastic poet increasingly out of step with black Americans. Following the events of September 11, 2001, Baraka's anti-Semitic pronouncements and his 2003 poem "Somebody Blew up America" regarding the complicity of Israeli politicians in the terrorist attacks against the United States did much to diminish his continued relevance or impact. As Cedric Johnson noted in *Monthly Review:* "Though he was as witty and defiant as ever, Baraka's latest publicity lacked the popular resonance and critical edge of his historical work. Unlike his black power activism which was intimately linked to mass mobilizations that sought to challenge domination and transform public institutions into more democratic and responsive bodies, this latest fiasco was more media circus than movement." Such reaction does not discredit the fact that during an earlier era Baraka's influence on younger writers was significant and widespread, and as a leader of the Black Arts movement of the 1960s he did much to define and support black literature's mission into the next century. His experimental fiction of the 1960s is yet considered some of the most significant contribution to black fiction since that of Jean Toomer, who wrote during the Harlem Renaissance of the 1920s. Writers from other ethnic groups have credited Baraka with opening "tightly guarded doors" in the white publishing establishment, noted Murice Kenney in *Amiri Baraka: The Kaleidoscopic Torch*, adding: "We'd all still be waiting the invitation from the New Yorker without him. He taught us how to claim it and take it."

■ Biographical and Critical Sources

BOOKS

Allen, Donald M., and Warren Tallman, editors, *Poetics of the New American Poetry,* Grove (New York, NY), 1973.

Anadolu-Okur, Nilgun, *Contemporary African American Theater: Afrocentricity in the Works of Larry Neal, Amiri Baraka, and Charles Fuller,* Garland (New York, NY), 1997.

Baraka, Amiri, *Tales,* Grove (New York, NY), 1967.

Baraka, Amiri, and Larry Neal, editors, *Black Fire: An Anthology of Afro-American Writing,* Morrow (New York, NY), 1968.

Baraka, Amiri, *Black Magic: Sabotage; Target Study; Black Art; Collected Poetry, 1961-1967,* Bobbs-Merrill (New York, NY), 1969.

Baraka, Amiri, *The Autobiography of LeRoi Jones/Amiri Baraka,* Freundlich Books, 1984.

Baraka, Amiri, and Charlie Reilly, *Conversations with Amiri Baraka,* University Press of Mississippi (Jackson, MS), 1994.

Benston, Kimberly A., editor, *Baraka: The Renegade and the Mask,* Yale University Press (New Haven, CT), 1976.

Benston, Kimberly A., editor, *Imamu Amiri Baraka (LeRoi Jones): A Collection of Critical Essays,* Prentice-Hall, 1978.

Bigsby, C. W. E., *Confrontation and Commitment: A Study of Contemporary American Drama, 1959-1966,* University of Missouri Press, 1968.

Bigsby, C. W. E., editor, *The Black American Writer, Volume II: Poetry and Drama,* Everett/Edwards, 1970, Penguin (Harmondsworth, England), 1971.

Bigsby, C. W. E., *The Second Black Renaissance: Essays in Black Literature,* Greenwood Press (Westport, CT), 1980.

Birnebaum, William M., *Something for Everybody Is Not Enough,* Random House (New York, NY), 1972.

Black Literature Criticism, Gale (Detroit, MI), 1991.

Brown, Lloyd W., *Amiri Baraka,* Twayne (New York, NY), 1980.

Concise Dictionary of American Literary Biography, Volume 1: *The New Consciousness,* Gale (Detroit, MI), 1987.

Contemporary Literary Criticism, Gale (Detroit, MI), Volume 1, 1973, Volume 2, 1974, Volume 3, 1975, Volume 5, 1976, Volume 10, 1979, Volume 14, 1980, Volume 33, 1985.

Cook, Bruce, *The Beat Generation,* Scribner (New York, NY), 1971.

Dace, Letitia, *LeRoi Jones (Imamu Amiri Baraka): A Checklist of Works by and about Him,* Nether Press, 1971.

Debusscher, Gilbert, and Henry I. Schvey, editors, *New Essays on American Drama,* Rodopi, 1989.

Dictionary of Literary Biography, Gale (Detroit, MI), Volume 5: *American Poets since World War II,* 1980, Volume 7: *Twentieth-Century American Dramatists,* 1981, Volume 16: *The Beats; Literary Bohemians in Postwar America,* 1983, Volume 38: *Afro-American Writers after 1955: Dramatists and Prose Writers,* 1985.

Dukore, Bernard F., *Drama and Revolution,* Holt (New York, NY), 1971.

Elam, Harry Justin, *Taking It to the Streets: The Social Protest Theater of Luis Valdez and Amiri Baraka,* University of Michigan Press (Ann Arbor, MI), 1997.

Ellison, Ralph, *Shadow and Act,* New American Library (New York, NY), 1966.

Emanuel, James A., and Theodore L. Gross, editors, *Dark Symphony: Negro Literature in America,* Free Press (New York, NY), 1968.

Fox, Robert Elliot, *Conscientious Sorcerers: The Black Post-modernist Fiction of LeRoi Jones/Baraka, Ishmael Reed and Samuel R. Delany,* Greenwood Press (Westport, CT), 1987.

Frost, David, *The Americans,* Stein & Day, 1970.

Gayle, Addison, editor, *Black Expression: Essays by and about Black Americans in the Creative Arts,* Weybright & Talley, 1969.

Gayle, Addison, *The Way of the New World: The Black Novel in America,* Anchor/Doubleday (New York, NY), 1975.

Gwynne, James B., editor, *Amiri Baraka: The Kaleidoscopic Torch,* Steppingstones Press, 1985.

Harris, William J., *The Poetry and Poetics of Amiri Baraka: The Jazz Aesthetic,* University of Missouri Press, 1985.

Haskins, James, *Black Theater in America,* Crowell (New York, NY), 1982.

Henderson, Stephen E., *Understanding the New Black Poetry: Black Speech, and Black Music as Poetic References,* Morrow (New York, NY), 1973.

Hill, Herbert, *Soon, One Morning,* Knopf (New York, NY), 1963.

Hill, Herbert, editor, *Anger, and Beyond: The Negro Writer in the United States,* Harper (New York, NY), 1966.

Hudson, Theodore, *From LeRoi Jones to Amiri Baraka: The Literary Works,* Duke University Press, 1973.

Inge, M. Thomas, Maurice Duke, and Jackson R. Bryer, editors, *Black American Writers: Bibliographic Essays; Richard Wright, Ralph Ellison, James Baldwin, and Amiri Baraka,* St. Martin's Press (New York, NY), 1978.

Jones, LeRoi, *Blues People: Negro Music in White America,* Morrow (New York, NY), 1963.

Jones, LeRoi, *The Dead Lecturer,* Grove (New York, NY), 1964.

Jones, LeRoi, *Home: Social Essays,* Morrow (New York, NY), 1966.

Keil, Charles, *Urban Blues,* University of Chicago Press (Chicago, IL), 1966.

King, Woodie, and Ron Milner, editors, *Black Drama Anthology*, New American Library (New York, NY), 1971.

Knight, Arthur, and Kit Knight, editors, *The Beat Vision*, Paragon House, 1987.

Kofsky, Frank, *Black Nationalism and the Revolution in Music*, Pathfinder, 1970.

Lacey, Henry C., *To Raise, Destroy, and Create: The Poetry, Drama, and Fiction of Imamu Amiri Baraka (LeRoi Jones)*, Whitson Publishing Company, 1981.

Lewis, Allan, *American Plays and Playwrights*, Crown (New York, NY), 1965.

Littlejohn, David, *Black on White: A Critical Survey of Writing by American Negroes*, Viking (New York, NY), 1966.

Magidson, Mark, *Baraka: A Visual Journal*, St. Ann's Press, 2000.

O'Brien, John, *Interviews with Black Writers*, Liveright (New York, NY), 1973.

Olaniyan, Tejumola, *Scars of Conquest/Masks of Resistance: The Invention of Cultural Identities in African, African-American, and Caribbean Drama*, Oxford University Press (New York, NY), 1995.

Ossman, David, *The Sullen Art: Interviews with Modern American Poets*, Corinth, 1963.

Rexroth, Kenneth, *With Eye and Ear*, Herder & Herder, 1970.

Rosenthal, M. L., *The New Poets: American and British Poetry since World War II*, Oxford University Press (New York, NY), 1967.

Sollors, Werner, *Amiri Baraka/LeRoi Jones: The Quest for a "Populist Modernism,"* Columbia University Press (New York, NY), 1978.

Stepanchev, Stephen, *American Poetry since 1945*, Harper (New York, NY), 1965.

Watts, Jerry Gafio, *Amiri Baraka: The Politics and Art of a Black Intellectual*, New York University Press (New York, NY), 2001.

Weales, Gerald, *The Jumping-off Place: American Drama in the 1960s*, Macmillan (New York, NY), 1969.

Whitlow, Roger, *Black American Literature: A Critical History*, Nelson Hall (New York, NY), 1973.

Williams, Sherley Anne, *Give Birth to Brightness: A Thematic Study in Neo-Black Literature*, Dial (New York, NY), 1972.

Woodard, Komozi, *A Nation within a Nation: Amiri Baraka (LeRoi Jones) and Black Power Politics*, University of North Carolina Press (Chapel Hill, NC), 1999.

PERIODICALS

African-American Review, summer-fall, 2003, special Baraka issue.

American Book Review, February, 1980; May-June, 1985.

Atlantic, January, 1966; May, 1966.

Avant Garde, September, 1968.

Black American Literature Forum, spring, 1980; spring, 1981; fall, 1982; spring, 1983; winter, 1985.

Black Issues Book Review, Robert Fleming, "Trouble Man," p. 22.

Black World, April, 1971; December, 1971; November, 1974; July, 1975.

Booklist, January 1, 1994, p. 799; February 15, 1994, p. 1052; October 15, 1995, p. 380.

Book Week, December 24, 1967.

Book World, October 28, 1979.

Boundary 2, number 6, 1978.

Callaloo, summer, 2003, Matthew Rebhorn, "Flying Dutchman: Maosochism, Minstrelsy, and the Gender Politics of Amiri Baraka's 'Dutchman,'" p. 796.

Chicago Defender, January 11, 1965.

Chicago Tribune, October 4, 1968.

Commentary, February, 1965.

Contemporary Literature, Volume 12, 1971; winter, 2001, Michael Magee, "Tribes of New York," p. 694.

Detroit Free Press, January 31, 1965.

Detroit News, January 15, 1984; August 12, 1984.

Dissent, spring, 1965.

Ebony, August, 1967; August, 1969; February, 1971.

Educational Theatre Journal, March, 1968; March, 1970; March, 1976.

Esquire, June, 1966.

Essence, September, 1970; May, 1984; September, 1984; May, 1985.

Jazz Review, June, 1959.

Journal of Black Poetry, fall, 1968; spring, 1969; summer, 1969; fall, 1969.

Library Journal, January, 1994, p. 112; November, 1995, pp. 78-79.

Los Angeles Free Press, May 3, 1968.

Los Angeles Times, April 20, 1990.

Los Angeles Times Book Review, May 15, 1983; March 29, 1987.

Monthly Review, December, 2004, Cedric Johnson, "Black Radical Enigma," p. 42.

Nation, October 14, 1961; November 14, 1961; March 13, 1964; April 13, 1964; January 4, 1965; March 15, 1965; January 22, 1968; February 2, 1970; November 18, 2002, Art Winslow, "Prosody in Motion," p. 11.

Negro American Literature Forum, March, 1966; winter, 1973.

Negro Digest, December, 1963; February, 1964; August, 1964; March, 1965; April, 1965; March, 1966; April, 1966; June, 1966; April, 1967; April, 1968; January, 1969; April, 1969.

Newsweek, March 13, 1964; April 13, 1964; November 22, 1965; May 2, 1966; March 6, 1967; December 4, 1967; December 1, 1969; February 19, 1973.

New York, November 5, 1979.

New Yorker, April 4, 1964; December 26, 1964; March 4, 1967; December 30, 1972; October 14, 2002, Nick Paumgarten, "Goodbye, Paramus."

New York Herald Tribune, March 25, 1964; April 2, 1964; December 13, 1964; October 27, 1965.

New York Post, March 16, 1964; March 24, 1964; January 15, 1965; March 18, 1965.

New York Review of Books, January 20, 1966; May 22, 1964; July 2, 1970; October 17, 1974; June 11, 1984; June 14, 1984.

New York Times, April 28, 1966; May 8, 1966; August 10, 1966; September 14, 1966; October 5, 1966; January 20, 1967; February 28, 1967; July 15, 1967; January 5, 1968; January 6, 1968; January 9, 1968; January 10, 1968; February 7, 1968; April 14, 1968; August 16, 1968; November 27, 1968; December 24, 1968; August 26, 1969; November 23, 1969; February 6, 1970; May 11, 1972; June 11, 1972; November 11, 1972; November 14, 1972; November 23, 1972; December 5, 1972; December 27, 1974; December 29, 1974; November 19, 1979; October 15, 1981; January 23, 1984; February 9, 1991.

New York Times Book Review, January 31, 1965; November 28, 1965; May 8, 1966; February 4, 1968; March 17, 1968; February 14, 1971; June 6, 1971; June 27, 1971; December 5, 1971; March 12, 1972; December 16, 1979; March 11, 1984; July 5, 1987; December 20, 1987.

New York Times Magazine, February 5, 1984.

Salmagundi, spring-summer, 1973.

Saturday Review, April 20, 1963; January 11, 1964; January 9, 1965; December 11, 1965; December 9, 1967; October 2, 1971; July 12, 1975.

Skeptical Inquirer, January-February, 2003, Kevin Christopher, "Baraka Buys Bunk," p. 8.

Studies in Black Literature, spring, 1970; Volume 1, number 2, 1970; Volume 3, number 2, 1972; Volume 3, number 3, 1972; Volume 4, number 1, 1973.

Sulfur, spring, 1992.

Sunday News (New York, NY), January 21, 1973.

Time, December 25, 1964; November 19, 1965; May 6, 1966; January 12, 1968; April 26, 1968; June 28, 1968; June 28, 1971.

Times Literary Supplement, November 25, 1965; September 1, 1966; September 11, 1969; October 9, 1969; August 2, 1991.

Tribune Books (Chicago, IL), March 29, 1987.

Village Voice, December 17, 1964; May 6, 1965; May 19, 1965; August 30, 1976; August 1, 1977; December 17-23, 1980; October 2, 1984.

Washington Post, August 15, 1968; September 12, 1968; November 27, 1968; December 5, 1980; January 23, 1981; June 29, 1987.

Washington Post Book World, December 24, 1967; May 22, 1983.

Washington Times, October 11, 2002, Ward Connerly, "Amiri Baraka Hits a New Low: New Jersey's Hateful Poet Laureate," p. A22.

ONLINE

Academy of American Poets Web site, http://www.poets.org/ (April 20, 2005), "Amiri Baraka."*

Elizabeth Barrett Browning

■ **Personal**

Born March 6, 1806, in Durham, England; died June 29, 1861, in Florence, Italy; daughter of Edward (a county squire) and Mary (Graham-Clarke) Moulton-Barrett; married Robert Browning (a poet and playwright), September 12, 1846; children: Robert Weidemann Barrett. *Education:* Tutored at home and self-educated.

■ **Career**

Poet.

■ **Writings**

POETRY

The Battle of Marathon, W. Lindsell (London, England), 1820.

(Published anonymously) *An Essay on the Mind, with Other Poems*, Duncan (London, England), 1826.

(Anonymously) *Prometheus Bound, Translated from the Greek of Aeschylus; and Miscellaneous Poems*, A. J. Valpy (London, England), 1833, Francis (New York, NY), 1851.

The Seraphim and Other Poems, Saunders and Otley (London, England), 1838.

Poems, two volumes, Moxon (London, England), 1844, published as *A Drama of Exile: And Other Poems*, two volumes, Langley (New York, NY), 1845.

Poems: New Edition (includes *Sonnets from the Portuguese*), two volumes, Chapman and Hall (London, England), 1850, published as *The Poems of Elizabeth Barrett Browning*, Francis (New York, NY), 1850.

Casa Guidi Windows: A Poem, Chapman and Hall (London, England), 1851.

Poems: Third Edition, two volumes, Chapman and Hall (London, England), 1853.

(With Robert Browning) *Two Poems*, Chapman and Hall (London, England), 1854.

Poems: Fourth Edition, three volumes, Chapman and Hall (London, England), 1856.

Aurora Leigh, Chapman and Hall (London, England), 1857, Francis (New York, NY), 1857, revised edition, Chapman and Hall, 1859.

Poems before Congress, Chapman and Hall (London, England), 1860, published as *Napoleon III in Italy, and Other Poems*, Francis (New York, NY), 1860.

Last Poems, Chapman and Hall (London, England), 1862.

(With Richard Hengist Horne) *Psyche Apocalypte: A Lyrical Drama*, [London, England], 1876.

New Poems by Robert and Elizabeth Barrett Browning, edited by Frederic G. Kenyon, Smith, Elder (London, England), 1914, Macmillan (New York, NY), 1915.

The Poet's Enchiridion, edited by H. Buxton Forman, Bibliophile Society (Boston, MA), 1914.

Elizabeth Barrett Browning: Hitherto Unpublished Poems and Stories, with an Unedited Autobiography, two volumes, edited by H. Buxton Forman, Bibliophile Society (Boston, MA), 1914.

PROSE

The Greek Christian Poets and the English Poets, Chapman and Hall (London, England), 1863, published as *Essays on the Greek Christian Poets and the English Poets,* Miller (New York, NY), 1863.

Diary by E. B. B.: The Unpublished Diary of Elizabeth Barrett Browning, 1831-1832, edited by Philip Kelley and Ronald Hudson, Ohio University Press (Athens, OH), 1969.

COLLECTIONS

The Poetical Works of Elizabeth Barrett Browning, six volumes, Smith, Elder (London, England), 1889-90.

The Poetical Works of Elizabeth Barrett Browning, edited by G. Kenyon, Smith, Elder (London, England), 1897.

The Complete Poetical Works of Elizabeth Barrett Browning, edited by Harriet Waters Preston, Houghton Mifflin (Boston, MA), 1900.

The Complete Works of Elizabeth Barrett Browning, six volumes, edited by Charlotte Porter and Helen A. Clarke, Crowell (New York, NY), 1900.

LETTERS

Letters of Elizabeth Barrett Browning Addressed to Richard Hengist Horne, two volumes, edited by S. R. Townshend, Bentley (London, England), 1877.

The Letters of Elizabeth Barrett Browning, two volumes, edited by Frederic G. Kenyon, Smith, Elder (London, England), 1897.

Letters to Robert Browning and Other Correspondents, edited by Thomas J. Wise, [London, England], 1916.

Elizabeth Barrett Browning: Letters to Her Sister, 1846-1859, edited by Leonard Huxley, Murray (London, England), 1929.

Letters from Elizabeth Barrett to B. R. Haydon, edited by Martha Hale Shackford, Oxford University Press (New York, NY), 1939.

Elizabeth Barrett to Miss Mitford: The Unpublished Letters of Elizabeth Barrett Browning to Mary Russell Mitford, edited by Betty Miller, Murray (London, England), 1954.

Elizabeth Barrett to Mr. Boyd: Unpublished Letters of Elizabeth Barrett Browning to Hugh Stuart Boyd, edited by Barbara P. McCarthy, Yale University Press (New Haven, CT), 1955.

Letters of the Brownings to George Barrett, edited by Paul Landis, University of Illinois Press (Urbana, IL), 1958.

The Letters of Robert Browning and Elizabeth Barrett, 1845-1846, two volumes, edited b Elvan Kintner, Harvard University Press (Cambridge, MA), 1969.

Invisible Friends: The Correspondence of Elizabeth Barrett Barrett and Benjamin Robert Haydon, 1842-1845, edited by Willard Bissell Pope, Harvard University Press (Cambridge, MA), 1972.

Elizabeth Barrett Browning's Letters to Mrs. David Ogilvy, 1849-1861, edited by Peter N. Heydon and Philip Kelley, Quadrangle/New York Times Books (New York, NY), 1973.

■ Sidelights

"How do I love thee? Let me count the ways/ I love thee to the depth and breadth and height / My soul can reach, when feeling out of sight." These lines from *Sonnets from the Portuguese* form the core of almost any literate person's knowledge of quotable poetry, yet many forget who wrote them. These are not from a sonnet by William Shakespeare, but rather from one by the Victorian poet Elizabeth Barrett Browning. As an essayist in the *Concise Dictionary of British Literary Biography* wrote, "among all women poets of the English-speaking world in the nineteenth century, none was held in higher critical esteem or was more admired for the independence and courage of her views than Elizabeth Barrett Browning." Married to poet and playwright Robert Browning, Barrett Browning out-produced her famous husband during the decade and a half they were married. Making their home in Florence, Italy, the couple was besieged by visitors from abroad; most of them made the pilgrimage to see Elizabeth. In fact Browning was one of the first poets to gain a simultaneous following both in her native England and in the United States.

Revered in her own lifetime as one of the finest poets in England and even touted as a possible poet laureate, Browning spiraled into obscurity in the late nineteenth and early twentieth century. However, after decades of being out of style and favor, Browning made a resurgence in the late twentieth century. *Dictionary of Literary Biographer* contributor Beverly Taylor explained Browning's re-emergence: "By the 1950s she was represented in anthologies or literary studies almost entirely by *Sonnets from the Portuguese,*. . . revered as a paean of devotion to her husband yet frequently derided for its supposed sentimentality. Her most ambitious work, *Aurora Leigh,* went through more than twenty editions by 1900 but none between 1905 and 1978. Although in anthologies and literary histories after 1900 the tendency of scholars to mention her as an appendix to discussions of Robert Browning and refer to her patronizingly as 'Mrs. Browning' or 'Elizabeth' has long obscured her significant literary achievement, since the 1970s Elizabeth Barrett Browning has increasingly been recognized as a powerful, independent voice of social criticism and an innovative poet whose experimentation with rhyme and rhythms (frequently lamented by reviewers in her day) anticipated movements in modern versification."

The Squire's Daughter

Born Elizabeth Barrett Moulton-Barrett on March 6, 1806, "Ba," as she was nicknamed, was the oldest of eleven surviving children of Edward Moulton-Barrett and Mary Graham-Clarke. Moulton-Barrett was by this time a country squire, his wealth based on Jamaican sugar plantations. Soon after Elizabeth's birth the family moved from Durham, England, to a proper squire's home at Hope End, in the Malvern Hills of Herefordshire. Hope End was an estate of almost 500 acres, with a Georgian house which the father converted into stables. He built a new mansion, Turkish in design, with all the finest and richest materials, and landscaped the grounds with ponds, grottos, and gardens, turning Hope End into an opulent family setting.

Here Elizabeth Barrett grew up pursuing many of the activities of the privileged classes: she and her brothers and sisters went for long walks, had picnics, and held amateur theatricals. She also rode her pony along the lanes of the estate. She was largely self-educated, borrowing her brother Edward's tutor at first, then later branching out for classical studies to a neighbor, Hugh Stuart Boyd, a blind scholar who formed a close relationship with the young girl. Unlike her more outdoors-loving siblings, Elizabeth formed an early love of books and began composing poetry at age four. By the time she was ten she had read the histories of Greece, Rome, and England, and had imbibed Shakespeare's best plays, as well as the work of Alexander Pope. At eleven she began her study of Greek, Latin, and French, reading the great authors of each language. She even learned enough Hebrew to read the Old

Browning's *Sonnets from the Portuguese,* a series of love poems first published in 1850, contains the famous line, "How do I love thee? Let me count the ways."

Testament in its original language. From the French she gleaned a sense of liberalism; her readings of Voltaire and Jean-Jacques Rousseau stuck with her throughout her life, as did the works of Thomas Paine and Mary Wollstonecroft.

At age eleven Elizabeth wrote her first book, *The Battle of Marathon,* a 1,500-line epic in heroic couplets celebrating that famous battle between the Athenians and the Persians. The poem was privately printed by her father. By age fifteen she had published two poems in the *New Monthly* magazine. However, that same year she fell ill from an undiagnosed complaint. Two of her sisters also suffered from this illness, but quickly recovered, while Elizabeth lingered in the sick bed long enough for her family to begin treating her as an invalid. Sent to a spa, she was treated for a year for a supposed spinal injury and returned home weakened, for she had been confined to bed for almost the entire time. Doctor's orders were for her to avoid any strenuous activity, which included reading and writing.

A Poet Emerges

Elizabeth Barrett ignored such prescriptions, setting to work on an ambitious 1,300-line poem in couplets that would trace the history of science, philosophy, and poetry from ancient Greece to the nineteenth century, and celebrate various liberal political movements as well as the poetry of Lord Byron.

AURORA LEIGH.

BY

ELIZABETH BARRETT BROWNING.

NEW YORK:
C. S. FRANCIS & CO., 554 BROADWAY.
BOSTON:—53 DEVONSHIRE STREET.
1857.

Browning's epic 1857 work *Aurora Leigh*, the tale of a successful female author who finds true love, has echoes of the poet's own life.

The resulting *An Essay on the Mind, with Other Poems* was published anonymously in 1826 and met critical appraisal that generally praised the author's erudition but decried the work as pretentious and arid intellectualism. As Taylor noted, such reviews "established what would become a theme in contemporary criticism [of Barrett's work]—Barrett's unusual, even 'unwomanly' erudition."

Barrett suffered personal setbacks with the death of her beloved mother in 1828 and then the forced sale of Hope End in 1832. The Jamaican sugar plantations had been badly mismanaged for years, and finally things came to a head; Hope End had to be liquidated. The sale was a humiliation for Barrett's father, though the family was left relatively well off. They moved first to the coastal town of Sidmouth, and then in 1835 to London, where Barrett would live until her marriage.

While residing at Sidmouth, Barrett anonymously published a translation of Aeschylus's drama about Prometheus together with some of her poems, *Prometheus Bound, Translated from the Greek of Aeschylus; and Miscellaneous Poems*. The *Concise Dictionary of British Literary Biography* essayist noted that the miscellaneous poems of the title "are all immature in content and expression and give little promise of their author's future distinction." Barrett completed the translation in two weeks, an exercise and a result of her work with Boyd, for the classicist lived nearby the family in Sidmouth and the two spent a great deal of time together, with Barrett helping the older man get his text on the Greek Christian Fathers ready for publication—much to the neglect of her own poetry.

Gains Public Renown

Settled in London, Barrett began work on another collection, *The Seraphim and Other Poems*, the first collection to bear her name at publication. The title poem of seventy-eight pages features the conversation of two angels discussing the Crucifixion and Christ's suffering on the cross. Taylor noted that the theme of the poem is "not heroic rebellion but the divine submission of Christ." She went on to observe: "Through Christ's humility and suffering the angels learn to value earthly pain above celestial tranquility." Among the shorter poems, "Isobel's Child," about the death of a three-month-old baby in its mother's arms, became an especial favorite of the critics and public alike. This collection brought the usual criticisms about poetry not being a woman's provenance, but also won praise in many influential journals, such as the *Athenaeum* and the *Quarterly Review*. Barrett had arrived on the London literary scene.

However, just as she was earning respect and a degree of renown, illness again intruded in the form of a bronchial infection. Barrett was sent to a warmer climate on the south coast of Devon to the town of Torquay. For the next three years she was largely bedridden, and the drowning death of her closest and dearest brother, Edward, in 1840, exacerbated matters. When she finally returned to London in 1841 she believed the rest of her life would be lived as an invalid. She repaired to her room, surrounded by busts of famous poets and accompanied by her dog, Flush, and stayed there for much of the next five years. She had a few friends who would come to visit, such as the poet John Kenyon and the writer Mary Russell Mitford. Otherwise she lived with her books, wrote letters, and continued to write poetry, freed at least by her illness from any domestic household duties.

In 1844 Barrett published the fruits of her recent labors in the two-volume *Poems,* a work that "established Barrett as one of the major poets of the day," according to Taylor. With the long poem "A Drama of Exile," she takes up John Milton's *Paradise Lost* where that great poet had left it. "Lady Geraldine's Courtship: A Romance of the Age," about a young poet who falls in love with an earl's daughter, "Bertha in the Lane," about the death of a jilted woman, and "The Cry of the Children," dealing with child labor, are other memorable works from this collection.

From Sick Bed to Motherhood

Publication of *Poems* brought not only further recognition, but also attracted the notice of young poet and playwright Robert Browning. Barrett had alluded to Browning's work in her "Lady Geraldine's Courtship," and Browning returned the compliment by writing to Barrett, expressing his admiration not only for her verses but for her as a person. Soon Browning was a regular visitor to the Barrett domicile at 50 Wimpole Street. Though six years younger than Barrett, he was strongly attracted to her. Barrett began composing poems detailing the progression of their love, later collected in *Sonnets from the Portuguese.* This courtship progressed despite the objections of Barrett's father, an autocrat who wanted his children to remain dependent on him. Barrett, however, knew her own mind. By September of 1845 she had agreed to marry the younger man; the following year they were joined in matrimony at a parish church not far from her home. Almost immediately, the couple left for the warmer climate of Italy.

In the more hospitable climate of Italy, Barrett bloomed. The couple settled first in Pisa, but by 1847 had moved on to Florence where they rented

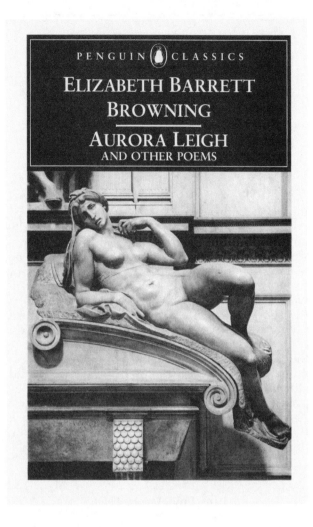

A verse narrative of 11,000 lines, *Aurora Leigh* is considered Browning's most ambitious work.

the second floor of an old city palace, the Casa Guidi. It was here where Barrett, now Barrett Browning, would live and work for the rest of her life. It was also the birthplace, in 1849, of her son, Robert Weidemann. Barrett was forty-three at the time. The couple were visited by friends and admirers from both sides of the Atlantic, including Thomas Carlyle, William Makepeace Thackeray, Owen Meredith, and Harriet Beecher Stowe.

The year of her son's birth Barrett showed her husband the love poems she had written during their courtship and he convinced her to publish them. The title *Sonnets from the Portuguese* was chosen to make it appear that these were not autobiographical, but rather translations. The first publication of the forty-four Petrarchan sonnets appeared in the 1850 new edition of *Poems.* Taylor commented that *Sonnets from the Portuguese* is "recognized as one of

---

If you enjoy the works of Elizabeth Barrett Browning, you may also want to check out the following:

The sonnets of William Shakespeare (1564-1616), the love poems of John Donne (1572-1631), and the poems of Emily Dickinson (1830-1866).

---

the finest sonnet sequences in English." The same critic also noted that "the sequence is markedly innovative. [Barrett] Browning breaks with the conventions of the Renaissance sonnet sequence . . . by making the speaker and lover a woman." Taylor further explained: "While readers have been perennially engrossed by the biographical components of the series, the sonnets' intricate artistry—which prompted critics to rank them with those of Shakespeare—is too often overlooked." Critical reaction to the new edition of *Poems* ranged from those who lamented what they considered obfuscations and clumsy rhymes (but which later reviewers see as presaging modern modalities and rhythms employed by poets such as Gerard Manley Hopkins), to those such as the critic for the *Athenaeum* who proposed her for the next poet laureate of England.

Pens Epic *Aurora Leigh*

The Italian years proved to be rich ones for Barrett in terms of her poetry. Two volumes of political poems, *Casa Guidi Windows* and *Poems before Congress,* deal with Italian independence and with issues such as slavery and women's rights. One of the major works of her later career is *Aurora Leigh,* a narrative of 11,000 lines telling the story of the eponymous heroine from her birth in Italy to her early years in rural England, her successful literary career in London, her move to Florence, and finally her marriage to her only true love. While using the broad outlines of Barrett's own life, the poem deals with hard-hitting topics such as the role of educated women in Victorian England, the possible dangers of extreme socialist philosophy, and the plight of the fallen woman. The last theme in particular, as articulated through the misadventures of a minor character in the drama, Marian Erle, who is kidnaped by a rival and sent to a French brothel, earned the work the reputation of a racy title with critics. The public, however, as well as fellow artists, championed the book, sending it through nineteen editions in its first twenty-eight years after initial publication. Taylor noted that *Aurora Leigh* is "simultaneously an epic and a novel." The work, in Taylor's opinion, "bluntly argues that the stuff of ambitious poetry should not be the remote chivalry of a distant past, neither King Arthur nor Charlemagne, but the pulsing life of the present day as experienced by ordinary people."

Illness plagued Barrett's final years. Devastated by the 1861 death of Italian statesman Camillo di Cavour, who Barrett saw as the one man who could unify Italy, she fell into a low state and caught a severe cold that went into her chest. She died in her husband's arms on June 29, 1861, acclaimed in obituary notices of the day as the greatest woman poet in English history.

■ Biographical and Critical Sources

BOOKS

Barnes, Warner, *A Bibliography of Elizabeth Barrett Browning,* University of Texas Press (Austin, TX), 1967.

Concise Dictionary of British Literary Biography, Volume 4: *Victorian Writers, 1832-1890,* Gale (Detroit, MI), 1991.

Dictionary of Literary Biography, Gale (Detroit, MI), Volume 32: *Victorian Poets before 1850,* 1984, pp. 53-89, Volume 199: *Victorian Woman Poets,* 1999, pp. 79-99.

Hayter, Alethea, *Mrs. Browning: A Poet's Work and Its Setting,* Faber and Faber (London, England), 1962.

Hewlett, Dorothy, *Elizabeth Barrett Browning: A Life,* Knopf (New York, NY), 1952.

Hudson, Gladys W., *An Elizabeth Barrett Browning Concordance,* four volumes, Gale (Detroit, MI), 1973.

Kelley, Philip, and Ronald Hudson, editors, *The Browning's Correspondence: A Checklist,* Browning Institute (New York, NY), 1978.

Lupton, Mary Jane, *Elizabeth Barrett Browning,* Feminist Press (Westbury, NY), 1972.

Mander, Rosalie, *Mrs. Browning: The Story of Elizabeth Barrett,* Weidenfeld and Nicolson (London, England), 1980.

Marks, Jeannette, *The Family of the Barrett: A Colonial Romance,* Macmillan (New York, NY), 1938.

Markus, Julia, *Dared and Done: The Marriage of Elizabeth Barrett and Robert Browning,* Knopf (New York, NY), 1995.

McAleer, Edward C., *The Brownings of Casa Guidi,* Browning Institute (New York, NY), 1979.

Moers, Ellen, *Literary Women,* Doubleday (Garden City, NY), 1976.

Peterson, William S., *Robert and Elizabeth Barrett Browning: An Annotated Bibliography, 1951-1970,* Browning Institute (New York, NY), 1974.

Radley, Virginia L., *Elizabeth Barrett Browning,* Twayne (New York, NY), 1972.

Stone, Marjorie, *Elizabeth Barrett Browning,* St. Martin's Press (New York, NY), 1995.

Stott, Rebecca, and Simon Avery, *Elizabeth Barrett Browning,* Longman (London, England), 2003.

Taplin, Gardner B., *The Life of Elizabeth Barrett Browning,* Yale University Press (New Haven, CT), 1957.

PERIODICALS

Biblio, April, 1998, Lucy Gordon, "Through Casa Guidi Windows," p. 16.

Biography, spring, 2003, Joseph Phelan, "Ethnology and Biography: The Case of the Brownings," p. 261.

English Review, February, 2003, Francis O'Gorman, "The Politics of Live in *Sonnets from the Portuguese,*" p. 28.

Philological Quarterly, winter, 2000, Sueann Schatz, "*Aurora Leigh* as Paradigm of Domestic-Professional Fiction," p. 91.

Studies in the Literary Imagination, fall, 2002, Natalie M. Houston, "Affecting Authenticity: *Sonnets from the Portuguese* and Modern Love," p. 99.

Texas Studies in Literature and Language, summer, 1997, Ranen Omer, "Elizabeth Barrett Browning and Apocalypse," p. 97.

Victorian Poetry, winter, 2001, Steve Dillon, "Barrett Browning's Poetic Vocation, p. 509;" fall, 2002, Marjorie Stone, "Elizabeth Barrett Browning," p. 290; fall, 2003, Marjorie Stone, "Elizabeth Barrett Browning," p. 377.

World and I, October, 2002, Michael Timko, "Love Lost and Found—The Lives of Elizabeth and Robert Browning," p. 302.

ONLINE

Academy of American Poets, http://www.poets.org/ (November 15, 2004), "Elizabeth Barrett Browning."

Victorian Web, http://www.victorianweb.com/ (November 15, 2004), "Elizabeth Barrett Browning."

Women's Studies Database, http://www.mith2.umd.edu/ (November 15, 2004), "Elizabeth Barrett Browning."*

Henri Cartier-Bresson

■ Personal

Born August 22, 1908, in Chanteloup, Seine-et-Marne, France; died August 3, 2004, in I'lle-sur-Sorgue, France; married Ratna Mohini (a dancer), 1937 (marriage ended); married Martine Franck (a photographer), 1970; children: one daughter. *Education:* Studied painting with Jean Cottenet and Jacques-Emile Blanche, 1922-23, and with Andre Lhote, Paris France, 1927-28; studied painting and literature at Cambridge University, 1928-29.

■ Career

Photographer, painter, and film maker. Assistant director to Jean Renoir, France, 1936, 1939; *Ce Soir,* Paris, France, staff photographer, 1937-39; Magnum Photos, cofounder, 1947; director of documentary *Le Retour,* 1947. *Exhibitions:* Individual photography exhibitions: Gallery Julien Levy, New York, NY, 1932; Club Atheneo, Madrid, Spain, 1932; Palacio de Bellas Artes, Mexico City, Mexico, 1934; *Documentary and Anti-Graphic,* Gallery Julien Levy, New York, NY, 1935; Museum of Modern Art, New York, NY (retrospective), 1946, 1968; Institute of Contemporary Arts, London, 1952; Art Institute of Chicago, 1954; Musée des Arts Decoratifs, Paris, France, 1955; Phillips Collection, Washington, DC, 1964; Asahi Gallery, Tokyo, Japan, 1965; *En France,* Grand Palais, Paris, then world tour, 1970; International Center of Photography, New York, NY, 1974, 1979; Fruit Market Gallery, Edinburgh, Scotland, 1978; Galerie Delpire, Paris, 1979; Zeit-Foto Salon, Tokyo, 1979, 1980; Kunsthaus, Zurich, Switzerland, 1981; Colorado Photographic Arts Center, Denver, 1981; Art University, Osaka, Japan, 1991; Palazzo Sanvitale, 1992; L'Amerique, FNAC, Paris, 1992; Muséo Camon Aznar, 1992; Hamburg, Germany, 1994; I.C. P., New York, NY 1994; La Caridad, Barcelona, Spain, 1994; National Portrait Gallery, London, 1998; Hayward Gallery, London, 1998; Bibliotheque Nationale de France, Paris, 2003; and Martin-Gropius-Bau Museum, Berlin, Germany, 2004. Exhibitions of drawings: Carlton Gallery, New York, NY, 1975; Bischofberger Gallery, Zurich, 1976; Forcalquier Galerie, Paris, 1976; Musée d'Art Moderne, Paris, 1981; Muséo Nacional de Belas Artes, Mexico City, 1982; French Institute, Stockholm, Sweden, 1983; Padiglione d'Arte Contemporanea, Milan, Italy, 1983; Museum of Modern Art, Oxford, England, 1984; Palais Liechtenstein, Vienna, and Salzburg, Austria, 1985; French Institute, Athens, Greece, 1985; Manheim, Germany, 1986; Herstand Gallery, New York, NY, 1987; École des Beaux Arts, Paris, 1989; Printemps Ginza, Tokyo, 1989; Musée d'Art Moderne, Taiwan, 1991; Parma, Italy, 1992; Saragosse, Logrono, 1993; and La Caridad, Barcelona, 1994. *Military service:* Served in French Army, 1930 and 1939-43; prisoner of war in Germany, 1940-43.

■ Member

American Academy of Arts and Sciences.

■ Awards, Honors

Overseas Press Club of America Award, 1948, 1954, 1960, 1964; American Society of Magazine Photographers Award, 1953; Prix de la Société Français de Photographie, 1959; D.Litt., Oxford University, 1975; Culture Prize, Deutsche Gesellschaft für Photographie, 1979; Hasselblad Award, 1983; Novecento Award, 1986; inducted into International Photography Hall of Fame, 2001.

■ Writings

The Photographs of Henri Cartier-Bresson, text by Lincoln Kersten, Museum of Modern Art (New York, NY), 1947.

The Decisive Moment, Simon and Schuster (New York, NY), 1952.

Les danses a Bali, text by Antonin Artaud, Delpire (Paris, France), 1954.

The Europeans, Simon and Schuster (New York, NY), 1955.

People of Moscow, Thames and Hudson (London, England), 1955.

China in Transition, Thames and Hudson (London, England), 1956.

Henri Cartier-Bresson: Fotografie, text by Anna Farova, Statni naklaatelstvi krasne (Prague, Czechoslovakia), 1958.

Photographs by Henri Cartier-Bresson, Grossman (New York, NY), 1963.

China, text by Barbara Miller, Bantam (New York, NY), 1964.

The World of HCB, Viking (New York, NY), 1968.

France, text by François Nourissier, Thames and Hudson (London, England), 1970.

The Face of Asia, introduction by Robert Shapien, John Weatherhill (New York, NY), 1972.

About Russia, Thames and Hudson (London, England), 1973.

Henri Cartier-Bresson, Aperture (New York, NY), 1976.

Henri Cartier-Bresson: Ritratti, text by Andre Pieyre de Mandiargues and Ferdinando Scianna, Gruppo Editoriale Fabbri (Milan, Italy), 1983.

Photoportraits, text by de Andre Pieyre de Mandiargues, Thames and Hudson (London, England), 1985.

Henri Cartier-Bresson in India, text by Yves Vequaud, Thames and Hudson (London, England), 1987.

L'Autre Chine, Centre National de la Photographie (Paris, France), 1989.

Line by Line: Henri Cartier-Bresson's Drawings, Thames and Hudson (London, England), 1989.

America in Passing, Bullfinch (New York, NY), 1991.

Alberto Giacometti photographie par Henri Cartier-Bresson, Franco Sciardelli (Milan, Italy), 1991.

A propos de Paris, text by Vera Feyder and Andre Pieyre de Mandiargues, Thames and Hudson (London, England), 1994.

Double Regard, text by Jean Leymarie, Le Nycatlope (Amiens, France), 1994.

Mexican Notebooks, text by Carlos Fuentes, Thames and Hudson (London, England), 1994.

Europeans, text by Jean Clair, Thames and Hudson (London, England), 1997.

Tete à tete, text by Ernst H. Gombrich, Thames and Hudson (London, England), 1998.

The Mind's Eye: Writings on Photography and Photographers, Aperture (New York, NY), 1999.

Landscape Townscape, text by Erik Orsenna and Gerard Mace, Thames and Hudson (London, England), 2001.

■ Sidelights

"Once Cartier-Bresson photographed something or someone," wrote *Newsweek* contributor Malcolm Jones, "you might as well have retired them as subjects: best picture of a man jumping over a puddle, best portrait of Sartre, best image of a picnic." Jones could have gone on with his list to include best shot of a child carrying two huge wine bottles or best picture of proletarian dancers in Moscow or of crowds of Chinese in Shanghai attempting to buy gold. Henri Cartier-Bresson's list of instantly recognizable black-and-white photographs is a long one, yet the French artist, who died in 2004, always claimed that he was not really a photographer at all. To prove his claim, he laid down his Leica in the early 1970s, and, except for the rare assignment, turned wholly to his first artistic passions: painting and drawing.

The world did not forget his work, however. As Sadanand Menon noted in the *New International* at the time of Cartier-Bresson's death, "For over 45 years, from when he began to work with a camera in 1932 until he stopped taking photographs in the mid-1970s, almost nothing significant seems to have happened in the world without Cartier-Bresson's signature presence there with his battered and taped Leica M 3 camera." In those years before television and the pervasiveness of instant electronic images, the work of Cartier-Bresson and other photojournalists was greedily consumed by the public. He was in Spain for that country's civil war, in Paris for the occupation and liberation in World War II, in China for the communist revolution, in India and Pakistan at the handover from England, in the Soviet Union as it began to lift the Iron Curtain, in Hungary for the 1956 revolution, in Cuba when Castro took over, in Berlin when the Wall went up, and in Prague in 1968. His portraits of famous people define them: he took the final photos of India's Gandhi, just minutes before that leader was assassinated; his portrait of Henri Matisse with birds is iconic. These images have entered the cultural psyche; Cartier-Bresson could not retire from them.

Cartier-Bresson was considered a pioneer of photography and perhaps one of the greatest ever. Writing in *Grove Art Online*, Mark Haworth-Booth noted that Cartier-Bresson "not only shaped and extended the concept of photography but through it achieved a psychological penetration and formal perfection equal to other kinds of serious image-making." During his lifetime, he was the stuff of legend, and his thousands of photographs have inspired several generations of younger photographers. Jones noted in *Newsweek* that Cartier-Bresson "set a standard for excellence that has yet to be matched. Art photography, portraiture, photojournalism—there was nothing he could not do with a camera." For *Time* writer James Nachtwey, Cartier-Bresson "made us see." Nachtwey further explained: "Through his eyes we see the universal in the specific, large issues in small things, mystery in the obvious, poetry in the mundane. We see infinity in the blink of an eye." Such a legacy was no accident, for as Cartier-Bresson himself noted in his book *The Decisive Moment*, there is a perfect instant for each shot. This moment comes with, as he noted, "the simultaneous recognition, in a fraction of a second, of the significance of an event as well as the precise organization of forms which gives that even its proper expression." Famed for shooting with available light and without a flash, sometimes even without using a light meter, Cartier-Bresson eschewed dark-room manipulation of his prints. Rather, the moment was caught in a frozen instant of insight by his lens, or not at all. As Vicky Hallett put it in *U.S. News and World Report*, "Captured through the lens of Henri Cartier-Bresson's 35-millimeter Leica, a photograph was never merely just a picture of a bicycle passing a spiral staircase, or a boy toting wine bottles down a street. It was an instant of serendipity, when subject, geometry, and motion aligned as they never would again." Cartier-Bresson's life also displayed this same serendipity.

Wealthy Origins

Born on August 22, 1908, in Chanteloup, France, Henri Cartier-Bresson came from a family whose wealth, for the French, equaled that of the Ameri-

can Rockefellers. The family was in the thread business on both sides, but this did not stop Cartier-Bresson's uncle or his father from their own artistic pursuits, albeit with the family firm always foremost in their thoughts. The same was expected of young Henri, but in this respect the rebellious youngster disappointed his parents. Growing up in Paris, he lost interest in his studies, failing to pass the exam for the prestigious Lycée Condorcet. Instead, he was interested in intellectual currents of the day, including the rise of surrealism, Nietzschean and Hindu philosophy, and psychoanalysis. His interest in painting began early, and by the age of twelve he was taking private lessons. One of his instructors introduced the young man to some of the artistic movers and shakers of the day, including Andre Breton, whose writings were shaping the surrealist school. Cartier-Bresson was greatly taken by this revolutionary art movement which held spontaneity as one of the highest goals and which also plumbed the unconscious mind with its strange visions. But most of all, Cartier-Bresson appreciated the social outcast role such surrealists enjoyed.

A pioneer in the art of photojournalism, Cartier-Bresson captured many memorable and startling images during a career that spanned five decades.

Using his hand-held 35-millimeter Leica camera, Cartier-Bresson photographs a trio of men in Brooklyn, New York.

In the late 1920s Cartier-Bresson began taking lessons with cubist painter Andre Lhote, served a compulsory years in the French Army, and then went to Africa. There he landed in the French Ivory Coast and headed for the interior, intending to make his living as a big-game hunter. Instead he caught malaria; after a year tramping in Africa, Cartier-Bresson returned to Europe, where he traveled in Central European countries. The rough-and-tumble life in Africa dissuaded him from a career in painting, but seeing a photograph of native boys diving into an African lake, he realized that photography was the medium for him.

Have Leica, Will Travel

In 1932 he bought a Leica camera small enough to hold in the hand and set about to hunt images to capture with it. He would use the Leica brand for the rest of his career, learning how to use it in a matter of days and forsaking such photographic equipment as the flash or tripod. Not long after purchasing the camera, he shot one of his most famous images, *Behind Gare St. Lazar,* "an iconic vision of a shadowy figure leaping across a puddle," as Hallett

described the photo. Here at the very outset of his career were the ingredients of what would make Cartier-Bresson famous: the perfect moment captured in mid-action, with the photographer perfectly positioned as if, as Cartier-Bresson was fond of saying, he did not take the picture, rather the picture took him. As a writer for the *Economist* noted, Cartier-Bresson "framed and preserved [such] less famous moments, elevating them with his genius so that they somehow seemed to capture the essence of life itself." Haworth-Booth noted of these early images that Cartier-Bresson "brought elements from Post-Impressionism and Surrealism to bear on the new technology in photographs taken first in the streets of Paris, then during his travels in Italy and Spain."

Cartier-Bresson did indeed travel in the next years, capturing street scenes in Spain, such as *Madrid* and *Seville,* both from 1933, and *Callejon of the Valencia Arena,* one of his most famous photos, showing a man looking through the wooden gate into a bull-fight arena. The sun is caught and reflected in one of the lenses of the man's glasses to make it appear as if the person has a hole in his head. Further travels in Mexico yielded *Alicante* and photos of the prostitutes if the Calle Cuahtemocztin. In 1935 Cartier-Bresson moved on to New York, where he exhibited with the American photographer Walker Evans, and where he first became interested in the possibilities of the cinema with fellow photographer Paul Strand.

Returning to France, he worked as an assistant to legendary film director Jean Renoir on films including *La vie est a nous* and *Le regle du jeu,* the latter in which the photographer also played the part of the English butler. Except for the post-war documentary *Le Retour,* and a couple of television documentaries in the United States, this was the extent of Cartier-Bresson's involvement in film. In 1937 he married Javanese dancer Ratna Mohini, and needing a steady income took a job as staff photographer for the leftist newspaper *Ce Soir.* There he met two other journalists who would prove important in his life: Robert Capa and David Seymour. He also continued his own photography of the everyday in addition to his photojournalism.

With the outbreak of World War II Cartier-Bresson joined the military, serving in a film and photography unit. Captured in 1940, he was shipped to Germany as a prisoner of war. After several unsuccessful attempts, he finally escaped and made his way back to Paris in 1943, joining the Resistance there until the liberation of his country in 1945. His philosophy of catching the exact right moment is demonstrated in his 1945 picture *Dessau: Exposing a Gestapo Informer.* According to Haworth-Booth, "few photographs of the 20th century encompass so much of its history. The image perfectly fulfills the aesthetics of the 'decisive moment.'"

Life after the War

Following the war, Cartier-Bresson established the photographic cooperative and agency Magnum, together with Capa and Seymour. He worked on assignments from India to China and Cuba. His photos had by this time become symbols of the twentieth century, were exhibited worldwide, and filled the pages of the many of photo books he published. In 1952 he published his book on photographic theory, *The Decisive Moment,* but always maintained a humble opinion of himself, noting that he was an amateur when it came to photography. Cartier-Bresson was one of the first Westerners allowed in the Soviet Union after a small thaw in the Cold War; his book *People of Moscow* details that

The celebrated photographer arranges a shot during the filming of "California Impressions by Henri Cartier-Bresson," a made-for-television film.

trip, as does his 1956 *China in Transition* for that other Communist country.

By 1966 Cartier-Bresson had grown weary of his duties at Magnum and left the agency, and from 1974 on he devoted himself primarily to drawing, his first love. He explained at the time that for him photography was "instant drawing," and he preferred the real thing. Remarried in 1970, Cartier-Bresson did not leave photography totally behind: his new wife was a photographer. He spent the remaining three decades of his life anonymously, living in Paris and in the south of France, preferring not to be photographed. He drew in the Louvre, published his drawings, and had many exhibitions.

If you enjoy the works of Henri Cartier-Bresson, you may also want to check out the following:

The images of pioneering photojournalists George Rodger (1908--), David Seymour (1911-1956), and Robert Capa (1913-1954).

However, in the final analysis, it was photography for which he was known and for which he will always be known. He was one of the true innovators of the photographic image, a "documentary photographer with a boxer's timing and an artist's eye," as Sarah Boxer noted in the *Smithsonian.* The 15,000 rolls of film he shot during his career document and give image to an entire generation. For Boxer there is always an "indecisiveness" to a Cartier-Bresson photograph. This quality is, in fact, according to Boxer, "a hallmark of many classic Cartier-Bresson shots. They are beautifully, even obsessively composed, yet when it comes to pinpointing what is going on, psychologically or even factually, they seldom yield." Boxer concluded that it is exactly this uncertainty that allows many of his pictures to function as icons "of postwar anxiety."

The year before his death in 2004, Cartier-Bresson was honored with a huge show at Paris's Bibliotheque Nationale de France. Describing the exhibition in *Time International,* Judy Fayard noted that Cartier-Bresson's "powerful black-and-white, natural-light photographs—formally rigorous, timeless and often enigmatic—adorn the BNF's vast exhibit space. . . . Here is the master class." At the

A playful Cartier-Bresson covers his face while receiving an honorary degree at Oxford University in 1975.

time of the photographer's death, no less a personage than French President Jacques Chirac joined in the mourning. As quoted in the *Economist*, Chirac said of his late compatriot: "With him, France loses a genius photographer, a true master, and one of the most gifted artists of his generation."

■ Biographical and Critical Sources

BOOKS

Bonnefoy, Yves, *Henri Cartier-Bresson Photographer*, Bullfinch (New York, NY), 1979.

Boot, Chris, editor, *Magnum Stories*, Phaidon Press (Boston, MA), 2005.

Clair, Jean, *Line by Line: The Drawings of Henri Cartier-Bresson*, Thames & Hudson, 1989.

Galassi, Peter, *Henri Cartier-Bresson: The Early Work*, Museum of Modern Art (New York, NY), 1987.

Galassi, Peter, and others, *Henri Cartier-Bresson: The Man, the Image, and the World*, Thames and Hudson (London, England), 2003.

Montier, Jean-Pierre, *Henri Cartier-Bresson and the Artless Art*, Thames and Hudson (London, England), 1994.

PERIODICALS

Artforum International, May, 2003, Miriam Rosen, "Henri Cartier-Bresson: Bibliotheque Nationale de France," p. 66.

Booklist, December 1, 1998, Ray Olson, review of *Tete à tete*, p. 643.

Economist, August 22, 1998, "Man of the Moment," p. 67; April 19, 2003, "Regarding Henri."

Library Journal, November 15, 1998, David Bryant, review of *Tete à tete*, p. 63; May 15, 2000, Douglas F. Smith, review of *The Mind's Eye: Writings on Photography and Photographers*, p. 88.

New Statesman, November 27, 1998, Charles Darwent, "Master of the Frozen Moment," p. 40.

Newsweek, June 2, 2003, Malcolm Jones, "The Man of the Moment," p. 56.

People, July 9, 2001, "Cheap Shots?," p. 115.

Print, January-February, 1999, Fred Ritchin, reviews of *Europeans* and *Tete à tete,* p. 32.

PSA Journal, January, 1992, George W. Cushman, review of *America in Passing,* p. 9; January, 2001, "Photography Hall of Fame Announces Latest Inductees," p. 9.

Smithsonian, November, 2003, Sarah Boxer, "Magic Moments," p. 21.

Time International, May 5, 2003, Judy Fayard, "Eternity in an Instant," p. 54.

ONLINE

Fondation Henri Cartier-Bresson, http://www.henri cartierbresson.org/ (November 15, 2004).

Grove Art Online, http://www.groveart.com/ (November 15, 2004), Mark Haworth-Booth, "Cartier-Bresson, Henri."

■ Obituaries

PERIODICALS

Afterimage, September-October, 2004, Bruno Chalifour, "Henri Cartier-Bresson's Last Decisive Moment," p. 2.

Art in America, October, 2004, p. 188.

Economist, August 7, 2004, "Kingdoms of the World in a Moment," p. 67.

New Internationalist, October, 2004, Sadanand Menon, "Master of the Moment," p. 34.

Newsweek, August 16, 2004, Malcolm Jones, "An Eye without Equal: Henri Cartier-Bresson, 1908-2004," p. 13.

People, August 23, 2004, p. 72.

Time, August 16, 2004, James Nachtwey, "Henri Cartier-Bresson, 1908-2004," p. 86.

U.S. News and World Report, August 16, 2004, p. 36.

Variety, August 9, 2004, p. 44.

Washington Times, August 7, 2004, J. Ross Baughman, "Cartier-Bresson: No Yes-Man, He Followed His Vision, and No Other," p. B1.*

Johnny Cash

■ Personal

Born February 26, 1932, in Kingsland, AR; died of complications from diabetes September 12, 2003, in Nashville, TN; son of Ray (a farmer) and Carrie (a homemaker; maiden name, Rivers) Cash; married Vivian Liberto, August 7, 1954 (divorced, c. 1967); married June Carter (a singer), March 1, 1968 (died May 15, 2003); children: (first marriage) Rosanne, Kathleen, Cindy, Tara; (second marriage) John Carter. *Education:* Attended Keegan School of Broadcasting, c. 1954; attended Evangel Temple in Goodlettsville, TN, c. 1975; received certificate from Christian International College. *Religion:* Baptist. *Hobbies and other interests:* Researching folklore, hunting, fishing, gardening, writing.

■ Career

Singer, songwriter, and musician. Worked in a General Motors auto assembly plant, Pontiac, MI, and in an oleomargarine factory in Evadale, AR, c. 1949-50; salesperson in Memphis, TN, c. 1954; artist with "Johnny Cash and the Tennessee Two," and "Johnny Cash and the Tennessee Three"; artist with Sun Records, 1955-58, Columbia Records, 1958-c. 1986, Polygram, c. 1986-c. 1993, and American Recordings Inc., 1993-2003. Host, *The Johnny Cash Show* (variety series), American Broadcasting Company (ABC), 1969-71; co-host of Muscular Dystrophy Telethon, 1972. Actor in television and film productions, including *A Gunfight,* Paramount Pictures, 1985, *Stagecoach,* Columbia Broadcasting System (CBS), 1986, *Johnny Cash Is Coming to Town* (special), CBS, 1987, and *Dr. Quinn, Medicine Woman,* CBS, 1993. President of House of Cash, and Song of Cash, Inc.; vice president of Family of Man Music, Inc. Member of advisory committee, Peace Corps, and John Edwards Memorial Foundation. Board member of National Music Foundation, Inc. *Military service:* U.S. Air Force, 1950-54, served as intercept radio operator in Germany; became staff sergeant.

■ Member

Country Music Association, National Rifle Association, American Legion, 100 Club.

■ Awards, Honors

Recipient of numerous Gold Records, including in 1963, for *Ring of Fire,* and 1964, for *I Walk the Line;* Grammy Award (with June Carter Cash) for best album notes, National Academy of Recording Arts and Sciences, 1968, for *Johnny Cash at Folsom Prison;*

named Entertainer of the Year, Male Vocalist of the Year, and Vocal Group of the Year (with June Carter Cash), all from Country Music Association (CMA), all 1969; Grammy Award (with Bob Dylan), 1969, for *Nashville Skyline*; Grammy Award for best male vocal performance, 1969, for "A Boy Named Sue"; H.H.D., Gardner-Webb College, 1971, and National University, 1975; Special Award of Merit, American Music Awards, 1977; named to Country Music Hall of Fame, 1980; Horatio Alger Award, Horatio Alger Association of Distinguished Americans, 1986; Grammy Award (with Carl Perkins, Jerry Lee Lewis, Roy Orbison, Sam Phillips, Rick Nelson, and Chips Morman) for best spoken word or non-musical recording, 1986, for *Interviews from the Class of '55—Recording Sessions*; Country Video Award (with Willie Nelson, Waylon Jennings, and Kris Kristofferson) for favorite video single, American Music Awards, 1986, for *Highwayman*; Golden Plate Award, American Academy of Achievement, 1988; Number-One Hit Song Award, CMA, 1988, for "Tennessee Flat Top Box"; named to Rock-n-Roll Hall of Fame, 1992; National Medal of Arts, presented by President George W. Bush, 2002; Founders Award, International Entertainment Buyers Association, 2002; Spirit of Americana Free Speech Award, First Amendment Center, 2002; CMA awards, 2003, for album of the year, for *American IV: The Man Comes Around*, and for single of the year and video of the year, both for song "Hurt"; Grammy Award for best short form music video, 2004, for "Hurt."

■ Writings

RECORDINGS; SONGWRITER, WITH OTHERS

Johnny Cash with His Hot and Blue Guitar, Sun, 1957.
The Fabulous Johnny Cash, Columbia, 1958.
Blood, Sweat and Tears, Columbia, 1963.
Ring of Fire, Columbia, 1963.
I Walk the Line, Columbia, 1964.
Bitter Tears: Ballads of the American Indian, Columbia, 1964.
Orange Blossom Special, Columbia, 1965.
Mean as Hell, Columbia, 1966.
Johnny Cash at Folsom Prison, Columbia, 1968.
The Holy Land, Columbia, 1969.
Johnny Cash at San Quentin, Columbia, 1969.
Show Time with the Tennessee Two, Sun, 1970.
Story Songs of Trains and Rivers with the Tennessee Two, Sun, 1970.
Hello, I'm Johnny Cash, Columbia, 1970.
The World of Johnny Cash, Columbia, 1970.

Singing Storyteller with the Tennessee Two, Sun, 1970.
(With June Carter Cash) *Jackson*, Columbia, 1970.
Rough Cut King of Country Music, Sun, 1970.
Man in Black, Columbia, 1971.
(With Jerry Lee Lewis) *Johnny Cash Sings Hank Williams*, Sun, 1971.
A Thing Called Love, Columbia, 1972.
Folsom Prison Blues, Columbia, 1972.
(With June Carter Cash) *Give My Love to Rose*, Harmony, 1972.
America, Columbia, 1972.
Any Old Wind That Blows, Columbia, 1973.
I Walk the Line, Nash, 1973.
(With June Carter Cash) *Johnny Cash and His Woman*, Columbia, 1973.
Ragged Old Flag, Columbia, 1974.
Junkie and Juicehead, Columbia, 1974.
Destination Victoria Station, Columbia, 1976.
Strawberry Cake, Columbia, 1976.
One Piece at a Time, Columbia, 1976.
Last Gunfighter Ballad, Columbia, 1977.
The Rambler, Columbia, 1977.
Silver, Columbia, 1979.
A Believer Sings the Truth, Columbia, 1980.
The Baron, Columbia, 1981.
(With Willie Nelson, Waylon Jennings, and Kris Kristofferson, as the Highwaymen) *Highwaymen*, 1985.
Believe in Him, Columbia, 1986.
(With Waylon Jennings) *Heroes*, 1986.
(With Jerry Lee Lewis, Carl Perkins, and Roy Orbison) *Class of '55 (Memphis Rock & Roll Homecoming)*, Mercury, 1986.
Johnny Cash Is Coming to Town, Mercury, 1987.
Water from the Wells of Home, Mercury, 1988.
(With Bob Dylan, George Harrison, Roy Orbison, and others) *The Traveling Wilburys*, 1988.
(With the Highwaymen) *Highwaymen 2*, 1990.
The Mystery of Life, Mercury, 1991.
American Recordings, American, 1994.
(With the Highwaymen) *The Road Goes on Forever*, Liberty, 1995.
Unchained, American, 1996.
Love, God, Murder, Columbia/Legacy, 2000.
American III: Solitary Man, American, 2000.
American IV: The Man Comes Around, American/Lost Highway, 2002.
At Madison Square Garden, Columbia, 2002.
The Essential Johnny Cash, Columbia, 2002.
Unearthed, American, 2003.

Also composer of music sound track for films *Little Fauss and Big Halsy*, *True West*, and *Pride of Jessie Hallam*. Co-writer of *Return to the Promised Land* (a musical), 1992. Composer of numerous songs, including "I Walk the Line," "A Boy Named Sue," "Folsom Prison Blues," "Man in Black," and "Tennessee Flat Top Box."

OTHER

(Composer) *True West* (documentary film), Columbia, 1965.

Songs of Johnny Cash, introduction by Christopher S. Wren, Dial (New York, NY), 1970.

(Co-writer, producer, and narrator) *Gospel Road* (documentary film), Twentieth Century-Fox, 1971.

Man in Black: His Own Story in His Own Words (autobiography), Zondervan (Grand Rapids, MI), 1975.

Man in White (novel), Harper (New York, NY), 1986.

(With Patrick Carr) *Cash: The Autobiography,* HarperSanFrancisco (San Francisco, CA), 1997.

Ring of Fire: The Johnny Cash Reader (interviews), edited by Michael Streissguth, Da Capo Press (New York, NY), 2002.

■ Sidelights

The "Man in Black"—as Johnny Cash has long been known—was one of the most influential figures in American country music during the last half of the twentieth century. He also reached a substantial audience of rock fans, thanks to his charismatic outlaw persona, deep, authoritative voice, and dark songs like "Folsom Prison Blues." After enjoying a string of hits in the 1950s and even greater success in the late 1960s, when he was briefly the best-selling recording artist in the world, Cash saw his edgy, close-to-the-bone style eventually go out of fashion. Even as his 1980s work was neglected, however, he retained a strong and loyal fan base worldwide. In 1994, well past his sixtieth birthday, Cash came roaring back with a sparsely recorded album that ranked among his best work and earned him a Grammy award. "Can you name anyone in this day and age who is as cool as Johnny Cash?" asked a writer for *Rolling Stone* rhetorically. "No, you can't."

Cash was born into an impoverished Arkansas family in 1932 and grew up working in the cotton fields. His Baptist upbringing meant that the music he heard was almost entirely religious, and the hymns sung by country greats like the Carter Family and Ernest Tubb reached him on the radio and made an indelible impression. "From the time I was a little boy," he recollected to Steve Pond in a *Rolling Stone* interview, "I never had any doubt that I was gonna

be singing on the radio." His brother Roy formed a band when he was young, increasing Johnny's determination to do the same one day.

Cash had no idea, though, what path would lead him to his destiny. He held a few odd jobs after graduating from Dyess High School in 1950, but eventually opted for a four-year stay in the U.S. Air Force. Stationed in Germany, he endured what he would later describe as a lonely, miserable period. Fortunately, he learned to play the guitar and began turning the poetry he had been writing into song lyrics. After viewing a powerful film about Folsom Prison, he sat down to write what would become one of his signature songs, "Folsom Prison Blues." Cash's empathy for prisoners and other marginalized people would consistently inform his work. With his powerful position in a generally conservative musical world, he also championed Native American rights and spoke out against various social ills.

Cash left the military in 1954 and married Vivian Liberto, whom he had met before joining the Air Force; they had corresponded throughout his tour of duty. The two lived in Memphis, Tennessee,

Famously known as the "Man in Black" for his dark wardrobe, Cash recorded such hits as "Folsom Prison Blues," "I Walk the Line," and "A Boy Named Sue."

This 1963 release collects a dozen of Cash's songs, including the classic "Ring of Fire."

where Cash earned a meager living selling appliances. "I was the worst salesman in the world," he confided to Pond. Nonetheless, he summoned the passion to sell himself as a singer, playing with a gospel group and canvassing radio stations for chances to perform on the air.

Makes First Recording

Eventually, Cash was granted an audience with trailblazing producer Sam Phillips, at whose Sun Studios the likes of Elvis Presley, Jerry Lee Lewis, Carl Perkins, and others made recordings that changed the course of popular music. Phillips was a hard sell, but Cash won the opportunity to record his first single, and "Cry, Cry, Cry" became a number 14 hit in 1955. Cash's group, the Tennessee Two, also played some local gigs with Presley. Pond describes Cash's early records as "stark, unsettling and totally original. The instrumentation was spare, almost rudimentary," featuring bass and lead guitar supplied by the Tennessee Two and Cash's rhythm guitar, which had "a piece of paper stuck underneath the top frets to give it a scratchy sound."

In 1956 Cash left his sales job and recorded the hits "Folsom Prison Blues"—containing the legendary and much-quoted lyric "I shot a man in Reno just to watch him die"—and "I Walk the Line." The next year saw the release of the one album released by Sun before Cash's departure from the label, *Johnny Cash with His Hot and Blue Guitar*. Cash and the Tennessee Two left the label after a string of hits and signed with CBS/Columbia Records in 1958; interestingly, singles he recorded on Sun at Phillips's insistence just before his contract lapsed continued to chart for years afterward, much to Cash's chagrin. Yet he charted on CBS as well with a bevy of singles and such albums as *Blood, Sweat, and Tears* and *Ring of Fire*.

Turns to God

In the midst of his success, however, Cash grew apart from Vivian and their children. He also grew dependent on alcohol and drugs, and his on-the-road lifestyle became increasingly dissolute. Such misery no doubt contributed force to such work as 1963's "Ring of Fire," which was co-written by musician June Carter, who also performed on the track. Cash and Carter, a scion of the famed musical Carter Family—became increasingly close, both professionally and personally. By 1966 Cash's marriage had collapsed, and that year he nearly died of an overdose. Cash attributed his subsequent rehabilitation to two factors: Carter and God. He and Carter wed in 1968 and later had a son, John.

Cash expanded his repertoire as the 1960s unfolded, incorporating folk music and protest themes. He recorded songs by folk-rock singer Bob Dylan and up-and-comers like Kris Kristofferson, but by the end of the decade, driven perhaps by his generally out-of-control lifestyle, his hits came largely from novelty songs like Shel Silverstein's "A Boy Named Sue." Even so, by 1969 Cash was the best-selling recording artist alive, outselling even rock legends the Beatles. That year saw him win two Grammy awards for *Johnny Cash at Folsom Prison*, a live album for a worshipful audience of prisoners that led to *Johnny Cash at San Quentin*. From 1969 to 1971 he hosted a smash variety program for television, *The Johnny Cash Show*.

The 1970s saw more career triumphs, notably a Grammy-winning duet with wife June Carter Cash on Tim Hardin's song "If I Were a Carpenter," a command performance for President Richard M. Nixon, acting roles in film and on television, a best-selling autobiography, and several more hit albums, including *Man in Black*, the title of which had become his permanent show-business moniker. While this label has been associated with his "outlaw" image, Cash and his bandmates originally wore black because they had nothing else that matched; besides, as Cash informed a writer for *Entertainment Weekly*, "black is better for church."

Cash appears with another country music legend, Tammy Wynette.

In Cash's 1975 autobiography, also titled *Man in Black,* he describes his years of fighting an addiction to drugs. He began to take amphetamines—"uppers"—to stay awake for the grueling tours and to provide a constant supply of energy for his concerts, and barbiturates—"downers"—to fall asleep afterward. Addicted for seven years, Cash saw his health deteriorate; he became violent, depressed, and suicidal. In 1967 he woke up in a jail cell in Lafayette, Georgia, and admitted he was addicted. With the help of his strong Christian faith, his doctor, and his soon to be bride June Carter, Cash successfully completed his withdrawal from drug dependency. Throughout the book Cash stresses "the religious aspects of his life," wrote a *Library Journal* reviewer, and he credits his ultimate salvation to his faith in Jesus Christ. According to a *Publishers Weekly* reviewer, Cash's account is a brutally honest version "that goes further in personal disclosure than anything written about him thus far." The book met with critical and popular success, selling over 250,000 hardcover copies.

In 1980 Cash was inducted into the Country Music Association Hall of Fame. He had become a music hero worldwide, appearing in eastern Europe before the fall of the Soviet empire and praising those who agitated for democracy. Yet during the 1980s, Cash became less and less of a priority for his record label; country music had come to be dominated by younger artists who were either pop-inclined or "roots" artists who favored more sophisticated production. These troubles led Cash to again struggle with drugs; he eventually checked into the Betty Ford clinic for rehabilitation. There, he said, he experienced a religious epiphany.

A Book about St. Paul

Cash's second book, *Man in White,* draws upon his personal struggle with drugs and is the result of almost ten years of research and writing. The manuscript—carried from city to city in saddlebags, and worked on in buses and hotel rooms—was written in longhand on yellow legal pads. It is the story of the biblical Saul of Tarsus, the Jewish Pharisee, who, in approximately 37 A.D., converted to Christianity after an encounter with "the man in white," or Jesus, on the Damascus road. In the book, Cash fictionalizes the three-year span of Saul's anti-Christian zealotry prior to his conversion, and the three-year interval afterward, during which Saul changed his name to Paul, built up relationships with the apostles, and prepared for the first of his numerous missionary journeys. Cash acknowledged that he was inspired to write the book because Paul's transforming experience so closely paralleled his own. After more than seven years of drug addiction and violence, Cash's rehabilitation was "like a new birth, a new lease on life," he was quoted as saying by William Griffin in a *Publishers Weekly* interview. "My mind was renewed . . . I was transformed, and I identified with Paul the apostle."

Many reviewers praised *Man in White* for its characterization and historical authenticity, and the novel was even optioned for a movie. John Lawson, a *School Library Journal* critic, wrote that "this well-researched novel breathes life into Paul," the disciples, and the high priest, making "the characters and times come alive." Rene H. Engel commented in the *Los Angeles Times Book Review* that, although Cash's music is the best descriptor of his personality, "if the reader considers Cash's powerful identification with Paul, then the *Man in White*, together with [Cash's] autobiography, does give us some insight into the convictions of the man in black."

During the 1980s Cash continued to indulge his eclectic musical tastes. Alongside Kristofferson, Willie Nelson, and Waylon Jennings, he participated in a collaborative album, *The Highwaymen*, which was followed by two other albums by the team. He also joined Jerry Lee Lewis, Carl Perkins, and country-rock giant Roy Orbison for a reunion recording called *Class of '55 (Memphis Rock & Roll Homecoming)*, which enjoyed solid sales. A daughter by his first marriage, Rosanne, became a country star in her own right; Johnny Cash himself, even as his solo albums sold poorly, was firmly established as a living legend of country music and a profound influence on rock and roll. In 1992 he was inducted into the Rock and Roll Hall of Fame.

Yet Cash tired of record-business priorities. "I kept hearing about demographics [market studies of consumers] until it was coming out my ears," the singer told Christopher John Farley of *Time*. The first label representative who seemed to understand Cash after this bitter experience was, ironically enough, a man best known for his work with hardcore rap, metal, and alternative acts. Rick Rubin had founded

A champion of the oppressed, Cash often performed for inmates, including those at the Cummins Prison Farm in Arkansas.

his own label, first called Def American and later changed to American Recordings, to support acts he believed in. Though not intimately acquainted with Cash's work, Rubin admired the singer's artistic persona. "I don't see him as a country act," Rubin told Farley. "I would say he embodies rock 'n' roll. He's an outlaw figure, and that is the essence of what rock 'n' roll is."

Rubin's appeal, to Cash, lay in the producer's idea for a record. After seeing one of the country legend's performances, Rubin "said he'd love to hear just me and my guitar," Cash told *Los Angeles Times* writer Robert Hilburn. These were the words the veteran artist had waited decades to hear; he had suggested such a minimal approach many times to country producers, only to have it vetoed immediately on commercial grounds. Rubin simply set up a tape machine in his Hollywood living room and allowed Cash to play guitar and sing.

Rubin "was a lot like Sam [Phillips], actually," Cash told Hilburn. "We talked a lot about the approach we were going to take, and he said, 'You know, we are not going to think about time or money. I want you to come out as much as you can.'" Freed from the constraints that had clipped Cash's wings in his Nashville years, he was able to experiment with a wide range of material. Recording over seventy songs, mostly at Rubin's house but also at his own cabin in Tennessee and at the trendy Los Angeles nightspot The Viper Room, Cash had a valedictory experience. He later told *Time*'s Farley that the work was his "dream album."

First Release on American Recordings

The recorded material was culled to thirteen tracks, including traditional songs, some Cash originals, and compositions by such diverse modern songwriters as Kristofferson, Leonard Cohen, Tom Waits, Nick Lowe, Glenn Danzig, and Loudon Wainright III. The lead-off track, "Delia's Gone," grimly describes the murder of a faithless woman; Rubin seemed to invite comparisons between Cash and the controversial metal and rap acts on his label. Titled *American Recordings*, the album was released in 1994; its artist was sixty two years old. The liner notes contained testimonials from both Rubin and Cash. "I think we made a brutally honest record," the producer declared. "Working with Rick," Cash averred, "all the experimenting, kinda spread me out and expanded my range of material. This is the best I can do as an artist, as a solo artist, this is it."

Critics seemed to agree. Karen Schoemer of *Mirabella* praised *American Recordings* as "a daring, deceptively simple album" that "operates on a mythic

Kirk Douglas (right) and Cash star as a pair of aging gunslingers in the 1971 film *The Gunfight*.

scale, which suits someone who's always been larger than life. What is breathtaking is Cash's ability to analyze his aging self, and the failures, weaknesses, strengths and wisdoms that time bestows." *Village Voice* critic Doug Simmons praised it as "fiercely intimate," while *Rolling Stone*'s Anthony DeCurtis called it "unquestionably one of his best albums," one which "will earn him a time of well-deserved distinction in which his work will reach an eager new audience."

While *American Recordings* sold only modestly well, it restored Cash's sense of mission. It also earned him a 1995 Grammy Award for best contemporary folk album. He played a sold-out engagement in Los Angeles just before his nomination, before an audience studded with such music stars as Tom Petty, Sheryl Crow, and Dwight Yoakam. And in September of 1996 he played a set at the CMA Music Marathon in Manhattan, previewing songs from a new album, *Unchained*, as well as performing cover versions from younger artists such as Beck and Soundgarden.

In later years, health problems caused Cash to limit his touring schedule. He began to suffer from Shy-Drager's syndrome, a degenerative nerve disease

that can cause blackouts, tremors, and muscle stiffness and made him prone to pneumonia. He was hospitalized with pneumonia twice in 1998 and again in October 1999. Yet, as the 1990s waned and the millennium turned over, Cash—now approaching the end of his seventh decade—returned to the recording studio and issued *American III: Solitary Man* in 2000; the title track from that album won a Grammy for best male country vocal performance. Also in 2000 he compiled a three-disc retrospective boxed set called *Love, God, Murder,* one of more than one hundred Cash retrospective packages compiled since the 1950s. Indeed, 1999 alone saw the release of nearly two dozen Cash collections, and that year he was honored also with the Grammy Lifetime Achievement Award from the National Academy of Recording Arts and Sciences.

Connects with Younger Generation

About the prospect of an "eager new audience" Cash himself—who seriously considered playing at the alternative-rock festival known as Lollapalooza before declining the offer—was philosophical. "I no longer have a grandiose attitude about my music being a powerful force for change," he told a contributor to *Entertainment Weekly*. Even so, he allowed, "I think [today's youth] sees the hypocrisy in government, the rotten core of social ills and poverty and prejudice, and I'm not afraid to say that's where the trouble is. A lot of people my age are." One thing remained constant, as he told *Rolling Stone:* "I feel like if I can just go onstage with my guitar and sing my songs, I can't do no wrong no matter where I am."

If you enjoy the works of Johnny Cash, you may also want to check out the following recordings:

Waylon Jennings, *Singer of Sad Songs*, 1970.
Willie Nelson, *Red Headed Stranger*, 1975.
Merle Haggard, *If I Could Only Fly*, 2000.

Cash continued to reach this new audience with a fourth effort in the American Recordings series, *American IV: The Man Comes Around.* Once again, the legendary country singer delved into the works of younger artists like Depeche Mode's "Personal Jesus" and Nine Inch Nails' "Hurt." The latter song also became a popular video, launching the song onto the Modern Rock Tracks chart. The video, directed by Mark Romanek, earned six nominations at the 2003 MTV Awards, and won in the best cinematography category. *American IV: The Man Comes Around* rose to number two on the Top Country Albums chart and was certified gold in 2003.

Cash's success, however, was mingled with continued health problems and personal tragedy. June Carter Cash, his wife of thirty-five years, died of complications following heart surgery on May 15, 2003. "After June died," friend Kris Kristofferson told a *People* contributor, "life was a struggle for him. His daughter told me he cried every night." Cash was eager to attend the MTV Awards in August of 2003, but had been re-admitted to the hospital due to complications from diabetes. On September 12, 2003, almost four months after the death of his wife, Cash died. A memorial service, held at Hendersonville, North Carolina, on September 15, 2003, was attended by friends, family, and his musical peers. "He stood up for the underdogs, the downtrodden, the prisoners, the poor, and he was their champion," Kristofferson told *People*. "He appealed to people all over the world."

■ Biographical and Critical Sources

BOOKS

Campbell, Garth, *Johnny Cash: He Walked the Line*, John Blake, 2004.

Cash, Johnny, *Man in Black: His Own Story in His Own Words*, Zondervan (Grand Rapids, MI), 1975.

Cash, Johnny, and Patrick Carr, *Cash: The Autobiography*, HarperSanFrancisco (San Francisco, CA), 1997.

Cash, Johnny, *Ring of Fire: The Johnny Cash Reader* (interviews), edited by Michael Streissguth, Da Capo Press (New York, NY), 2002.

Contemporary Musicians, Volume 46, Gale (Detroit, MI), 2004.

Cusic, Don, *Johnny Cash: The Songs*, Thunder's Mouth Press, 2004.

Lewry, Peter, *I've Been Everywhere: A Johnny Cash Chronicle*, Helter Skelter Publishing, 2001.

McCall, Michael, and Nicholas Maier, *Johnny Cash: An American Legend*, AMI Books, 2003.

Miller, Bill, *Cash: An American Man*, CMT, 2004.

Moriarty, Frank, *Johnny Cash*, MetroBooks (New York, NY), 2000.

Streissguth, Michael, *Johnny Cash at Folsom Prison: The Making of a Masterpiece*, Da Capo Press (New York, NY), 2004.

Turner, Steve, *The Man Called Cash: The Life, Love, and Faith of an American Legend*, W Publishing Group, 2004.

Urbanski, Dave, *The Man Comes Around: The Spiritual Journey of Johnny Cash*, Relevant Books, 2003.

PERIODICALS

Billboard, March 30, 2002, Wes Orshoski, "Johnny Cash: An American Original," p. 1.

Booklist, October 1, 1997, Mike Tribby, review of *Cash: The Autobiography*, p. 274.

Entertainment Weekly, February 18, 1994, pp. 57-67.

Kirkus Reviews, July 15, 1986, p. 1039.

Library Journal, November 1, 1975, review of *Man in Black*, p. 2042; June 1, 2002, Eric Hahn, review of *Ring of Fire: The Johnny Cash Reader*, p. 154.

Los Angeles Times, April 28, 1984; April 25, 1994, Robert Hilburn, pp. F1, F5.

Los Angeles Times Book Review, September 12, 1986, Rene H. Engel, review of *Man in White*, p. 7.

Mirabella, July, 1994, Karen Schoemer, review of *American Recordings*.

New York Times, March 25, 1979, p. 28.

People, November 3, 1986, Andrea Chambers, "Johnny Cash Changes His Tune: From 'A Boy Named Sue' to a Saint Named Paul," p. 67; September 29, 2003, talk with Kris Kristofferson, p. 78.

Publishers Weekly, July 18, 1986, William Griffin, interview with Cash, p. 81; October 3, 1986, Sybil Steinberg, review of *Man in White*, pp. 94-95; October 6, 1997, review of *Cash: The Autobiography*, p. 66.

Rolling Stone, November 21, 1985, p. 75; December 10, 1992, Steve Pond, interview with Cash, pp. 118-25, 201; May 5, 1994, p. 14; May 19, 1994, pp. 97-98; June 30, 1994, p. 35.

School Library Journal, September, 1970; January, 1976, p. 58; December, 1986, John Lawson, review of *Man in White*, p. 125.

Time, May 9, 1994, Christopher John Farley, "Dream Album," pp. 72-74.

Village Voice, May 18, 1994, Doug Simmons, review of *American Recordings*.

■ Obituaries

PERIODICALS

Chicago Tribune, September 13, 2003, Section 1, pp. 1, 6.

Los Angeles Times, September 13, 2003, pp. A1, A16-17.

New York Times, September 13, 2003, pp. A1, A12.

Times (London, England), September 13, 2003.

Washington Post, September 13, 2003, pp. A1, A10.*

Monte Cook

■ Personal

Male. Married; wife's name, Sue. *Education:* Graduate, Clarion West writer's workshop, 1999. *Hobbies and other interests:* Game playing, runs games, watches DVDs, builds dioramas out of LEGO building bricks, paints miniatures, reads comics.

■ Addresses

Agent—c/o Wizards of the Coast, P.O. Box 707, Renton, WA 98057. *E-mail*—monte@montecook.com.

■ Career

Game designer, author. Iron Crown Enterprises, Charlottesville, VA, game designer, editor, 1988-92; TSR, Inc., game designer and Wizards of the Coast, Renton, WA, game designer to 1994-2002; Malhavoc Press, founder, 2003.

■ Awards, Honors

Origins Award, 2000, for Third Edition *Dungeons & Dragons* Game Design; Nigel D. Findley Award, 2000, for Third Edition *Dungeons & Dragons Player's Handbook;* EN World Award, 2001, for *The Book of Eldritch Might;* nominee, Origins Award, 2001, for *Of Aged Angels;* EN World Award, 2002, for *Call of Cthulhu d20 Roleplaying Game;* Pen and Paper Fan Award, 2002, En World Award, 2003, for *The Banewarrens;* Fan Favorite Author/Designer, Pen and Paper Fan Awards, 2002, 2003; EN Award, Best Publishers, 2003, Malhavoc Press; Weird Gamewyrd Award, 2003, Pen and Paper Fan Award, 2003, for *Arcana Unearthed;* inclusion in Pen and Paper Fan Award Hall of Fame.

■ Writings

GAME DESIGN CREDITS

Creatures and Treasures II, Iron Crown Enterprises (Charlottesville, VA), 1990.

Champions in 3-D, Iron Crown Enterprises (Charlottesville, VA), 1990.

Rolemaster Companion IV, Iron Crown Enterprises (Charlottesville, VA), 1990.

Dark Space, Iron Crown Enterprises (Charlottesville, VA), 1991.

Rolemaster Character Records, Iron Crown Enterprises (Charlottesville, VA), 1991.

European Enemies, Iron Crown Enterprises (Charlottesville, VA), 1991.

Rolemaster Companion V, Iron Crown Enterprises (Charlottesville, VA), 1991.

Spell User's Companion, Iron Crown Enterprises (Charlottesville, VA), 1992.

Champions Universe, Iron Crown Enterprises (Charlottesville, VA), 1992.

Elminster's Ecologies, TSR Inc. (Renton, WA), 1994.

Glantri, Kingdom of Magic, TSR Inc. (Renton, WA), 1995.

Windriders of the Jagged Cliffs, TSR Inc. (Renton, WA), 1995.

Labyrinth of Madness, TSR Inc. (Renton, WA), 1995.

Planewalker's Handbook, TSR Inc. (Renton, WA), 1996.

Hellbound: The Bloody War, TSR Inc. (Renton, WA), 1996.

A Hero's Tale, TSR Inc. (Renton, WA), 1996.

A Guide to the Astral Plane, TSR Inc. (Renton, WA), 1996.

The Great Modron March, TSR Inc. (Renton, WA), 1997.

Dead Gods, TSR Inc. (Renton, WA), 1998.

Planescape Monstrous Compendium III TSR Inc. (Renton, WA), 1998.

A Paladin in Hell, TSR Inc. (Renton, WA), 1998.

Faction War, TSR Inc. (Renton, WA), 1998.

Tales from the Infinite Staircase, TSR Inc. (Renton, WA), 1998.

Vecna Reborn, TSR Inc. (Renton, WA), 1998.

The Inner Planes, TSR Inc. (Renton, WA), 1998.

Dark Matter, Wizards of the Coast (Renton, WA), 1999.

D & D Third Edition, Dungeon Master's Guide, Wizards of the Coast (Renton, WA), 2000.

Return to the Temple of Elemental Evil, Wizards of the Coast (Renton, WA), 2001.

The Book of Eldritch Might, Malhavoc Press, 2001.

Demon God's Fane, Malhavoc Press, 2001.

Beyond the Veil, Atlas Games, 2001.

The Book of Eldritch Might II, Malhavoc Press, 2002.

Queen of Lies, Fiery Dragon Productions, 2002.

Call of Cthulhu d20 Roleplaying Game, Wizards of the Coast (Renton, WA), 2002.

HeroClix: Marvel Comics Collectible Miniatures Game, WizKids, 2002.

The Banewarrens, Malhavoc Press, 2002.

Requiem for a God, Malhavoc Press, 2002.

The Book of Vile Darkness, Wizards of the Coast (Renton, WA), 2002.

Book of Eldritch Might III, Malhavoc Press, 2002.

The Book of Hallowed Might, Malhavoc Press, 2002.

Ghostwalk, Wizards of the Coast (Renton, WA), 2003.

Monte Cook's Arcana Unearthed: A Variant Player's Handbook, Malhavoc Press, 2003.

A Plague of Dreams, Fiery Dragon Productions, 2003.

Arcana Unearthed DM's Screen and Player's Guide, Malhavoc Press, 2003.

The Diamond Throne, Malhavoc Press, 2003.

Chaositech, Malhavoc Press, 2003.

The Complete Book of Eldritch Might, Malhavoc Press, 2004.

Legacy of the Dragons, Malhavoc Press, 2004.

Book of Hallowed Might II, Malhavoc Press, 2004.

Beyond Countless Doorways, Malhavoc Press, 2004.

Monte Cook's Arcana Evolved, Malhavoc Press, 2005.

OTHER

The Glass Prison (novel), Wizards of the Coast (Renton, WA), 1999.

Of Aged Angels (novel), Wizards of the Coast (Renton, WA), 2001.

Contributor of articles and short stories to magazines including *Dragon Magazine, Dungeon Magazine, Amazing Stories, Forgotten Realm,* and *Game Trade Magazine.* Contributor of stories to anthologies including *Realms of the Arcane,* TSR Inc. (Renton, WA), 1997, *Realms of Mystery,* TSR Inc. (Renton, WA), 1998, *Best of the Realms,* Wizards of the Coast, 2003, and *Children of the Rune,* Malhavoc Press, 2004. Editor of numerous games and game rule books for Iron Crown Enterprises.

■ **Sidelights**

Monte Cook is a game designer who has worked on over one hundred titles since his professional start in 1988. Best known for his work on the core titles of the *Dungeons & Dragons* (*D & D*) game, he has also worked on various individual titles for game companies, including Iron Crown Enterprises, TSR Inc., and Wizards of the Coast. In 2002 he set off on his own to found a design studio, Malhavoc Press, and with that imprint has brought out games and manuals, including *The Book of Eldritch Might, Banewarrens,* and *Monte Cook's Arcana Unearthed.* Cook told Kosala Ubayasekara in an interview for *Silven Cross* that he doesn't look upon game design as "a science, it's an art." Cook further noted that "there isn't a right/wrong way to do something. What might be 'wrong' in a WotC (Wizards of the Coast) product could be just right for an independent publisher.... A smaller company can take more risks because they can easily survive with a smaller audience. It's like with movies. The big studios have to put out the big blockbusters to pull in the large audiences. But the smaller, independent studios can do more cutting-edge, really 'different' movies." Such a philosophy and a lot of hard work and long hours have earned Cook numerous industry and fan awards and made his one of the foremost names in game designers.

From Monopoly to Dungeons

Cook told Ubayasekara that he "started gaming when I was about ten." In an interview with Michael Burnaugh for *GamingReport.com*, he further explained, "I come from a game-playing family who loved all kinds of card games, chess, board games like Monopoly, Risk, Payday, and so on. From an extremely early age, about as soon as I could write, I was designing my own board games—the kind where you roll a die and move that many spaces and then follow the instructions on that space." As a youth Cook invented hundreds such games, all with little squares drawn on paper, some of them "quite involved," as he told Burnaugh. From these he graduated to role-play games (RPG) such as *Dungeons & Dragons,* the first game of its kind, invented in 1974. In a profile piece on the *Wizards of the Coast* Web site, Cook recalled how an early *D & D* book, *The Temple of Elemental Evil,* got him excited about the RPG scene. "I begged for [the book]," he noted. "I loved this adventure when it came out. I got it for my birthday when I was in high school and read it from cover to cover immediately. It was the first adventure that really went into depth about the organization of the creatures that lived there. This wasn't just some old ruined dungeon and some orcs in one room and beholder across the hall. Here, they all worked together, they had enemies and allies in the dungeon—it was a microcosm. It introduced me to the idea that a 'dungeon' can really have a sort of working ecology ... , a dynamic set of politics, and pretty complex theme. It was the next step in *D & D* adventure evolution." Later, as a professional game designer himself, Cook would have the opportunity to update this adventure with the *Return to the Temple of Elemental Evil.*

Cook first worked professionally in the burgeoning gaming industry in 1988, while still in college. With Iron Crown Enterprises he was an editor on games including *Rolemaster* and *Champions.* He stayed with that firm for several years, then went freelance for a time before taking a position as game designer with the originators of *Dungeons & Dragons,* TSR Inc. That company was later bought out by Wizards of the Coast. Here he worked on game design for the third edition of *Dungeons & Dragons,* which brought RPG into the mainstream of gaming with more simplistic and realistic play and characters. Cook also authored the *Dungeon Master's Guide* for the third edition of the game.

Sets Out on His Own

Wizards of the Coast developed what is known as the d20 system for their third edition of *Dungeons & Dragons,* which takes its name for a twenty-sided die used for the chance part of the game. The d20 system is an open system, meaning other designers may use it free of charge in an attempt to bring a new generation into gaming and RPG. Cook took advantage of this Open Gaming License to set up his own design studio, Malhavoc Press, with himself and his wife as the two principles. "I can't tell you how wonderful it is to have the creative freedom to write and produce what I want without anyone looking over my shoulder, wanting to make changes just for their own gratification, or because of some silly imposed rules," Cook told Burnaugh. He also explained the operations at Malhavoc: "I still spend the vast majority of my time writing, which is exactly the way I want it. My wife, Sue, handles most of the 'running of the company' types

Cook, a game designer, penned two of the stories contained in this 2004 anthology based on his popular role-playing game.

of duties, like contracting artists, mappers, dealing with the printer." Malhavoc contracted a joint deal with Sword & Sorcery Studios for storage and distribution of their book products. Other products from Malhavoc are sold directly to customers over the company Web site as a PDF file, or Portable Document Format, which allows formatted documents to be transmitted via the Internet. The goal of his press, as Cook told Joe G. Kushner in an interview for *OgreCave.com,* is to release "quality, imaginative work. I don't like writing bland, 'just what you expect' sorts of material, and I don't think most people want to buy it. I want every product to trod new ground. I want every product to be so good that no one's faith in Malhavoc is ever so much as shaken." Cook further commented, "I don't have dreams of becoming some big publisher. The point, ultimately, is to have fun and put out cool, high-quality books."

Speaking with Ubayasekara, Cook noted that "in the beginning, I never thought that Malhavoc Press would actually amount to too much. Sales of our first product blew me away. I am indeed very proud—both of the ... content of our books and the success of Malhavoc Press." Some of the most popular titles from Malhavoc were the 2003 *Monte Cook's Arcana Unearthed: A Variant Player's Guide,* and the 2004 *Monte Cook's Arcana Evolved,* each of which offer new and improved magic systems for traditional *D & D* gaming. Also popular are the numerous titles and downloadable articles supporting the game of *Ptolus,* based in an ancient city with a long and very complex history.

Cook himself prefers RPGs with a mixture of action/conflict and with characterization that brings out the emotion in the participating character (PC). Speaking with James Rozee on *Gaming System Design* Web site, Cook noted that playtesting is vital to a good game, and he and his team try out their own products thoroughly before publishing them. Ideas come to Cook from many sources, as he told Rozee: "Personally, I'm influenced by everything around me. It's common that a scene in a movie or book will inspire some part of an adventure. For example, if I see a movie with characters running around in a volcano dealing with explosions and lava flows, I might decide that an adventure (or part of an adventure) should be set in a volcano. Lots of times, visual media—movies and comic books—inspire a vivid scene or character." For Cook it is important, as he explained to Rozee, to "push the limits" in design. "Don't set a fight encounter in an empty room when you can set it in a room with a fire pit and a swinging pendulum blade. Surprise the reader."

If you enjoy the works of Monte Cook, you may also want to check out the following:

Nobilis, a role playing game by R. Sean Borgstrom.
In Nomine by Steven Jackson Games.
The *Magic--The Gathering* series of role playing games.

Cook has also ventured into novel writing, publishing *The Glass Prison* in 1999 and *Of Aged Angels* in 2001, both with Wizards of the Coast. On the *Wizards of the Coast* Web site Cook characterized the writing of the latter novel as "painful and pleasant at the same time." The book includes many of his favorite themes: "modern day conspiracies, secret societies, and cutting-edge occult matters." Cook further explained that *Of Aged Angels* has a "character that uses his laptop computer to help him create chaos magick rituals, and investigations into the Knights Templar. And it's got Jim Morrison. So really, what's not to like?" Speaking with Burnaugh, Cook noted the difference for him between game design and writing novels: "Gaming products are more fun, but fiction is somehow a bit more satisfying."

For the future Cook intends to continue in both fields, publishing short fiction in his house imprint along with the game books. In a *GameWyrd.com* interview Cook elaborated on the future of d20 games: "I'm generally excited about the gaming industry right now. I'm excited by the d20 industry because it seems that all the obvious books are out of the way—the fighter book, the dwarf book, etc. We're done with that now.... This forces designers (I hope) to get more creative, which can only lead to cooler products." Cook concluded to Kushner, "I hope that a few years from now d20 and Malhavoc are still going strong. I'm having tons of fun and wouldn't mind seeing it continue at all. That's my hope."

■ Biographical and Critical Sources

ONLINE

Gamegrene.com, http://www.gamegrene.com/ (June 13, 2003), "Yes, That Monte."

GameWyrd.com, http://www.gamewyrd.com/ (October 4, 2003), "Monte Cook Interview for Downloader Monthly."

GamingReport.com, http://www.gamingreport.com/ (May 25, 2003), Michael Burnaugh, "Interview with Monte Cook of Malhavoc Press."

Gaming System Design, http://www.gdse.com/ (November 21, 2004), James Rozee, "Interview with Monte Cook of Wizards of the Coast."

Official Monte Cook Web Site, http://www.montecook.com/ (November 21, 2004).

OgreCave.com, http://www.ogrecave.com/ (May 26, 2003), Joe G. Kushner, "Interviews: Monte Cook/Malhavoc Press."

Silven Crossroads, http://www.silven.com/ (May 1, 2003), Kosala Ubayasekara, "Q & A Session with Monte Cook"; (November 21, 2004), Bradford Ferguson, "GenCon 2003: Weekend with Malhavoc Press."

Wizards of the Coast, http://www.wizards.com/ (November 21, 2004), Michael Ryan, "Monte Cook Interview" and "Ghostwalk Designers"; (November 22, 2004), "Product Spotlight: Monte Cook."

Atom Egoyan

■ Personal

Surname is pronounced "Eh-goy-en"; born July 19, 1960, in Cairo, Egypt; immigrated to Canada, 1962; naturalized Canadian citizen; son of Joseph (a furniture store manager) and Shushan (a furniture store manager; maiden name, Devletian) Egoyan; married Arsinee Khanjian (an actress); children: Arshile (son). *Education:* Trinity College, University of Toronto, B.A., 1982. *Hobbies and other interests:* Classical guitar.

■ Addresses

Home—Toronto, Ontario, Canada. *Office*—Ego Film Arts, 80 Niagara St., Toronto, Ontario, Canada M5V 1C5.

■ Career

Director, producer, film editor, actor, and writer. Associated with Playwrights Unit in Toronto, Ontario, Canada. Director of Ego Film Arts, Toronto, beginning 1982. Director of films, including *Howard in Particular*, 1979; *After Grad with Dad*, 1980; *Peep Show*, 1981; (and producer and editor) *Next of Kin*, 1984; *Men: A Passion Playground*, 1985; (and producer and editor) *Family Viewing*, 1987; *The Final Twist*, 1987;

Speaking Parts, Cinephile, 1989; (and producer) *The Adjuster*, Orion Classics, 1991; "En passant" in *Montreal vu par*, 1991; (and producer and coeditor) *Calendar*, Zeitgeist, 1992; (and producer) *Exotica*, Miramax, 1994; *A Portrait of Arshile* (short), 1995; *The Sweet Hereafter*, 1997; *Bach Cello Suite #4: Sarabande*, 1997; *Felicia's Journey*, 1999; *The Line* (short), 2000; *Diaspora* (short), 2001; and *Ararat*, 2002. Director of television movies, including *Open House* (broadcast as part of *Canadian Reflections* series), Canadian Broadcasting Corporation (CBC), 1982; *In This Corner*, 1985; *Looking for Nothing*, 1989; and *Gross Misconduct*, CBC, 1992. Director of episodes of television shows, including *Alfred Hitchcock Presents* and *Twilight Zone*; director of stage productions, including *Salome*, 1996. Actor in motion pictures, including *Next of Kin*, 1984; *La boite a soleil*, 1988; *Calendar*, Zeitgeist, 1992; and *Camilla*, Miramax, 1994. Member of jury for Cannes International Film Festival, 1996.

■ Member

Academy of Canadian Television and Radio Artists, Directors Guild of Canada.

■ Awards, Honors

Grant from University of Toronto's Hart House Film Board; prize from Canadian National Exhibition's film festival, for *Howard in Particular*; grants from

Canadian Council and Ontario Arts Council; Gold Ducat Award, Mannheim International Film Week Festival, 1984, for *Next of Kin*; Toronto City Award for excellence in a Canadian production, Toronto Film Festival, 1987, International Critics Award for Best Feature Film, Uppsala Film Festival, 1988, and Priz Alcan from Festival du Nouveau Cinema, 1988, all for *Family Viewing*; prize for best screenplay, Vancouver International Film Festival, 1989, for *Speaking Parts*; Special Jury Prize, Moscow Film Festival, Golden Spike, Vallodolid Film Festival, Toronto City Award, Toronto Film Festival, and award for best Canadian film, Sudbury Film Festival, all 1991, all for *The Adjuster*; Golden Gate Award, San Francisco Film Festival, 1992, for *Gross Misconduct*; prize for best film in "new cinema," International Jury for Art Cinema, and prize from Berlin International Film Festival, both 1994, both for *Calendar*; Genie awards for best picture, best director, and best writer, International Film Critics Award, Cannes Film Festival, Prix de la Critique for best foreign film, and Toronto City Award, Toronto International Film Festival, all 1994, all for *Exotica*; eight Genie Awards, including for best picture and best director, grand prize and International Critics Award, Cannes Film Festival, and Academy Award nominations for writing and directing, all 1997, all for *The Sweet Hereafter*; Genie Award for screenplay adaptation, and Golden Palm nomination, Cannes Film Festival, both 1999, both for *Felicia's Journey*; Order of Canada Medal, 1999; first prize, Golden Apricot Film Festival, 2002, for *Ararat*.

■ Writings

SCREENPLAYS

(And director) *Howard in Particular*, 1979.

(And director, producer, and editor) *Next of Kin*, 1984.

(And director, producer, and editor) *Family Viewing*, 1987.

(And director) *Speaking Parts* (produced by Cinephile, 1989), published with essays and interviews, Coach House Press (Toronto, Ontario, Canada), 1993.

(And director and producer) *The Adjuster*, Orion Classics, 1991.

(And director, producer, and coeditor) *Calendar*, Zeitgeist, 1992.

(And director of "En passant" segment) *Montreal vu par*, 1992.

(And director and producer) *Exotica* (produced by Miramax, 1994), with interview with Egoyan, introduction by Geoff Pevere, Coach House Press (Toronto, Ontario, Canada), 1995.

(And director and producer) *The Sweet Hereafter*, Fine Line Features, 1997.

(And director) *Felicia's Journey*, Marquis Films, 1999.

(And director) *Ararat* (produced by Miramax, 2002), Newmarket Press, 2002.

Also director and writer of short films, including *Open House* (broadcast as part of Canadian Reflections series), Canadian Broadcasting Corporation, 1982.

OTHER

(Editor with Ian Balfour) *Subtitles: On the Foreignness of Film*, MIT Press, 2004.

Also author of plays, including *The Doll*.

■ Sidelights

Filmmaker Atom Egoyan gained a following with critics and cinema buffs in the 1980s with his atmospheric, haunting, darkly humorous, and intellectual works dealing with alienation, loss, and the search for identity. With efforts such as *Family Viewing* and *Speaking Parts*, he explores the issue of human bonding and how media such as video and film can serve to deepen an individual's detachment. Though he is still not exactly mainstream, Egoyan's

Egoyan received both the Grand Prize and the International Critics Award at the 1997 Cannes Film Festival for *The Sweet Hereafter*.

Earl Pastko and Arsinee Khanjian portray grieving parents whose child is killed in a school bus accident in the 1997 drama *The Sweet Hereafter.*

works became better known after the release of his breakthrough film, *Exotica,* an intricate investigation of several characters and subplots surrounding a strip club. Subsequently, the filmmaker's name got its biggest boost to date, as well as an Academy Award nomination, with his release of 1997's *The Sweet Hereafter,* adapted from the book by Russell Banks. He has also been hailed for his 1999 effort, *Felicia's Journey.*

Egoyan was born on July 19, 1960, in Cairo, Egypt, the oldest of two children born to Joseph and Shushan Yeghoyan; the family changed their surname to Egoyan to make it easier to pronounce. When the parents named their daughter Eve, it led to a barrage of jokes on the theme of Atom—which sounds like "Adam"—and Eve. Egoyan's parents were Armenian refugees and aspiring artists who operated a thriving furniture store in Cairo; they gave their

son his unconventional name in honor of the onset of nuclear energy in Egypt.

When Egoyan was three years old, the family relocated to Victoria, British Columbia, Canada, where they opened another furniture business. Both parents were creative, which helped to inspire their children; Eve Egoyan eventually became a concert pianist. Egoyan's mother once had a painting accepted by the National Gallery of Armenia, while his father had attended classes at the Chicago Art Institute at age sixteen, and staged his last major art show when Egoyan was ten. "They gave him the whole second floor of the provincial museum in Victoria, and his show was just images of dead birds," the filmmaker recalled to Brian D. Johnson in *Maclean's.* "The year before, our house was full of dead birds. It did not go over well. He would pose them around the house and paint them." Egoyan added, "I think I had a very early exposure to a very excessive mentality."

Assimilating to his new country, Egoyan enrolled in hockey school and soon refused to speak Armenian. Later, though, he joined an Armenian campus group at college and began to take private Armenian language courses, eventually becoming fluent again in his native language. Meanwhile, Egoyan showed an early interest in the arts, learning classic guitar, which he still plays, and beginning to write plays in his early teens. Among his influences he counts Harold Pinter, Samuel Beckett, and Eugene Ionesco.

College Films Lead to Television Work

At age eighteen Egoyan headed east and enrolled at Trinity College, Toronto, where he earned a bachelor of arts degree in international relations in 1982. In addition to writing film reviews for the student newspaper, he joined the Trinity College Dramatic Society and began to direct his own works, which did not prove to be the most popular campus productions. "I was trying to prove that I had something to express," Egoyan told Patricia Pearson in *Saturday Night*, "but at the same time I never wanted to bend to what was popular." Still, he pressed on, starting to create short films and submitting them to festivals. His first project, the fourteen-minute *Howard in Particular*, was financed by a small grant and filmed using equipment from the Hart House Film Board and the University of Toronto. The film focuses on an old man who is retiring from a fruit cocktail factory when its line becomes automated. In Egoyan's senior year, he created a 30-minute short, *Open House*, about a young man who tries to express his love for his father. This film was televised in the early 1980s by the Canadian Broadcasting Corporation (CBC) as part of its *Canadian Reflections* series.

A lonely, pregnant teenager (Elaine Cassidy) falls under the spell of a predatory older man (Bob Hoskins) in Egoyan's 1999 film *Felicia's Journey.*

In the meantime, Egoyan worked in Toronto with the Tarragon Theatre, where he studied playwrighting. After *Open House* aired, he was given $37,000 in grants from the Ontario Arts Council and the Canada Council, allowing him to shoot his first feature film. Egoyan thus put together *Next of Kin*, about a bored young man who pretends to be the long-lost son of an Armenian couple. This established what would become recurring themes in his work: alienation, loss, and identity. The film was accepted for showing at Toronto's Festival of Festivals in 1984, and then won the Gold Ducat Award at the Mannheim Film Festival in Germany the same year. In addition, Egoyan was nominated for a Genie Award, Canada's version of the Academy Award, as best director.

While planning *Next of Kin,* which was released in 1984, Egoyan cast actor Arsinee Khanjian, an Armenian who immigrated to Canada from Lebanon at age seventeen. Though she was married at the time to an Armenian dental student who also had a part in the film, she and Egoyan began a romantic relationship. After Khanjian's marriage broke up, the two later married. She has appeared in all of Egoyan's films, and serves as his artistic muse. The couple has a son, Arshile, who was born in 1993.

Despite *Next of Kin*'s exposure in Toronto and Mannheim and the fact that it found favor among critics, it did not transform Egoyan into an overnight sensation. For a time after its release, he worked as a porter at University of Toronto's Massey College for $5 an hour. However, he soon landed work directing a 1985 television movie titled *In This Corner,* which is about an Irish-Canadian boxer who gets involved with an Irish Republican Army gunman. After that, he was hired as a freelance director on episodes of *Alfred Hitchcock Presents, The Twilight Zone,* and other American television series, as well as some Canadian programs.

In 1987, with financial help from the Ontario Film Development Corporation, Egoyan made his second feature film, *Family Viewing.* This unsettling drama involves a man who has split with his Armenian wife and tries to erase his past by taping over old home videos with scenes of him and his new lover engaging in sexual acts. Meanwhile, the man's mistress repeatedly propositions the son. The son, in turn, moves in with a woman who works as a telephone sex operator, who counts his father as one of her clients. Attempting to find some stability in his life, the son begins visiting his maternal grandmother in a nursing home, where she has been placed by the father, and devises a plan to restore some semblance of order to his family.

In 1999 Egoyan was inducted into the Order of Canada by Governor General Romeo LeBlanc.

Family Viewing gained praise at film festivals worldwide and won an award for best Canadian feature film at the Toronto Film Festival in 1987. Even more astounding, at the Festival of New Cinema in Montreal, legendary director Wim Wenders, who was accepting an award for *Wings of Desire,* offered his prize money to Egoyan, boosting the young film maker's reputation even more. However, as Egoyan pointed out to Pearson, "The great myth was that he loved my film so much that he wanted the world to embrace me, but actually he hadn't seen the film. What he really wanted to embrace was the notion that a young film maker needed money more than he did."

In 1989 Egoyan released *Speaking Parts,* which continues to explore notions of voyeurism and deception. It is set in a hotel, a venue Egoyan became familiar with as a teenager when he worked in housekeeping at a hotel in Victoria. The film involves a chambermaid who is obsessed with a coworker, an actor who has had bit parts in some films. She rents and replays his movies nightly. Meanwhile, the actor tries to impress a screenwriter staying at the hotel, and manages to win a part in her upcoming film after seducing her. This enigmatic film moves at a deliberately slow pace and offers a purposely stilted acting style, prompting viewers to remain conscious of the fact that they were watching a film, not a slice of reality, as Hollywood products attempt to do. When *Speaking Parts* first aired at the Cannes International Film Festival in 1989, the third reel burst into flames and the audience had to wait 40 minutes to see the conclusion. The delay did not water down the critics' praise, however.

Egoyan was inspired to do his next project, *The Adjuster,* after a fire destroyed his parents' home and store on New Year's Eve in 1989. The story focuses on an alienated insurance adjuster who gets emotionally involved in his clients' lives. His wife, meanwhile, works as a government film censor and often tapes portions of the pornographic films she is assigned to watch. This dark comedy won a Toronto Film Festival Award and a Special Jury Prize at the Moscow Film Festival in 1991. Afterward, Egoyan embarked on a low-budget project resembling a home movie called *Calendar,* in which he also stars as a photographer who takes shots of Armenian churches for calendars. While overseas, his wife abandons him for a tour guide. This intimate effort, with a clever combination of unscripted moments and a postmodern sensibility, was made with help from German television network ZDF. It gained a small following among art-house circles and attracted applause from critics.

Just before Egoyan's wife became pregnant with their son, he started filming *Exotica,* the tale of a grief-stricken father who has lost a young daughter and frequents a striptease club where he talks to the performers. The plot is complex, also weaving in a character who smuggles exotic pets and a love triangle involving the dancer, the club disc jockey, and the club owner. By the time shooting began on the film, his wife, actress Khanjian, was seven months pregnant. "It was such a perverse film for a new parent to have made," Egoyan remarked to Brian D. Johnson in *Maclean's.* "But it wasn't conceived that way." As it turned out, *Exotica* won the International Critics Prize and was voted best foreign film at Cannes in 1994, in addition to reaping Genies for best picture, best director, and best writer, along with another Toronto Film Festival Award. It also became Egoyan's first widespread commercial success.

Adaptation Earns Major Awards

In 1997 Egoyan won even more acclaim for *The Sweet Hereafter,* about a group of grief-stricken people in a small Canadian town who try to rebuild their lives after a traumatic school bus accident. The film is adapted from a novel written by Russell Banks. It was the first time Egoyan directed a feature film script that he did not also write, but the film is nevertheless stamped with his trademark hypnotic style. However, the work also branches away from the director's earlier coldness to delve into the emotion of the characters; Owen Glieberman in *Entertainment Weekly* described *The Sweet Hereafter* as a "metaphysical soap opera." Indeed, Egoyan himself told Johnson, "What makes this film such a huge step forward is that for the first time you can identify with the characters. You're not outside them. In all my other films, the characters have been fragments of aspects of my personality. They were people looking for their own identity through rituals or gestures. But they were just shells." *The Sweet Hereafter* reaped a total of eight Genie awards, including for best picture and best director, and won the grand prize and International Critics Award at Cannes, among other honors at various festivals. It was also nominated for Academy awards for writing and directing. As Richard Porton noted in *Cineaste,* "While Egoyan had enjoyed a cult following during the 1980s, *The Sweet Hereafter* appeared on more than 200 'Ten Best' Lists in 1998 and won him a much larger audience."

Egoyan's next endeavor, *Felicia's Journey,* is also an adaptation, this time of a prize-winning novel by William Trevor. The film concerns a pregnant, destitute Irish girl who ventures to England to locate the boyfriend who abandoned her. Visiting the factory where he has told her he works, Felicia instead meets up with Joseph Hilditch, an older man who works in the factory cafeteria. While seemingly a gentle soul, Hilditch is actually a psychotic killer of homeless girls. "Unable to know themselves, out of place in their societies, these two characters never-

Egoyan discusses a scene with an actor on the set of the 2002 film *Ararat.*

theless form a temporary world of their own," according to Stuart Klawans, reviewing *Felicia's Journey* in *Nation*. Calling the film "a small masterpiece of literary creepiness," Patricia Hluchy in *Maclean's* concluded: "*Felicia's Journey* emphatically is not a feel-good experience. But it is an exquisite film." Reviewing the film for *Entertainment Weekly*, Lisa Schwarzbaum stated: "Egoyan has a talent for locating the dream-state perversity that runs just under the surface of everyday life," while Klawans described the film as "droll, disquieting, enigmatic." According to an essayist for the *International Dictionary of Films and Filmmakers*, "*The Sweet Hereafter* and its successor, *Felicia's Journey*, marked a departure in Egoyan's career, adapting material by others . . . instead of working to his own original scripts. Both films are sensitively crafted, keeping faith with their originals while further exploring his perennial themes of loss and disaffection." For *Felicia's Journey*, Egoyan won a Genie award for screenplay adaptation and was nominated for a Golden Palm award at Cannes.

Armenian Tragedy Presented on Film

Egoyan returned to his Armenian roots in the 2002 film *Ararat*, the story of the 1915 slaughter of one million Armenians by the Turks. He tells the story through present-day Canadians of Armenian heritage who seek to discover who they are by learning of their people's past. The story follows a film director, an art historian, and their children, all of whom must confront the past to understand the present. Within *Ararat* is another film, an historical film about the tragic events of 1915, being shot by a Toronto director of Armenian descent. As Schwarzbaum noted in *Entertainment Weekly*, Egoyan's film is a "difficult, dense, passionate drama. It's a story only he would tell this way, circling round and into the painful past through the stories of vivid characters in the crisp Canadian present of multicultural Toronto." Todd McCarthy, writing in *Variety*, called it an "ambitious, time-jumping mosaic," while Maryann Bird in *Time International* described *Ararat* as "a contemporary tale of two families' searches for truth and reconciliation as they struggle with uncertainty, insecurity and the legacy of denial." Writing in the *Hollywood Reporter*, Michael Rechtshaffen found *Ararat* to be "an intricately scripted, beautifully photographed meditation on redemption and reconciliation."

Egoyan told Bird that he was moved to make *Ararat* because of a question asked by his young son. When the boy was six or seven years old, Egoyan first told him about the genocide of 1915. But when the boy asked whether the Turks had apologized for

If you enjoy the works of Atom Egoyan, you may also want to check out the following films:

The Ice Storm, directed by Ang Lee, 1997.
Affliction, starring Nick Nolte, 1997.
A Map of the World, starring Sigourney Weaver, 1999.

this atrocity, Egoyan was startled. The Turks still refuse to admit any wrongdoing in the events, attributing the many deaths of the time to the fortunes of war. "I realized that by telling him the answer, the trauma of denial that I had been raised with would be transferred to him," Egoyan told Bird. "I understood that I wanted to talk about how this trauma lives on today."

■ Biographical and Critical Sources

BOOKS

Desbarts, Carole, editor, *Atom Egoyan*, Dis Voir, 1994.

International Dictionary of Films and Filmmakers, Volume 2: *Directors*, 4th edition, St. James Press (Detroit, MI), 2000.

Ismert, Louise and Michael Tarantino, *Atom Egoyan: Out of Use*, Musée d'art contemporain de Montréal, 2002.

Romney, Jonathan, *Atom Egoyan*, British Film Institute (London, England), 2003.

PERIODICALS

Artforum International, November, 1999, Steve Erickson, review of *Felicia's Journey*, p. 59.

Catholic New Times, February 9, 2003, Rosemary Ganley, "*Ararat*: An Egoyan Masterpiece," p. 16.

Cineaste, December, 1997, interview with Egoyan; winter, 1999, Richard Porton, "The Politics of Denial" (interview), p. 39.

Entertainment Weekly, March 24, 1995, review of *Exotica*, pp. 46-47; December 19, 1997, Owen Gleiberman, review of *The Sweet Hereafter*, p. 57; November 19, 1999, Lisa Schwarzbaum, review of *Felicia's Journey*, p. 111; November 22, 2002, Lisa Schwarzbaum, "Haunting History," p. 54.

Film Comment, January 1, 1998, Kent Jones, "The Cinema of Atom Egoyan," p. 32.

Hollywood Reporter, May 21, 2002, Michael Rechtshaffen, review of *Ararat,* p. 10.

Interview, March, 1995, Laura Winters, "Atom Egoyan Is Watching Us," p. 58.

Jeune Cinema, April, 1995, Marcus Rothe, interview with Egoyan.

Maclean's, October 3, 1994, pp. 45-47; April 6, 1998, "Atom's Oscar Diary: A Director Basks in Cinema's Biggest Spotlight," p. 61; November 15, 1999, Patricia Hluchy, "Starvation of the Soul: Atom Egoyan's Latest Is a Troubling Minor Masterpiece," p. 148.

Narrative, January, 2002, Katherine Weese, "Family Stories: Gender and Discourse in Atom Egoyan's *The Sweet Hereafter,*" p. 69.

Nation, July 13, 1992, Stuart Klawans, review of *The Adjuster,* p. 64; March 21, 1994, Stuart Klawans, review of *Calendar,* pp. 190-192; October 13, 1997, Stuart Klawans, review of *The Sweet Hereafter,* p. 34; December 6, 1999, Stuart Klawans, review of *Felicia's Journey,* p. 50.

National Post, November 6, 1999, Rick McGinnis, "The 'Egoyanesque' Atom Egoyan," p. 4.

National Review, February 9, 1998, John Simon, review of *The Sweet Hereafter,* p. 59.

New Statesman and Society, September 22, 1989, Suzanne Moore, review of *Speaking Parts,* p. 43.

Opera Canada, March 22, 2004, Wayne Gooding, "Forging the Ring: Atom Egoyan in Pre-Rehearsal Rehearsals for *Die Walkure,*" p. 14.

Parachute, July-September, 2001, Jacinto Lageira and Stephen Wright, "Relocating the Viewer" (interview), pp. 51-71.

Saturday Night, April, 1998, Patricia Pearson, interview with Egoyan, p. 67.

Sight and Sound, October, 1997, Tony Rayns, interview with Egoyan.

Take One, September 22, 1999, Marc Glassman, "Atom Egoyan's Delusional *Felicia's Journey,*" pp. 12-16; September 1, 2002, Tom McSorley, "Faraway, So Close: Atom Egoyan Returns Home with *Ararat,*" p. 8.

Time, November 22, 1999, Richard Corliss, review of *Felicia's Journey,* p. 108.

Time International, April 28, 2003, Maryann Bird, "Moving the Mountain: A Meditation on Memory and Denial, Atom Egoyan's *Ararat* Explores the Armenian Genocide of 1915," p. 92.

Variety, May 13, 2002, Brendan Kelly, "*Ararat* Draws Ire: Egoyan's Hot Button Screens out of Competition," p. 14; June 3, 2002, Todd McCarthy, review of *Ararat,* p. 26.

Written By, February, 1998, S. B. Katz, interview with Egoyan.

ONLINE

Egoyan Nucleus, http://www2.cruzio.com/~akreyche/atom.html/ (April 20, 2005).*

Milos Forman

■ Personal

Born Jan Tomas Forman, February 18, 1932, in Caslav, Czechoslovakia; came to United States, 1968, became U.S. citizen, 1975; son of Rudolf (a teacher) and Anna (Svabova) Forman; married Jana Brejchova (an actress; divorced, 1956); married Vera Kresadlova (a singer), 1964 (divorced); married Martina Zborilova, November 28, 1999; children: (second marriage) Petr, Matej (twin sons); (third marriage) Andrew, James (twins). *Education:* Prague Film Faculty, diploma, 1954.

■ Addresses

Home—The Hampshire House, 150 Central Park South, New York, NY 10019. *Agent*—Robert Lantz, Ltd., 888 Seventh Ave., New York, NY 10022.

■ Career

Director of motion pictures, including Taking Off, 1971; *One Flew over the Cuckoo's Nest,* 1975, *Hair,* 1979, *Ragtime,* 1982, *Amadeus,* 1984, *Valmont,* 1989,

The People vs. Larry Flynt, 1996, and *Man on the Moon,* 1999. Theater director for Laterna Magika, Prague, 1958-62; production assistant for Barrandov Studios, Czechoslovakia, 1962-63. Member of Sebor-Bor Film Producing Group, c. 1963. Actor in films, including *Heartburn,* 1986, and *New Year's Day,*1989. Honorary chairman of Columbia University Department of Film, 1975.

■ Awards, Honors

Prize from Czechoslovakian film critics, 1963, first prize from Locarno International Film Festival's young critics, 1964, and first prize in twentieth anniversary celebration for liberation of Czechoslovakia, and young critics prize from film competition, Öberhausen, both 1965, all for *Cerny Petr;* CIDALC Prize from French Film Festival, 1965, and Grand International Prize from French Film Academy, and Trilobite from Union of Czechoslovakian Film and Television Artists, both 1966, all for *Lasky jedne plavovlasky;* Cannes Film Festival jury prize, 1971, for *Taking Off;* Academy Award for Best Director, Academy of Motion Picture Arts and Sciences, Best Director Award, Directors Guild of America, and Silver Ribbon Award, Italian National Syndicate of Film Journalists, all 1975, all for *One Flew over the Cuckoo's Nest;* Academy Award for Best Director, 1984, and Golden Globe Award, Cesar Award (France) for Best Foreign Film, and Silver Ribbon for Best Director of a Foreign Film, Italian National Syndicate of Film Journalists, all 1985, all for *Ama-*

deus; Eastman Kodak Second Century Award, 1990; Freedom of Expression Award, 1996; Golden Globe for Best Director, Golden Berlin Bear, Berlin International Film Festival, and Karlovy Vary International Film Festival prize, all 1997, all for *The People vs. Larry Flynt;* John Huston Award for Artist Rights, 1997; Silver Berlin Bear, 2000, for *Man on the Moon;* Lifetime Achievement Award, Palm Springs International Film Festival, 2000; Lifetime Achievement Award, Netherlands Film by the Sea Festival, 2004; Billy Wilder Award, National Board of Review of Motion Pictures, 2004; Award for Lifetime Achievement in Directing, San Francisco International Film Festival, 2004; Legion d'Honour, Cannes Film Festival, 2004.

■ Writings

SCREENPLAYS

(With Ivan Passer) *Konkurs* (two short films), Filmstudio Barrandov, 1963, released in English as *Audition,* 1963.

(With Jaroslav Papousek) *Cerny Petr* (title means "Black Peter"), Altura Films, 1971, released in English as *Peter and Pavla,* Srebo, 1964.

(With Ivan Passer and Jaroslav Papousek) *Lasky jedne plavovlasky,* Sebor-Bor/Filmstudio Barrandov, 1965, released in English as *Loves of a Blonde,* Prominent Films, 1966.

(With Ivan Passer and Jaroslav Papousek) *Hori, ma panenko,* Filmstudio Barrandov/Carlo Ponti, 1967, released in the United States as *The Fireman's Ball,* Cinema V, 1968, released in England as *Like a House on Fire,* 1968.

(With John Guare, Jean-Claude Carriere, and John Klein) *Taking Off* (also see below), Universal, 1971.

(With others) *Visions of Eight* (contains *Decathlon* by Forman), Cinema V, 1973.

Also author, with Jean-Claude Carriere, of *La prince . . . Ongles,* 1969, and of screenplays produced in Czechoslovakia with translated titles "Leave It to Me," 1955, and "Puppies," 1957.

OTHER

(With Nancy Hardin) *Taking Off* (adapted from the screenplay directed by Forman and co-authored by Forman, John Guare, Jean-Claude Carriere, and John Klein; released by Universal, 1971), New American Library (New York, NY), 1971.

(With Antonin J. Liehm) *The Milos Forman Stories,* International Arts and Sciences Press, 1975.

(With Jan Novak) *Turnaround: A Memoir,* Villard (New York, NY), 1994.

■ Work in Progress

Directing a screen adaptation of Sandor Marai's novel *Embers.*

■ Sidelights

Milos Forman is one of only a few foreign film directors to achieve box-office success with American audiences. His films, including the Academy Award winners *One Flew over the Cuckoo's Nest* and *Amadeus,* display a sense of empathy for people caught up in cruel societal systems over which they have

Forman composes a shot on the set of his 1971 film *Taking Off,* a satirical look at American society.

Forman (right) and John Turturro discuss *Amadeus: The Director's Cut*, the 2002 re-release of the Academy Award-winning 1984 film.

little control. Despite the serious content of many of his films, Forman has also distinguished himself as a master of ironic comedy and rich visual effects.

Early Love of Theater and Film

Forman described his first experience with cinema in an interview published in the *UNESCO Courier.* "It was unforgettable," he recalled. "One Saturday night, when I was four or five years old, my parents took me to see a film in Caslav, the city where I was born in the country that was then called Czechoslovakia. I found out later that it was a documentary about Smetana's opera *The Bartered Bride.* Oddly enough, it was a silent film. On the screen gigantic people opened enormous mouths from which no sound emerged. But the audience knew the opera by heart and began to sing louder and louder. The women were in tears. It was an extraordinary introduction to the cinema!"

Forman's life was soon torn apart by the Nazi invasion of Czechoslovakia. He was orphaned when his father, a Jewish professor, was taken to the Buchenwald concentration camp, where he died in 1944. His mother, a Protestant, was imprisoned and perished at Auschwitz. Forman's brother Pavel was also wanted by the Gestapo; while hiding from Nazi authorities Pavel worked as part of an underground theater group. "It was thanks to him that I saw my first play, which struck a deep emotional chord," Forman was quoted as saying in the *UNESCO Courier.* "He also took me backstage. That was extremely disconcerting: the young women undressing before my eyes, the jokes, the music, the smell of starch and mothballs and sweat. It was a revelation to me and I decided there and then that the theatre, this other world, would be my life."

When the German occupation ended in Chechoslovakia, Forman had the opportunity to see American films, and became enthralled with them. In 1950, while in his final year of secondary school at Dejvice, he organized a drama club and staged a musical about French poet François Villon that was presented at numerous small venues around Prague. After graduation, he enrolled in the Film Institute at the University of Prague, and from there he went on to work as a director and screenwriter for Czech television. By the 1960s he had moved into film work, and was establishing himself as one of the leading figures of the Czech "New Wave" film renaissance, as well as one of Eastern Europe's finest, and most sardonic, filmmakers.

Cerny Petr, or *Black Peter,* Forman's first film to garner much attention, earned international honors for its humorous depiction of a dispirited floorwalker who arbitrarily reports numerous shoplifters. *Lasky jedne plavovlasky,* released in English as *Loves of a Blonde,* was another early success and features a young woman named Andula, who is disillusioned and haphazard in her pursuit of pleasure. Andula falls in love with a young pianist and pursues him to Prague, where she creates a crisis by confronting his parents with an account of her tryst with their son. A reviewer for the *New York Times* called *Loves of a Blonde* "delightful and unusual—comic and sad and comprehending in a curiously inarticulate way." The reviewer added that the film "is human, true but understated—inconclusive, indeed, as is life— and it leaves one amused and wistful over the romantic hopes of its little blonde."

Hori, ma panenko—released in translation as *The Firemen's Ball* and *Like a House on Fire*—was Forman's third major success from the mid-1960s and focuses on a ceremony conceived to honor a retiring fire chief. The celebration in the man's honor is disrupted, however, by a beauty contest, a marching band, and a raffle. Even a fire interrupts the proceedings; while the owner of the burning home sits and watches, thoughtful neighbors turn his chair away to lessen the shock, then move the fellow closer to the fire to warm him. A *New York Times* writer described *The Firemen's Ball* as "a hilarious shaggy dog story, with the pessimism of the exquisite logic that leads nowhere." "That a director who sees things so bitterly and clearly can be this funny," the critic added, ". . . may mean that we are in for a comic renaissance after all."

The **Firemen's Ball** was released in 1967 and banned by the Communist authorities in Czechoslovakia.

Exile to America

Forman's life, and his career, were once again disrupted by European politics when, in 1968, Soviet troops invaded Czechoslovakia. He had already been forced to publicly apologize to the 40,000 firemen who had walked off their jobs after the release of *The Firemen's Ball* and assured these workers that the film was actually a political allegory. However, the increasingly repressive Communist rule signaled the end of a period where the subtleties of allegory would be tolerated. Forman was in Paris when the Soviets entered his country, and he remained abroad rather than return home to live under communism. Eventually, he headed to the United States and Hollywood. Hoping to film an adaptation of Franz Kafka's *Amerika,* he was unable to recruit producers. A project featuring actor Jimmy Durante as a wealthy bear hunter roaming the Slavic woodlands also failed to interest appropriate producers.

Then, in 1968, Forman was enlisted by Paramount Pictures to direct one of his own works. Together with several other writers, including playwright John Guare, Forman fashioned *Taking Off,* a film

Jack Nicholson starred in Forman's film adaptation of *One Flew Over the Cuckoo's Nest*.

that earned the same acclaim accorded his Slavic works. The film depicts the increasingly permissive American society of the late 1960s, as personified by staid businessman Larry Tyne and his family. When Tyne's daughter, Jeannie, becomes involved in a Greenwich Village theater production and decides to stay in the Village, Larry and his wife try to become better acquainted with their daughter's environment in an attempt to woo her into returning home. Their adventures take them to a meeting of the Society for Parents of Fugitive Children, where they learn how to smoke marijuana, and into the Village, where they are appalled by the inhabitants' casual attitude toward sex and drugs. A *New York Times* critic hailed *Taking Off* as a "charming" work, adding: "Forman's America is made up of neighborhood bars to which lonely ladies come accompanied by their Siamese cats; of the sort of mother who, when told her daughter has shoplifted a portable Japanese TV set, asks whether it's a Sony."

Despite favorable reviews of *Taking Off*, Forman was unable to obtain funding for another project. In 1972 he filmed decathlon competitors at the Olympics for inclusion in the omnibus production *Visions of Eight*, but that proved to be his sole production throughout the next two years. Forman fell into a deep depression, and it was at this low point that he was approached by producers Saul Zaentz and Michael Douglas to direct Bo Goldman's adaptation of the Ken Kesey novel *One Flew over the Cuckoo's Nest*.

In interpreting the novel, Forman fashioned a compelling portrait of the individual against the system, and his effort earned a host of awards, including an Academy Award for Forman's direction and the award for Best Picture. The film was driven by Jack Nicholson's performance as R. P. McMurphy, an irrepressible con man who has managed to convert a jail sentence into a period of treatment in a state mental institution. What McMurphy does not realize at first is that he has been committed and will not be released until those in charge of the hospital deem him fit to rejoin society. The con man finds himself pitted against Nurse Ratched, a domineering woman who seeks total control over her patients. Ratched's interactions with McMurphy lead to violence, and, eventually, to a tragic and ironic ending. In addition to being a critical success, the film was a tremendous box-office hit. Suddenly well known in his adopted country, Forman became an American citizen.

Forman next worked with playwright Michael Weller on the films *Hair* and *Ragtime. Hair,* which had been a phenomenally successful Broadway musical, captured the mood of rebellion and affection that fostered the youth movement of the late 1960s. Although some critics felt the film was anachronis-

tic by the time it was made, a *New Yorker* writer believed "it is no accident that Forman took on the direction of *Hair,*" since "the score, with—to his ears— its newness and its eloquence about his adopted country, must have sung strongly to him. So, clearly, did moments of ease and fun that he catches on to in the book and lyrics."

Ragtime, in contrast, is a painstaking presentation of E. L. Doctorow's popular novel about a true-life murder involving some of the most well-known New York socialites of the early 1900s. Some critics felt that Forman's European background was a handicap in making such an American film. A *New Yorker* columnist contended that "Forman simply didn't have the storehouse of associations to make a *Ragtime,*" and added: "It's limp—it always seems to be aiming about halfway to Doctorow's effects." A more enthusiastic *Newsweek* reviewer called *Ragtime* "high-class," but "oddly tamed and domesticated."

In 2004 Forman was made a member of the French Legion d'Honneur for his contributions to cinema.

Wins Second Academy Award for *Amadeus*

In 1979 Forman returned to Czechoslovakia for the first time since his voluntary exile. A few years later he went to his native country to film what would be one of his greatest successes: the film adaptation of Peter Schaffer's play *Amadeus,* about the life and death of great composer Wolfgang Amadeus Mozart. The film focuses on the rivalry between Salieri, a court composer with limited talent but a great devotion to his art, and Mozart, a natural genius who, in Salieri's view, seems an unworthy recipient of his incredible talent. The film was a runaway hit, winning eight Academy Awards and boosting the sales of Mozart's music appreciably. According to *New Republic* reviewer Stanley Kauffmann, Forman's screen version is a marked improvement over the theater production, utilizing "a more straightforward narrative" to create "a visually lively piece."

With another Academy Award to his credit, it seemed that Forman was at the pinnacle of his career, but his next film, *Valmont,* was widely panned and generated little interest among moviegoers. The project was an adaptation of Choderlos de Laclose's novel *Les Liasons Dangereuses,* which had earlier been adapted for film as *Dangerous Liasons.* The story is one of ruthless games of seduction in French society, but according to *Maclean's* reviewer Brian D. Johnson, Forman "has warmed its cold heart with a blush of romance." Comparing *Valmont* to *Dangerous Liasons,* Johnson commented, "The erotic scenes are less graphic, and the film's artists of sexual treachery are sympathetic and vulnerable. Finally, he has added an upbeat twist to the story's dark ending." Despite such positive assessments, *Valmont* marked the beginning of a long inactive spell for Forman as a director. He acted in a few films and busied himself with other projects, but he did not direct again until 1996.

Freedom of Expression

In the mid-1990s Forman again became the topic of discussion, this time for taking a cinematic risk despite his many years of inactivity. Involving a complex subject and an unlikeable—even reviled— protagonist, *The People vs. Larry Flynt* is based on the legal battles of Larry Flynt, publisher of the hardcore pornographic magazine *Hustler.* Forman's movie takes the position that no matter how objectionable the content of Flynt's publications, it is essential to protect the right to free speech. The theme was particularly meaningful to Forman, who had lived under Communist censorship. His film evoked

If you enjoy the works of Milos Forman, you may also want to check out the following films:

Five Easy Pieces, starring Jack Nicholson, 1970.
American Beauty, directed by Sam Mendes, 1999.
Chicago, starring Richard Gere and Catherine Zeta-Jones, 2002.

strong response, both positive and negative. It won awards, yet it was also strongly condemned by many, including feminist Gloria Steinem, who criticized it for making a hero out of a man who routinely debases women in his publications. John Simon, reviewing *The People vs. Larry Flynt* for the *National Review,* called it "a resounding vindication of free speech in America, something that cannot be tested in a nonsubversive or inoffensive context." Simon added that most of the film is made up of "good dialogue and direction, idiomatic performances, and virtually no visible flesh."

Again profiling a well-known individual, Forman presents a marginally likeable character in his 1999 film *Man on the Moon,* which is about the life and career of comedian Andy Kaufmann. Known for bizarre performances that frequently irritated or puzzled audiences, Kaufmann died of a rare form of cancer at an early age. Forman's film, according to *Time* reviewer Richard Schickel, does a fine job of capturing Kaufmann's "self-destructive and endlessly confrontational relationship with networks, concert managers and audiences," which Schickel maintained "was the great theme of his career. He was always disconcertingly catching everyone between laughter and outrage. And the cookies-and-milk treat he sometimes offered later never quite healed that ambiguity. *Man on the Moon* doesn't either. It just gives us Andy, the pop postmodernist, and permits us to make what we will of him, which is a fascinating activity."

Good Guy Always Wins

Discussing the differences between American and European films with Steven Gaydos of *Variety,* Forman commented that while both usually revolve around a struggle between good and evil, "in American movies the good guys mostly win at the end, [but] the European films pride themselves in the fact that at the end nobody wins. You can loosely describe the majority of European movies as being basically a masochistic slice of dreary life, while American movies are basically macho fairy tales."

The filmmaker looked back on his life in *Turnaround: A Memoir,* published in 1994. His memories of his traumatic childhood years remain sharp and moving, according to *Entertainment Weekly* writer D. A. Ball, while he employs a more relaxed style when discussing his film career. Ball concluded: "Good directors are good storytellers, and this storyteller is a good autobiographer." A *Publishers Weekly* contributor described it as "a wonderful political and artistic odyssey," and concluded: "The memoir is a treat for movie buffs, cultural historians and lovers of the American dream."

■ Biographical and Critical Sources

BOOKS

Encyclopedia of World Biography Supplement, Volume 20, Gale (Detroit, MI), 2000.

Forman, Milos, *Turnaround: A Memoir,* Villard Books (New York, NY), 1994.

International Dictionary of Films and Filmmakers, Volume 2: *Directors,* St. James Press (Detroit, MI), 2000.

Poizot, Claude, *Milos Forman,* Dis voir, 1987.

Slater, Thomas J., *Milos Forman: A Bio-Bibliography,* Greenwood Press (New York, NY), 1987.

PERIODICALS

Booklist, January 1, 1994, Lindsay Throm, review of *Turnaround: A Memoir,* p. 798.

Canadian Dimension, March-April, 1997, Karen Sawatzky, review of *The People vs. Larry Flynt,* p. 39.

Christian Century, April 23, 1997, Margaret R. Miles, review of *The People vs. Larry Flynt,* p. 419.

Cineaste, fall, 1996, Richard Porton, interview with Foreman, p. 28; spring, 2000, David Sterritt, review of *Man on the Moon,* p. 52.

Columbia Journalism Review, January-February, 1997, James Boylan, review of *The People vs. Larry Flynt,* p. 15.

Commonweal, October 19, 1984, Tom O'Brien, review of *Amadeus,* p. 557-558; December, 1989, Tom O'Brien, "Better and Better than Bland," pp. 670-671.

Daily Variety, April 29, 2004, "Forum Fetes Forman: Helmer among Trio Tapped for Europe Day," p. 8; July 14, 2004, Marlene Edmunds, "Netherlands Fest Will Fete Film Duo," p. 9; December 9, 2004, Ian Mohr, "Pair Pluck Special NBR Nods," p. 4.

Entertainment Weekly, March 4, 1994, D. A. Ball, review of *Turnaround,* p. 60; December 10, 1999, Jeff Jensen, review of *Man on the Moon,* p. 50; June 2, 2000, Troy Patterson, review of *Man on the Moon,* p. 57.

Film Comment, September-October, 1984, Michael Walsh, review of *Amadeus,* pp. 51-52.

Hollywood Reporter, September 26, 2002, Glenn Abel, review of *Amadeus,* p. 57; August 6, 2002, Chris Gardner, "'Embers' Burning for Forman," p. 6; March 5, 2004, "Forman's Lifetime," p. 6.

Interview, January 20, 1967; January, 2000, Courtney Love, interview with Forman, p. 86.

Journal of American History, December, 1997, Kathryn H. Fuller, review of *The People vs. Larry Flynt,* pp. 1185-1186.

Life, September, 1984, "Madcap Mozart," p. 66; spring, 1989, "Director: Milos Forman Makes the Scene in Paris," p. 70.

Los Angeles Times, September 19, 1984, Sheila Benson, review of *Amadeus,* pp. 1, 6.

Maclean's, November 20, 1989, Brian D. Johnson, review of *Valmont,* p. 82; December 30, 1996, Brian D. Johnson, review of *The People vs. Larry Flynt,* p. 99.

Memphis Business Journal, January 13, 1997, Linda Romine, interview with Forman, p. 3.

Nation, December 11, 1989, Stuart Klawans, review of *Valmont,* p. 727; February 3, 1997, Katha Pollitt, review of *The People vs. Larry Flynt,* p. 9.

National Review, October 19, 1984, John Simon, review of *Amadeus,* p. 56; January 22, 1990, John Simon, review of *Valmont,* p. 56; Februrary 24, 1997, John Simon, review of *The People vs. Larry Flynt,* p. 53.

New Republic, October 22, 1984, Stanley Kauffmann, review of *Amadeus,* p. 30; December 11, 1989, Stanley Kauffmann, review of *Valmont,* p. 24; January 6, 1997, Hanna Rosin, review of *The People vs. Larry Flynt,* p. 20; January 20, 1997, Stanley Kauffmann, review of *The People vs. Larry Flynt,* p. 24; May 8, 2000, Jonathan Romney, review of *Man on the Moon,* pp. 41-42.

New Statesman, April 4, 1997, Marcel Berlins, review of *The People vs. Larry Flynt,* p. 36; April 11, 1997, Jonathan Coe, review of *The People vs. Larry Flynt,* pp. 40-41.

Newsweek, November 23, 1981; December 23, 1996, David Ansen, review of *The People vs. Larry Flynt,* p. 62, Jonathan Alter, "The Right to Be Wrong," p. 64.

New Yorker, April 16, 1979; November 23, 1981.

New York Times, October 23, 1966; September 30, 1968; March 23, 1971; April 18, 1971; May 14, 1971; November 11, 1971; November 23, 1971.

People, October 1, 1984, review of *Amadeus,* p. 14; October 8, 1984, John Stark, "Going Home to Prague to Film *Amadeus* Evokes Bittersweet Memories for Milos Forman," p. 113; January 20, 1997, Tom Gliatto, review of *The People vs. Larry Flynt,* p. 18.

Publishers Weekly, December 13, 1993, review of *Turnaround,* p. 53.

Reason, January, 1997, Charles Paul Freund, "Market Culture: Bashed and Unabashed," p. 54.

Sight & Sound, spring, 1985, review of *Amadeus,* pp. 142-143; March, 1997, Stella Bruzzi, review of *The People vs. Larry Flynt,* pp. 58-59; April, 2000, Leslie Felperin, review of *Man on the Moon,* p. 58.

Time, April 8, 1985, Gerald Clarke, "Eight Cheers for the Music Man," p. 74; July 8, 1985, Richard Corliss, "Magic Shadows from a Melting Pot," p. 92; November 20, 1989, Richard Schickel, review of *Valmont,* p. 92; March 18, 1996, Belinda Luscombe, "Sex, Lies and Free Speech," p. 101; December 30, 1996, Richard Corliss, review of *The People vs. Larry Flynt,* p. 140; December 31, 1999, Richard Schickel, review of *Man on the Moon,* p. 232.

Times Literary Supplement, November 29, 1991, Malcolm Bowie, "Rites of Passage Romp," p. 21; April 18, 1997, Adam Newey, review of *The People vs. Larry Flynt,* p. 18.

UNESCO Courier, July-August, 1995, interview with Forman, p. 18.

Variety, January 10, 2000, Steven Gaydos, "Forman Brings Euro Touch to U.S. Movies," p. 74; August 5, 2002, Cathy Dunkley, "Helmer Sifts through 'Embers' for Next Pic," p. 6; July 14, 2003, "Thesps Stoked for Forman's 'Embers,'" p. 2.

Video Business, September 30, 2002, interview with Forman, p. 6.

ONLINE

Director's Chair, http://www.industrycentral.net/director_interviews/ (January 28, 2005), Joseph McBride, interview with Forman.

Reel.com, http://www.reel.com/ (April 20, 2005), Ray Greene, "Milos Forman: The Man behind *Man on the Moon.*"

Scene 360: The Film and Arts Online Magazine, http://www.scene360.com/ (April 20, 2005), biography of Forman.

OTHER

The Directors: Milos Forman (film), Winstar Entertainment, 2000.*

Donald Hall

writer, 1975—. Bennington College graduate Writing Seminars, poet-in-residence, 1993—. Broadcaster on British Broadcasting Corporation radio programs, 1959-80; host of *Poets Talking* (television interview series), 1974-75; has given poetry readings at colleges, universities, schools, and community centers.

■ Personal

Born September 20, 1928, in New Haven, CT; son of Donald Andrew (a businessman) and Lucy (Wells) Hall; married Kirby Thompson, September 13, 1952 (divorced 1969); married Jane Kenyon (a poet), April 17, 1972 (died April 22, 1995); children: (first marriage) Andrew, Philippa. *Education:* Harvard University, B.A., 1951; Oxford University, B. Litt., 1953; attended Stanford University, 1953-54.

■ Addresses

Home—Eagle Pond Farm, Danbury, NH 03230. *Agent*—Gerald McCauley Agency, Inc., Box 844, Katonah, NY 10536.

■ Career

Harvard University, Cambridge, MA, junior fellow in Society of Fellows, 1954-57; University of Michigan, Ann Arbor, 1957-75, began as assistant professor, became professor of English; full-time freelance

■ Member

PEN, American Academy and Institute of Arts and Letters.

■ Awards, Honors

Newdigate Prize, Oxford University, 1952, for poem "Exile"; Lamont Poetry Prize, Academy of American Poets, 1955, for *Exiles and Marriages*; Edna St. Vincent Millay Award, Poetry Society of America, 1956; Guggenheim fellowship, 1963-64, 1972-73; *New York Times* Notable Children's Books citation, 1979, and Caldecott Medal, 1980, both for *Ox-Cart Man*; Sarah Josepha Hale Award, 1983, for writings about New England; *Horn Book* Honor List, 1986, for *The Oxford Book of Children's Verse in America*; Lenore Marshall Prize, 1987, for *The Happy Man*; National Book Critics Circle Award for poetry, and *Los Angeles Times* Book Prize in poetry, both 1989, both for *The One Day*; named poet Laureate of New Hampshire, 1984-89, 1995—; Associated Writing Programs Poetry Publication Award named in Hall's honor.

■ Writings

FOR CHILDREN

Andrew the Lion Farmer, illustrated by Jane Miller, F. Watts (New York, NY), 1959, illustrated by Ann Reason, Methuen (London, England), 1961.

Riddle Rat, illustrated by Mort Gerberg, Warne (London, England), 1977.

Ox-Cart Man, illustrated by Barbara Cooney, Viking (New York, NY), 1979.

The Man Who Lived Alone, illustrated by Mary Azarian, Godine (New York, NY), 1984.

(Editor) *The Oxford Book of Children's Verse in America*, Oxford University Press, 1985.

The Farm Summer 1942, illustrated by Barry Moser, Dial (New York, NY), 1994.

I Am the Dog, I Am the Cat, illustrated by Barry Moser, Dial (New York, NY) l, 1994.

Lucy's Christmas, illustrated by Michael McCurdy, Harcourt Brace (New York, NY), 1994.

Lucy's Summer, illustrated by Michael McCurdy, Harcourt Brace (New York, NY), 1995.

When Willard Met Babe Ruth, illustrated by Barry Moser, Harcourt Brace (New York, NY), 1996.

Old Home Day, illustrated by Emily Arnold McCully, Harcourt Brace, (New York, NY) 1996.

The Milkman's Boy, illustrated by Greg Shed, Walker (New York, NY), 1997.

POETRY

Fantasy Poets No. 4, Fantasy Press, 1952.

Exile, Fantasy Press, 1952.

To the Loud Wind and Other Poems, Pegasus, 1955.

Exiles and Marriages, Viking (New York, NY), 1955.

The Dark Houses, Viking (New York, NY), 1958.

A Roof of Tiger Lilies, Viking (New York, NY), 1964.

The Alligator Bride: Poems, New and Selected, Harper (New York, NY), 1969.

The Yellow Room: Love Poems, Harper (New York, NY), 1971.

The Gentleman's Alphabet Book (limericks), illustrated by Harvey Kornberg, Dutton (New York, NY), 1972.

The Town of Hill, Godine (New York, NY), 1975.

A Blue Wing Tilts at the Edge of the Sea: Selected Poems, 1964-1974, Secker & Warburg (London, England), 1975.

Kicking the Leaves, Harper (New York, NY), 1978.

The Toy Bone, BOA Editions, 1979.

Brief Lives: Seven Epigrams, William B. Ewart, 1983.

The Twelve Seasons, Deerfield Press, 1983.

Great Day in the Cow's House, illustrated with photographs by T. S. Bronson, Ives Street Press, 1984.

The Happy Man, Random House (New York, NY), 1986.

The One Day, Ticknor & Fields, 1988.

Old and New Poems, Ticknor & Fields, 1990.

The Museum of Clear Ideas, Ticknor & Fields, 1993.

The Old Life, Houghton (Boston, MA), 1996.

Without, Houghton (Boston, MA), 1998.

The Purpose of a Chair, Brooding Heron Press (Waldron Island, WA), 2000.

The Painted Bed, Houghton (Boston, MA), 2002.

Contributor of poetry to numerous periodicals, including the *New Yorker, New Republic, New Criterion, Kenyon Review, Iowa Review, Georgia Review, Ohio Review, Gettysburg Review, Nation*, and *Atlantic Monthly*.

PROSE

String Too Short to Be Saved: Recollections of Summers on a New England Farm (autobiography), illustrated by Mimi Korach, Viking (New York, NY), 1961, expanded edition, Godine (New York, NY), 1979.

Henry Moore: The Life and Work of a Great Sculptor, Harper (New York, NY), 1966.

As the Eye Moves: A Sculpture by Henry Moore, illustrated with photographs by David Finn, Abrams (New York, NY), 1970.

Marianne Moore: The Cage and the Animal, Pegasus, 1970.

The Pleasures of Poetry, Harper (New York, NY), 1971.

Writing Well, Little, Brown (Boston, MA), 1974, 9th edition (with Sven Birkerts), HarperCollins (New York, NY), 1997.

(With others) *Playing Around: The Million-Dollar Infield Goes to Florida*, Little, Brown (Boston, MA), 1974.

(With Dock Ellis) *Dock Ellis in the Country of Baseball*, Coward (New York, NY), 1976.

Goatfoot Milktongue Twinbird: Interviews, Essays, and Notes on Poetry, 1970-76, University of Michigan Press (Ann Arbor, MI), 1978.

Remembering Poets: Reminiscences and Opinions—Dylan Thomas, Robert Frost, T. S. Eliot, Ezra Pound, Harper (New York, NY), 1978, revised edition published as *Their Ancient Glittering Eyes*, Ticknor & Fields, 1992.

To Keep Moving: Essays, 1959-1969, Hobart & William Smith Colleges Press, 1980.

To Read Literature, Holt (New York, NY), 1980.

The Weather for Poetry: Essays, Reviews, and Notes on Poetry, 1977-1981, University of Michigan Press (Ann Arbor, MI), 1982.

Fathers Playing Catch with Sons: Essays on Sport (Mostly Baseball), North Point Press, 1985.

Seasons at Eagle Pond, illustrated by Thomas W. Nason, Ticknor & Fields, 1987.

Poetry and Ambition, University of Michigan Press (Ann Arbor, MI), 1988.

Here at Eagle Pond, illustrated by Thomas W. Nason, Ticknor & Fields, 1990.

Life Work, Beacon Press (Boston, MA), 1993.

Death to the Death of Poetry: Essays, Reviews, Notes, Interviews, University of Michigan Press (Ann Arbor, MI), 1994.

Principle Products of Portugal: Prose Pieces, Beacon Press (Boston, MA), 1995.

Breakfast Served Any Time All Day: Essays on Poetry New and Selected, University of Michigan Press (Ann Arbor, MI), 2003.

Willow Temple: New and Selected Stories, Houghton (Boston, MA), 2003.

Contributor of short stories and articles to numerous periodicals, including the *New Yorker, Esquire, Atlantic, Playboy, Transatlantic Review,* and *American Scholar.*

PLAYS

An Evening's Frost, first produced in Ann Arbor, MI; produced Off-Broadway, 1965.

Bread and Roses, produced in Ann Arbor, MI, 1975.

Ragged Mountain Elegies (produced in Peterborough, NH, 1983), revised version published as *The Bone Ring* (produced in New York, NY, 1986), Story Line, 1987.

EDITOR

The Harvard Advocate Anthology, Twayne (New York, NY), 1950.

(With Robert Pack and Louis Simpson) *The New Poets of England and America*, Meridian Books, 1957.

Whittier, Dell (New York, NY), 1961.

Contemporary American Poetry, Penguin (London England), 1962, Penguin (Baltimore, MD), 1963.

(With Robert Pack) *New Poets of England and America: Second Selection*, Meridian Books, 1962.

A Poetry Sampler, F. Watts (New York, NY), 1962.

(With Stephen Spender) *The Concise Encyclopedia of English and American Poets and Poetry*, Hawthorn, 1963.

(With Warren Taylor) *Poetry in English*, Macmillan (New York, NY), 1963.

The Faber Book of Modern Verse, revised edition, Faber & Faber (London, England), 1965.

A Choice of Whitman's Verse, Faber & Faber (London, England), 1968.

Man and Boy, F. Watts (New York, NY), 1968.

The Modern Stylists: Writers on the Art of Writing, Free Press (New York, NY), 1968.

American Poetry: An Introductory Anthology, Faber & Faber (London, England), 1969.

(With D. L. Emblem) *A Writer's Reader*, Little, Brown (Boston, MA), 1969, 9th edition, Longman (New York, NY), 2002.

The Pleasures of Poetry, Harper (New York, NY), 1971.

The Oxford Book of American Literary Anecdotes, Oxford University Press (Oxford, England), 1981.

To Read Literature: Fiction, Poetry, Drama, Holt (New York, NY), 1981, 3rd edition, Harcourt (New York, NY), 1992.

Claims for Poetry, University of Michigan Press (Ann Arbor, MI), 1982.

To Read Poetry, Holt (New York, NY), 1982, revised edition published as *To Read a Poem*, Harcourt (New York, NY), 1992.

The Contemporary Essay, St. Martin's Press (New York, NY), 1984, 3rd edition, 1995.

The Oxford Book of Children's Verse in America, Oxford University Press (New York, NY), 1985.

To Read Fiction, Holt (New York, NY), 1987.

(With Pat Corrington Wykes) *Anecdotes of Modern Art: From Rousseau to Warhol*, Oxford University Press (New York, NY), 1990.

Peter Davison, *One of the Dangerous Trades: Essays on the Work and Workings of Poetry, 1963-1990*, University of Michigan Press (Ann Arbor, MI), 1991.

Andrew Marvell, *The Essential Marvell*, Ecco Press (New York, NY), 1991.

Edwin Arlington Robinson, *The Essential Robinson*, Ecco Press (New York, NY), 1993.

Oxford Illustrated Book of American Children's Poems, Oxford University Press (New York, NY), 1999.

Former poetry editor, *Paris Review.* Former member of editorial board, Wesleyan University Press poetry series; editor, University of Michigan "Poets on Poetry" series.

■ Sidelights

Considered one of the major American poets of his generation, Donald Hall explores a longing for the more bucolic past and his verse reflects his abiding reverence for nature. Although Hall gained an early success with his 1955 poetry collection *Exiles and Marriages*, his mature recent poetry has generally been regarded as the best of his career. Often compared favorably with such writers as James Dickey,

Robert Bly, and James Wright, Hall uses simple, direct language to evoke surrealistic imagery. In addition to his poetry, Hall has build a respected body of prose work that includes essays, short fiction, plays, and a number of children's books. Hall, who lives on the New Hampshire farm he visited in summers as a boy, is also noted for the anthologies he has edited and is a popular teacher, speaker, and reader of his own poems.

A New England Childhood

Born in 1928, Hall grew up in Hamden, Connecticut, a child of the Great Depression of the 1930s, though not greatly affected by it. Hall spent his boyhood in Connecticut and New Hampshire. The Hall household was marked by a volatile father and a mother who was "steadier, maybe with more access to depths because there was less continual surface," as Hall explained in an essay for *Contemporary Authors Autobiography Series* (*CAAS*). "To her I owe my fires, to my father my tears. I owe them both for their reading." In "Finally Only the Art of Love," an essay published in the *New York Times Book Review,* Hall spoke of the childhood influences on his writing career and two of the houses he remembered living in as a boy. "When I was in my snooty teens I would have denied it," he wrote, "but these houses were bookish." The reading matter consisted of Book-of-the-Month-Club "masterpieces," *Reader's Digest* and *Collier's.* "I felt superior," the poet confessed, realizing only later his good fortune in living with "people who continually gazed at print" and having a mother who read poems to him. Hall remembers too his discovery of the poet and short story writer Edgar Allan Poe: "I read Poe and my life changed," he remarked in *CAAS.* Another strong influence in Hall's early years was his maternal great-grandfather's farm in New Hampshire, where he spent many summers. The pull of nature became a compulsion in him so strong that decades later he bought that same farm and settled there as a full-time writer and poet.

Hall attended Philips Exeter Academy and despite early frustrations had his first poem published at age sixteen. He was a participant at the prestigious Bread Loaf Writer's Conference that same year. From Exeter, Hall went to Harvard University, where he attended class alongside other poets-in-training, among them Adrienne Rich, Robert Bly, Frank O'Hara, and John Ashbery; he also studied for a year with Archibald MacLeish. In his time at Oxford University, Hall became one of the few Americans to win the coveted Newdigate contest for his poem "Exile."

Returning to the United States, Hall spent three years at Harvard and there assembled *Exiles and Marriages,* a collection crafted in a tightly structured style on which Hall imposes rigid rhyme and meter. In 1957 he took a position as assistant professor of English at the University of Michigan, where he remained until 1975. During those years he wrote volumes of poetry and essays, and edited several important anthologies. Hall's conservative posture informed the influential anthology he edited with Robert Pack and Louis Simpson, *The New Poets of England and America.* This book, with an introduction by Robert Frost, exhibited the academic taste then in vogue and stood in rigid opposition to contemporary innovative work such as that gathered three years later in Donald Allen's anthology *The New American Poetry.* These two books were widely seen as defining an unbridgeable chasm in American poetry: in fact, no poet appeared in both. Hall eventually modified his view, and his later anthology, *Contemporary American Poetry,* published in 1962, included a number of poets, such as John Ashbery, who would have been uncomfortable in the earlier volume. Nonetheless, Hall has continued to be seen as a spokesman for the more conventional side of American poetry.

During his teaching career at the University of Michigan, Hall had always contemplated returning to the rural paradise that he had found as a youth in New Hampshire. Finally he was in a position to make this a reality, and when his grandmother, who owned Eagle Pond Farm, passed away, he bought the farm, left teaching, and moved there with his second wife, poet Jane Kenyon. With one child in college at the time and another having not yet started, the move to New Hampshire was a risky one. Giving up the relative security of a tenured position at Michigan was a difficult decision, "but I did not hesitate, I did not doubt," Hall recalled in *CAAS.* "I panicked but I did not doubt." The collections *Kicking the Leaves* and *The Happy Man* reflect Hall's happiness at his return to the family farm, a place rich with memories and links to his past. Many of the poems explore and celebrate the continuity between generations, as the narrative voice in his poetry often reminisces about the past and anticipates the future.

Most of Hall's major poetry was written after his return to New Hampshire. Many of these poems evoke the durable, seemingly immutable character of this region as seen through a deeply meditative or reflective sensibility. The books of this period include *Kicking the Leaves* (1978), *The Happy Man* (1986), *The Museum of Clear Ideas* (1993), and *The Old Life* (1996). The 1988 collection *The One Day,* a series of linked poems in blank verse, earned Hall the presitigious National Book Critics Circle Award.

Some of Hall's feelings about his move to New Hampshire were expressed in *Kicking the Leaves*, which Brent Spencer described in *Poet and Critic* as "mostly poems about memory, yet not mere reminiscence. The effort in these poems is to look for that part of the past that lives on into the present. They are, for the most part, poems about the gifts the past brings to us, the gifts of the dead." A prose relative of the poetry collection, *String Too Short to Be Saved,* contains stories or reminiscences about Hall's boyhood summers on the farm. "Ultimately the prose book expresses a moral imperative that goes beyond mere nostalgia and personal need," Barry Wallenstein elaborated in *American Book Review.* "The author realizes the insight that 'to be without history is like being forgotten.'" "The

With a New Preface

"A book of extraordinary nobility and wisdom. It will remain with me always." — Louis Begley *The New York Times Book Review*

Hall recounts his life as a poet, essayist, and critic in this 1993 memoir.

stories show both of the main characteristics of Hall's poetry—the attention to language and to detail," Spencer wrote. "And they show a real storyteller at work, something we get a taste of in *Kicking the Leaves.* Each book throws light on the other, both coming as they do from the same source."

The Happy Man, winner of the Lenore Marshall Prize, also centers on Hall's life on the family farm. As William Logan explained in the *New York Times Book Review*, the poems in this collection continue the "New Hampshire pastoral" of *Kicking the Leaves*, "but in a landscape of reversion and collapse. . . . The tone of these poems veers wildly between mania and depression." Alicia Ostriker also acknowledged this quality. "Where *Kicking the Leaves* was elegiac," she wrote in the *Nation*, "this book begins to grapple with monsters: fear, guilt, despair." Ostriker praised the collection for its depiction of rural New England life, exclaiming that Hall "paints scenes with the reverent earthliness of a Dutch master, getting all the textures right." Again providing a prose counterpart to a book of poems is the slim collection of essays titled *Seasons at Eagle Pond.* In this book Hall evoked his native New England "as eloquently as any living writer," in the opinion of Frank Levering in the *Washington Post Book World*, who praised the author for taking on picture-postcard characteristics of rural New England and making them fresh for the reader.

An Award-Winning Collection

Hall's 1988 book of poetry, *The One Day*, was published on his sixtieth birthday and won the National Book Critics Circle Award for poetry, the *Los Angeles Times Book Prize* in poetry, and a Pulitzer Prize nomination. Composed of 110 ten-line stanzas divided into three parts, *The One Day* is an ambitious work in which Hall speaks in several narrative voices about mid-life crisis. Reviewing the book for the *Los Angeles Times Book Review*, Liam Rector claimed that "Hall has long kept his eye and ear upon what is old, what is historical, what seems behind us yet is still living with us, and with *The One Day* he moves out into a different terrain from his recent mature books, *Kicking the Leaves* and *The Happy Man.*"

In an *American Poetry Review* interview with Rector, Hall explained that *The One Day* "began with an onslaught of language back in 1971. Over a period of weeks I kept receiving messages. I filled page after page of notebooks. . . . It was inchoate, sloppy, but full of material: verbal, imaginative, recollected."

DONALD HALL

In 1998 Hall published this collection of poems, an emotional tribute to his late wife, Jane Kenyon.

After approaching this material in several different ways over a period of seventeen years, Hall went on, he developed the 110 ten-line stanzas and worked with them for about four more years before he thought of structuring the long narrative poem into three parts.

The One Day, Daniel Mark Epstein wrote in *America,* is "Donald Hall's poem of the mid-life crisis, a painful time for men and women alike." Epstein observed that Hall "uses mid-life as a metaphor that works on several levels—personal, historical and mythic." Both a male and a female voice speak in *The One Day,* but they appear to be aspects of one voice—perhaps the poet's persona, as Stephen Sandy suggests in the *Boston Review*—that works through despair, rage, and cynicism before settling into a calm that embodies acceptance of inevitable death. In the *Washington Post Book World,* David Lehman praised the book as "loud, sweeping, multi-

tudinous, an act of the imperial imagination" and declared that "high on Hall's thematic agenda are age and aging, rage and raging against the dying of the light, but his powerful rhetorical gestures and dazzling juxtapositions communicate a pleasure even beyond the skillful treatment of such themes." *Ploughshares* contributor Liam Rector dubbed the book to be "an eloquent consummation of Modernism."

Poems Inspired by Universal Joys, Personal Sorrows

Two years after the success of *The One Day,* Hall's *Old and New Poems* was published. Richard Tillinghast, writing in the *New York Times Book Review,* labeled the book a "magnificent collection" and "Praise for Death," the closing poem, "perhaps the finest sustained evocation of death in American poetry." Reviewing the book in the *Times Literary Supplement,* Dick Davis declared that "few writers could have taken such apparently slight anecdotes of country life and made them, so unobtrusively but surely, into such profoundly authoritative icons of human experience."

The Museum of Clear Ideas was published in 1993 and includes Hall's poem "Baseball," his ode to the game. The poem is based on the nine innings of a baseball game: marked by nine stanzas, nine syllables per line, and so on. John Skott of *Time* noted of Hall: "He is besotted by baseball and, like all the other writers who crowd the box seats, assumes dreamily that everyone will accept this." The collection also includes poetry on such topics as love, sex, family, aging, and poetry. As Susanne Keen commented in *Commonweal,* "Hall does not eschew the ordinary; he inhabits it. Books and poems and language belong in this poet's everyday world, so we find poems about old affairs or old friends cheek by jowl with his criticism of contemporary poetry." High praise came from Vernon Shetley of the *Yale Review:* "Hall's latest book should encourage us all: live long enough, work hard and sincerely, and eventually the muse will pay you back by giving you poems as wonderful as these."

Tragically for Hall, the life he shared with Kenyon, which was chronicled by journalist Bill Moyers in the 1993 film *A Life Together,* was not to last. While his works had focused on baseball, the joys of community, and family, they now took on a more somber tone, as he and Kenyon fought against the leukemia that would ultimately take her life in 1995 at age forty-seven. Written following Kenyon's death, *Without* reflects on the first changes the absence of

If you enjoy the works of Donald Hall, you may also want to check out the following books:

Robert Frost, *A Witness Tree*, 1942.
Richard Wilbur, *Things of This World: Poems*, 1956.
Sharon Olds, *The Father: Poems*, 1992.

his wife brought to the poet's life. *The Painted Bed* finds Hall in another phase of the grieving process, the poems included showcasing the poet's "distinctive musical mark" and "exhibiting the terrible suffering of the bereaved with dignity and beauty," according to *Book* contributor Stephen Whited.

Speaking of Hall's overall work as a poet, an essayist for *Contemporary Poets* explained: "In a country like the United States that eschews aging and casts an amnesiac's eye on its past and traditions, in a country that increasingly focuses on the right now and the self at the expense of historical perspective and compassion for neighbors, Hall's poetry, and especially his verse since 1978, reminds us of what is most enduring in our culture.... A poet is ultimately judged on his ability to tell the true stories of his tribe. In late middle age Hall transcended the pack of popular academic plodders all around him to become a solitary singer whose remarkable vision has included us all."

In addition to his accomplishments as a poet, Hall is respected as an academic who, through writing, teaching, and lecturing, has made significant contributions to the study and craft of writing. As Rector explained, Hall "has lived deeply within the New England ethos of plain living and high thinking, and he has done so with a sense of humor and eros." In *Remembering Poets: Reminiscences and Opinions*, a 1978 work that was expanded as *Their Ancient Glittering Eyes: Remembering Poets and More Poets*, Hall recounts his relationship with fellow poets such as T. S. Eliot, Ezra Pound, Dylan Thomas, and Robert Frost. His books on the craft of writing include *Writing Well*—in its ninth edition by 1998—and *Death to the Death of Poetry. Life Work* is Hall's memoir of the writing life and his tenure at Eagle Pond Farm, while his children's book *Ox-Cart Man* is one among several works that have established him in the field of children's literature. A fable on the cyclical nature of life, *Ox-Cart Man* expresses for readers "the sense that work defines us all, connects us with our world, and we are all rewarded . . . in measure of our effort," according to Kristi L. Thomas in *School Library Journal*.

Hall continues to live and work on his New Hampshire farm, a site which serves as both his abode and an inspiration for much of his work. Following his wife's tragic death in the spring of 1995, Hall appeared at several tributes to Jane Kenyon's work, and composed an afterword to a posthumous collection of her poetry, *Otherwise: New and Selected Poems*. His work, much of which continues to be inspired by memories of Kenyon and their life together, frequently appears in such periodicals as *Poetry, Ploughshares,* and *Kenyon Review.*

■ Biographical and Critical Sources

BOOKS

Children's Books and Their Creators, edited by Anita Silvey, Houghton Mifflin (Boston, MA), 1995.

This 2002 volume, a follow-up to *Without,* focuses on grief, acceptance, and renewal.

Contemporary Authors Autobiography Series, Volume 7, Gale (Detroit, MI), 1988, pp. 55-67.

Contemporary Literary Criticism, Gale (Detroit, MI), Volume 13, 1980, Volume 37, 1986, Volume 59, 1989.

Contemporary Poets, St. James Press (Detroit, MI), 7th edition, 2001.

Dictionary of Literary Biography, Volume 5: *American Poets since World War II,* Gale (Detroit, MI), 1980.

Hall, Donald, *Riddle Rat,* Warne (London, England), 1977.

Hall, Donald, *The Man Who Lived Alone,* Godine (New York, NY), 1984.

Hall, Donald, *I Am the Dog, I Am the Cat,* Dial (New York, NY), 1994.

Rector, Liam, editor, *The Day I Was Older: Collected Writings on the Poetry of Donald Hall,* Story Line Press, 1989.

PERIODICALS

America, June 17-24, 1989, Daniel Mark Epstein, review of *The One Day.*

American Book Review, March-April, 1981, Barry Wallenstein, review of *String Too Short to Be Saved.*

American Poetry Review, January-February, 1989, Liam Rector, interview with Hall.

Book, May-June, 2002, Stephen Whited, review of *The Painted Bed,* p. 85.

Booklist, July 15, 1977, p. 1728; June 1, 1994, p. 1816; August, 1994, p. 2051; September 15, 1994, p. 132; March 15, 1996, Bill Ott, review of *When Willard Met Babe Ruth,* p. 1262; September 1, 1996, p. 724; March 15, 2000, Gillian Engberg, review of *The Oxford Illustrated Book of American Children's Poems,* p. 1380; March 1, 2002, Ray Olson, review of *The Painted Bed,* p. 1079; April 15, 2003, Ellen Loughran, review of *Willow Temple: New and Selected Stories,* p. 1448.

Boston Globe Magazine, May 26, 1985.

Boston Review, October, 1988, Stephen Sandy, review of *The One Day.*

Bulletin of the Center for Children's Books, February, 1980, Zena Sutherland, review of *Ox-Cart Man,* p. 110; March, 1985, pp. 126-27; July, 1994, Deborah Stevenson, review of *The Farm Summer 1942,* p. 358; October, 1994, Roger Sutton, review of *Lucy's Summer,* pp. 48-49; December, 1994, Roger Sutton, review of *I Am the Dog, I Am the Cat,* p. 129; June, 1996, p. 336; October, 1996, p. 61.

Christian Science Monitor, October 2, 1958.

Commonweal, September 24, 1993, Susanne Keen, review of *The Museum of Clear Ideas,* p. 21; December 2, 1994, p. 29.

Emergency Librarian, March, 1995, p. 44; January, 1996, p. 55.

Encounter, March, 1965.

Horn Book, February, 1982, Mary M. Burns, review of *Ox-Cart Man,* pp. 44-45; July-August, 1994, Nancy Vasilakis, review of *The Farm Summer 1942,* p. 441; September-October, 1994, Ann A. Flowers, review of *I Am the Dog, I Am the Cat,* p. 577; November-December, 1994, Elizabeth S. Watson, review of *Lucy's Christmas,* p. 711; May, 1995, pp. 324-325; November, 1996, pp. 724-725.

Iowa Review, winter, 1971.

Junior Bookshelf, December, 1980, review of *Ox-Cart Man,* pp. 283-284.

Kirkus Reviews, August 15, 1994, review of *I Am the Dog, I Am the Cat,* p. 1129; October 15, 1994, review of *Lucy's Christmas,* pp. 1420-1421; November 1, 1984, review of *The Man Who Lived Alone,* p. 88; March 1, 1996, review of *When Willard Met Babe Ruth,* pp. 374-375; July 15, 1996, review of *Old Home Day,* p. 1048; July 15, 1997, p. 1111; March 15, 2003, review of *Willow Temple,* p. 416.

Library Journal, April 15, 2003, review of *Willow Temple,* p. 128; December, 2003, review of *Breakfast Served Any Time All Day,* p. 118.

Los Angeles Times Book Review, February 5, 1989, Liam Rector, review of *The One Day;* April 30, 1995, p. 6; August 4, 1996, p. 11.

Nation, August 30, 1986, Alicia Ostriker, review of *The Happy Man.*

New Republic, February 14, 1994.

New Statesman, November 27, 1964.

New Yorker, June 28, 1993; October 11, 1993.

New York Review of Books, March 24, 1994.

New York Times Book Review, January 13, 1985, Thomas Powers, review of *The Man Who Lived Alone,* p. 26; January 18, 1987, William Logan, review of *The Happy Man;* February 24, 1991, Richard Tillinghast, review of *Old and New Poems;* October 3, 1993; April 30, 1995, p. 22.

Ploughshares, fall, 2001, Liam Rector, "About Donald Hall," p. 270.

Poet and Critic, Volume 12, number 3, 1980, Brent Spencer, review of *Kicking the Leaves.*

Poetry, May, 1971; December, 2003, review of *Breakfast Served Any Time All Day,* p. 177.

Publishers Weekly, June 13, 1977, review of *Riddle Rat,* p. 108; April 11, 1994, review of *The Farm Summer 1942,* p. 65; April 10, 1995, review of *Lucy's Summer,* p. 62; August 12, 1996, review of *Old Home Day,* p. 82; July 14, 1997, review of *The Milkman's Boy,* p. 83; February 25, 2002, review of *The Painted Bed,* p. 56; March 31, 2003, review of *Willow Temple,* p. 39.

Quill and Quire, May, 1995, review of *Lucy's Summer,* p. 51.

School Library Journal, September, 1977, p. 108; October, 1979, Kristi L. Thomas, review of *Ox-Cart Man,* p. 140; February, 1985, Anna Biagioni Hart, review of *The Man Who Lived Alone*, p. 64; September, 1994, p. 101; May, 1996, p. 113; October, 1996, p. 96; January, 2000, Margaret Bush, review of *The Oxford Illustrated Book of American Children's Poems*, p. 121.

Sewanee Review, summer, 1994; winter, 2000, review of *Without*, p. 6.

Tennessee Poetry Journal (special Donald Hall issue), winter, 1971.

Time, December 5, 1955; March 22, 1993, p. 70, John Skott, review of *The Museum of Clear Ideas*.

Times Literary Supplement, November 1, 1991, Dick Davis, review of *Old and New Poems*.

Virginia Quarterly Review, spring, 1965; spring, 1970.

Washington Post Book World, December 17, 1987, Frank Levering, review of *Seasons at Eagle Pond*; August 28, 1988, David Lehman, review of *The One Day*; September 12, 1993, p. 4; January 22, 1995, p. 12.

World Literature Today, summer, 1995, p. 593.

Yale Review, October, 1993, Vernon Shetley, review of *The Museum of Clear Ideas*, p. 151.

OTHER

A Life Together (documentary by Bill Moyers about Jane Kenyon and Donald Hall), broadcast on PBS, December, 1993.*

Marsden Hartley

■ Personal

Born Edmund Hartley, January 4, 1877, in Lewiston, ME; died September 2, 1943, of a heart ailment in Ellsworth, ME; son of Thomas (a cotton spinner and theater bill-poster) and Eliza Jane (Horbury) Hartley. *Education:* Attended Cleveland Institute of Art, 1892; attended William Merritt Chase School, New York, NY, 1898-99, and National Academy of Design, 1900; studied privately with John Semon. *Hobbies and other interests:* Traveling.

■ Career

Painter and poet.

■ Writings

Adventures in the Arts; Informal Chapters on Painters, Vaudeville, and Poets, Boni & Liveright (New York, NY), 1921, reprinted, Hacker Art Books (New York, NY), 1972.
Twenty-five Poems, Contact (Paris, France), 1923.

Androscoggin, Falmouth Publishing House (Portland, ME), 1940.
Sea Burial, Leon Tebbetts Editions (Portland, ME), 1941.
Selected Poems, Viking (New York, NY), 1945.
Eight Poems and One Essay, Bates College (Lewiston, ME), 1976.
On Art, edited and introduced by Gail R. Scott, Horizon Press (New York, NY), 1982.
Heart's Gate: Letters between Marsden Hartley and Horace Traubel, 1906-1915, edited by William Innes Homer, Jargon Society (Highlands, NC), 1982.
The Collected Poems of Marsden Hartley, edited by Gail R. Scott, Black Sparrow Press (Santa Rosa, CA), 1987.
Somehow a Past: The Autobiography of Marsden Hartley, edited and with an introduction by Susan Elizabeth Ryan, MIT Press (Cambridge, MA), 1996.
My Dear Stieglitz: Letters of Marsden Hartley and Alfred Stieglitz, 1912-1915, edited by James Timothy Voorhies, University of South Carolina (Columbia, SC), 2002.

Contributor of poems to literary magazines, including *Poetry, Little Review, Others, Contact,* and *Dial.*

■ Sidelights

Marsden Hartley was a prolific painter whose most acclaimed works depict the coast of Maine and the rugged fishermen who lived and worked there dur-

Some of Hartley's most acclaimed paintings, including *Maine Seascape*, depict the rugged coastline of his home state.

ing Hartley's lifetime. Widely acknowledged as being among the finest of American artists, he also won esteem for his poetry, and moved in a circle of influential twentieth-century artists and writers, including William Carlos Williams, Ernest Hemingway, and Gertrude Stein.

A Lonely Childhood

Hartley's parents were born in Staleybridge, Lancashire, England, but had immigrated to Maine in 1857. His father found work only sporadically, and his mother also worked to try to support the family. She died when Hartley was eight years old, an event that devastated the young boy; as an adult, death would often be the subject of many of his most striking works. Four years after his mother's death, Hartley's father married Martha Marsden, another immigrant from Staleybridge. While Hartley had been christened Edmund Hartley, he adopted his stepmother's maiden name as his own. As a teen living a somewhat secluded rural life, he found great solace in the flowers, mountains, and seascapes of Maine, and at the age of thirteen he made a series of drawings for a local naturalist. By the age of fourteen, Hartley had left school and begun working in a shoe factory. Meanwhile, his father moved to Cleveland, leaving his son behind in the care of an older sister.

In 1892, the fifteen-year-old Hartley went west to be reunited with his family. Once in Cleveland, he began work in the office of a marble quarry. Continu-

ing his education, as well as his art, in 1898, he won a scholarship to the Cleveland School of Art, where he studied under Nina Waldeck and Cullen Yates. He later went on to the New York School of Art, the National Academy of Design, and the Art Students League. During this period his teachers included William Merritt Chase, Frank Vincent DuMond, George Maynard, and Edgar M. Ward, and he also became acquainted with many in the social circle surrounding poet Walt Whitman; Hartley's earliest extant painting is of Whitman's house in Camden, New Jersey. One of the most pivotal events of his school years occurred when a teacher gave Hartley a collection of essays by Ralph Waldo Emerson. He was so captivated by Emerson's writing that he carried the volume with him almost constantly, and read it daily, for the next five years. During this period, he alternated busy winters in New York with solitary summers at remote locations in his home state of Maine.

As a young man Hartley was troubled by many insecurities, and in 1905, he slid into a deep depression. During this time he painted a series of canvases depicting suicidal themes. This period in his work then gave way to one in which he did small, impressionistic mountain landscapes. Fre-

Hartley incorporated Native American themes into his 1914 work "Indian Composition," completed during the artist's stay in Berlin, Germany. ("Indian Composition," painting by Marsden Hartley. Frances Lehman Loeb Art Center, Vassar College, Poughkeepsie, New York. Gift of Paul Rosenfeld. 1950.1.5. Reproduced by permission.)

In addition to his work as a painter, Hartley was recognized as an accomplished poet.

quent stylistic changes such as these would mark Hartley's entire career. In 1909 he had his first major art exhibition at Gallery 291, a New York gallery owned by noted photographer Alfred Stieglitz. Included in the show were Hartley's brooding Maine seascapes. Approval from Stieglitz gained the young artist entry into the artistic elite of the day, which included such influential figures as Alfred Mauer, Max Weber, and Arthur Dove. From such companions he was exposed to European trends in modern art. In 1912 he had a second exhibition at Gallery 291, and in that year he also traveled to Paris, where he met Gertrude Stein, Alice B. Toklas, and other emigré writers at Stein's salon. When Stein visited Hartley's studio to look at his paintings, she declared that she would hang his work among her Picasso and Matisse paintings.

Hartley soon moved on from Paris to Berlin, and inspired by the powerful images in Germany's military and industrial cultures, he began including them in his art. A series of works with war motifs followed, including one of his most famous paintings, *Portrait of a German Officer*. This was a memorial to a German soldier named Karl von Freyburg, who was a friend and possibly a romantic interest of Hartley's. However, not surprisingly, in the wake of World War I, Hartley's German-influenced work was not well received in New York. Although he continued to paint, he also traveled abroad through-

out the 1920s and much of the 1930s, and it was during this time that he began to reveal his literary talents.

From Art to Poetry

The book *Adventures in the Arts* features Hartley's essays on a wide range of topics. Published in 1921, it contains the well-traveled artist's thoughts on such diverse topics as the declining popularity of acrobats, Walt Whitman and Paul Cezanne, and modern art in America. In 1923 Hartley released *Twenty-five Poems*. This chapbook features a poetic style that, in the words of Joel Lewis in the *American Book Review*, showcase Hartley's "absorption of the new, Cubist-inspired poetics of Williams, Mina Loy, and Walter Arensberg." Hartley continued to publish the occasional poem in journals, but he did not release another collection until 1940. That year, *Androscoggin* was published to favorable reviews.

By this time in his life, the road-weary Hartley was again creating art that celebrated his native land of Maine. In the aesthetic spirit of the Objectivists, Hartley's poetry also gave voice to the natural world. In the poem "Return of the Native," for example, Hartley embraces the rugged landscape of

This heavily-illustrated 1998 work examines Hartley's life and art.

If you enjoy the works of Marsden Hartley, you may also want to check out the following:

The paintings of Paul Cezanne (1839-1906), Albert Pinkham Ryder (1847-1917), and Giovanni Segantini (1858-1899), who were major influences on Hartley.

Maine. *Sea Burial,* another chapbook featuring work drawn from the author's home region, was published in 1941. Hartley died two years later of heart failure, and his ashes were scattered into the Androscoggin River. He told his own story posthumously in *Somehow a Past: The Autobiography of Marsden Hartley.* According to Bob Roehr, writing in the *Lambda Book Report,* "*Somehow a Past* is most successful when Hartley writes of the profession of art, not his own work on which he is near completely silent, but of the works of artists who have affected him, Cezanne and Piero della Francesca in particular. His account of time in Mexico on a fellowship (1932) is also masterful, perhaps because it was closest to the time of his writing the first draft of this work." Roehr found Hartley's memoir too reserved, but stated that, despite this flaw, "The poet in Hartley could be a very skilled writer, and there are passages of the autobiography that are a joy to read for their sheer use of language."

Though he was recognized as an artistic force during his lifetime, appreciation for Hartley's cultural contributions increased to new levels in the 1980s and 1990s. In 1982, Gail R. Scott produced *On Art,* a book that collects Hartley's writings and provides glimpses into his personal feelings on art and the social scenes of his time. In 1987, Scott edited *The Collected Poems of Marsden Hartley.* A contributor to *Christian Science Monitor* declared that there "is a melody in Hartley's poems . . . a solitary tune mingling with the strains created by American poets as they celebrate the vast silences and solitude of their native land."

Assessing Hartley's literary significance in the *Dictionary of Literary Biography,* Robert K. Martin mused that the poet "never lost his Thoreau-like ability to capture the precise details of a scene." Martin further observed that "true to his transcendentalist heritage, he was also always tempted to 'read' the scene and find its meaning." While reflecting that "Hartley the poet is now almost completely forgotten," Martin praised Hartley's poetic contributions, particularly his "use of the sea and its rhythms,"

which "provided him with a means for the recognition of death and human tragedy. The strength that he derived from his immersion in life is reflected in the hard lines and bold forms of these poems that seem to echo the sharp objectivity of his painting. Not, surely, as important a poet as a painter, he remains a voice in modern American poetry that is worth rediscovering."

■ Biographical and Critical Sources

BOOKS

Dictionary of Contemporary American Artists, St. Martin's Press (New York, NY), 1994.

Dictionary of Literary Biography, Volume 54: *American Poets, 1880-1945, Third Series,* Gale (Detroit, MI), 1987.

Encyclopedia of World Biography, 2nd edition, Gale (Detroit, MI), 1998.

Gay and Lesbian Literature, 2nd edition, St. James Press (Detroit, MI), 1998.

Haskell, Barbara, *Marsden Hartley,* Whitney Museum of American Art (New York, NY), 1980.

Kornhauser, Elizabeth, *Marsden Hartley: American Modernist,* Yale University Press (New Haven, CT), 2003.

Ludington, Townsend, editor, *Marsden Hartley: The Biography of An American Artist,* Little, Brown (Boston, MA), 1992.

Ludington, Townsend, *Seeking the Spiritual: The Paintings of Marsden Hartley,* Cornell University (Ithaca, NY), 1998.

MacCausland, Elizabeth, *Marsden Hartley,* University of Minnesota Press (Minneapolis, MN), 1952.

Robertson, Bruce, *Marsden Hartley,* Abrams (New York, NY), 1995.

Ryan, Susan Elizabeth, editor, *Somehow a Past: The Autobiography of Marsden Hartley,* MIT Press (Cambridge, MA), 1996.

Turner, Elizabeth Hutton, *In the American Grain: Arthur Dove, Marsden Hartley, John Marin, Georgia O'Keeffe, and Alfred Stieglitz : The Stieglitz Circle at the Phillips Collection,* Counterpoint, 1995.

Weinberg, Jonathan Edman, *Speaking for Vice: Homosexuality in the Art of Charles Demuth, Marsden Hartley, and the First American Avante-Garde,* Yale University Press (New Haven, CT), 1993.

PERIODICALS

Advocate, April 1, 2003, David Ehrenstein, "Confessions of a Modernist Mind," p. 66.

American Book Review, September-October, 1987, p. 7.

Art in America, March, 1983, p. 17; November, 2003, Robert Berlind, "Hartley's Indicative Objects," p. 148.

Chicago Tribune, June 26, 2003, Michael Kilian, "Phillips Features Controversial Modernist Marsden Hartley."

Christian Science Monitor, January 18, 1941, p. 11; July 3, 1987, p. B3.

Gay & Lesbian Review Worldwide, July-August, 2003, Ken Gonzales-Day, "An American Back from Paris," p. 37.

Insight on the News, July 22, 2003, Stephen Goode, "Hartley's Talent," p. 36.

Lambda Book Report, March, 1997, Ulysses D'Aquila, review of *Somehow a Past: The Autobiography of Marsden Hartley,* p. 20; October, 1998, Bob Roehr, review of *Somehow a Past,* p. 23.

Library Journal, January, 2003, Eric Linderman, review of *My Dear Stieglitz: Letters of Marsden Hartley and Alfred Stieglitz, 1912-1915,* p. 101.

Magazine of Art, November, 1948, Donald Gallup, "Weaving of a Pattern: Marsden Hartley and Gertrude Stein," pp. 256-261.

New Criterion, March, 2003, James Panero, "Marsden Hartley and American Modernism," p. 49.

New England Quarterly, December, 1958, Robert Burlingame, "Marsden Hartley's *Androscoggin: Return to Place,*" pp. 447-462.

Newsweek, April 14, 1980, p. 109.

New York, March 31, 1980, p. 73; December 6, 1982, p. 154.

New Yorker, December 29, 1945, p. 68; February 3, 2003, Peter Schjeldahl, "The Searcher," p. 93.

New York Times, May 7, 2000, Helen A. Harrison, "Through His Drawings, Hartley's Delicate Side," p. 22; May 30, 2003, Grace Glueck, "The Heart of the Matter—The Still Lifes of Marsden Hartley," p. E36.

New York Times Book Review, December 22, 1996, p. 22.

Publishers Weekly, December 2, 1996, review of *Somehow a Past,* p. 48.

Quarterly Review of Literature, winter, 1944, Henry W. Wells, "The Poetry of Marsden Hartley," pp. 100-106.

Seattle Post-Intelligencer, February 4, 2005, Regina Hackett, "Hartley Collection Traces the Career of a Modern Pioneer," p. 16.

Seattle Times, January 16, 2005, Sheila Farr, "An American Original," p. K1.

Time, July 14, 1980, p. 68.*

Jasper Johns

■ Personal

Born May 15, 1930, in Augusta, GA; son of Jasper (a farmer) and Jean (Riley) Johns. *Education:* Attended University of South Carolina, 1948-49; attended commercial art school in New York, NY, 1949.

■ Addresses

Home—New York, NY. *Agent*—c/o Leo Castelli Gallery, 420 West Broadway, New York, NY 10012.

■ Career

Painter, printmaker, and sculptor. Bookstore salesman and window display artist, New York, NY, 1952-59. Foundation for Contemporary Performance Arts, director, 1963—; Merce Cunningham Dance Company, New York, NY, ballet designer in productions, including *Walkabout*, 1968, *Second Hand*, 1970, *TV Re-Run*, 1970, *Borst Park*, 1972, and *Un Jour ou Deux*, 1973. *Exhibitions:* Individual exhibitions: Leo Castelli Gallery, New York, NY, 1958, 1960-61, 1963,

1966, 1970, 1976, 1984; Galerie Rive Droite, Paris, France, 1959, 1961; Galleria d'Arte del Naviglio, Milan, Italy, 1959; Tweed Gallery, Minneapolis, MN, 1960; Columbia Museum of Art, South Carolina, SC, 1960; Everett Ellin Gallery, Los Angeles, CA, 1962; Galerie Ileana Sonnabend, Paris, 1962; Jewish Museum, New York, NY, 1964; Whitechapel Art Gallery, London, England, 1964; Pasadena Museum of Art, CA, 1965; Minami Gallery, Tokyo, Japan, 1965; American Embassy, London, 1965; Ashmolean Museum, Oxford, England, 1965; Smithsonian Institution, Washington, DC, 1966; Galerie Ricke, Cologne, Germany, 1968; Galerie Buren, Stockholm, Sweden, 1968, 1972; Museum of Modern Art, New York, NY, 1968, 1970-71, 1972, 1996-97; Castelli Graphics, New York, NY, 1969, 1971, 1976-77, 1980, 1982; Kunstmuseum, Basel, Switzerland, 1969, 1979; University of New Mexico, Albuquerque, 1969; Los Angeles County Museum of Art, CA, 1969; Castelli-Whitney Gallery, New York, NY, 1969; David Whitney Gallery, New York, NY, 1969; New Gallery, Cleveland, OH, 1970; Philadelphia Museum of Art, PA, 1970; University of Iowa, Iowa City, 1970; Kunsthalle, Bern, Switzerland, 1971; Minneapolis Institute of Arts, MN, 1971; Dayton's Gallery 12, Minneapolis, 1971; Museum of the Sea, Hilton Head, SC, 1971; Museum of Contemporary Art, Chicago, IL, 1971; Marion Koogler McNay Art Institute, San Antonio, TX, 1971; Museum of Fine Arts, Houston, TX, 1972; Heath Gallery, Atlanta, GA, 1972; South Texas Art Museum, Corpus Christi, 1972; Fendrick Gallery, Washington, DC, 1972; Emily Lowe Gallery, Hofstra University, Hempstead, NY, 1972; Gertrude Kasle Gallery, Detroit, MI, 1973; Galerie de Gestlo, Hamburg, Germany, 1974; Knoedler Contemporary

Prints, New York, NY, 1974; Lo Spazil-Galleria d'Art, Rome, Italy, 1974; Lucio Amelio Modern Art Agency, Naples, Italy, 1974; Galerie Folker Skulima, Berlin, Germany, 1974; Museum of Modern Art, Oxford, England, 1974; Mappin Art Gallery, Sheffield, England, 1974; Herbert Art Gallery, Coventry, England, 1974; Walker Art Gallery, Liverpool, England, 1974; City Art Gallery, Leeds, England, 1975; Serpentine Gallery, London, 1975; Janie C. Lee Gallery, Houston, 1976; Brooke Alexander Inc., New York, NY, 1977, 1985; Whitney Museum of American Art, 1977; Museum Ludwig, Cologne, Germany, 1978; Georges Pompidou Center, Paris, 1978; Hayward Gallery, London, England, 1978; Seibu Museum of Art, Tokyo, 1978; San Francisco Museum of Modern Art, 1978; Margo Leavin Gallery, Los Angeles, 1978; Galerie Nancy Gillespie, Paris, 1978; Galerie Valeur, Nagoya, 1978, 1979; Center for the Arts, Wesleyan University, Middletown, CT, 1978; John Berggruen Gallery, San Francisco, 1978; Janie C. Lee Gallery, Houston, 1979; Stätliche Graphische, Munich, 1979; Stadtische Galerie, Stadelschen Kunstinstitut, Frankfurt, Germany, 1979; Kunstmuseum, Hannover, Germany, 1979; Tucson Museum of Art, AZ, 1979; Statens Museum for Kunst, Copenhagen, Denmark, 1980; Moderna Museet, Stockholm, 1980; Tyler Museum of Art, TX, 1980; Tate Gallery, London, 1981; L. A. Louver Gallery, Venice, CA, 1982; Akira Ikeda Gallery, Tokyo, 1983; Delahunty Gallery, Dallas, 1983; Fondation Maeght, St. Paul de Vence, France, 1986; St. Louis Art Museum, MO, 1986; Centro Reina Sofia, Madrid, Spain, 1987; United States pavilion, *43rd Biennale*, Venice, 1988; National Gallery of Art, Washington, DC, 1990; Horodner Romley Gallery, New York, NY, 1995; and Cleveland Museum of Art, OH, 2003-04. Also participated in numerous group exhibitions worldwide. Permanent collections: Museum of Modern Art; Whitney Museum; Guggenheim Museum, New York, NY; Albright-Knox Art Gallery, Buffalo, NY; San Francisco Museum of Modern Art; Tate Gallery, London; Stedelijk Museum, Amsterdam, Netherlands; Kunstmuseum, Basel; Moderna Museet, Stockholm; and Seibu Museum, Tokyo. *Military service:* Served in U.S. Army in Japan, 1949.

■ **Awards, Honors**

First Prize, *Print Biennale*, Ljubljana, Yugoslavia, 1967; Prize, *São Paulo Bienal*, 1967; Skowhegan Award for Painting, 1972; Skowhegan Award for Graphics, 1977; Mayor's Award of Honor for Art and Culture, New York, NY, 1978.

■ **Writings**

(Illustrator) Samuel Beckett, *Fizzles,* Whitney Museum (New York, NY), 1977.

Jasper Johns: Writings, Sketchbook Notes, Interviews, edited by Kirk Varnedoe, Museum of Modern Art/Harry Abrams (New York, NY), 1996.

Jasper Johns: A Retrospective, edited by Kirk Varnedoe and Roberta Bernstein, Museum of Modern Art (New York, NY), 2003.

Contributor of articles to magazines and journals, including *Artforum, ARTnews, Art in America,* and *Juilliard.*

■ **Sidelights**

One of the leading figures of the American Pop art movement of the mid-twentieth century, Jasper Johns became instantly famous for turning everyday objects into art tropes. Writing in the *New York Times,* Deborah Solomon noted that "no artist was ever catapulted into fame more suddenly than Johns." In 1958, at the tender age of twenty-eight, Johns had a one-man show at the Leo Castelli Gallery in New York that overnight turned him into a pioneer of modern art, the next stage in art development after abstract expressionism. He took iconic objects—the American flag, targets, numbers—and by using wax-based paint and a technique known as encaustic, he transformed these mundane objects into art, "focusing attention," as an essayist in the *International Dictionary of Art and Artists* wrote, "on the act of painting and bringing out the profound ambiguity between image and object, and the constant interplay between painted illusion and real object." Such a style influenced the next generation of painters, including minimalist Frank Stella and pop artists such as Andy Warhol, with his paintings of Campbell soup cans, Claes Oldenburg, and his hamburger sculpture, and Roy Lichtenstein, who "elevated comic book blondes to the realm of high art," as Solomon further noted. These artists "were all exploring the ideas set forth in Johns' . . . paintings of commonplace objects," according to Solomon.

A Conflicting Legacy

Though Johns is acknowledged as one of the great American painters, some critics see that appellation as somewhat inflated. Eric Gibson, for example, writing in *World and I,* allowed the originality of his

A leader in the Pop Art movement, Johns stands besides his mixed-media painting *Target*, one of his most familiar motifs.

early paintings: "They were so deadpan and so literally figuratively down-to-earth that it was as though somebody had turned on the lights and turned off the music at the Abstract Expressionist party." These early paintings have, as Gibson noted, a "surprising power." Gibson further explained, however, that "in the years since, Johns' reputation has largely rested on that fantastic breakout ahead of the pack. Hardly mentioned is the fact that for the next decade he did little more than ring a series of changes on his initial subjects in a variety of media." There were the crosshatching paintings of the 1970s and then the collage or multiple image paintings of the 1980s and 1990s with their hidden meanings, like a "kind of coded diary," according to Gibson. This "hermetic" turn to Johns's painting is, for Gibson, also a turn off: "It's hard to get interested in someone who wants to talk only about themselves but doesn't want you to know what he's saying." Similarly, Jed Perl, writing in the *New Republic*, called much of Johns's art "stalemates and dead-ends and insoluble puzzles; they're headaches waiting to happen."

For Perl, Johns's oeuvre is a watered-down version of that of Dadaist artist Marcel Duchamp. "Over and over again, Johns replays the same old Dadaist is-it-art-or-not? routines, until the everything-is-nothing mantra has turned your mind to mush." Perl did allow a "certain fidgety elegance" to Johns's work, but also complained that "now Johns is such

a pervasive influence that it is sometimes difficult for people to separate his send-ups from the real thing." *Time* magazine's Robert Hughes, reviewing a 1996 retrospective of Johns's work at New York's Museum of Modern Art (MoMA) also wondered about Johns's reputation versus his actual work. "Is there, or has there ever been a modern American artist with a more peculiarly sacrosanct reputation than Jasper Johns? If so, none spring to mind," Hughes noted. In fact, Hughes went on to observe, "We are so used by now to being told that Johns is an artist of the utmost profundity and difficulty that we assume, on peering into the well of his talent, that the fault for not recognizing masterpieces lies with ourselves." In fact, however, Hughes pointed out that "you can't traverse this [retrospective exhibition] without getting a sense of decline, of gradual burnout. . . . Time and again, after the late '80s, one comes up against Johnses that seem to have no raison d'etre, and are valued merely because Johns did them."

Johns certainly has his champions, as well. *Newsweek* contributor Peter Plagens felt that the 1996 retrospective was a "grand, meaty show," and that it took "an artist so radical on the inside that he's not afraid to look conservative on the outside" to "pull it off." *Nation* writer Arthur C. Danto, reviewing the same retrospective, felt that Johns's career is "remarkable in itself in part because eyes are a lot less innocent today than when *Flag* was painted, and this is due in no small measure to Johns himself." Like most critics, Danto had high praise for Johns's early work, which included painted flags, targets, maps, letters, and numerals: "The representation/reality ambiguity for this class of objects made Johns's work of this period intoxicating, witty and brilliant." And it was not simply a matter of wit for Danto. The critic further noted that "Johns's handling of paint was simply marvelous. He could have been an Abstract Expressionist if he had wanted to; the brushwork had the lyricism of its greatest exponents. Simply as painting, *Flag* is delicious." And for Danto, Johns's talent did not lessen over the years: "Johns has never relinquished his Abstract Expressionist credentials in the subsequent adventure of his art, and his brushwork remains one of the aesthetic glories of our time." Danto also had praise for the artist's "increasingly esoteric subjects" of the 1980s and 1990s, finding that he was able to master this new genre "without losing either his philosophical intuitiveness or his marvelous touch."

Thus two camps emerge: those who find Jasper Johns a pioneer of modern art and those who find him a bit of a charlatan. It is a paradox, a "representation/reality ambiguity" the like of which Johns himself is fond of investigating in his own paintings.

Reviewing a 1990 exhibition of Johns's work at the National Gallery of Art in Washington, D.C., Mark Stevens noted in the *New Republic* that since 1960 "the art of Jasper Johns has been scrutinized. And scrutinized. And scrutinized. . . . What explains such obsessive attention? . . . Even if one considers him a great artist, and many still do not, history has often treated great artists with indifference or doled out attention inconsistently." Stevens answered his own question in part by going back to the seminal work of this twentieth-century painter, *Flag*. "By transforming the national symbol into an individual, changing, evanescent image," Stevens wrote, "Johns became the emblematic artist of his period." In an earlier *New Republic* article, Stevens also examined Johns's standing in the art world. "For many," Stevens wrote, "Jasper Johns has become the last Great Artist in the modernist tradition." Stevens explained that Johns "occupies this position because he paints well, but also because he fits certain stereotypes. . . . Johns fought the last big battle in postwar art. In place of [Jackson] Pollock's and [Willem] De Kooning's warm spontaneity, he proposed a cool reserve. Instead of the private scribble

Using a technique known as encaustic, Johns transformed iconic objects such as targets, numbers, and flags into works of art. (Art © Jasper Johns/Licensed by VAGA, New York, NY.)

of the self, he offered the 'given' or public image. . . . He became a father to the subsequent styles of pop, minimal, and conceptual art."

Southern Beginnings

Born in Augusta, Georgia, in 1930, Johns was the son of a farmer. His early years were ones of loss: he was just a year old when his mother left his alcoholic father. However, soon, his mother discovered that she could not provide for her only son and sent him to live with his grandfather in Allendale, South Carolina. "My family were very narrow in a sense, provincial, sort of country people," Johns told Helen Dudar in *Smithsonian* magazine. "The men were all farmers and the women schoolteachers." Then, almost finished with the third grade, Johns lost his grandfather and was shipped back to his remarried mother and her new family. After a year there he again moved to live with an aunt who was a schoolteacher. He spent six years with her and then moved back in with his mother to finish high school.

After high school graduation Johns spent a few semesters at the University of South Carolina. Though he demonstrated an early interest in art, he still had no real direction. Then he moved to New York where he attended an art school, but was later drafted into the U.S. military, serving in Japan. During his service he developed an appreciation for Japanese art. Back in New York, he took work in a bookstore, painting in his spare time. In 1954 he met the artist Robert Rauschenberg, who introduced the younger man to some of the avant-garde of the city, including composer John Cage and his companion, Merce Cunningham, the choreographer. Johns would ultimately design sets for Cunningham's ballets, but in the meantime he was working along with Rauschenberg as a window designer for stylish shops. The two also lived in the same building and thus saw and critiqued one another's work daily.

Johns destroyed all his early work in 1954, wanting to get a fresh start. Then, inspired by a dream, came his painting *Flag*, exhibited that same year. He chose this well-known object so that he did not have to deal with design, but could instead focus on the surface of the painting. Thereafter came other flags and paintings of everyday images including alphabets, numerals, targets, and maps. His *Green Target* was exhibited at the Jewish Museum in New York in a group show, and attracted the attention of gallery owner Leo Castelli, who gave the young artist his own show the following year. The show was a huge success; critics immediately perceived that

Johns meets with art dealer Leo Castelli, who helped the artist to fame, and his wife in New York City in 1966.

Johns was presenting the next stage in the developing exploration of the meaning of art, rejecting the rigidly non-representational aesthetic in order to depict objects that were transformed by the simple act of representation. Commentators also noted the subtle ironic humor in Johns' method of elevating a simple figure to the stature of art. Collectors, too, approved of Johns' approach; all the paintings in the exhibit were sold, and the Museum of Modern Art purchased four of his works. Deborah Solomon, in a 1988 appreciation in the *New York Times*, wrote: "No artist was ever catapulted into fame more suddenly than Johns."

Seasons of an Artist

Since that time Johns's work has gone through three distinct phases: the pop work of the 1960s; the abstract crosshatching paintings of the 1970s; and the multiple image work of his later career. Johns's pop work picturing everyday objects and images lasted through the 1960s, focusing the viewer's attention onto the surface of the canvas. Here he used oil, encaustic, or acrylic paints. He also sculpted mundane objects such as a light bulb. In 1959 he met Duchamp and came more under the influence of Dadaist principles, experimenting with found objects such as brooms and pieces of ceramic, which he glued onto the canvas and labeled. He was also influenced by the philosophy of Austrian Ludwig Wittgenstein. "Johns focuses attention on the painting as an object," noted a contributor for *Contemporary Artists*, "a thing in its own right, rather than a representation." A major motif in his work is "the theme of illusion versus reality and the constant questioning of reality and identity," according to this same critic. In *False Start* from 1959, Johns deals with visual puns, using swatches of blue, orange, red, and yellow, and then stenciling the names of other colors over these. In *Fool's House* he inserts a broom into the middle of the painting and labels it, as if asking whether or not the broom is an actual broom now that it no longer has the function of "broom."

In 1964, only six years after his first solo exhibition, Johns' works were displayed in retrospectives at the Jewish Museum in New York and the Whitechapel Gallery in London, an exceedingly unusual event for an artist of Johns' relatively young age. In 1977, another retrospective, this time at the Whitney Museum in New York, drew 4,100 visitors and subsequently travelled to San Francisco, Cologne, Paris, and Tokyo.

By the 1970s Johns was verging into abstraction, employing a crosshatching technique to create an image. *The Dutch Wives* of 1975, is an example of this style, in which the artist employs wide brush strokes to cover the entire canvas in crosshatching. This technique again focuses the viewer's eye on the technical aspects of the medium, rather than focusing on the content. He famously said of this period that he was attempting to "make paintings about painting."

More psychological in content are the multiple image paintings of his later period. These paintings often employ multiple panels as well, sometimes joined by visible hinges. Homage to earlier painters is paid up in such paintings, with references to Pablo Picasso, Paul Cezanne, Leonardo da Vinci, or Edvard Munch. His *Racing Thoughts* from 1983, includes a painted illusion of the *Mona Lisa,* a photograph of his agent, Leo Castelli, one of his own crosshatch paintings, a nail, a faucet, some pottery, and a print by another artist, Barnett Newman. "The painting is a kind of interior monologue," according to Gibson. For this same critic, "the overarching theme of [Johns's] work is of a highly introverted artist quietly probing and articulating his own doubt in the face of the world—both the art world and the world at large." *The Seasons* from 1986, incorporates a shadowy figure of Johns's body. Some critics call this an homage to Picasso and his own 1954 work, *The Shadow.* This more personal and self-referential work is in stark contrast to the early period of Johns's creativity in which the focus was away from the artist and placed on the work. In that early work, as *Grove Art Online* contributor Michael Crichton noted, "He emphasized the ready-made and impersonal elements of his creations: the pre-existing imagery, the stenciled lettering, the un-mixed primary colors, things that were 'not mine, but taken.'"

Over the years, Johns has also designed sets and costumes for the Merce Cunningham Dance Company in New York—the inspiration for his painting *Dancers on the Plane.* He collaborated with Cunningham and John Cage on the ballet *Un Jour ou Deux* in 1973. One of Johns' most fruitful collaborations was with the renowned author Samuel Beckett; the 1977 volume *Fizzles* features five stories by Beckett and 33 etchings by Johns, considered to be among his finest works in that medium.

If you enjoy the works of Jasper Johns, you may also want to check out the following:

The Pop Art of Roy Lichtenstein (1923-1997), Robert Rauschenberg (1925--), and Andy Warhol (1928-1987).

Johns's works continue to be highly sought-after; in 1980, *Flag* was purchased by the Whitney Museum for $1 million. In 1988 his *Diver* sold for $4.2 million, the highest sum ever paid for the work of a living artist at that time.

Dudar noted that "one of the hallmarks of a master is that he never stops exploring," and in that sense Johns is a modern master. "Few artists juggle such a range of materials," Dudar further observed. In addition to his works in oil and his sculptures and prints, Johns has also produced a large body of drawings. "Pen, pencil, charcoal, crayon, chalk, pastel, watercolor, and collaged scraps of newspapers may be put to the service of his drawings," according to Dudar. For Stevens "Johns is hardly jolly, but he is a playful pessimist, whose work has much in common with the game of hide-and-seek." This "playful pessimist" may not be to everyone's liking, but all agree that he profoundly altered the direction of modern painting. Stevens concluded: "Obviously Johns is not a painter who enters easily into either art or life. He is the prototypical intellectual, standing slightly apart, the outsider looking in. His playing will not charm those who like their art torn from the inside out. Nor will it appeal to activists with firm convictions. But Johns will delight those who feel that, in all seriousness, life is a game of mysterious rules played on the edge of chaos—and who take pleasure in some beautiful fiddling."

■ Biographical and Critical Sources

BOOKS

Barton, Stephanie and Lynn Zelevansky, *Jasper Johns to Jeff Koons: Four Decades of Art from the Broad Collections,* Harry M. Abrams (New York, NY), 2001.

Bernstein, Roberta, *Jasper Johns' Paintings and Sculptures, 1954-1974: "The Changing Focus of the Eye,"* UMI Research (Ann Arbor, MI) 1985.

Bernstein, Roberta, *Jasper Johns: Numbers,* Cleveland Museum of Art (Cleveland, OH), 2003.

Castleman, Riva, *Jasper Johns: A Print Retrospective* (exhibition catalogue), Museum of Modern Art/ Little, Brown (Boston, MA), 1986.

Contemporary Artists, 4th edition, St. James Press (Detroit, MI), 1996.

Crichton, Michael, *Jasper Johns,* revised edition, Harry M. Abrams (New York, NY), 1994.

Field, Richard S., *Jasper Johns: Prints, 1960-1970* (exhibition catalogue), Philadelphia Museum of Art (Philadelphia, PA), 1970.

Francis, Richard, *Jasper Johns,* Abbeville Press (New York, NY), 1984.

Garrels, Gary, *Jasper Johns: New Paintings and Works on Paper,* San Francisco Museum of Modern Art (San Francisco, CA), 1999.

International Dictionary of Art and Artists, St. James Press (Detroit, MI), 1990.

Jasper Johns (exhibition catalogue), Jewish Museum (New York, NY), 1964.

Jasper Johns: Drawings (exhibition catalogue), Arts Council of Great Britain (London, England), 1974.

Jasper Johns: 19 avril-4 juin, 1978 (exhibition catalogue), Centre Georges Pompidou (Paris, France), 1978.

Jasper Johns: 35 Years [with] Leo Castelli (exhibition catalogue), edited by Susan Brundage, Leo Castelli Gallery/Harry N. Abrams (New York, NY), 1993.

Johnston, Jill, *Jasper Johns: Privileged Information,* Thames and Hudson (New York, NY), 1996.

Kozloff, Max, *Jasper Johns,* Harry N. Abrams (New York, NY), 1972.

Orton, Fred, *Figuring Jasper Johns,* Harvard University Press (Cambridge, MA), 1994.

Rothfuss, Joan, editor, *Past Things and Present: Jasper Johns since 1983,* Walker Art Center, 2003.

Seventeen Monotypes/Jasper Johns (exhibition catalogue), text by Judith Goldman, ULAE (West Islip, NY), 1982.

Shapiro, David, *Jasper Johns Drawings, 1954-1984,* Harry N. Abrams (New York, NY), 1984.

Steinberg, Leo, *Jasper Johns,* G. Wittenborn (New York, NY), 1963.

Varnedoe, Kirk, *Jasper Johns: A Retrospective,* Museum of Modern Art (New York, NY), 2003.

PERIODICALS

America's Intelligence Wire, February 5, 2004, Jessica Witkin, "U. Southern California: Jasper Johns Paints Art with 'Numbers'."

Art Business News, August, 2004, "Exhibit Explores Pop Art's Cultural Impact," p. 58.

Artforum International, March, 1994, Wayne Kostenbaum, "Jasper Johns: 'In Memory of My Feelings'—Frank O'Hara, 1961," p. 74; March, 1996, Richard Shiff, "Jasper Johns' 'Alley Oop,' 1958," p. 88; September, 1996, Rosalind E. Krauss and Christopher Knight, "Split Decision," p. 78; September, 2003, Katy Siegel, "Past Things and Present: Jasper Johns since 1983," p. 81.

Art in America, May, 1995, Raphael Rubinstein, "Full Circle," p. 108; April, 1997, Roni Feinstein, "Jasper Johns: The Examined Life," p. 78, David Sylvester, "Shots at a Moving Target," p. 90; October, 2004, Joe Fyfe, "Jasper Johns at the Cleveland Museum of Art," p. 162.

Entertainment Weekly, January 15, 1993, Hilton Kramer, "Jasper Johns: Ideas in Print," p. 58.

Financial Times, August 11, 2004, Lynn Macritchie, "A Painter of Unconscious Insight," p. 13.

Interiors, April, 1999, Andrea Truppin, "Numbers Crunching," p. 23.

Lancet, December 18, 1999, John McConnell, "Jasper John's Strings," p. 2177.

Modernism Magazine, winter, 2003, David Rago, "Jasper Johns: Numbers," p. 20.

Nation, April 27, 1985, Arthur C. Danto, "The 1985 Biennial Exhibition," p. 501; January 27, 1997, Arthur C. Danto, "Jasper Johns," p. 32.

New Republic, May 18, 1987, Mark Stevens, "Jasper Johns," p. 26; January 9, 1989, Mark Stevens, "Pessimist at Play," p. 25; July 30, 1990, Mark Stevens, "The Seducer of Certainty," p. 28; December 2, 1996, Jed Perl, "Flag Burning," p. 42.

New Statesman, July 5, 1996, Michael Bywater, "Wham Bam Thank You Ma'am!," p. 38.

Newsweek, October 28, 1996, Peter Plagens, "Rally round the Flag, Boys," p. 72.

New York Times, June 19, 1988, Deborah Solomon, "The Unflagging Artistry of Jasper Johns," p. 20.

Smithsonian, June, 1990, Helen Dudar, "Enigmatic, Distant, Jasper Johns Is at the Top of His Form," p. 56.

Time, July 25, 1988, Robert Hughes, "The Venice Biennale Bounces Back," p. 84; September 9, 1996, "Jasper Johns' Grand Old Retrospective," p. 64; November 11, 1996, Robert Hughes, "Behind the Sacred Aura," p. 76.

Time International, April 2, 2001, "Art Goes Pop," p. 74.

World and I, March, 1997, Eric Gibson, "The Inflation of Jasper Johns," p. 96.

ONLINE

Artchive.com, http://www.artchive.com/ (November 19, 2004), "Jasper Johns."

Museum of Modern Art, http://www.moma.org/ (November 19, 2004), "Jasper Johns: A Retrospective."*

Lynn Johnston

trator of "For Better or for Worse" cartoon strip syndicated by Universal Press Syndicate, 1979—. President, Lynn Johnston Productions, Inc.

■ Personal

Born May 28, 1947, in Collingwood, Ontario, Canada; daughter of Mervyn (a jeweler) and Ursula (an artisan; maiden name, Bainbridge) Ridgway; married first husband (a cameraman), c. 1975 (divorced); married John Roderick Johnston (a dentist and pilot), February 15, 1977; children: (first marriage) Aaron Michael; (second marriage) Katherine Elizabeth. *Education:* Attended Vancouver School of Arts, 1964-67. *Religion:* Unitarian-Universalist. *Hobbies and other interests:* Travel, doll collecting, playing the accordion, co-piloting and navigating aircraft.

■ Addresses

Home—Corbeil, Ontario, Canada. *Office*—c/o Andrews & McMeel Publishing, 4520 Main St., Kansas City, MO 64111.

■ Career

McMaster University, Hamilton, Ontario, Canada, worked as a medical artist, 1968-73; freelance commercial artist and writer, 1973—; author and illus-

■ Member

National Cartoonists Society (president, 1995).

■ Awards, Honors

Reuben Award, National Cartoonists Society, 1986, for outstanding cartoonist of the year, and 1991, for best newspaper comic strip; Gemini Award, 1987, for television special *The Bestest Present;* named member of the Order of Canada, 1992; Pulitzer Prize nomination, 1993; Reuben Award finalist, 1995, for outstanding cartoonist of the year; inducted into International Museum of Cartoon Art Hall of Fame, 1997; Media Human Rights Special Award, League for Human Rights of B'nai Brith, 2001; Quill Award, National Association of Writing Instrument Distributors; Inkpot Award, San Diego Comics Convention; EDI Award; two honorary degrees.

■ Writings

SELF-ILLUSTRATED COMIC COLLECTIONS

David! We're Pregnant!, Potlatch Publications (Hamilton, Ontario, Canada), 1973, published as *David! We're Pregnant!: 101 Cartoons for Expecting Parents,* Meadowbrook (Deephaven, MN), 1977, revised edition, 1992.

Hi, Mom! Hi, Dad!: The First Twelve Months of Parenthood, P. Martin Associates (Toronto, Ontario, Canada), 1977, revised edition, Meadowbrook (Deephaven, MN), 1977.

Do They Ever Grow Up?, Meadowbrook (Deephaven, MN), 1978, published as *Do They Ever Grow Up?: 101 Cartoons about the Terrible Twos and Beyond*, 1983.

"FOR BETTER OR FOR WORSE" COMIC COLLECTIONS

I've Got the One-More-Washload Blues, Andrews & McMeel (Kansas City, MO), 1981.

Is This "One of Those Days," Daddy?, Andrews & McMeel (Kansas City, MO), 1982.

It Must Be Nice to Be Little, Andrews & McMeel (Kansas City, MO), 1983.

More than a Month of Sundays: A For Better or for Worse Sunday Collection, Andrews & McMeel (Kansas City, MO), 1983.

Our Sunday Best: A For Better or for Worse Sunday Collection, Andrews & McMeel (Kansas City, MO), 1984.

Just One More Hug, Andrews & McMeel (Kansas City, MO), 1984.

The Last Straw, Andrews & McMeel (Kansas City, MO), 1985.

Keep the Home Fries Burning, Andrews & McMeel (Kansas City, MO), 1986.

It's All Downhill from Here, Andrews & McMeel (Kansas City, MO), 1987.

Pushing Forty, Andrews & McMeel (Kansas City, MO), 1988.

A Look Inside: For Better or for Worse: The Tenth Anniversary Collection, Andrews & McMeel (Kansas City, MO), 1989.

It All Comes out in the Wash (contains reprints from previous books), Tor Books (New York, NY), 1990.

If This Is a Lecture, How Long Will It Be?, Andrews & McMeel (Kansas City, MO), 1990.

For Better or for Worse: Another Day, Another Lecture (contains reprints from previous books), Tor Books (New York, NY), 1991.

What, Me Pregnant?, Andrews & McMeel (Kansas City, MO), 1991.

For Better or for Worse: You Can Play in the Barn, but You Can't Get Dirty (contains reprints from previous books), Tor Books (New York, NY), 1992.

For Better or for Worse: You Never Know What's around the Corner (contains reprints from previous books), Tor Books (New York, NY), 1992.

Things Are Looking Up, Andrews & McMeel (Kansas City, MO), 1992.

For Better or for Worse: It's a Pig-Eat-Chicken World (contains reprints from previous books), Tor Books (New York, NY), 1993.

For Better or for Worse: Shhh—Mom's Working! (contains reprints from previous books), Tor Books (New York, NY), 1993.

But, I Read the Destructions!: For Better or for Worse, T. Doherty Associates (New York, NY), 1993.

"There Goes My Baby!": A For Better or for Worse Collection, Andrews & McMeel (Kansas City, MO), 1993.

It's the Thought That Counts: For Better or for Worse Fifteenth Anniversary Collection, Andrews & McMeel (Kansas City, MO), 1994.

Starting from Scratch, Andrews & McMeel (Kansas City, MO), 1995.

Love Just Screws Everything Up, Andrews & McMeel (Kansas City, MO), 1996.

Remembering Farley: A Tribute to the Life of Our Favorite Cartoon Dog, Andrews & McMeel (Kansas City, MO), 1996.

Growing like a Weed: A For Better or for Worse Collection, Andrews & McMeel (Kansas City, MO), 1997.

Middle Age Spread: A For Better or for Worse Collection, Andrews & McMeel (Kansas City, MO), 1998.

The Lives behind the Lines: Twenty Years of For Better or for Worse, Andrews & McMeel (Kansas City, MO), 1999.

Sunshine & Shadow: A For Better or for Worse Collection, Andrews & McMeel (Kansas City, MO), 1999.

The Big 5-0: A For Better or for Worse Collection, Andrews & McMeel (Kansas City, MO), 2000.

Isn't He Beautiful?, Andrews & McMeel (Kansas City, MO), 2000.

Isn't She Beautiful?, Andrews & McMeel (Kansas City, MO), 2000.

All about April: Our Little Girl Grows Up!: A For Better or for Worse Special Edition, Andrews & McMeel (Kansas City, MO), 2001.

Graduation, a Time for Change: A For Better or for Worse Collection, Andrews & McMeel (Kansas City, MO), 2001.

A Perfect Christmas: A For Better or for Worse Little Book, Andrews & McMeel (Kansas City, MO), 2001.

Family Business: A For Better or for Worse Collection, Andrews & McMeel (Kansas City, MO), 2002.

Reality Check: A For Better or for Worse Collection, Andrews & McMeel (Kansas City, MO), 2003.

With This Ring: A For Better or for Worse Collection, Andrews & McMeel (Kansas City, MO), 2003.

Suddenly Silver: A For Better or for Worse Collection, Andrews & McMeel (Kansas City, MO), 2004.

So You're Going to Be a Grandma!: A For Better or for Worse Collection, Andrews & McMeel (Kansas City, MO), 2005.

Striking a Chord: A For Better or for Worse Collection, Andrews & McMeel (Kansas City, MO), 2005.

ILLUSTRATOR

Bruce Lansky, editor, *The Best Baby Name Book in the Whole Wide World*, Meadowbrook Press (Deephaven, MN), 1979.

Vicki Lansky, *The Taming of the C.A.N.D.Y. Monster*, revised edition, Book Peddlers (Deephaven, MN), 1988.

Vicki Lansky, *Practical Parenting Tips for the First Five Years*, revised and enlarged edition, Meadowbrook Press (Deephaven, MN), 1992.

OTHER

(With Andie Parton) *Leaving Home: Survival of the Hippest*, Andrews & McMeel (Kansas City, MO), 2003.

(With Brenda Wegmann) *Laugh 'n' Learn Spanish: Featuring North America's Most Popular Comic Strip "For Better or for Worse,"* McGraw-Hill (New York, NY), 2004.

Has also contributed one story and a cover illustration to *Canadian Children's Annual*.

■ Adaptations

Ottawa's Funbag Animation Studios produced a weekly animated series based on "For Better or for Worse," 2000.

■ Sidelights

Lynn Johnston's comic strip "For Better or for Worse" has captured the imaginations and hearts of readers throughout North America. Focusing on humorous and dramatic moments in the life of the fictional Patterson family, Johnston has ranged from sight-gag humor to serious storylines about death, aging, and discrimination. Printed daily in hundreds of newspapers across the United States and Canada, "For Better or for Worse" has won numerous top awards, is regularly named one of the top five strips in reader polls, and even earned Johnston a Pulitzer Prize nomination.

Drawing Provided Escape, Laughter

Though Johnston's comic is marked by gentle humor, she began drawing in her youth to escape feelings of intense anger within her. In an interview with Tom Heintjes for *Hogan's Alley Online*, the cartoonist described her mother as "a brilliant, talented lady with potential beyond belief," but her mother was also a frustrated person from an abusive home. Her discipline of her children's real and imagined transgressions was frequently brutal. Johnston's father did not intervene, but was a gentle, comic presence "with the ability to dance and sing and charm and analyze poetry," Johnston remembered. When the children grew too large for their mother to physically beat them, the abuse became verbal.

Filled with dark and negative feelings, Johnston would express them in drawings and find her spirits lifted. "If I wanted to draw funny pictures, I would draw them, and I remember loving watching my brother laugh at them," she recalled to Heintjes. "My brother was a great audience, and if he liked the picture, he would laugh and laugh and laugh, and he would want to keep the picture. Making people laugh with an image I had created . . . what power that was!"

Despite the violence in the home, Johnston's parents were both very supportive of their children's creative aspirations. Art classes were a regular activity even when money was scarce. Johnston's father encouraged her to analyze the humor in comics, seeing how timing and setting played an important part in the humor of a piece. She didn't care for superhero comics, but told Heintjes, "I loved the Little Lulu stories, where she would fantasize that her bedroom rug would turn into a pool of water, and she could dive down into the center of the world. Or Scrooge McDuck with his money bin. I loved all that stuff. It was wonderful fantasy that seemed achievable by a child. And it wasn't ugly. There were no villains with guns." Johnston also enjoyed the more raucous humor of the Three Stooges and *Mad* magazine, although her mother disapproved of these.

Johnston eventually enrolled in the Vancouver School of Art, but left her studies before graduation to take employment in animation and illustration. She married and moved to Hamilton, Ontario, where she found a job as a medical illustrator, a source of invaluable experience for her. Her first marriage was not a happy one, however. Johnston's low-self-esteem led her into anorexia, and her husband left her while she was pregnant. Faced with the challenges of single parenthood, Johnston found herself struggling to cope.

Breaking into Comics

After her divorce, Johnston started to do freelance work out of her home and soon found her business booming. Oddly enough, it was her obstetrician

A pregnant Ellie Patterson ponders her baby's future in Johnston's popular comic strip, *For Better or for Worse*.(For Better Or For Worse (c) 1991 Lynn Johnston Productions. Dist. By Universal Press Syndicate. Reprinted with permission. All rights reserved.)

who started a chain of events that would eventually lead to her being offered a contract for a comic strip. Knowing that she was a comic artist, he challenged her to come up with some cartoons to be put on the ceiling above his examining tables. She produced eighty drawings for the doctor, and with a friend's help, found a publisher for the illustrations. They appeared in three books: *David, We're Pregnant!*, *Hi Mom! Hi Dad!: The First Twelve Months of Parenthood*, and *Do They Ever Grow Up?* Submissions editors at Universal Press Syndicate were impressed with the quality and humor in her drawings. They were searching for a comic strip that could compete with the family-oriented "Blondie" and "Hi and Lois" and thought Johnston might be an ideal candidate. She was contacted and asked if she could produce in a four-frame format.

Johnston was both excited and nervous about the proposition. She had never written in a daily format, but was willing to give it a try. Shortly after Universal Press's offer, she sent them samples of a strip she had developed based loosely on her own family life. To her surprise, they accepted her submissions and offered her a daily, syndicated strip. She received a one-year development contract with which she was allowed to work on her strip for a year before it was published. After the year, she was offered a twenty-year contract.

"When I got the contract, I was totally blown out of the water," she told Jeanne Malmgren of the *St. Petersburg Times Floridian*. "It was the opportunity of a lifetime, but at the same time, it was terrifying. I never thought I would be able to come up with funny gags 200 or 300 times a year." She turned to her friend Cathy Guisewite, the creator of the very successful "Cathy" comic strip, for some friendly advice. Guisewite suggested that before doing the art she should write all the dialogue down as if she were doing script. "I had a tremendously good relationship with her on the phone," Johnston once remarked. "She gave me lots of hints on how she worked and then I went from there."

Over 150 papers signed on to carry "For Better or for Worse," even before the strip debuted. "It's hard to sell a new feature to papers, and many new cartoonists only start with about fifty papers, and maybe they never get past that," the cartoonist said. "I know now some young people who are struggling and they cannot seem to get past their fifty papers. So for me to start with 150 was quite an exciting thing. But then it was one of the first of the family strips that was not done by a man and also was done in a contemporary style. So I was breaking new ground in a way. . . . I was very fortunate."

As her comic career was developing, another story had been brewing as well. A few years before, while driving along with her young son, she happened to spot a small plane flying overhead. She loved flying and small aircraft, so on a whim she drove to the airport to see the plane land. She began chatting with the pilot, who then invited her to fly to the next airport with him for a hamburger. In 1976, she married the pilot, Rod Johnston. He adopted her son, Aaron, and the two soon had a daughter of their own. When Rod completed dental school, they moved to northern Manitoba. Lynn Johnston credits her husband's down-to-earth, stable personality, along with his sense of humor, as being an essential influence on her career, and her life in general. She has stated that the move to a remote area was also probably a good thing, at a time when she was suddenly famous.

Patterson Family Mirrors Johnston's

The Patterson family, featured in "For Better or for Worse," developed out of many of Johnston's real-life situations and concerns. There are two parents: Elly, the harried mother, and John, a dentist who flies a plane. Michael and Elizabeth, the two original children in the strip, carry the middle names of Johnston's real-life children and are just slightly younger than their real-life counterparts. Both families are Canadian, and the Johnstons once owned an English sheep dog named Farley, as did the Pattersons. Elly's brother Phil is a wayward trumpet player just like Johnston's brother, Alan Philip Ridgway. Johnston herself has said that both she and Elly want to be rescuers, and are motivated to try to fix everyone and everything in their family.

Johnston's emotional closeness to her characters has made them very real to her, but at a certain point, the parallels end. "I find that somehow the characters develop their personalities independently of me," Johnston told Janice Dineen in the *Toronto Star*. Rod Johnson also noted the differences, telling Malmgren that Lynn has more polish than her fictional character, and that she "is much more of a businessperson. And she's more in charge of our family than Elly is." Johnston's children "both look very, very different from the characters in the strip, and their lives are very different," Johnston commented in an interview for *Authors and Artists for Young Adults*.

Unlike some comic strips, where the characters do not age, the Patterson family has seen many changes. Michael has married, grown, and become a father; Elizabeth has graduated from college and

This strip appears in the silver anniversary edition *Suddenly Silver* published in 2004, which presents strips from twenty-five years of *For Better or for Worse*. (For Better Or For Worse © 2004 Lynn Johnston Productions. Dist. By Universal Press Syndicate. Reprinted with permission. All rights reserved.)

begun a job. Elly's mother died, and her father remarried. The death of Farley, the dog, was a major milestone in the strip, one which not all readers welcomed. The addition of daughter April represented Johnston's way of working out her desire to have a baby later in life. "I brought the baby into the strip," Johnston remarked to Janice Dineen in the *Toronto Star*, "because for a while I really wanted another baby. I thought about adopting but instead, in the end, I made my baby up." When writing about Michael and Elizabeth, who really were based on her children, Johnston is always conscious of protecting the privacy of their real-life counterparts. With April, however, Johnston felt freer to explore her inner life and be more playful with the character. April is the only one who is totally fictional. "I can have a lot more fun with her and reveal a lot more about her private life because in reality she doesn't exist, so it's not as though I'm opening up a closet that no one has a right to see in," Johnston once told *AAYA*.

Serious Issues on the Comics Page

Johnston's early comics were very simple sketches of the Pattersons. They dealt with the normal daily routine of a growing family, parents and children in conflict, exhaustion, and household clutter. As time went on, however, Johnston tackled more complex and controversial issues in her strip. At one point, Elly had to deal with the problem of her friend, who gave birth to a baby with six fingers on both hands. Race relations were explored when an Asian family moved into the house across the street from the Pattersons. In a 1992 story line, Mike Patterson finds out that his friend, Gordon, is being abused by his father. Johnston admitted that the strip was taken from an incident that had happened to a friend of her daughter. She told John Przybys in the *Las Vegas Review-Journal*: "It was an experience I had and it bothered me. And, sometimes, when experiences bother you, you know how you tend to dream about them? For me, the dreaming came out on paper."

Johnston tackled another difficult topic in a 1993 strip series. In it, family friend Lawrence Poirier tells his family that he is gay. Unfortunately, his parents react badly, denying the news and eventually kicking him out of the house. This topic choice was partly inspired by Johnston's brother-in-law, Ralph, who is gay. Ralph revealed his feelings to the family years before, but the admission of his homosexuality changed her family forever. "What happens when you hear this news is you change," Johnston told John Tanasychuk of the *Detroit Free Press*. "You change because your point of view is shattered. You think one thing about the person and then this comes along. Then you realize that they haven't changed. It's you."

Johnston was a catalyst for family healing when this situation happened. By writing a series of strips about a gay character, the cartoonist hoped to reach her readers with this same sort of information and sharing she had discovered. However, because of the controversial topic, forty papers took alternate material, and nineteen cancelled the strip outright. About this reaction, Johnston commented to Tanasychuk, "It surprises me in today's environment that people would want to [keep] something like that out of a newspaper. I think that the readers should be able to decide for themselves whether they want to read that."

Johnston received more than 3,000 letters after the strips were published, two thirds of which praised her for having the courage to address the issue. However, there was also a significant amount of negative backlash. She told Hentjes that whatever the reaction, she simply had to do the storyline because it felt right. "I wrote it from experience," she said. "My brother-in-law is gay. It certainly has not been by design, but so very many of my friends have been gay, all the way through school, art school, even in my husband's dental class—our very best friend, who graduated with Rod, was gay and is now HIV-positive. He's been thrown out of his home. We've been part of the private lives of so many people who have had to deal with this. I know this story. I know it's a true one, and I know the dialogue by heart."

In general, Johnston receives a lot of positive feedback from her more controversial strips. "If I do something of a serious nature, I'll get one letter against and 20 letters for," she told Przybys. "People are really comfortable reading about [serious] stuff as long as I'm careful to treat it with dignity and in a light way, because it is an entertainment medium and people do read comics for fun." One problem with confronting a controversial issue is that other special interest groups have sometimes requested that Johnston give equal time to their causes. "[A] lot of people want me to go further: 'Oh gosh, if she's willing to talk about child abuse, let's have her champion the abortion issue.' It's dangerous, when you do realistic things, turning the strip into a soapbox and people wanting you to champion their cause. You can't do that."

Johnston has won numerous awards and accolades throughout her career. In 1986, she won the prestigious Reuben Award for outstanding cartoonist of the year from the National Cartoonists Society, making her the first female and the youngest person ever to win. At the time, Johnston felt a little cowed by winning the award, feeling she could not live up to what would now be expected of her. She found her whole studio looked different after winning the award, and she began to write a letter to "Peanuts" creator Charles M. Schulz, one of the most successful cartoonists of all time. That same morning, Schulz telephoned her, and the two began a long and profound friendship.

Besides the accolades she has received from fellow comic strip artists, Johnston has fared well with newspaper readers as well. In comic strip popularity polls held by many newspapers in the early 1990s, "For Better or for Worse" consistently placed in the top five, and, even more consistently, the top two spots. Johnston's strip was picked number one by readers of such newspapers as the *Detroit Free Press*, *The Oregonian*, the *Toronto Star*, the *Los Angeles Daily News*, Denver's *Rocky Mountain News*, the *Norfolk Virginian Pilot*, the *Cincinnati Enquirer*, and the Monterrey County, California, *Herald*.

If you enjoy the works of Lynn Johnston, you may also want to check out the following comic strips:

Zits by Jerry Scott and Jim Borgman.
Baby Blues by Jerry Scott and Rick Kirkman.
Jump Start by Robb Armstrong.

Johnston works in a studio near the log home she and her husband now own on a lake in northern Ontario. It takes her about one or two days to write the dialogue for one week of her comic strip, a task that is especially trying for her. "There's a fine line between what makes something funny and what makes something just barely amusing. I think it takes a sort of acting ability to be able to set up a scene, get the expressions and then bring it to a punch line. All in four frames. It's a knack that's taken me a long time to develop," she confided to Malmgren. Johnston feels that over the course of a week, one or two strips will be significantly funny, while the rest just build the story line.

After the writing process, she sets to work creating the art. "I waste almost no paper. I draw it in pencil, then I go over it with India ink pens, and then I

put on the Lettra film, with the little dots that gives you the gray tones," she told Malmgren. "You have to be the characters as you are drawing," the artist also explained to Dineen. "You have to feel what the character is feeling." Johnston admitted to Dineen that she loves her job: "It keeps me in touch with people and their lives. I get to make people laugh." And besides being a profession, it is also a means of self-expression. "This is my way of communicating. Some people use music or dance or literature. I use cartooning." Despite her love for her characters and her readers, Johnston planned to end "For Better or For Worse" after a twenty-eight-year run; her contract expires in 2007.

■ Biographical and Critical Sources

BOOKS

Encyclopedia of World Biography Supplement, Gale (Detroit, MI), 1998.

PERIODICALS

Austin American-Statesman, August 19, 1997, Patrick Beach, "'Better or Worse' Gay Storyline Brings Debate," p. E1.
Bookwatch, February, 2005, review of *Suddenly Silver*.
Capital Times (Madison, WI), October 16, 1999, "Cartoonist's Book to Take Us behind 'For Better' Scenes," p. 1D.
Chatelaine, February, 1987; June, 1989; March, 1997, p. 41.
Detroit Free Press, March 17, 1993, John Tanasychuk, "Gay Teen Comes out in 'For Better or for Worse'"; August 8, 1993, pp. 1J, 4J.
Editor & Publisher, April 3, 1993, David Astor, "Comic with Gay Character Is Dropped by Some Papers: But Most 'For Better or For Worse' Clients Decide to Publish the Sequence," p. 32; April 10, 1993, David Astor, "More Papers Cancel Controversial Comic," p. 34; March 11, 1995, p. 40; September 13, 1997, David Astor, "'For Better' Creator Explains Her Move," p. 36; February 20, 1999, David Astor, "'Better' Bests Competitors in Survey of Major Papers," p. 37; October 16, 1999, David Astor, "Canadian Lynn Johnston Addresses Feature Editors in Her Home Country," p. 41; December 4, 2000, David Astor, "'Better' Creator in the Canadian Club of Celebrity," p. 45; September 10, 2001, Dave Astor, "Gown Appears and Lawrence Returns in 'FB,'" p. 25; November 26, 2001, Dave Astor, "'Better' Is Best of the Family Comics," p. 14.

Florida Times Union, December 2, 1999, Susan P. Respess, review of *The Lives behind the Lines,* p. D6.

Fresno Bee (Fresno, CA), May 1, 1999, John C. Davenport, "Drawing on Real Life the Creator of a Popular Comic Strip Shows Many Sides of Life, *For Better or for Worse,*" p. E1.

Houston Chronicle, March 4, 1998, Dai Huynh, "Comic Strip Experiences Death," p. 3.

Las Vegas Review-Journal, May 31, 1992, John Przybys, "Getting Serious."

Los Angeles Times Book Review, November 26, 1989; September 13, 1992.

Maclean's, November 6, 2000, "For Better, Not Worse," p. 83.

Milwaukee Journal Sentinel, April 16, 2002, Mary-Liz Shaw, "She's in 'toon: Cartoonist Draws Way into Hearts of Fans," p. 1; April 18, 2002, Kathy Flanigan, "Comic Art Imitates Life," p. 6.

People, September 15, 1986, Ned Geeslin, "For Better or Worse, Canadian Cartoonist Lynn Johnston Draws Her Inspiration from Reality."

Philadelphia Inquirer, September 13, 2001, Denise Cowie, "Bridal Gown Goes from Comic Strip to Shops."

St. Louis Post-Dispatch, July 9, 2004, Daniel P. Finney, "Readers Are Clear: It's 'For Better,' Not Worse," p. E1.

St. Petersburg Times Floridian, February 1, 1989, Jeanne Malmgren, "It's Getting 'Better.'"

Seattle Times, February 19, 2003, John C. Davenport, "For Better or for Worse, Cartoonist's Life Differs from Comic," p. F1.

Tampa Tribune, September 5, 2001, "Comic's Story Line Comes Out Again," p. 1.

Toronto Star, October 9, 1992, Janice Dineen, "Better than Ever."

Variety, January 1, 1986.

Washington Post, April 7, 1996, Charles Truehart, "In Lynn Johnston's Drawing Room," p. F1.

Wind Speaker, January, 2005, Deirdre Tombs, "Cartoonist's Ordinary Native People Celebrated," p. 21.

ONLINE

For Better or for Worse, http://www.fbofw.com/ (February 3, 2005).

Hogan's Alley Online, http://www.cagle.com/ hogan/ (Volume 1, number 1), Tom Heintjes, interview with Johnston.

Suite101.com, http://www.suite101.com/ (April 19-May 2, 2002), Susanna McLeod, interview with Johnston.*

Jane Kenyon

■ Personal

Born May 23, 1947, in Ann Arbor, MI; daughter of a jazz musician and a singer; died of leukemia April 23, 1995, in Wilmot, NH; married Donald Hall (a poet), April 17, 1972; children: (stepchildren) Philippa Smith, Andrew Hall. *Education:* University of Michigan, B.A., 1970, M.A., 1972.

■ Career

Poet. Associate faculty member at Bennington College, beginning 1994.

■ Awards, Honors

Avery and Julia Hopwood Award for poetry, University of Michigan; fellow, National Endowment for the Arts, 1981, and New Hampshire Commission on the Arts, 1984; Guggenheim Foundation fellowship, 1992-93.

■ Writings

POEMS

From Room to Room, Alice James Books (Cambridge, MA), 1978.

The Boat of Quiet Hours, Graywolf Press (St. Paul, MN), 1986.

Let Evening Come, Graywolf Press (St. Paul, MN), 1990.

Constance, Graywolf Press (St. Paul, MN), 1993.

Otherwise: New and Selected Poems, Graywolf Press (St. Paul, MN), 1996.

OTHER

(Translator) *Twenty Poems of Anna Akhmatova,* Eighties Press (St. Paul, MN), 1985.

A Hundred White Daffodils: Essays, the Akhmatova Translations, Newspaper Columns, Notes, Interviews, and One Poem, Graywolf Press (Saint Paul, MN), 1999.

Work represented in anthologies, including *The Third Coast: Contemporary Michigan Poetry,* 1976. Contributor to periodicals, including *Atlantic Monthly, Harvard* magazine, *New Criterion, New Republic, New Yorker, Pequod, Ploughshares,* and *Poetry.*

■ Adaptations

Some of Kenyon's poetry was set to music by William Bolcom as *Briefly It Enters: A Cycle of Songs from the Poems of Jane Kenyon for Voice and Piano, 1994-96,* Bolcom Music, 1996.

The Boat of Quiet Hours

POEMS BY JANE KENYON

Kenyon focuses on everyday concerns in this 1986 poetry collection.

■ Sidelights

Poet Jane Kenyon was noted for creating verse that probes the inner psyche, particularly demons of depression such as those that plagued her throughout much of her adult life. Kenyon was not a prolific writer, publishing just four volumes of poetry in her lifetime: *From Room to Room, The Boat of Quiet Hours, Let Evening Come,* and *Constance.* Although her output was limited, her work is notable for its power and precision.

Born in Ann Arbor, Michigan, Kenyon spent her first two decades in the Midwest, attending the University of Michigan in her home town, and completing a master's degree there. While a student, she met her future husband, poet Donald Hall, who was an instructor at the university. They married and took up residence at Eagle Pond Farm, a New Hampshire property that had been in Hall's family for generations. It would be Kenyon's main residence until her death from leukemia at the age of forty-seven. The setting inspired stoic portraits of domestic and rural life; as essayist Gary Roberts noted in *Contemporary Women Poets,* her poetry was "acutely faithful to the familiarities and mysteries of home life, and it is distinguished by intense calmness in the face of routine disappointments and tragedies."

Discussing Kenyon's first published collection, *From Room to Room,* Robin M. Latimer, writing in the *Dictionary of Literary Biography,* called it "the poetic diary of a honeymoon, in which a young wife explores the spaces between her and her husband, and her new and former homes." As Kenyon was a generation younger than her husband, she had a great deal of his past to assimilate into her life. The poems' subjects include the gender gap, a husband's absence, and a wife examining some of his possessions. Latimer went on: "The overlay of the new on the old continues as the main character progresses through her first anniversary, chronicled in 'Year Day,' revamping room after room of her new home. As she does so, she encounters the emblems, both universal and personal, of her female lineage, a grandmother's tablecloth here, an heirloom thimble there." Latimer concluded, "The fact that it manages to sidestep all of its potential triteness lies in Kenyon's craft—her haikulike precision in rendering an effect and her clear regard for smooth sound."

Kenyon's next collection, *The Boat of Quiet Hours,* was praised by Carol Muske in the *New York Times:* "These poems surprise beauty at every turn and capture truth at its familiar New England slant. Here, in Keats's terms, is a capable poet." In fact, Kenyon's work has often been compared with that of English Romantic poet John Keats; Roberts dubbed her a "Keatsian poet" and noted that, "like Keats, she attempts to redeem morbidity with a peculiar kind of gusto, one which seeks a quiet annihilation of self-identity through identification with benign things."

A Poet's Poet

Latimer pointed out that Keats is actually a character in Kenyon's *Let Evening Come,* "evoked, in the speaker's knowledgeable reconstruction of his last days, in various reposes. This reference to Keats is refreshing on the part of Kenyon because it clarifies her awareness that she is subject, as was he, to the criticism that she is a poet's poet. She baits this criticism in her poems in which the speaker registers alarm at or resistance to public places, events, the uneducated, and the unwashed." Latimer further noted that in the collection, "as one has come to expect, Kenyon's craft in sound and image is consummate. The poems, pointedly arranged so as not to concentrate linked themes and subjects, invite a slow, unaggressive reading, one that recapitulates the rhythms of water, leaf, and wind—despite all the clamor for something more stimulating. Faith and meaning, Kenyon urges, as in all of her works, lie in a rhythm so constant one might view it as cliché."

The cycles of nature held special significance for Kenyon, who returned to them again and again, both in her variations on Keats's ode "To Autumn," and in other pastoral verse. In *Let Evening Come*, the poet took what a *Poetry* essayist called "a darker turn," exploring nature's cycles in other ways: the fall of light from day to dusk to night, and the cycles of relationships with family and friends throughout a long span of years brought to a close by death. *Let Evening Come* "shows [Kenyon] at the height of her powers," wrote Muske in a review of the 1990 volume for the *New York Times Book Review,* the critic adding that the poet's "descriptive skills" are "as notable as her dramatic ones. Her rendering of natural settings, in lines of well-judged rhythm and simple syntax, contribute to the [volume's] memorableness."

Constance began Kenyon's study of depression, and her work in this regard has been compared with that of the late poet Sylvia Plath. Comparing the two, Breslin wrote that "Kenyon's language is much quieter, less self-dramatizing" than that of Plath, and where the earlier poet "would give herself up, writing her lyrical surrender to oblivion, . . . Kenyon fought to the end." Breslin noted the absence of self-pity in Kenyon's work, and the poet's ability to separate from self and acknowledge the grief and emotional pain of others, as in her poems "Coats," "Sleepers in Jaipur," and "Gettysburg: July 1, 1863," which imagines a mortally wounded soldier lying in wait for death on the historic battlefield.

Struggles with Illness

After Kenyon and Hall had been married for some time, Hall contracted colon cancer, which spread to his liver. The prognosis for his recovery was very poor, and part of his liver was removed. As Hall's

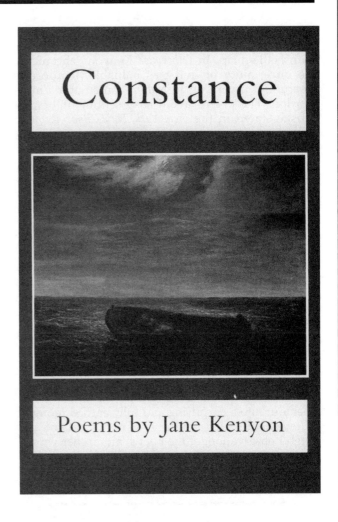

The poems in this 1993 volume, the final work Kenyon published in her lifetime, examine depression, grief, and death.

friend Liam Rector recalled in *American Poetry Review:* "We didn't think he had long to live. I orchestrated a tribute to Don's work at Old Dominion University in Virginia. Because we thought Don was soon to be a goner, there was something of a memorial service in this, while Don was still alive. Don accepted all this cheerfully (if a bit ruefully), gratefully, and great swarms of his many friends came to speak. There were other tributes, in different places. But, as fate would have it, Don recovered; Don endured." Ironically, after standing by her husband throughout his illness and treatment, Kenyon herself was eventually diagnosed with leukemia, which brought about her early death.

Kenyon's last work was collected in *Otherwise: New and Selected Poems,* a posthumous collection containing twenty poems written just prior to her death, as well as several taken from her earlier books. Kenyon herself selected the poems during her last months, with Hall's help. In *Otherwise* Kenyon "chronicles the uncertainty of living as culpable, temporary creatures," according to *Nation* contributor Emily Gordon. The poems avoid easy sentimentality, as Muske stated in the *New York Times Book Review:* "The poet here sears a housewife's apron, hangs wash on the line, walks a family dog and draws her thought from a melancholy, ecstatic soul as if from the common well, 'where the fearful and rash alike must come for water.' In ecstasy," Muske continued, Kenyon "sees this world as a kind of threshold through which we enter God's wonder."

Reviewing *Otherwise* for *World Literature Today*, Sandra Cookson wrote: "Kenyon's poems are the earnest, spare, often moving record of a life of work at her craft, of years of struggling with painful depression, of the daily bearing witness in the intimacy of the New Hampshire countryside where she lived. Given the limited range and voice of Kenyon's poetry, she is at her best in the brief lyric, which in some of these poems opens into the apercu that is the reward of closely observed details. . . . Many of the best poems in the collection are lighted by or open out into a surprising and fully earned moment of revelation. Such are the rewards of patient and careful observation, of the poet's faith in her work."

If you enjoy the works of Jane Kenyon, you may also want to check out the following books:

Edward Thomas, *Collected Poems*, 1920.
Sylvia Plath, *Ariel*, 1965.
Carol Muske, *Red Trousseau*, 1993.

Another posthumous work, *A Hundred White Daffodils*, collected some of Kenyon's prose writings, including the newspaper column she produced for several years before her death. Reviewing the collection for *Booklist*, Ray Olson stated, "They are exquisite little essays, mostly on seasonal events, especially in the garden, for Kenyon was an ardent flower gardener." In Olson's opinion, the newspaper columns in *A Hundred White Daffodils* "are the heart of this companion to her deeply moving final selection of her poems, *Otherwise*." A reviewer for *Publishers Weekly* also gave the book a strong recommendation, finding that "the woman who comes to life in these pages is witty, guileless, humble and heartbreakingly intelligent. One is left wanting more, as if continuing the interviews could restore this vibrant person to life."

In 2002 Kenyon's publisher, the Graywolf Press, presented "Jane Kenyon: A Celebration in Words and Song," a multimedia tribute to the late poet held in Minneapolis. The event included Hall reading some of Kenyon's poems, classical musicians performing musical settings, and the premier of J. Mark Scearce's "American Triptych," based on three of Kenyon's poems about New England.

■ Biographical and Critical Sources

BOOKS

Carruth, Hayden, *Letters to Jane*, Ausable Press (Keene, NY), 2004.
Contemporary Poets, St. James Press (Detroit, MI), 6th edition, 1996.
Contemporary Women Poets, St. James Press (Detroit, MI), 1998.
Dictionary of Literary Biography, Volume 120: *American Poets since World War II, Third Series*, Gale (Detroit, MI), 1992.
Hall, Donald, *Without*, Houghton (Boston, MA), 1998.
Timmerman, John H., *Jane Kenyon: A Literary Life*, Eerdmans (Grand Rapids, MI), 2002.

PERIODICALS

American Poetry Review, November-December, 1994, Robin Becker, review of *Constance*, p. 23; November-December, 2004, Liam Rector, "Remembering Jane Kenyon," p. 57.
Booklist, April 1, 1996, Ray Olson, review of *Otherwise: New and Selected Poems*, p. 1340; November 1, 1998, review of *Otherwise: New and Selected Poems*, p. 483; September 1, 1999, Ray Olson, review of *A Hundred White Daffodils*, p. 58.
Library Journal, September 1, 1999, review of *A Hundred White Daffodils*, p. 191.
Nation, April 29, 1996, Emily Gordon, review of *Otherwise: New and Selected Poems*, p. 28.
New York Times Book Review, June 21, 1987, p. 13; March 24, 1991; January 5, 1997.
Poetry, July, 1997, pp. 226-240; November, 2004, Donald Hall, "The Third Thing," p. 113.

Publishers Weekly, March 30, 1990, Penny Kaganoff, review of *Let Evening Come,* p. 56; July 12, 1993, review of *Constance,* p. 75; February 26, 1996, review of *Otherwise,* p. 101; July 19, 1999, review of *A Hundred White Daffodils,* p. 171.

Star Tribune (Minneapolis, MN), October 27, 2002, Gwendolyn Freed, "Poetic Tribute," p. 11F.

Virginia Quarterly Review, winter, 1979.

Wisconsin State Journal, December 4, 1996, John Aehl, "Poetic License: Blending Words, Music, Voice," p. 1D.

World Literature Today, spring, 1997, Sandra Cookson, review of *Otherwise,* p. 390.

OTHER

A Life Together (documentary film by Bill Moyers), broadcast on PBS, December, 1993.

■ **Obituaries**

PERIODICALS

Washington Post, April 25, 1995, p. B7.*

Barbara Kesel

■ Personal

Born October 2, 1960; married; husband's name, Karl (a comic book artist and writer). *Education:* Graduated from college (in drama), 1983.

■ Addresses

Office—CrossGen Entertainment, 4023 Tampa Rd., Suite 2400, Oldsmar, FL 34677.

■ Career

Graphic novelist. DC Comics, New York, NY, former editor; Dark Horse Comics, Milwaukie, OR, began as editor, became managing editor and liaison to "Legends" series; CrossGen Comics, Oldsmar, FL, head writer, 1999-2003, director of creative development, 2003—.

■ Writings

GRAPHIC NOVELS: AUTHOR OF TEXT

(With husband, Karl Kesel) *Hawk and Dove*, DC Comics (New York, NY), 1993.

Elseworld's Finest, Volume 2: Supergirl & Batgirl, DC Comics (New York, NY), 1997-98.
Sigil: Mark of Power, CrossGen Comics (Oldsmar, FL), 2001.
(With Mark Waid) *Sigil: The Marked Man*, CrossGen Comics (Oldsmar, FL), 2002.
(With others) *Hell Boy: Seed of Destruction*, Dark Horse Comics (Milwaukie, OR), 2004.
Solus: Radiant, CrossGen Comics (Oldsmar, FL), 2004.

"MERIDIAN" SERIES; AUTHOR OF TEXT

Meridian: Flying Solo, CrossGen Comics (Oldsmar, FL), 2001.
Meridian: Going to Ground, CrossGen Comics (Oldsmar, FL), 2002.
Meridian: Taking the Skies, CrossGen Comics (Oldsmar, FL), 2002.
Meridian: Coming Home, CrossGen Comics (Oldsmar, FL), 2002.
Meridian: Minister of Cadador, CrossGen Comics (Oldsmar, FL), 2003.
Meridian: The Mystery of Sheristan, CrossGen Comics (Oldsmar, FL), 2004.
Meridian: Changing Course, CrossGen Comics (Oldsmar, FL), 2004.

"FIRST" SERIES; AUTHOR OF TEXT

The First: Two Houses Divided, CrossGen Comics (Oldsmar, FL), 2001.

The First: Magnificent Tension, CrossGen Comics (Oldsmar, FL), 2002.

The First: Sinister Motives, CrossGen Comics (Oldsmar, FL), 2002.

The First: Futile Endeavors, CrossGen Comics (Oldsmar, FL), 2003.

The First: Liquid Alliances, CrossGen Comics (Oldsmar, FL), 2003.

The First: Ragnarok, CrossGen Comics (Oldsmar, FL), 2004.

OTHER

Also author of *Savant Garde* comic book series, 1997.

■ Sidelights

Barbara Kesel has been an influential voice in bringing young female readers into the comic-book scene. Working as a freelancer, as well as an editor and story developer at DC Comics, Dark Horse Comics, and at the Florida-based CrossGen Comics, she had consistently endeavored to create storylines and protagonists that transcend gender and generation. The series titles she has personally written—at CrossGen in particular, where she pens the "Meridian," "The First," and "Solus" series—all feature strong female characters either as comic-book heroes or major secondary characters. Additionally, as head writer and then director of creative development at CrossGen, Kesel has played a large role in directing that more-recently established publishing house in the production of story lines and series that would attract female as well as male readers.

Becomes Comic-Book Afficionado

Born Barbara Randall in 1960, Kesel first "discovered comic books through TV," as she told Jennifer M. Contino in a *SequentialTart.com* interview. "I remember getting up early to watch Superman (George Reeves) on TV. Then came Aquaman on Saturday morning." From real-life or animated versions of comic-book heroes, Kesel moved on to the real thing, and became particularly interested in "Wonder Woman" comics. Even her Barbie dolls were turned into superheroes in her games. As she told Contino, her childhood was full of "constant motion, rollerskating." But her youth was also full of words. She was fond of "writing stories and plays that the neighborhood kids would put on." And there was in addition her old standby activity,

"reading, reading, reading. . . . I grew up moving just often enough that my childhood 'friends' are certain books that were always in the local libraries." Kesel's taste in books ranged from works by C. S. Lewis to the books of Madeleine L'Engle and Harlan Ellison.

In high school the predominant culture was "anti-learning, pro-jock worship," as Kesel recalled to Contino. She found a place for herself in a drama class and was inspired by the energy of her drama teacher, who had the class put on shows with real professional intensity. "It was the only area in my school where I felt like anybody cared about trying to do something to the best of their ability as opposed to the easiest way possible, and it offered me a venue to write, and a group of really good friends who have stayed connected ever since." Kesel took this new-found enthusiasm with her to college, majoring in theater with plans of perhaps becoming a high school drama teacher herself. All the while however, she knew that she also wanted to write. "I never realized I 'wanted to be [a writer],'" she told Contino. "I just always WAS one. I can't remember a time before telling and writing stories."

Initially the urge to write seemed destined to find an outlet in the transformation of Kesel into a famous playwright, but then came a fateful day at the mall in Pomona, California, in 1979. Pestered by a stranger, she fled into a used bookstore and there re-connected with DC Comics. However, through more sophisticated eyes, she now saw how poor the characterization of women was presented in many of these titles. The owner of the bookstore agreed and suggested Kesel write her complaints to DC. With the characteristic naivete of a college sophomore, Kesel did just that, penning a ten-page critique to Dick Giordano at DC Comics demonstrating how such characterizations could be remedied. Her letter was not lost in the void; in fact Giordano replied with an offer for Kesel to write a back-up "Batgirl" story for *Detective.* Kesel's version appeared in the magazine in 1981.

A Strong Voice in the Comics World

Since updating the image of Batgirl, Kesel has become a major fixture in the world of comics and graphic novels. Graduating from college in 1983, she took a job with DC as an associate editor, moving to the company's headquarters in New York City, where she worked from 1984 to 1989. At DC she had a hand in virtually every series, including "Watchmen." She also met her comic-book artist husband, Karl Kesel, in New York; the couple collaborated on the "Hawk and Dove" series for the company and saw the series published in graphic-novel format in 1993. Soon, however, Kesel found herself spending most of her time working as part of a development group and no longer able to have a direct hand in creating the superhero comics that she loves. Not a great fan of Manhattan in the first place, she decided to leave DC and move west again. After several years spent working as a freelance comics writer, she took another full-time job, this one with Dark Horse Comics in Portland, Oregon, where she eventually rose to managing editor. "When I started at Dark Horse, I was the fifteenth employee and it was a small shop where we all got to do everything," Kesel recalled to Contino. Success, however, changed that. After a few years a more corporate atmosphere evolved, and Kesel again responded by going freelance. Then, in 1999, she accepted a job as head writer for CrossGen Comics after the company's chief operating officer attended Kesel's scriptwriting seminar at an annual San Diego Comic Convention. Once again, she moved from coast to coast, settling in Florida where CrossGen is headquartered. As head writer, Kesel was responsible not only for her own titles, but also for helping to train new writers and building a stable of professionals to generate all titles in house.

At CrossGen Kesel has helped develop a range of titles, mostly in the categories of science fiction and fantasy. As a writer, she is well known for her work on the "Meridian" series. Set on one of the city-states floating above the poisoned planet of Demetria, the series focuses on Sephie, daughter of the minister of Meridian. When her father dies, Sephie inherits his position and his mysterious sigil, a sign that the link between the character and a source of cosmic power has been activated. Sephie's sigil gives her powers of renewal. But her scheming Uncle Ilahn also has a sigil, with powers of decay, and he has every intention of using it in a grand plan to master all of Demetria by controlling its trade. Sephie and Ilahn are soon a collision course in a series of adventures that provides female comic book fans a heroine to respect and identify with.

The "Meridian" series has been published in a number of book-length collections. Reviewing the first collection, *Meridian: Flying Solo*, *Booklist* reviewer Cathy Buskar called the volume an "appealing coming-of-age story." Buskar also significantly noted that "young women, a group not usually counted among graphic novel enthusiasts, may be especially intrigued" with the "Meridian" saga. Of *Meridian: Going to Ground* and *Meridian: Taking the Skies*, *School Library Journal* reviewer Susan Salpini wrote, "these titles are a coming-of-age story on a richly imagined world with appealing characters." Also reviewing *Taking the Skies*, *Library Journal* con-

tributor Steve Raiteri concluded, "Demetria is the most fully realized of all of CrossGen's invented worlds, and Sephie herself is the publisher's most endearing character." A contributor to *Publishers Weekly* had similar praise, commenting on the series' "fascinating" characters, and Kesel's scripting, which "gives the action more moral weight than usual in a mass market comic." This same contributor concluded that "Meridian" is a "superior value" within the graphic-novel market because of its "beautiful art and strong scripting." Writing about the fifth installment in the "Meridian" series, *Meridian: Minister of Cadador*, *School Library Journal* reviewer Salpini again praised the "lush-colorful artwork" that "complements the text," while a *Publishers Weekly* contributor was pleased that "the creators of Meridian are not content to endlessly repeat themselves."

If you enjoy the works of Barbara Kesel, you may also want to check out the following comic books:

The "Mystic" series by Ron Marz.
The "Crux" series by Mark Waid.
The "Negation" series by Tony Bedard.

Another major series penned by Kesel is "The First," about a group of god-like beings that inhabited the Earth before humans. These superhumans, however, are not perfect; in fact they are "as quarrelsome and horny as the ancient Greek gods of Olympus," according to a reviewer for *Publishers Weekly*. Bickering among themselves, they separate into two rival houses. The debut "First" collection, published in 2001 as *The First: Two Houses Divided*, deals with the battles between the House of Dexter, home to the more selfless gods, and the House of Sinister, home to the more selfish ones. The sigil bearers also play an important role in these books, while the action is a bit more intense and dominant than in the "Meridian" titles. Reviewing series title *The First: Sinister Motives*, a contributor for *Publishers Weekly* called the volume a "cross between a soap opera and a WWF tag-team extravaganza." Hillias J. Martin, writing in *School Library Journal*, noted that Kesel "packs all of the traditional superhero-comics tricks" into the story, but the critic also complained that the dialogue contains an overly large portion of "flat cinematic clichés and overbearingly collegiate vocabulary."

Kesel has also created the comic-book series "Solus," featuring pencils by George Perez. The series features a female character, an all-powerful sigil bearer, named Sousandra (aka Andra Radiant), who seems to have lost her memory and also needs increased sigil power. This new series ended prematurely in 2003, as CrosGen Comics reorganized its publishing output, requiring Kesel to find appropriate endings for her books much earlier than expected. With the company's major reorganization, she also had to gear up for a new job in creative development. "What it all means is that I'm now one of these cell-phone people," she told Carrie Landers in an interview for *SequentialTart.com.* Kesel remains optimistic about her career, however, and continues to view her main role within the comic-book industry as finding ways to attract young female readers to comic books. The "Meridian [series] may be finite," she noted to Landers, "but what's there will continue to be around to draw in other readers, both male and female."

■ Biographical and Critical Sources

PERIODICALS

Booklist, April 1, 2003, Cathy Buskar, review of *Meridian: Flying Solo,* p. 1390.

Library Journal, November 1, 2002, Steve Raiteri, review of *Meridian: Taking the Skies,* p. 66; July, 2003, Steve Raiteri, review of *Meridian: Traveler Edition: Flying Solo,* p. 68.

Publishers Weekly, September 23, 2002, review of *Meridian: Taking the Skies,* p. 52; March 10, 2003, review of *The First: Sinister Motives,* p. 55; August 11, 2003, review of *Meridian: Minister of Cadador,* p. 259.

School Library Journal, October, 2002, Susan Salpini, review of *Meridian: Going to Ground,* p. 198; March, 2003, Susan Salpini, review of "Coming Home," p. 262; May, 2003, Hillias J. Martin, review of *The First: Sinister Motives,* p. 182; July, 2003, Susan Salpini, review of *Meridian: Minister of Cadador,* p. 154.

ONLINE

CrossGen, http://www.crossgen.com/ (November 17, 2004).

Pipeline Reviews, http://www.nic.com/~augie/pipeline/ (September 28, 1997), Augie De Blieck, Jr., review of *Savant Garde.*

SequentialTart.com, http://www.sequentialtart.com/ (May, 2000), Jennifer M. Contino, "The Accidental Writer: Barbara Kesel"; (November, 2003) Carrie Landers, "Meridian's Mom: Barbara Kesel."

Silver Bullet Comic Books, http://www.silverbulletcomicbooks.com/ (April 21, 2005), Tim Hartnett, review of *Solus #4.*

Titan's Tower, http://www.titanstower.com/ (November 17, 2004), "The Kesels on *Hawk & Dove II.*"*

Haven Kimmel

■ Personal

Born 1965, in Mooreland, IN; married three times (divorced); children: Katie; (third marriage) Obadiah. *Education:* Ball State University, B.A.; attended Earlham School of Religion and North Carolina State College. *Religion:* Society of Friends ("Quaker").

■ Addresses

Home—Durham, NC. *Agent*—Bill Clegg, Burnes & Clegg, Inc., 1133 Broadway, Suite 1020, New York, NY 10010.

■ Career

Writer.

■ Awards, Honors

Nominee, Orange Prize (England), 2003, for *The Solace of Leaving Early;* has received two National Endowment for the Arts (NEA) grants.

■ Writings

A Girl Named Zippy: Growing up Small in Mooreland, Indiana (memoir), Doubleday (New York, NY), 2001.

The Solace of Leaving Early (first novel in trilogy), Doubleday (New York, NY), 2002.
Orville: A Dog Story (picture book), illustrated by Robert Andrew Parker, Clarion Books (New York, NY), 2003.
Something Rising (Light and Swift) (second novel in trilogy), Free Press (New York, NY), 2004.

Contributor to *Killing the Buddha: A Heretic's Bible,* edited by Peter Manseau and Jeff Sharlet, Free Press (New York, NY), 2004, and *Remarkable Reads: 35 Writers and Their Adventures in Reading,* edited by J. Peder Zane, Norton (New York, NY), 2004. Contributor of poetry, as Haven Koontz, to journals, including *Hopewell Review, Sycamore Review, Yellow Silk,* and *Ball State University Forum.*

■ Adaptations

The Solace of Leaving Early was optioned for a film, to be directed by Mike Nichols.

■ Work in Progress

Third novel in the trilogy which includes *The Solace of Leaving Early* and *Something Rising (Light and Swift).*

■ Sidelights

"If there is ever going to be a Midwestern gothic, it will not be written by me," author Haven Kimmel told *Book* contributor Lisa Levy. "I don't see the

Midwest as a place filled with bumbling, malignant, stupid people." Kimmel has firsthand knowledge of the region, having been born and raised in Indiana, and she has also used the area as the setting for three books. Her memoir, *A Girl Named Zippy: Growing up Small in Mooreland, Indiana*, put Kimmel's name and face on the literary map. A "love letter" to her hometown, as *Library Journal* contributor Pam Kingsbury described the book, *A Girl Named Zippy* found readership both in the United States and in England, and was noted for demonstrating a compassionate voice with all the characters. This same voice was at play in Kimmel's first novel, *The Solace of Leaving Early,* also set in Indiana, and in her second novel, *Something Rising (Light and Swift).* Levy commended the author for populating her books with "extremely literate, philosophical and spiritually curious people" that are perhaps not unlike Kimmel herself.

A Hoosier Background

Kimmel was born in Mooreland, Indiana, in 1965. With a population of only a few hundred and boasting three churches and one gas station, the town was small enough for a young girl to explore thoroughly as she grew up, and to come to know all the inhabitants. As Kimmel told Karen Valby in *Entertainment Weekly*, there was nothing to do on Friday nights "except get drunk, drive around, crash into tombstones, and get pregnant." Growing up, Kimmel had no dreams of becoming a writer. Instead, her "only real dream," as she related to Kelley Kawano in *Bold Type*, "was to be a rodeo star. Wait, that's not true. There was a time I thought I'd make a good prison guard, and my sister agreed with me." Nonetheless, Kimmel began writing at age nine, "automatically and without intention—like a savant," she explained to Kawano. Except in Kimmel's case, writing was in fact copying stories out of a story collection by Ray Bradbury, then showing the results to her mother and claiming them to be her creations. "It is, perhaps, rare for a person to be both a savant and a plagiarist," Kimmel quipped to Kawano. Plagiarist or not, Kimmel was supported in her creative endeavors by an understanding parent. Finally, she decided that copying stories was boring, and that she could even see places where she could improve the plot by, for example, having a girl's nose serve as a howitzer.

She remained in Indiana for her undergraduate studies, attending Ball State University in Muncie, where she graduated with degrees in English and creative writing. "I would say," Kimmel told Kawano, "with only a slight measure of hysteria and hyperbole, that by the time I was twenty-one I

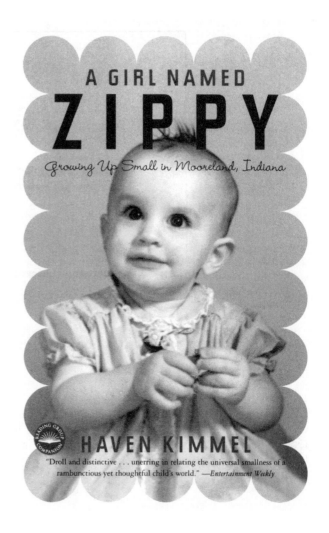

Kimmel reminisces about her upbringing in small-town Indiana in this 2001 memoir.

had given my life over to poetry." One early publication was a poem titled "Heartland," published in the *Sycamore Review.* This poetry phase lasted for fifteen years.

A lifelong Quaker, Kimmel, at age twenty-six, entered a seminary at the Earlham School of Religion. As she further recounted for Valby, "I called the dean and said, 'I am a heathen and a hopeless sinner, and I fall short of the grace of God every single day, and I will never be the type of believer anyone wants me to be, but I want to come to your school.'" The dean welcomed her to attend, but she ultimately dropped the studies, having already begun writing what would become her first novel by penning a chapter about an eccentric neighbor, Edythe Koontz. Thereafter she attended North Carolina

State, studying creative writing, but also stopped these studies after a time. However, she did stay on in her new state, settling in Durham. Along the way she also had three marriages and two children. And she continued to work on the tales and remembrances that would, after much revision, form the heart of her first book, *A Girl Named Zippy*.

Memoirs and Novels

In Kimmel's memoir she writes of a young girl who is nicknamed Zippy for her rather vigorous miming of a monkey. Zippy's first words begin at age three, but thereafter they come fast and furious. Like Kimmel, Zippy was born in 1965 in Moorehead, Indiana, a town populated by strange and loving people, and the young girl's world is also populated by a wide variety of animals. Kingsbury wrote that Kimmel's book is "filled with good humor, fine storytelling, and acute observations of small town life." Similarly, *Booklist*'s Mary Carroll felt that despite its "awful" title, "Kimmel's childhood memoir rings true," and went on to conclude that the "simple, poignant memoir, reads like fine historical fiction." And in *Publishers Weekly*, a contributor noted that Kimmel's "smooth, impeccably humorous prose evokes her childhood as vividly as any novel." Kimmel's narrator's voice carries the day, as she tells of her first bike or recalls looking at comic books at the drugstore. "There is no single element in *Zippy* I worked on harder, longer, or with more conscious deliberation than the voice," Kimmel told Kawano. "And, as you've noticed, the voice dictated the content." Whatever the secret formula, *A Girl Named Zippy* took off, was chosen by television's *Today Show* for its book club, and reached the top of national bestseller charts.

By the time of publication of *A Girl Named Zippy* Kimmel was already hard at work on a proposed trilogy of novels set in Indiana. The first, *The Solace of Leaving Early*, features another heroine drawn closely from Kimmel's own life. Langston Braverman comes back to her Indiana hometown after walking out on her doctoral oral exams. It does not help that she has also been dumped by her professor boyfriend. But once back home she finds that her childhood friend, Alice, has been shot by her estranged husband. In the same town, Amos Townsend is a preacher who was counseling Alice and is a man who feels bereft now that he was unable to stop the violence. Out of this crisis in two separate lives, a new romance is formed. Thrown together when Langston begins to take care of Alice's two children, Amos and Langston "are forced to confront their own demons," according to a *Publishers Weekly* reviewer, who also found this debut novel "intelligent and compassionate."

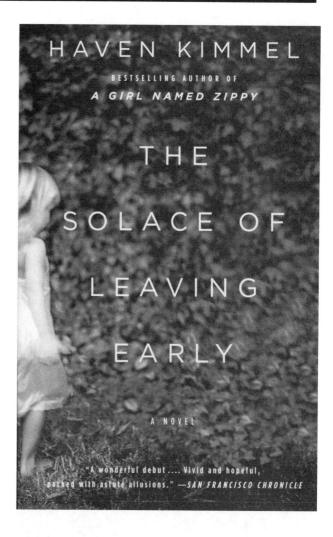

In this 2003 novel, a young woman who walked out on a promising career returns to her hometown to find her childhood friend murdered, leaving her to care for the friend's two daughters.

Some critics of Kimmel's first novel, such as Alfred Hickling of London's *Guardian*, found Langston to be "one of the most precocious intellectual prigs in literature." Likewise, a writer for *Kirkus Reviews* described Kimmel's protagonist as "a humorless intellectual snob further burdened by wooden dialogue never spoken on earth or in heaven." However, *Library Journal*'s Colleen Lougen called this same dialogue "clever and sleek," and further praised Kimmel's novel as a "heartwarming story about troubled individuals who struggle with their problems while finding solace and a degree of peace in one another." Kristine Huntley, writing in *Booklist*, felt that "Kimmel's debut novel boasts vast theological and philosophical thought as well as unusual but compelling characters." Connie Ogle, reviewing *The Solace of Leaving Early* in *Knight Ridder/Tribune News Service*, found the novel "engaging," and went on to note that the author "has found an offbeat, original voice with which to tell her bittersweet story." Similarly, George Walden of London's *Sunday Telegraph* called *The Solace of Leaving Early* an "arresting first novel," and further observed that "in these relentlessly marketeering times it is good to see a writer dare to intersperse the intellectual with the small dramas of daily life, and to do it unselfconsciously."

Kimmel continues her exploration of small town Midwestern life with the 2004 novel *Something Rising (Light and Swift)*, a book in which, according to Robin Vidimos of the *Denver Post*, the author "takes a small slice of society, confined to an unremarkable piece of real estate, and captures the reader's heart with unexpected events and characters both famil-

Abandoned by her father, Cassie Claiborne supports her fragile mother and her neurotic sister by shooting pool in this coming-of-age tale, published in 2004.

If you enjoy the works of Haven Kimmel, you may also want to check out the following books:

Ivan Klima, *Lovers for a Day*, 1999.
Michael Ondaatje, *Anil's Ghost*, 2000.
Gao Xingjian, *One Man's Bible*, 2002.

iar and unique." Cassie Claiborne is ten when the reader meets her, and dotes on her mostly absent pool-shark father. She takes the opportunity during her father's visits to learn pool, and by the time he finally abandons his family, Cassie herself has become a pool hustler. At age eighteen she can support herself and her family with her winnings. The story then jumps ahead to catch a further snapshot of Cassie at age thirty, embarking "on a journey that will free her from her past and launch her as her own adult," according to Vidimos.

Judith Kicinski, writing in *Library Journal*, noted that Kimmel relates more of a "rough-and-tough" story with *Something Rising (Light and Swift)* than she did in her previous books. Kicinski also felt that "more development of Cassie's character would have helped." *Guardian* contributor Carrie O'Grady also had mixed praise for this second novel, commending the poetry of the author "which lingers on the landscape and the rough-edged details of Cassie's progress down a difficult path." Still, for O'Grady "if Kimmel had pared down the poetry and stepped up the action, she could have told quite a story." Mark Kamine, writing in the *New York Times*, complained of "occasional clunky sentences, their meanings elusive, their locutions dubious." Similarly, a critic for *Kirkus Reviews* summed up the book as "too lugubrious for an elegy, a bit too lighthearted for a caper; [but] still, a serviceable account of a young woman finding her own way in a twilit world of regret and loss."

Other reviewers felt more positive about *Something Rising (Light and Swift)*. Ogle called it *compelling*, while *Booklist*'s Kristine Huntley found it "evocative and fresh," and a "beautiful coming-of-age story." A contributor for *Publishers Weekly* noted that Kimmel's "characters are sympathetic and believable, and the author proves herself equally deft at conveying smalltown desolation and the physics of pool." *Entertainment Weekly* reviewer Alyssa Lee joined the chorus of praise, observing that in the novel Kimmel "takes aspects of the everyday and renders them transcendent." And for Malcolm Jones of *Newsweek*, the "loveliness of *Something Rising* has nothing to do with talking points and everything to do with the acquaintance of Cassiopeia Claiborne, a young woman growing up in Indiana." Jones concluded that "if this book were a pool game, Kimmel would run the table all night long."

Kimmel has also written a children's book, *Orville: A Dog Story*, that was actually a chapter that would not fit in her memoir, *A Girl Named Zippy*. Thus all her published works have focused on the Midwest. In an interview with Dave Weich for *Powells.com*, she expanded on the trilogy she is creating that celebrates that region. "The Midwest is a simple geographic point in some ways, and in other ways it's very, very complicated—who landed there and why, and what those lives became. . . . Since this is a trilogy, what I saw as one of my charges was to be as truthful about the place as I could be. In the third book, the next novel, the characters are all different again. If I listened and paid attention, I think it could go on and on."

■ Biographical and Critical Sources

PERIODICALS

Atlanta Journal-Constitution, August 11, 2002, David Kirby, review of *The Solace of Leaving Early*, p. F4.

Book, January-February, 2003, Lisa Levy, "The New Carson McCullers: Haven Kimmel," p. 39.

Booklist, March 15, 2001, Mary Carroll, review of *A Girl Named Zippy: Growing up Small in Mooreland, Indiana*, p. 1351; June 1, 2002, Kristine Huntley, review of *The Solace of Leaving Early*, p. 1684; September 15, 2003, Hazel Rochman, review of *Orville: A Dog Story*, p. 246; October 15, 2003, Kristine Huntley, review of *Something Rising (Light and Swift)*, p. 357; June 1, 2004, Rosalind Reisner, review of *A Girl Named Zippy*, p. 1695.

Capital Times (Madison, WI), August 9, 2002, Deborah Hirsch, review of *The Solace of Leaving Early*, p. A13; May 30, 2003, Heather Lee Schroeder, "Author's First Novel Draws High Acclaim," p. A11.

Denver Post, January 18, 2004, Robin Vidimos, review of *Something Rising (Light and Swift)*, p. F12.

Detroit Free Press, August 11, 2002, Connie Ogle, review of *The Solace of Leaving Early*.

Entertainment Weekly, January 23, 2004, Allyssa Lee, review of *Something Rising (Light and Swift)*, p. 103; February 27, 2004, Karen Valby, "Just a Small Town Girl," p. 67.

Georgia Review, winter, 2002, Sanford Pinsker, review of *A Girl Named Zippy*.

Guardian (London, England), November 15, 2003, Alfred Hackling, review of *The Solace of Leaving Early*, p. 30; June 5, 2004, Carrie O'Grady, review of *Something Rising (Light and Swift)*, p. 27.

Kirkus Reviews, May 1, 2002, review of *The Solace of Leaving Early*, p. 612; September 1, 2003, review of *Orville*, p. 1126; October 15, 2003, review of *Something Rising (Light and Swift)*, p. 1244.

Kliatt, November, 2003, Susan Allison, review of *The Solace of Leaving Early*, p. 16.

Knight Ridder/Tribune News Service, July 10, 2002, Nancy Pate, review of *A Girl Named Zippy*, p. K1084; August 7, 2002, Connie Ogle, review of *The Solace of Leaving Early*, p. K1809; January 21, 2004, Connie Ogle, review of *Something Rising (Light and Swift)*, p. K0316.

Library Journal, February 1, 2001, Pam Kingsbury, review of *A Girl Named Zippy*, p. 103; June 1, 2002, Colleen Lougen, review of *The Solace of Leaving Early*, p. 196; September 15, 2003, Judith Kicinski, review of *Something Rising (Light and Swift)*, p. 92.

Newsweek, January 26, 2004, Malcolm Jones, review of *Something Rising (Light and Swift)*, p. 59.

New York Times, February 22, 2004, Mark Kamine, review of *Something Rising (Light and Swift)*, p. 16.

Plain Dealer (Cleveland, OH), June 16, 2002,, Karen Sandstrom, review of *The Solace of Leaving Early*, p. J11.

Publishers Weekly, January 15, 2001, review of *A Girl Named Zippy*, p. 60; May 27, 2002, review of *The Solace of Leaving Early*, p. 37; September 23, 2002, Daisy Maryles, "Yippy for Zippy," p. 16; September 8, 2003, review of *Orville*, p. 76; December 8, 2003, review of *Something Rising (Light and Swift)*, p. 46, Ann Abel, "Pool Shark," p. 47.

Raleigh News and Observer, January 4, 2004, Erin McGraw, review of *Something Rising (Light and Swift)*.

San Francisco Chronicle, June 16, 2002, Miriam Wolf, review of *The Solace of Leaving Early*.

School Library Journal, November, 2003, Wendy Woodfill, review of *Orville*, p. 102.

Sewanee Review, spring, 2003, review of *A Girl Named Zippy*.

Sunday Telegraph (London, England), March 16, 2003, George Walden, review of *The Solace of Leaving Early*.

USA Today, January 13, 2004, Bob Minzesheimer, review of *Something Rising (Light and Swift)*.

Vail Daily, April 8, 2004, Alessandra Mayer, "Meet the Author: Haven Kimmel."

ONLINE

Book Page, http://www.bookpage.com/ (July, 2002), Amy Scribner, review of *The Solace of Leaving Early*; (January, 2004), Amy Scribner, review of *Something Rising (Light and Swift)*.

Crescent Blues, http://www.crescentblues.com/ (April 21, 2005), Dawn Goldsmith, review of *A Girl Named Zippy.*

Glide Magazine, http://www.glidemagazine.com/ (February 26, 2003), Jessica Ward, review of *The Solace of Leaving Early.*

Houghton Mifflin, http://www.houghtonmifflin books.com/ (November 13, 2004), "Haven Kimmel."

Official Haven Kimmel Web Site, http://www.haven kimmel.com/ (November 13, 2004).

Our Land, Our Literature, http://www.bsu.edu/ ourlandourlit/Literature/ (April 21, 2005), biography of Kimmel.

Powells.com, http://www.powells.com/ (March 2, 2004), Dave Weich, "Haven Kimmel Builds Books to Last" (interview).

Random House, http://www.randomhouse.com/ (November 13, 2004), Kelly Kawano, interview with Kimmel.

Southern Scribe, http://www.southernscribe.com/ (April 21, 2005), Pam Kingsbury, "A Rising Literary Star: An Interview with Haven Kimmel."*

Elizabeth Laird

■ Personal

Born October 21, 1943, in Wellington, New Zealand; daughter of John McLelland (a general secretary) and Florence Marion (a homemaker; maiden name, Thomson) Laird; married David Buchanan McDowall (a writer), April 19, 1975; children: Angus John, William Alistair Somerled. *Ethnicity:* "Caucasian." *Education:* University of Bristol, B.A. (with honors), 1966; University of Edinburgh, M.Litt., 1972. *Religion:* Church of England. *Hobbies and other interests:* Gardening, travel, reading, patchwork, films.

■ Addresses

Agent—Rosemary Sandberg, 6, Bailey St., London, WCIB 3HB England.

■ Career

Bede Mariam School, Addis Ababa, Ethiopia, teacher, 1967-69; Pathway Further Education Centre, Southall, London, England, lecturer, 1972-77. Former violinist with the Iraq Symphony Orchestra; has taught in India and Malaysia.

■ Awards, Honors

Burnley Express Book Award, 1988, for *Red Sky in the Morning;* Glass Globe Award, Royal Dutch Geographical Society, and the Sheffield Book Award, both for *Kiss the Dust;* Smarties Young Judges Award for *Hiding Out;* Carnegie Medal Shortlist, British Library Association, 1996, for *Secret Friends;* Lancashire Book Award, 1997, for *Jay; Jake's Tower* was shortlisted for the *Guardian* Children's Fiction Prize, 2002; Scottish Arts Council Children's Book of the Year Award and the Stockport Children's Book Award, both 2004, both for *The Garbage King.*

■ Member

Society of Authors, Anglo-Ethiopian Society.

■ Writings

English in Education, Oxford University Press (Oxford, England), 1977.

Welcome: To Great Britain and the U.S.A., Longman (New York, NY), 1983.

Faces of Britain, Longman (New York, NY), 1986.

Faces of the U.S.A., photographs by Darryl Williams, Longman (New York, NY), 1987.

Loving Ben, Delacorte (New York, NY), 1989, published as *Red Sky in the Morning,* Heinemann (London, England), 1989.

Arcadia (historical novel), Macmillan (New York, NY), 1990.

Jake's Tower, Macmillan (New York, NY), 2001.

The Garbage King, Macmillan (New York, NY), 2003.

FOR CHILDREN

Anna and the Fighter, illustrated by Gay Galsworthy, Heinemann Educational (London, England), 1977.

The House on the Hill, illustrated by Gay Galsworthy, Heinemann Educational (London, England), 1978.

The Garden, illustrated by Peter Dennis, Heinemann Educational (London, England), 1979.

The Big Green Star, illustrated by Leslie Smith, Collins (London, England), 1982.

The Blanket House, illustrated by Leslie Smith, Collins (London, England), 1982.

The Doctor's Bag, illustrated by Leslie Smith, Collins (London, England), 1982.

(With Abba Aregawi Wolde Gabriel) *The Miracle Child: A Story from Ethiopia,* Holt (New York, NY), 1985.

The Cubby Bears' Birthday Party, illustrated by Carolyn Scrace, Collins (London, England), 1985.

The Cubby Bears Go Camping, illustrated by Carolyn Scrace, Collins (London, England), 1985.

The Cubby Bears Go on the River, illustrated by Carolyn Scrace, Collins (London, England), 1985.

The Cubby Bears Go Shopping, illustrated by Carolyn Scrace, Collins (London, England), 1985.

The Dark Forest, illustrated by John Richardson, Collins (London, England), 1986.

The Long House in Danger, illustrated by John Richardson, Collins (London, England), 1986.

Henry and the Birthday Surprise, illustrated by Mike Hibbert, photographs by Robert Hill, British Broadcasting Corp. (London, England), 1986.

The Road to Bethlehem: A Nativity Story from Ethiopia, foreword by Terry Waite, Holt (New York, NY), 1987.

Work and Play, Children's Press Choice (Chicago, IL), 1987.

Prayers for Children, illustrated by Margaret Tempest, Collins (London, England), 1987.

Time for Fun, Children's Press Choice (Chicago, IL), 1987.

Things to Do, Children's Press Choice (Chicago, IL), 1987.

Busy Day, Children's Press Choice (Chicago, IL), 1987.

Wet and Dry, Pan Books (London, England), 1987.

Hot and Cold, Pan Books (London, England), 1987.

Light and Dark, Pan Books (London, England), 1987.

Heavy and Light, Pan Books (London, England), 1987.

(With Olivia Madden)*The Inside Outing,* Barron's (New York, NY), 1988.

Happy Birthday! A Book of Birthday Celebrations, illustrated by Satomi Itchekawa, Collins (London, England), 1987, Philomel (New York, NY), 1988.

Hymns for Children, illustrated by Margaret Tempest, Collins (London, England), 1988.

Sid and Sadie, Collins (London, England), 1988.

(With Olivia Madden) *The Inside Outing,* Barron's Educational Services (Woodbury, NY), 1988.

Crackers, Heinemann (Portsmouth, NH), 1989.

Rosy's Garden, illustrated by Satomi Itchekawa, Putnam (London, England), 1990.

The Day the Ducks Went Skating, Tambourine Books (New York, NY), 1990.

The Day Veronica Was Nosy, Tambourine Books (New York, NY), 1990.

The Day Sydney Ran Off, Tambourine Books (New York, NY), 1990.

The Day Patch Stood Guard, Tambourine Books (New York, NY), 1990.

The Pink Ghost of Lamont, Heinemann (Portsmouth, NH), 1991.

Kiss the Dust, Dutton, 1992, Puffin (New York, NY), 1994.

Hiding Out, Heinemann (Portsmouth, NH), 1993.

Secret Friends, Hodder & Stoughton (London, England), 1996.

Jay, Heinemann (Portsmouth, NH), 1997.

Forbidden Ground, Hamish Hamilton (London, England), 1997.

On the Run, Mammoth (Rochester, NY), 1997.

Gabriel's Feather, illustrated by Bettina Patterson, Scholastic (New York, NY), 1998.

A Book of Promises, DK Publishing (New York, NY), 2000.

When the World Began, Oxford University Press (New York, NY), 2000.

A Little Piece of Ground, Macmillan (New York, NY), 2003.

The Ice Cream Swipe, Oxford University Press (New York, NY), 2003.

Beautiful Bananas, Peachtree (Atlanta, GA), 2004.

Hot Rock Mountain (short stories), Egmont Books (London, England), 2004.

Paradise End, Macmillan (London, England), 2004.

Author of ten volumes in the "Wild Things" series, published by Macmillan (New York, NY), 1999-2000, including *Leopard's Trail, Baboon Rock, Elephant Thunder, Rhino Fire, Red Wolf, Zebra Storm, Parrot Rescue, Turtle Reef, Chimp Escape,* and *Lion Pride.* Also writer for television, including *The Toucan 'Tecs* and *Testament.*

■ Sidelights

Elizabeth Laird is a well-respected and award-winning author of children's picture books and easy readers, but she is best known for her novels for young adults. She has paired a love of travel with a love for books in a long list of novels about Muslim countries, the Middle East, and East Africa. Born in New Zealand, she moved with her parents to England as a child. At the age of eighteen she took a job teaching in Malaysia, where she suffered a nearly fatal snake bite. After returning to school for a while, she took another teaching job, this time in Ethiopia, where she traveled to remote regions by horseback and bus. It was at this point that her writing began in earnest in the form of diaries and letters.

"I always had a burning desire to travel," Laird once explained, "and as soon as I possibly could, at the age of eighteen, I took off from home (with my parents' blessing!) and went to Malaysia where I spent a year as a teacher's aide in a boarding school for Malay girls. That experience only gave me a taste for more, so after I had graduated in French (which involved a wonderful spell as a student in Paris) I headed off to Ethiopia, and worked for two years in a school in Addis Ababa. In those days the country was at peace, and it was possible to travel to the remotest parts by bus and on horseback."

World Traveler

Two years after returning from Ethiopia, Laird got on a plane for India, heading for a summer teaching job. She became very airsick on the flight, and the man in the seat next to her was kindly and helpful. A year later, she married that passenger, a man named David McDowall, who worked for the British Council. They began their married life in Baghdad, where Laird played violin with the Iraq Symphony Orchestra. The couple then moved on to Beirut, but were eventually evacuated from that war-torn area and sent to Vienna. Once they became the parents of two sons, they moved back to London to raise their family. Laird had already published some historical nonfiction books and reading text for non-English speakers; once in London, she began writing fiction.

Laird's first novel for young adults was inspired by the birth and death of a younger brother. *Loving Ben* (published in England as *Red Sky in the Morning*) tells the story of Anna, the twelve-year-old narrator, whose brother, Ben, is born brain damaged. Through

Anna, Laird recreates the family struggle of raising a handicapped child and the confusing feelings of pain and release experienced when the child dies. "Anna's voice rings true throughout as she moves from awkwardness and judgmental statements to a more mature empathy," wrote Barbara Chatton in a *School Library Journal* review. Critics also praised the author's rendering of the adult characters outside Anna's family. The adults who help Anna understand new aspects of human nature "are sufficiently real, and the story homely and natural enough for the wisdom of the moral lessons conveyed to be palatable," wrote a *Junior Bookshelf* reviewer. A critic in *Horn Book* concluded that the story, told in Anna's "wise and witty voice tugs at the heart."

A PUFFIN BOOK

Kiss the Dust

Tara and her family must flee the only home they have ever known. . . .

ELIZABETH LAIRD

A thirteen-year-old Kurdish girl and her family flee from the dangers in their homeland of Iraq in this 1992 novel, inspired by the author's visit to Kurdistan.

Laird's training in linguistics has been greatly helpful to her as she has sought out native tales in various countries. She won praise for her two books recounting Ethiopian religious tales. In *The Miracle Child: A Story from Ethiopia* she tells the story of Takla Haymanot, a thirteenth-century Ethiopian saint known for praying on one leg after the other withered away, and for performing such miracles as healing the sick and raising the dead. Laird's captions, which accompany the book's reproductions of eighteenth-century paintings by Ethiopian monks, are "informative and explain many of the artistic conventions of Ethiopian paintings in a manner so simple as to be understandable to a child and yet interesting to an adult," according to Vincent Crapanzano of the *New York Times Book Review*. In *The Road to Bethlehem: A Nativity Story from Ethiopia*, Laird offers a retelling of Ethiopian accounts of Jesus Christ's birth and the life of the Holy Family. Rosemary L. Bray, an editor of the *New York Times Book Review*, called the book "delightful" for children because of Laird's "graceful" storytelling and insightful captions. In *When the World Began*, Laird recorded stories she collected on her travels in remote regions of Ethiopia, and in *The Garbage King*, she portrayed street children living in the modern-day Ethiopian city of Addis Ababa. "Both their tragedies and triumphs are painted in vivid, authentic, and often horrific detail," according to Genevieve Gallagher in *School Library Journal*.

A Modern War Story

Kiss the Dust was inspired by Laird's visit to Kurdistan, made when she lived in Iraq. The Kurds were subject to persecution at that time, and many fled their country. The story is told from the point of view of Tara Khan, a thirteen-year-old girl who has grown up in middle-class comfort similar to that of an American child. She is shaken when her father becomes involved in the Kurdish struggle, and is soon caught up in it herself, as her family must flee first to the Kurdish strongholds in the mountains, then to a refugee camp in Iran, and finally to London, where they seek political asylum. "The story is captivating and will shed some light on a tragic situation about which most Americans have little knowledge," wrote a reviewer for *Faces: People, Places, and Cultures*. A *Publishers Weekly* reviewer commented, "Even those familiar with political problems in Iraq and Iran may be shocked by the graphic depiction of tyranny."

In an interview with Joseph Pike for *Jubilee Books*, Laird discussed *Kiss the Dust*, recalling, "I wanted to write a war story, a modern war story, as I thought that there's so many stories about the Sec-

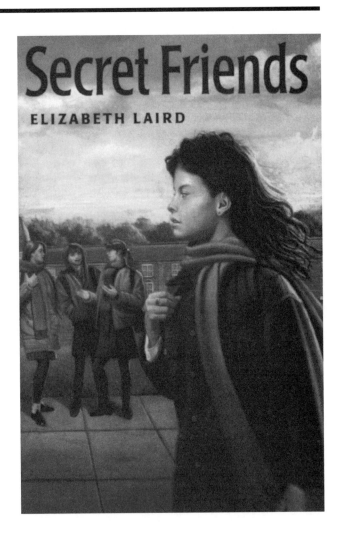

In this 1996 work, a pair of middle school students overcome a painful misunderstanding to form an unlikely friendship.

ond World War, which happened 50 years ago, and we don't seem to have moved on to wars that are happening all over the world now." She added: "It took me a year to research that book and I felt enormously worried that Kurdish people would object. I wondered if they'd be patronised by it, or worried about a foreigner writing about them. I spoke to Kurdish people practically every day and I really inched my way ahead in that book."

Jake's Tower, Laird's 2002 novel set in England, concerns a young boy, Jake, who lives in fear of his mother's abusive boyfriend. To escape his misery, Jake often dreams of a secret hideaway, and he also creates a fantasy involving Danny, his biological father, who, as a teenager, abandoned Jake's mother, Marie. After a particularly violent beating, Jake and Marie realize they need help, and they move in with

Danny's mother, who has always denied that her son is Jake's father. Jake and his grandmother forge a strong bond, however, and Jake learns to deal with some uncomfortable truths about his father. Jennifer Ralston, reviewing the story in *School Library Journal,* praised Laird for creating "believable characters" and noted that "the book conveys the tension and terror of living with abuse."

In her young adult novel published in 2003, *The Garbage King,* Laird focuses on the street children of Ethiopia. Dani, a wealthy, spoiled boy who runs away from home, and Mano, an orphan who escapes after being sold into slavery, meet in a cemetery in Addis Ababa. The pair soon join a gang of homeless children led by Million, a young tough who teaches them the ways of the street, including how to beg for money and scavenge food from the garbage. According to *School Library Journal* reviewer Genevieve Gallagher, "the boys become a family and both their tragedies and triumphs are painted in vivid, authentic, and often horrific detail." Though some critics faulted the book's upbeat ending, most found the tale compelling and praised the authenticity of the characters. In the words of *Booklist* critic Hazel Rochman, "It's the elemental friendship story of fear and hope that will draw in readers."

If you enjoy the works of Elizabeth Laird, you may also want to check out the following books:

Sonia Levitin, *The Return,* 1987.
Chris Lynch, *Gypsy Davey,* 1994.
Frances Temple, *Tonight, By Sea,* 1995.

A young boy who lives in fear of his mother's abusive boyfriend creates an imaginary hideaway in this 2001 novel.

Laird created some controversy with her 2003 title *A Little Piece of Ground,* the story of Karim, a Palestinian boy who lives under the harsh restrictions of Israeli occupation. While playing football with his friends, the boys become trapped outside during curfew, a dangerous situation when Israeli tanks move in to seal off the area. When Karim's father is stripped and humiliated by soliders, Karim and his friends join in a protest against Israeli occupation. According to Imman Laksari-Adams in the *Guardian,* Laird "manages to give the story through one person's point of view so that every emotion is shown." The book drew fire from Jewish organizations for its sympathetic portrait of the Palestinian cause. Speaking to the *Guardian,* Laird explained: "This is an important story that should be told. It shows a child under military occupation. It's terrible for the occupiers, and terrible for the occupied. I hope I have shown how awful it is for the soldiers too."

Discussing the life of a writer, Laird once stated: "The older I become, the more I realize that being a writer is not a voluntary condition. I didn't decide to become a writer, I discovered that I was one. This slow revelation, after years of teaching in Britain and abroad, has brought me much joy and many anxieties. The joy comes not only from the satisfactions of the creative process, but also from the freedom that being a writer brings, the ability to choose one's own subjects, to travel in search of inspiration, to meet fellow authors, and receive the responses of readers. The anxieties rise from the insecurity of the writer's life, the erratic income, the uncertain response of reviewers, the fear that inspiration, when the current project is finished, might never come back again."

■ Biographical and Critical Sources

PERIODICALS

Booklist, March 15, 1990, Carolyn Phelan, review of *Rosy's Garden*, p. 1446; June 1, 1991, p. 1879; January 15, 1995, p. 946; January 1, 1999, Hazel Rochman, review of *Secret Friends*, p. 878; February 15, 2001, review of *When the World Began: Stories Collected in Ethiopia*, p. 1148; December 1, 2003, Hazel Rochman, review of *The Garbage King*, p. 667; May 1, 2004, John Peters, review of *Beautiful Bananas*, p. 1563.

Books for Keeps, January, 1998, George Hunt, review of *Forbidden Ground*, pp. 19-20; September, 1998, p. 22.

Bulletin of the Center for Children's Books, January, 1988, review of *The Road to Bethlehem*; October, 1989, p. 36.

Faces: People, Places, and Cultures, March, 1999, review of *Kiss the Dust*, p. 43.

Guardian (London, England), June 14, 2003, Diane Samuels, review of *The Garbage King*, p. 33, August 23, 2003, Fiachra Gibbons, "Children's Author Faces Jewish Wrath," p. 3; June 12, 2004, Nicola Morgan, review of *Paradise End*, p. 33; January 18, 2005, Lindsey Fraser, review of *Hot Rock Mountain*, p. 11.

Horn Book, July, 1989, review of *Loving Ben*, p. 77.

Independent (London, England), July 29, 2000, Susan Elkin, review of *When the World Began*, p. 11.

Junior Bookshelf, August, 1988, review of *Red Sky in the Morning*, p. 197.

Kirkus Reviews, October 1, 1989, p. 1476; March 1, 1990, p. 349; April 15, 1992, review of *Kiss the Dust*, p. 539; February 1, 2004, review of *Beautiful Bananas*, p. 135.

Magpies, July, 1999, Lyn Linning, "Know the Author: Elizabeth Laird," pp. 14-15.

New York Times Book Review, November 10, 1985, Vincent Crapanzano, review of *The Miracle Child: A Story from Ethiopia*; December 6, 1987, Rosemary L. Bray, review of *The Road to Bethlehem: A Nativity Story from Ethiopia*.

Publishers Weekly, January 11, 1991, review of *The Day Patch Stood Guard* and *The Day Sidney Ran off*, p. 100; April 27, 1992, review of *Kiss the Dust*, p. 269; January 4, 1999, review of *Secret Friends*, p. 91; April 10, 2000, review of *A Book of Promises*, p. 98; November 10, 2003, review of *The Garbage King*, p. 63; March 15, 2004, review of *Beautiful Bananas*, p. 74.

Race and Class, Imman Laksari-Adams, review of *A Little Piece of Ground*, p. 139.

School Librarian, spring, 1997, Chris Stephenson, review of *On the Run*, p. 34; November, 1997, Sarah Mears, review of *Forbidden Ground*, p. 21.

School Library Journal, September, 1989, Barbara Chatton, review of *Loving Ben*, p. 252; November, 2000, Ann Welton, review of *When the World Began*, p. 172; October, 2002, Jennifer Ralston, review of *Jake's Tower*, p. 168; December, 2003, Genevieve Gallagher, review of *The Garbage King*, p. 156; April, 2004, Margaret R. Tassia, review of *Beautiful Bananas*, p. 118.

Times Literary Supplement, November 29, 1985.

ONLINE

Jubilee Books, http://www.jubileebooks.co.uk/ (June, 2002), Joseph Pike, interview with Elizabeth Laird.

Staffordshire Learning Net, http://www.sln.org.uk/ english/ (February 1, 2005), Elizabeth Laird, "Hidden Riches from the Horn of Africa."

Barry Lopez

■ Personal

Born January 6, 1945, in Port Chester, NY; son of Adrian Bernard and Mary (Holstun) Lopez; married Sandra Jean Landers (a bookwright), June 10, 1967 (divorced, January 16, 1999). *Education:* University of Notre Dame, B.A. (cum laude), 1966, M.A.T., 1968; University of Oregon, graduate study, 1968-69.

■ Addresses

Home—OR. *Agent*—Steven Barclay Agency, 12 Western Ave., Petaluma, CA 04052

■ Career

Full-time writer, 1970—. Associate at Media Studies Center (formerly Gannett Foundation Media Center), Columbia University, New York, NY, 1985—; Eastern Washington University, Cheney, Distinguished Visiting Writer, 1985; University of Iowa, Iowa City, Ida Beam Visiting Professor, 1985; Carleton College, Northfield, MN, Distinguished Visiting Naturalist, 1986; University of Notre Dame, Notre Dame, IN, W. Harold and Martha Welch Visiting Professor of American Studies, 1989. Sino-American Writers Conference in China, delegate, 1988.

■ Member

PEN American Center, Authors Guild, Authors League of America, Poets and Writers.

■ Awards, Honors

John Burroughs Medal for distinguished natural history writing, Christopher Medal for humanitarian writing, and Pacific Northwest Booksellers award for excellence in nonfiction, all 1979, and American Book Award nomination, 1980, all for *Of Wolves and Men;* Distinguished Recognition Award, Friends of American Writers, 1981, for *Winter Count;* National Book Award in nonfiction, 1986; Christopher Book Award, Pacific Northwest Booksellers award, National Book Critics Circle award nomination, *Los Angeles Times* book award nomination, American Library Association notable book citation, *New York Times Book Review* Best Books listing, and American Library Association Best Books for Young Adults citation, all 1986, and Francis Fuller Victor Award in nonfiction from Oregon Institute of Literary Arts, 1987, all for *Arctic Dreams: Imagination and Desire in a Northern Landscape;* Award in Literature, American Academy and Institute of Arts and Letters, 1986, for body of work; Guggenheim fellow, 1987; National Science Foundation grants, 1987, 1988, 1991, 1992; L.H.D., Whittier College, 1988; Parents' Choice Award, 1990, for *Crow and Weasel;* Lannan Foundation Award in nonfiction, 1990, for body of work; Governor's Award for Arts, 1990; Best Geographic Educational Article designation, National Council for Geographic Education, 1990, for "The American Geographies"; L.H.D., University of Portland, 1994; Fiction Award, Pacific Northwest Booksellers, 1995; National Magazine Award in Fiction finalist, 1998, for "The Letters of Heaven"; Lannan residency fellowship, 1999; John Hay Award, Orion Society, 2002.

■ Writings

FICTION

Desert Notes: Reflections in the Eye of a Raven (fictional narratives; also see below), Sheed, Andrews & McMeel (Kansas City, KS), 1976.

Giving Birth to Thunder, Sleeping with His Daughter: Coyote Builds North America (Native American trickster stories), Sheed, Andrews & McMeel (Kansas City, KS), 1977.

River Notes: The Dance of Herons (fictional narratives; also see below), Andrews & McMeel (Kansas City, KS), 1979.

Winter Count, Scribner (New York, NY), 1981.

Crow and Weasel (fable), illustrated by Tom Pohrt, North Point Press, 1990.

Desert Notes: Reflections in the Eye of a Raven [and] *River Notes: The Dance of Herons*, Avon (New York, NY), 1990.

Field Notes: The Grace Note of the Canyon Wren, A. A. Knopf (New York, NY), 1994.

Lessons from the Wolverine (short story), illustrated by Tom Pohrt, University of Georgia Press (Athens, GA), 1997.

Light Action in the Caribbean (short stories), Knopf (New York, NY), 2000.

Resistance, Knopf (New York, NY), 2004.

"The Letters from Heaven" and "Ruben Mendoza Vega . . ." were produced in limited editions, Pacific Editions.

NONFICTION

Of Wolves and Men, Scribner (New York, NY), 1978.

Arctic Dreams: Imagination and Desire in a Northern Landscape, Scribner (New York, NY), 1986.

Crossing Open Ground (essays), Scribner (New York, NY), 1988.

The Rediscovery of North America, University Press of Kentucky (Lexington, KY), 1990.

Apologia (essay), University of Georgia Press (Athens, GA), 1998.

About This Life: Journeys on the Threshold of Memory, Random House (New York, NY), 1998.

OTHER

Desert Reservation (chapbook), Copper Canyon Press, 1980.

Coyote Love (chapbook), Coyote Love Press (Portland, ME), 1989.

(With Jim Leonard, Jr.) *Crow and Weasel* (play; adapted from Lopez's work of the same title), with music by John Luther Adams, produced at Children's Theatre, Minneapolis, MN, 1993.

Vintage Lopez (fiction and nonfiction selections), Vintage Books (New York, NY), 2004.

Also author of catalog essays for painter Alan Magee, 1990, potter Richard Rowland, 1997, and mask maker Lillian Pitt, 1999. Author of "Disturbing the Night," a short story included on CD *Dark Wood* by David Darling, ECM Records. Collaborator with photographer Frans Lanting on large-format calendars, BrownTrout Publishers, 1994-96. Work appears in numerous anthologies, including *On Nature: Nature, Landscape, and Natural History*, edited by Daniel Halpern, North Point Press, 1987, *Modern American Memoirs*, edited by Annie Dillard and Cort Conley, HarperCollins (New York, NY), 1995, and *Writers Harvest 3*, edited by Tobias Wolff and William Spruill, Dell (New York, NY), 2000.

Contributor to numerous periodicals, including *Harper's, New York Times, National Geographic, American Short Fiction*, and *Paris Review*. Correspondent, *Outside*, 1982—. Contributing editor, *North American Review*, 1977—, and *Harper's*, 1981-82, 1984—; guest editor of special section, "The American Indian Mind," for *Quest*, September-October, 1978; advisory editor, *Antaeus*, autumn, 1986.

Lopez's books have been translated into numerous languages, including Chinese, Dutch, Finnish, French, German, Italian, Japanese, Norwegian, Spanish, and Swedish.

■ Adaptations

Composer John Luther Adams consulted with Lopez and others to create a stage adaptation of *Giving Birth to Thunder*, which was performed in Juneau, AK, in 1987; three stories from *River Notes* have been recorded with accompanying music by cellist David Darling; portions of *Desert Notes* and *Arctic Dreams* have been adapted for the stage by modern dance companies. Many of Lopez's writings have been recorded as audio books.

■ Sidelights

Barry Lopez is a writer with a deep commitment to social issues involving the environment, natural history, and humankind's relationship to both. Lopez's work has been favorably compared to that of such distinguished naturalist authors as Edward Hoagland, Peter Matthiessen, and Edward Abbey. Early in his career, he focused on natural history in a traditional, scientific sense, but as his writing developed, he incorporated philosophical content as well. In such works as *Of Wolves and Men* and *Arctic Dreams: Imagination and Desire in a Northern Landscape* the author uses natural history as a metaphor for discussing larger moral issues. In his fiction, too, he explores man's relationship to his world. "A writer has a certain handful of questions," Lopez explained in a *Seattle Review* interview. "Mine seem to be the issues of tolerance and dignity. You can't sit down and write directly about those things, but if they are on your mind and if you're a writer, they're going to come out in one form or another." His award-winning work has proven popular with readers and critics. "For Lopez, nature is a religion, a source of orientation and inspiration," assessed a writer for the *Los Angeles Times Book Review,* while a *New York Times* reviewer stated that "Lopez possesses a deep, almost mystical reverence for nature and the land."

From Country to City

Lopez was born in Port Chester, New York, in 1945, but the family moved to California's San Fernando Valley three years later. Two years later, his parents divorced, and his father disappeared from the lives of Barry and his younger brother, Dennis. Their mother remained in California, working as a teacher and dressmaker to support the family. The two boys enjoyed playing outdoors in this pleasant, rural area. Their mother made a point of taking them on trips beyond their valley as well, driving on weekends to the desert, to lakes, and to coastal towns. During this time, he began to feel a bond with nature and animals. He once described this feeling: "I was mesmerized by animals and the other-than-obvious dimension of the natural world when I was a child. I grew up in a rural part of California, and I was around animals from the time I was very young…. Animals were very special to me." Lopez also enjoyed looking through the family's world atlas and planning extravagant journeys around the globe. "This early interest in travel and fascination with place descriptions manifested itself much later in his own writings, and his experience living in both rural and urban landscapes proved to be crucial to his development as a writer," commented Susan M. Lucas in *Dictionary of Literary Biography.*

Lopez was eleven years old when his mother married Adrian Bernard Lopez, who adopted the two boys. Their new stepfather soon moved the family across the country to live in a Manhattan penthouse. The change in lifestyle could hardly have been more dramatic, but Lopez adapted well to his new world. He attended a Catholic preparatory school that emphasized the arts and "cultivated a skepticism of authoritative ways of knowing—two traits that still mark his thinking," commented Lucas. He excelled academically there, became a letterman in three varsity sports, and was president of his senior class. After graduation, he spent the summer traveling around Europe with a group of classmates. In the fall he began his freshman year at Notre Dame. On the weekends he continued to follow his urge to travel, taking frequent road trips. By the time he graduated in 1966, he had visited every state in the union except for Alaska, Hawaii, and Oklahoma.

Beginning to write seriously during his last two years at Notre Dame, Lopez published a few short

In this collection of short fiction, first published in 1981, Lopez examines humankind's relationship with nature.

stories and articles during his senior year. He felt certain he wanted writing to be his profession, but he knew that he would also need some other means of support. For a time he considered entering a monastery, for it was crucial to him to feel he would be leading a life of service. But in 1967, he married Sandra Landers and returned to Notre Dame for a master's degree, having decided to teach. In 1968, they moved west so that Lopez could earn a master's in fine arts at the University of Oregon. As it turned out, he spent only one semester in that program, but he did get a chance to study with legendary folklorist Barre Toelken. Toelken had a profound influence on Lopez, introducing him to anthropological research and opening up his world view. His first book, *Giving Birth to Thunder, Sleeping with His Daughter* came out of his graduate studies in folklore. The work, which includes sixty-eight stories about the fabled creature, provides Lopez's English-language adaptations of oral Indian tales.

Describing the essence of Coyote in the book's introduction, Lopez wrote that the character "was not necessarily a coyote, nor even a creature of strict physical dimensions. He was known as the Great Hare among many eastern tribes and as Raven in the Pacific Northwest.... He was Trickster, Imitator, First Born, Old Man, First Creator, Transformer and Changing Person in the white man's translations— all names derived from his powers, his habits and his acts." Quoting early twentieth-century Swiss psychologist and psychiatrist Carl Jung, Lopez noted that Coyote "was 'in his earliest manifestations, a faithful copy of an absolutely undifferentiated human consciousness, corresponding to a psyche that has hardly left the animal eye. He is,' continued Jung, 'a forerunner of the savior, and like him, God, man and animal at once. He is both subhuman and superhuman, a bestial and divine being.'" The tales presented in the work provide vivid descriptions of Coyote's adventures, whether as trickster, jester, creator, or hero. The situations in which Coyote finds himself range from his building of the earth and universe, to his deception of others for personal gain, to his humiliation as his outrageous pranks backfire. Featuring the legends of a number of Native American tribes—such as the Menomini, Arapaho, Blackfoot, Cheyenne, Plains Cree, and Nez Perce—*Giving Birth to Thunder* has been acknowledged by critics as a comprehensive study of Coyote, complete with details of a sexual nature that are frequently omitted from similar works. Such depictions include Coyote's marriage to his stepdaughter, his wife-swapping with a beaver, and his matrimony with a man.

In presenting the stories, Lopez tries to remain as true to the original tales as he can without violating sacred tribal customs associated with the telling.

His success in this endeavor is described in the book's foreword, written by former *Journal of American Folklore* editor J. Barre Toelken: *Giving Birth to Thunder* "does not pretend to be an 'Indian book.' It does not provide the original language, the ritual detail, the full context; in short, it does not betray the magic of the actual storytelling event. Instead, the stories are retold in a way that is both faithful to native concepts of Coyote and how his stories should go." For example, in the Wasco Indian fable "Coyote Places the Stars," Lopez describes five wolf brothers who see two animals in the night sky and want to investigate. Coyote assists them by shooting many arrows into the air, which stick to one another and form a ladder from the earth into space. When the wolves and a pet dog climb into the sky with Coyote, they discover the two animals are grizzly bears. Initially apprehensive, the wolves and dog eventually sit with the bears. Lopez explained: "Coyote wouldn't come over. He didn't trust the bears. 'That makes a nice picture, though,' thought Coyote. 'They all look pretty good sitting there like that. I think I'll leave it that way for everyone to see. Then when people look at them in the sky they will say, "There's a story about that picture," and they will tell a story about me....' He took out the arrows as he descended so there was no way for anyone to get back.... They call those stars the Big Dipper now."

Giving Birth to Thunder is dedicated "To the Native Peoples of North America that we may now share a little of each other's laughter in addition to all our tears." Described by Toelken as a nonscholarly work, although it contains bibliographic notes for further study, the book fared well with reviewers. A critic for *Publishers Weekly* praised the work for providing a glimpse of the "lighthearted side of Indian culture." A *Kliatt* reviewer, observing the book's nonacademic nature, called the stories "vulgar, amusing, ironic, and philosophical." The critic further stated that "each short tale is delightful," providing illumination into the various forms of Native American oral tradition. A commentator for *Choice* magazine lauded the author's "clear, concise prose."

Shift to Journalism

After compiling *Giving Birth to Thunder*, Lopez quit graduate school in 1969, opting to pursue a career as a full-time, freelance writer. Taking up permanent residence in Oregon with his wife, Sandra, the author began preparing articles for a variety of periodicals, including the *New York Times*, *Popular Science*, and *Washington Post*. He also established a solid reputation as an environmental writer through his features for the Audubon Society, Sierra Club, and Not Man Apart publications. Initiating a long association as a writer for *Harper's* and *North American Review,* he also penned some original folktales and reworked Native American legends for issuance in magazines such as *Northwest Review, Contemporary Literature in Transition, Tales,* and *Chouteau Review.* His list of publications expanded during the mid-1970s and 1980s to include the *New York Times Book Review, Outside, Vogue, GEO, National Geographic,* and *Life.* Speaking of his choice to pursue a freelance writing career, Lopez told Douglas Marx of *Publishers Weekly,* "In journalism, to write an editorial, for example, you sat down at a table that had a typewriter bolted to it, and the task was to write in 600 words something that was coherent and convincing. And you sat there until you did it. I like journalism because it's a grown-up world—deadlines, responsibilities. Freelance writing forces you to focus on the responsibility you have to write cleanly and clearly. It inclines against self-indulgence."

A 1974 assignment for *Smithsonian* magazine led to Lopez's first major book, *Of Wolves and Men.* His research for that article "catalyzed a lot of thinking about human and animal relationships which had been going on in a vague way in my mind for several years," he explained in an interview. "I realized that if I focused on this one animal, I might be able to say something sharp and clear." In his book, Lopez attempts to present a complete portrait of the wolf. He includes not only scientific information but also wolf lore from aboriginal societies and an overview of the animal's role in literature, folklore, and superstition.

The result, noted many critics, is a book that succeeds on several levels. First, Lopez has gathered "an extraordinary amount of material," wrote a contributor to the *New York Review of Books,* making *Of Wolves and Men* one of the most comprehensive sources of information on these animals ever published. Second, in showing readers the many diverse images of the wolf, the author reveals how man "creates" animals by projecting aspects of his own personality onto them. Third, Lopez illustrates how undeserved is Western civilization's depiction of the wolf as a ruthless killer. His observations showed him that the Eskimos' conception of the wolf is much closer to the truth; among them, wolves are respected and emulated for their intelligence and strong sense of loyalty. What society thinks about the wolf may reveal something about itself, concludes Lopez, for while Western man has reviled the wolf as a wanton killer, he himself has brutally and pointlessly driven many animals to extinction. Whitley Streiber, writing for the *Washington Post,* called *Of Wolves and Men* "a very important book by a man who has thought much on his

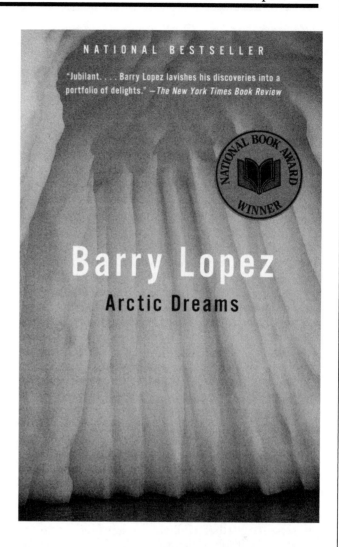

This 1986 work, winner of the National Book Award for nonfiction, examines the wonders of the Far North.

subject. Above all he has listened to many people who claim to know about wolves. In coming to terms with the difference between what we know and what we imagine about the wolf, Lopez has shed light on some painful truths about the human experience. By laying no blame while facing the tragedy for what it is, he has made what we have done to the wolf a source of new knowledge about man."

Arctic Dreams Wins National Book Award

Lopez found that he was strongly drawn to the Arctic even after *Of Wolves and Men* was completed. Over the next four years he made several more trips north, and in 1986 he published an account of his travels titled *Arctic Dreams: Imagination and Desire in a Northern Landscape,* which won the National Book Award for nonfiction that same year. While the book provides a wealth of factual information about the Arctic region, it is, according to a *New York Times* reviewer, "a book about the Arctic North in the way that 'Moby-Dick' is a novel about whales." In *Arctic Dreams* Lopez restates the deeper themes found in *Of Wolves and Men,* but while *Of Wolves and Men* focused tightly on man's relationship with a specific animal, *Arctic Dreams*'s scope is wider, exploring man's relationship with what Lopez refers to as "the landscape." He explained to Jim Aton in *Western American Literature,* "By landscape I mean the complete lay of the land—the animals that are there, the trees, the vegetation, the quality of soils, the drainage pattern of water, the annual cycles of temperature, the kinds of precipitation, the sounds common to the region."

Arctic Dreams drew many favorable reviews, both for its vivid descriptions of the North and for the questions it raises about man's place in nature. "The writing, at times, is luminous, powerful and musical. Lopez infuses each sentence with grace," stated a writer in the Toronto *Globe & Mail.* "It is a lyrical geography and natural history, an account of Eskimo life, and a history of northern explorations," said a *Los Angeles Times Book Review* contributor. "But mainly, it is a . . . reflection about the meaning of mankind's encounter with the planet. . . . Its question, starting as ecology and working into metaphysics, is whether civilization can find a way of adapting itself to the natural world, before its predilection for adapting the natural world to itself destroys self and world, both." Lopez elaborated on the feelings that prompted him to write *Arctic Dreams* in his interview with Aton: "I think if you can really see the land, if you can lose your sense of wishing it to be what you want it to be, if you can strip yourself of the desire to order and to name and see the land entirely for itself, you see in the relationship of all its elements the face of God. And that's why I say the landscape has an authority."

Fiction Wins Recognition

Man's interactions with "the landscape" are often highlighted in Lopez's fiction as well as in his nonfiction, and his short story collections have drawn particular praise from reviewers. For example, in a *Detroit News* review of *River Notes: The Dance of Herons,* David Graber wrote: "Lopez delicately surveys the terrain of shared experience between a man and place, in this case a river in the Pacific North-

west. . . . [The author] has an unsentimental naturalist's knowledge combined with profound love-of-land. . . . [His] writing has a dreamlike quality; the sensuality of his words, his . . . playful choice of simile serve as counterpoint to his precisely accurate portrayals of salmon spawning and herons fishing, of Douglas fir falling to the chainsaw and willow crowding the riverbank." A *Miami Herald* writer said that in *River Notes* "Lopez transmogrifies the physical characteristics of the river—the bend, the falls, the shallows, the rapids—into human experience: the bend as a man seriously ill for a long time who suddenly, for no reason as the river bends for no reason, decides he will recover. The falls is a strangely gothic convolution of the original fall from grace, brought up to date by a vagabond with mythic yearnings who ends his search at the high brink of the river's falls. . . . Lopez's nice shallows become deep reflecting mirrors, their images multiplying beyond ease. . . . Not since Ken Kesey's drastically different novel, *Sometimes a Great Notion,* has a writer so caught and pinned the mossy melancholy of Oregon." In his *Progressive* review, David Miller made the point that, despite the book's deceptively simple title, it is no mere study of herons. He wrote that *River Notes* "is about a small world of relationships among people, herons, salmon, cottonwoods—and all creatures drawn to this rushing, tumbling, powerful, and endangered emblem of natural life, the river. . . . [The book] is a thing of beauty in itself, as tantalizingly real and yet as otherworldly as your own reflection on a river's surface. . . . It is a rare achievement; perhaps—I've never said this before and know that only time will tell—it is a work of genius."

A *Saturday Review* commentator believed that *Winter Count,* another collection of short fiction, is the book that will win for Lopez "recognition as a writer who like, say, Peter Matthiessen or Edward Hoagland, goes to the wilderness in order to clarify a great deal about civilization." Cheuse commends Lopez for weaving "a style reminiscent of some important contemporary Latin American magical realists" and for turning "the sentiments of a decade's worth of ecology lovers into a deeply felt and unnervingly powerful picture of reality." A *Los Angeles Times* reviewer wrote: "There's a boundary, no wider than a pinstripe, where fact and fiction barely touch. With so much room on either side and assorted areas where overlap is expected, few writers choose to confine themselves to that fine line where the two simply meet. Lopez is one of those few. He makes that delicate border his entire territory. *Winter Count* is a small and perfectly crafted collection of just such encounters between imagination and reality. . . . Lopez's observations are so acute the stories expand of their own accord, lingering in the mind the way intense light lingers on the retina." A *New York Times Book Review* contributor said that *Winter Count* is "full of solid, quiet, telling short works. Each of the stories . . . is as economical in design, as painstakingly crafted and as resonant as a good classical guitar. . . . [Lopez's] fiction is as spare, as pared down and elemental as the lives it describes, the values it celebrates. One of his characters says, 'I've thrown away everything that is no good,' and this perilously righteous algorithm seems a key part of the author's own epic."

Lopez revised a number of previously published essays for 1988's *Crossing Open Ground*, which includes writings about Alaska, the American Southwest, Native American culture, folklore, endangered species, and other topics of environmental importance. Showcasing Lopez's reverence for the natural world, the volume presents the author's belief that in harming nature, we only cripple ourselves. These writings also denote Lopez's notion that western civilization generally lacks the proper respect for nature, suggesting that many people are at odds with the environment. All too often, Lopez offers, humans fail to realize their kinship and relationship with nature—that they are a part of the earth. In *Crossing Open Ground*, Lopez is "a clear and patient observer," announced a *Time* reviewer. Proclaiming the volume "intimate" and "inviting," *New York Times Book Review* contributor Edwin Dobb suggested that Lopez's esays will "both delight and alarm."

In 1990 Lopez wrote a novella-length fable, *Crow and Weasel,* composed in the form of a Native American tale and illustrated by Tom Pohrt, an artist Lopez had met ten years earlier. "When I first came across Tom's line drawings, I could see that he saw animals in a different way than any artist ever had," recalled Lopez in an interview with *Publishers Weekly* contributor Michael Coffey. "I was intrigued." *Crow and Weasel,* the result of their first collaboration, became a bestseller. The story charts the adventures of two young men during a time when animals and humans spoke a universal language. In order to evoke this mythical time and place, Lopez and Pohrt describe the protagonists as human in the text and depict them as a crow and weasel adorned in Indian attire in the illustrations. A coming-of-age saga, the book follows the characters as they embark on their spiritual and physical journey—"to travel farther north than anyone had ever gone, farther north than their people's stories went." The work interweaves a moral outlook about the land and its inhabitants in the youths' quest to understand the earth and themselves.

In *The Rediscovery of North America,* Lopez charts the progression of environmental pillage from the hands of the Spanish, to nineteenth-century industrialists and twentieth-century entrepreneurs. He records the continuation of abusive treatment bestowed upon indigenous peoples, flora and fauna, land, and other natural resources in the name of greed. Contending that humankind needs to regain respect for the earth and all its inhabitants, Lopez urges readers "to be intimate with the land" and to "rediscover" its worth. "What we need is to discover the continent again," Lopez concluded in the book. "We need to see the land with a less acquisitive frame of mind. We need to sojourn in it again, to discover the lineaments of cooperation with it. We need to discover the difference between the kind of independence that is a desire to be responsible to no one but the self—the independence of the adolescent—and the independence that means the assumption of responsibility in society, the indepen-

VINTAGE LOPEZ

This 2004 volume presents both fiction and nonfiction from three decades of writing.

dence of people who no longer need to be supervised. We need to be more discerning about the sources of wealth. And we need to find within ourselves, and nurture, a profound courtesy, an un-alloyed honesty."

In *Field Notes* Lopez presented a collection of twelve stories, completing a trilogy that also includes *Desert Notes* and *River Notes*. Critics emphasized the collection's portrayal of civilized man at odds with the natural world, noting Lopez's imaginative combination of elements of folklore, myth, and natural science. A writer for the *New York Times Book Review* praised the "purity and power of Mr. Lopez's imagery." In all the stories, characters must deal with extreme situations: tragedy, grief, brushes with death. Nature seems to provide divine guidance, as in the story "Introduction: Within Birds' Hearing," in which the song of a wren leads a man, lost in the desert and near death, to some life-giving water.

In 1998 Lopez published *About This Life: Journeys on the Threshold of Memory*, a collection of essays written during the period from 1981-1998. With the exception of four new pieces, the essays were originally published in periodicals, including *Harpers* and *North American Review*. Reviewing the collection for *Antioch Review*, Carolyn Maddux commented positively on Lopez's penchant for digression into "the mythic or metaphysical," writing that the author's "prose is always more than natural history, exposition, autobiography." Maddux concluded: "The seventeen pieces vary widely in form, though they have in common Lopez's characteristic lucidity of prose. Here is delight for the connoisseur of essays."

Lopez demonstrated his range when he published *Light Action in the Caribbean*, a work praised by Donna Seaman in *Booklist* as a "breath-takingly luminous and versatile collection, Lopez's strongest book of fiction to date." Many of the stories in the book are narrated by men who are trying to improve their understanding of life by applying themselves to a craft, or by reflecting on nature. In one, a prison inmate sets others free with this prayers and his storytelling; in another, a lawyer retreats to a monastery and becomes absorbed in building a very special model ship. In yet another, a gardener disturbs his clients with his great generosity. "The stories here are terse and tough and offer food for thought," affirmed Robert E. Brown in *Library Journal*.

Resistance, published in 2004, serves as another significant addition to Lopez's fiction canon. Set in a world dominated by fundamentalism and capital-

If you enjoy the works of Barry Lopez, you may also want to check out the following books:

Edward Abbey, *Down the River*, 1982.
Annie Dillard, *The Living*, 1992.
Farley Mowat, *High Latitudes*, 2002.

ism, the book is comprised of nine vignettes, each narrated by someone who has been detained by the fictional Office of Inland Security. The book's characters are all activists of some sort, and are charged with the crime of terrorizing the imagination of the citizenry; for their own part, each narrator recalls the moment when he or she realized the injustices of the world. *Library Journal* reviewer David Hellman found this book marred by some "heavy-handed polemics," and warned that many of the narrators seem "self-absorbed and unpleasantly righteous." A *Publishers Weekly* writer took a more enthusiastic view of the book, explaining: "Passionate in feeling but cool in rhetoric, these testimonials feel like haunting fragments of committed lives; though not always satisfying as straight fiction, they are powerful as artistic argument." Seaman also lauded *Resistance*, declaring: "Dramatic, unique, and provocative, these are essential stories for polarized times."

Discussing his fiction with Aton, Lopez commented: "My interest in a story is to illuminate a set of circumstances that bring some understanding of human life, enough at least so that a reader can identify with it and draw some vague sense of hope or sustenance or deep feeling and in some way be revived." He stated that it was very important to him "to go into a story with a capacity for wonder, where I know I can derive something 'wonder-full' and then bring this into the story so that a reader can feel it and say, 'I am an adult. I have a family, I pay bills, I live in a world of chicanery and subterfuge and atomic weaponry and inhumanity and round-heeled politicians and garrulous, insipid television personalities, but still I have wonder. I have been brought to a state of wonder by contact with something in a story.'" In his interview with Marx, he emphasized the centrality of writing and storytelling in his life, saying: "My themes will always be dignity of life, structures of prejudice, passion, generosity, kindness and the possibility of the good life in dark circumstances."

■ Biographical and Critical Sources

BOOKS

Cooley, J., editor, *Earthly Words: Essays on Contemporary American Nature and Environmental Writers,* University of Michigan Press (Ann Arbor, MI), 1994.

Dictionary of Literary Biography, Volume 256: *Twentieth-Century American Western Writers, Third Series,* Gale (Detroit, MI), 2002; Volume 275: *Twentieth-Century American Nature Writers: Prose,* Gale (Detroit, MI), 2003.

Lopez, Barry Holstun, *Arctic Dreams: Imagination and Desire in a Northern Landscape* (nonfiction), Scribner (New York, NY), 1986.

Lopez, Barry Holstun, *About This Life: Journeys on the Threshold of Memory,* Random House (New York, NY), 1998.

Lueders, Edward, editor, *Writing Natural History: Dialogues with Authors,* University of Utah Press (Salt Lake City, UT), 1989.

O'Connell, Nicholas, *At the Field's End: Interviews with Twenty Pacific Northwest Writers,* Madrona, 1987.

Paul, Sherman, *Hewing to Experience: Essays and Reviews on Recent American Poetry and Poetics, Nature and Culture,* University of Iowa Press (Iowa City, IA), 1989.

PERIODICALS

Albuquerque Journal, June 27, 2004, David Steinberg, review of *Resistance,* p. F6.

Alternatives Journal, spring, 1999, Martin von Mirbach, review of *About This Life: Journeys on the Threshold of Memory,* p. 37.

Antioch Review, winter, 1999, Carolyn Maddux, review of *About This Life,* p. 103.

Atlanta Journal-Constitution, August 8, 2004, Carlo Wolff, review of *Resistance,* p. L4.

Backpacker, August, 1995, Jeff Rennicke, review of *Field Notes: The Grace Note of the Canyon Wren,* p. 94.

Bloomsbury Review, January-February, 1990; January-February, 1998.

Booklist, April, 1998, Donna Seaman, review of *About This Life,* p. 1276; December 1, 1998, p. 627; December 15, 1998, p. 720; December 1, 1999, p. 681; October 15, 2000, Donna Seaman, review of *Light Action in the Caribbean,* p. 418; May 1, 2004, Donna Seaman, review of *Resistance,* p. 1547.

Chicago Tribune, November 5, 1978; March 30, 1986.

Choice, October, 1978, review of *Giving Birth to Thunder, Sleeping with His Daughter: Coyote Builds North America,* p. 1051.

Christian Science Monitor, February 12, 1979.

Commonweal, March 24, 2000, Nicholas O'Connell, "At One with the Natural World," p. 11.

Denver Post, June 13, 2004, Ron Franscell, review of *Resistance,* p. F11.

Detroit News, November 4, 1979.

English Journal, April, 1989.

Environmental Journal, January-February, 1991.

Esquire, November, 1994, p. 136.

Gazette (Colorado Springs, CO), April 11, 2005, Dave Philipps, "Author Poses Concerns over Man's 'Progress,'" p. L1.

Globe & Mail (Toronto, Ontario, Canada), May 31, 1986.

Grand Rapids Press (Grand Rapids, MI), August 1, 2004, Maria Sudekum Fisher, review of *Resistance,* p. J6.

Guardian, April 2, 2005, Robert Macfarlane, "Robert Macfarlane on Barry Lopez, Whose Language Grips an Arctic Wilderness Now under Threat," p. 36.

Harper's, December, 1984.

Kirkus Reviews, April 15, 2004, review of *Resistance,* p. 352.

Kliatt, fall, 1981, review of *Giving Birth to Thunder,* pp. 31-32.

Library Journal, May 15, 1998, Nancy Patterson, review of *About This Life,* p. 86; January, 2000, p. 141; October 1, 2000, Robert E. Brown, review of *Light Action in the Caribbean,* p. 149; June 15, 2004, David Hellman, review of *Resistance,* p. 59.

Los Angeles Times, November 12, 1978; May 9, 1981.

Los Angeles Times Book Review, March 2, 1986; February 14, 1988; April 2, 1995, p. 6; September 17, 1995, p. 8.

Miami Herald, September 30, 1979; March 29, 1986.

Missouri Review, Volume 11, number 3, 1988.

Nation, November 11, 1978.

New Republic, June 30, 1979.

Newsweek, October 16, 1978.

New Yorker, February 26, 1979; March 17, 1986; November 26, 1990.

New York Review of Books, October 12, 1978.

New York Times, January 4, 1979; February 12, 1986; March 29, 1986; July 4, 2004, Jeff Turrentine, review of *Resistance,* p. 16.

New York Times Book Review, November 19, 1978; June 14, 1981; February 16, 1986; April 24, 1988, Edwin Dobb, review of *Crossing Open Ground;* November 25, 1990; November 20, 1994, p. 22; June 21, 1998, p. 6.

North Dakota Quarterly, winter, 1988.

Observer (London, England), June 24, 1979.

Orion Nature Quarterly, summer, 1990.

Pacific Northwest, March-April, 1980.

Poets and Writers, March-April, 1994.

Progressive, May, 1980, David Miller, review of *River Notes.*

Publishers Weekly, January 16, 1978, review of *Giving Birth to Thunder,* p. 83; October 11, 1985; June 23, 1989; July 27, 1990, Michael Coffey, interview with Lopez; September 26, 1994, Douglas Marx, interview with Lopez, p. 41; May 11, 1998, review of *About This Life,* p. 57; September 7, 1998, p. 97; January 10, 2000, p. 46; May 22, 2000, p. 90; May 3, 2004, review of *Resistance,* p. 167.

Register-Guard (Eugene, OR), April 21, 2002, Kimber Williams, "Natural Reaction," p. L1.

St. Petersburg Times, May 24, 2004, Carlo Wolff, review of *Resistance,* p. 1E.

Saturday Review, April, 1981, Alan Cheuse, review of *Winter Count.*

Seattle Post-Intelligencer, June 4, 2004, Scott Driscoll, review of *Resistance,* p. 24.

Seattle Review, fall, 1985, Nick O'Connell, interview with Lopez.

Sierra, November, 1998, p. 58.

Star Tribune (Minneapolis, MN), October 10, 2004, Kristin Tillotson, review of *Resistance,* p. 11F.

Studies in Short Fiction, summer, 1996, David Starkey, review of *Field Notes,* p. 433.

Time, March 10, 1986, review of *Arctic Dreams,* p. 74; February 29, 1988, review of *Crossing Open Ground,* p. 90; October 10, 1994, p. 90.

Times Literary Supplement, December 7, 1979; August 8, 1986.

Tribune Books (Chicago, IL), November 23, 1979.

U.S. Catholic, June, 1998, Maureen Abood, "God between the Lines: Five Writers of Fiction, Nonfiction, and Poetry Talk about the Spiritual Source of Their Art," pp. 18-24.

Washington Post, November 27, 1978; November 18, 1986; November 24, 1986.

Washington Post Book World, March 9, 1986.

Western American Literature, spring, 1986, Jim Aton, interview with Lopez.

World Literature Today, fall, 1997, p. 800.

ONLINE

12Gauge.com, http://www.12gauge.com/ (February 1, 2005), Mark Mordue, interview with Lopez.

Calypso Consulting Web site, http://www.calypso consulting.com/lopez.htm/ (February 1, 2005), interview with Lopez.

January Online, http://www.januarymagazine.com/ (April, 2001), Linda Richards, interview with Lopez.

OTHER

Barry Lopez Interview with Kay Bonetti (audio recording), American Audio Prose Library (Columbia, MO), 1985.*

Sam Mendes

■ Personal

Born August 1, 1965, in Reading, Berkshire, England; son of Jameson Peter (a university professor) and Valery Helene (a children's book author; maiden name, Barnett) Mendes; married Kate Winslet (an actress), May, 2003; children: Joe. *Education:* Cambridge University, 1987.

■ Addresses

Home—Stow-on-the-Wold, Cotswolds, England.

■ Career

Director of theater and film. Chichester Festival Theatre, director of stage productions, including *Cherry Orchard;* Royal Shakespeare Company, director of productions including *Troilus and Cressida* and *Richard III;* Donmar Warehouse Theatre, London, England, artistic director, 1992-2002, director of productions, including *The Glass Menagerie, Cabaret,* and *Blue Room;* director of *Gypsy,* 2004. Director of films, including *American Beauty,* 1999, and *Road to Perdi-* *tion,* 2002. Scamp Productions (theatre and film production company), cofounder, 2004. Director of advertising shorts for eBay, 2004.

■ Awards, Honors

London Critics Circle Award, 1989, Best Newcomer for *Cherry Orchard;* London Critics Circle Theatre Award, Best Director, 1995, for *The Glass Menagerie,* and 2002, for *Uncle Vanya* and *Twelfth Night;* Laurence Olivier Theatre Award, 1996, for *The Glass Menagerie,* 2003, for Artistic Contributions and for Best Director, for *Twelfth Night* and *Uncle Vanya;* Academy Award for Best Director, Amanda Award (Norway) for Best Foreign Feature Film, British Academy of Film and Television Artists Award for best director nominee, Broadcast Film Critics Association Award for Best Director, Chicago Film Critics Association Award for Best Director, Dallas-Forth Work Film Critics Association award for Best Director, Directors Guild of America Award for Outstanding Directorial Achievement, and Golden Globe Award for Best Director, all 2000, all for *American Beauty;* named commander, Order of the British Empire, 2000; London *Evening Standard* Theatre Award for Best Director, 2002, for *Uncle Vanya* and *Twelfth Night.*

■ Writings

FILM DIRECTOR

Cabaret (television film), British Broadcasting Corporation, 1993.

Company (television film), British Broadcasting Corporation, 1996.

American Beauty, Dreamworks, 1999.

Road to Perdition, Twentieth Century-Fox, 2002.

STAGE DIRECTOR

The Cherry Orchard, produced by Royal Shakespeare Company, 1989.

The Plough and the Stars, produced by Royal Shakespeare Company, 1991.

Troilus and Cressida, produced by Royal Shakespeare Company, 1991.

The Alchemist, produced by Royal Shakespeare Company, 1991.

The Sea, produced at National Theatre Company,1991.

The Rise and Fall of Little Voice, produced at Lyttleton Theatre, 1992.

Assassins, produced by Royal Shakespeare Company, 1992.

Richard III, produced by Royal Shakespeare Company, 1993.

The Tempest, produced by Royal Shakespeare Company 1993.

The Birthday Party, produced at Lyttelton Theatre, 1994.

Cabaret, produced by Royal Shakespeare Company,1994; produced on Broadway, 1996.

Oliver!, produced at London Palladium, 1994.

The Glass Menagerie, produced, 1995.

Company, produced, 1996.

The Fix, produced, 1997.

Othello, produced by Royal Shakespeare Company, 1998.

The Blue Room, produced in London, England, 1998.

Wise Guys, produced in London, 2000.

To the Green Fields and Beyond, produced, 2000.

Uncle Vanya, produced, 2002.

Twelfth Night, produced by Royal Shakespeare Company, 2002.

Gypsy, produced in London, England, 2003, produced on Broadway, 2004.

■ **Work in Progress**

Directing films *Jarhead, Sweeney Todd,* and *The Kite Runner;* directing *Shrek, the Musical*

■ **Sidelights**

Dubbed "Britain's answer to Orson Welles" by *Spectator* contributor Toby Young, theater and film director Sam Mendes, like Welles, made a name for

himself directing Shakespeare fresh out of college. By the age of twenty-three he had two hits running simultaneously on London's West End, went on to the Royal Shakespeare Company for half a decade, and developed a "craft free of theatrical folderol," as *Time*'s Richard Zoglin noted. Still in his twenties, Mendes was made artistic director of the Donmar Warehouse Theatre in London, turning it into a chic theatrical haven. From theater, Mendes, again like Welles, progressed to film with great success, winning an Academy Award for his debut directorial job with the 1999 movie *American Beauty,* and garnering further praise for his direction of the 2002 film *Road to Perdition,* starring Paul Newman and Tom Hanks.

"Wunderkind" is another term often bandied about in connection with Mendes, whose productions of *Cabaret* and *The Blue Room* charmed audiences on both sides of the Atlantic. In early 2003, he scored a brilliant triumph, winning three Olivier awards for his directorial work in the theatre. That same year he left the Donmar behind and set out with his own production company, Scamp, producing both theatre work and film. Married to film star Kate Winslet, Mendes also became a father in late 2003. Comparing the relative strengths of both film and theatre, Mendes, as quoted by *New Yorker* contributor Hilton Als, has said, "Movies live and breathe and walk among us. . . . Theatre lives in the

Theater and film director Mendes first made his mark at age twenty-three with his production of *The Cherry Orchard,* **for which he received the London Critics Circle Award.**

memory, which can be very powerful, but is not the same. A movie puts you in the center of the culture. And that's the challenge—the game. You are playing with immortality."

The Only Child

Mendes was born in 1965, in Reading, England, where his father was a university professor of English and his mother wrote children's books. There were further literary connections in the Mendes line: his grandfather, Alfred Mendes, wrote novels and helped found the literary magazine *Beacon* in Trinidad. His childhood was marred by the divorce of his parents in 1970; he thereafter lived with his mother and early on attended Magdalene College in Oxford. There he developed a love of sport, both cricket and soccer, as well as of reading and watching movies. At age fourteen his mother took him to see a Royal Shakespeare Company production of *The Merchant of Venice* at Stratford upon Avon. At first uncomfortable in the theater with his mother, Mendes soon came to love the experience. "The theatre became a stabilizing influence in a rather unstable childhood," he told Valerie Grove of the London *Times.*

Graduating from prep school, he took a year off to work at the Guggenheim in Venice, and by the time he entered Cambridge University he had decided to major in English. During his years at Cambridge, Mendes became involved in the theater, directing student productions, which sparked an interest in the young man for a career in drama. In 1987, after graduating from Cambridge, he took a low-level production job at the Chichester Theatre, hired more for his athletic prowess than his theatre skills, for the director of Chichester wanted a good cricket player on his team to take on that of the Royal Shakespeare Company.

A Life in the Theater

In any event, his job with Chichester opened doors for him; when a director was sick, he was able to stand in for him and directed a Chekhov play to rave reviews. Thereafter, Mendes was given his own theatre to work with. He was just twenty-three years old. Then came work with various London theaters, directing *London Assurance* and *The Cherry Orchard* in the same season. The latter play starred the famous British actress Judi Dench, and won him his first London Critics Circle Award, introducing him as a new director to be reckoned with. Work with the Royal Shakespeare Company followed, direct-

Mendes's revival of the stage musical *Cabaret* in the mid-1990s thrilled audiences on both sides of the Atlantic.

ing actors such as Ralph Fiennes in *Troilus and Cressida,* an "arresting production," according to Jeremy Kingston in the London *Times.* Then in 1992 he was offered the artistic directorship of the new Donmar Warehouse, a leading non-profit studio theater in London, and over the next decade he turned that into one of the best stages in London. As Matt Wolf noted in the *Times,* Mendes's direction was successful in "spawning numerous West End and Broadway hits and turning a 251 seat studio playhouse into a venue whose influence is vastly disproportionate to its size." Susannah Clapp of the *New Statesman* quoted Mendes as saying that he wanted to create "a huge experience in a small room."

One of his biggest successes at the Donmar was a revival of the musical *Cabaret,* which traveled to Broadway in 1998. Zoglin found that the Mendes version of the play "is likely to give it a jolt. The sex is raw and upfront." *Variety*'s Chris Jones felt that "Mendes is clearly trying to rescue what he sees as the dark soul of *Cabaret* from the layers of showbiz kitsch that have shrouded its sharp-edged portrait of decadent Berlin on the cusp of Nazi domination." Jones further noted, "Mendes' ideas not only work very well, but have the effect of making one reconsider the dramaturgy of a Broadway masterpiece that has a narrative sophistication well beyond the more transitory appeal of its splashy production numbers." Another transatlantic hit was *The Blue Room,* an adaptation of an Arthur Schnitzler play, which featured film actress Nicole Kidman in the buff.

From the Stage to Film

When Steven Spielberg saw Mendes's production of *Cabaret,* he knew he had his director for a new film project. In 1999 Mendes took on the role of film director with the movie *American Beauty,* which is about the mid-life crisis of Lester Burnham, who

falls in love with a sexy young cheerleader and turns his life upside down in order to consummate his desire for her. Shot for only $15 million, the film earned $350 million. Part of the reason for the movie's success was the fact that Mendes identified strongly with the project. It had "resonance with his own suburban upbringing," as Jeff Dawson noted in the London *Sunday Times.* The depiction of Lester's dysfunctional family also had reverberations for Mendes with his own family.

Critical opinion varied on the quality of the movie, but most reviewers had praise for Mendes's directorial debut. While *Commonweal*'s Richard Alleva argued that "you can't make a masterpiece by cartooning some of your characters while insisting that the rest be taken as three-dimensional," the critic went on to note that *American Beauty* "is the best nonmasterpiece I've seen in a long, long time." *Nation* reviewer Stuart Klawans was less complimentary, however, commenting that Mendes "seems to lack any instinct for linking one shot to another."

Kevin Spacey and Annette Bening starred in the Academy Award-winning 1999 film *American Beauty,* Mendes's major motion picture debut.

If you enjoy the works of Sam Mendes, you may also want to check out the following films:

Miller's Crossing, directed by the Coen Brothers, 1990.
The Virgin Suicides, starring Kirsten Dunst, 1999.
House of Sand and Fog, starring Ben Kingsley, 2003.

For Klawans, Mendes's "camera placement is expressive only when formulaic . . . , and camera movement is simply beyond him." Stanley Kauffmann, of the *New Republic,* however, saw a stage director's hand at work in "helping [the film's actors] to dig into themselves." Kauffmann also had praise for Mendes's self-restraint: "He has sensibly concentrated on his actors. Some newcomers to film directing, after theater acclaim, try to prove themselves cinematically with all sorts of fussiness—odd camera angles, intrusive montage, and so on. Mendes simply tells his story clearly." *Newsweek* reviewer David Ansen had higher praise, observing that Mendes "uses the screen like a born filmmaker." For Ansen, "the beauty of *American Beauty* is how wickedly entertaining it makes this bleak diagnosis." And *Entertainment Weekly* reviewer Owen Gleiberman concluded that "Mendes has a filmmaker's essential, seductive gift: He doesn't just tell a story—he gives great surface." Awards committees agreed with the critics: Mendes earned an Academy award as well as a Golden Globe award for best director.

His first success with film did not put an end to Mendes's theatrical career, however. He continued to work at the Donmar, mounting productions such as Anton Chekhov's *Uncle Vanya* and Shakespeare's *Twelfth Night,* that drew appreciative crowds and won awards for the still young impresario. Sheridan Morely, writing in the *New Statesman,* called Mendes's production of *Twelfth Night* a "revelation and a revolution," while a reviewer for the *Economist* praised the director for his "rare qualities: directness, clarity, richness of feeling." These two plays were his farewell to the Donmar; he left that theater in 2003.

Mendes's second film work came with 2002's *Road to Perdition,* a somber gangster film based on a graphic novel about a hit man on the run with his son from his former boss and from a killer sent to deal with him. Reviewers again were mixed in their opinions about the quality of the film. Robert Koe-

hler, writing in *Daily Variety,* found it to be an "expressive, deeply felt drama about criminality, destiny and family." Kauffmann, in the *New Republic,* described the film's screenplay as "laden with cliches and improbabilities," but that Mendes's directing is good enough that "the triteness of the ideas in the work went largely unnoticed," just as with *American Beauty.* Kauffmann concluded that Mendes's film "is a flawed account of foul lives, aesthetically aggrandized." *Film Journal* reviewer Shirley Sealy had higher praise, calling *Road to Perdition* a "grand symphony of a movie." For David Denby, writing in the *New Yorker,* the movie is a "solemnly beautiful art concept—perhaps the most thoroughly stylized gangster picture since the Coen brothers' *Miller's Crossing.*" However, this tone wore on Denby: "There isn't a joke or a touch of wit anywhere in the movie," he complained, further commenting that "there's not much spontaneity in it, and the movie's flawless surface puts a stranglehold on meaning." Similarly, *Newsweek* reviewer Ansen felt that the same film was "self-conscious to the point of suffocation" and concluded: "Mendes has talent to burn; maybe in his next film he won't feel so anxious to prove it."

Mendes formed his own production company in 2004, and has since worked on both stage and film projects. He had his first Broadway flop with a reprise of the musical *Gypsy,* which is about striptease artist Gypsy Rose Lee, that closed after a half-year run, losing close to $4 million. For others this might be a tragedy, but for Mendes, whose successes were so many in such a short time, it was viewed as only a temporary setback. Other film and theater productions were in the works by 2004, and the director's love for the theater remained as strong as ever. As Mendes told Matt Wolf in the London *Sunday Times:* "A great night in the theatre is as memorable, if not more so, than a movie, because you can't take it down from a video shelf. It only lives in your head. That is my belief in the theatre—it is a great art form—and I don't think I could have made movies without what I've learnt from it."

■ Biographical and Critical Sources

PERIODICALS

Atlanta Journal-Constitution, July 12, 2002, Bob Longino, review of *Road to Perdition,* p. P1.
Back Stage, February 20, 2004, Leonard Jacobs, "Mendes Sets up Scamp," p. 8.
Cineaste, spring, 2000, Paul Arthur, review of *American Beauty,* p. 51.

In 2002 Mendes directed Tom Hanks (left) in *Road to Perdition,* a gritty thriller based on the graphic novel by Max Allan Collins.

Commonweal, November 5, 1999, Richard Alleva, review of *American Beauty,* p. 19.

Daily Mail (London, England), March 28, 2000, Tim Woodward, "Broken Home That Still Haunts the One and Only Mr. Mendes," p. 8; September 22, 2000, Baz Bamigboye, "Sam Proves Again That He's the Man," p. 51.

Daily Telegraph (London, England), July 13, 2002, John Hiscock, interview with Mendes, p. 2; February 4, 2004, Nigel Reynolds, "Mendes Loses Midas Touch on Broadway."

Daily Variety, December 11, 2002, Robert Koehler, review of *Road to Perdition,* p. 22; March 6, 2003, Matt Wolf, "Donmar Duty Set Stage for Role in Film," p. B8; July 18, 2003, Michael Fleming, "D'works on Cutup 'Todd,,'" p. 1; April 26, 2004, Michael Fleming, "Mendes Enlists in Gulf War Drama," p. 1.

Economist, January 4, 2003, review of *Twelfth Night.*

Entertainment Weekly, September 17, 1999, Owen Gleiberman, review of *American Beauty,* p. 49; July 19, 2002, Lisa Schwarzbaum, review of *Road to Perdition,* p. 44; February 28, 2003, Joshua Rich, review of *Road to Perdition* (video release), p. 63; May 23, 2003, Scott Brown, review of *Gypsy,* p. 85.

Film Journal, August, 2002, Shirley Sealy, review of *Road to Perdition,* p. 35.

Guardian, September 20, 2002, Peter Bradshaw, review of *Road to Perdition,* p. 12.

Independent (London England), April 10, 2000, David Lister, "The Rout Goes On," p. 5; June 8, 2004, Louise Jury, "Mendes' Run of Successes Ends as Black Comedy Succumbs to the May Blues," p. 7.

Nation, October 11, 1999, Stuart Klawans, review of *American Beauty,* p. 34.

New Republic, October 11, 1999, Stanley Kauffmann, review of *American Beauty,* p. 36; August 5, 2002, Stanley Kauffmann, review of *Road to Perdition,* p. 24.

New Statesman, April 25, 1997, Susannah Clapp, "The Fix," p. 42; November 4, 2002, Sheridan Morely, review of *Twelfth Night,* p. 48.

Newsweek, September 27, 1999, David Ansen, review of *American Beauty,* p. 68; July 15, 2002, David Ansen, review of *Road to Perdition,* p. 56.

New Yorker, July 15, 2002, David Denby, review of *Road to Perdition;* February 3, 2003, Hilton Als, "Playing for Immortality," p. 84.

New York Observer, July 22, 2002, Andrew Sarris, review of *Road to Perdition,* p. 21.

New York Post, April 18, 2003, "Jitters Over 'Gypsy': Director Makes Unusual Plea to Critics," p. 41; June 27, 2003, "The Great Green Way: Dreamworks Putting 'Shrek' on the Stage," p. 53.

Observer (London, England), September 22, 2002, Philip French, review of *Road to Perdition,* p. 7; October 27, 2002, Susannah Clapp, "A Glorious *Twelfth:* Sam Mendes Bows Out with Class at the Donmar While the Children of Ghent Are Seen but Not Heard," p. 12.

People, July 29, 2002, Michelle Tauber, "Road to Love," p. 69; May 3, 2004, "On the Block," p. 24.

Spectator, September 21, 2002, Toby Young, review of *Uncle Vanya,* p. 56.

Star-Ledger (Newark, NJ), July 26, 2003, "Winslet and Mendes Blessed with Beautiful News," p. 8.

Sunday Times (London, England), November 28, 1999, Jeff Dawson, "The Return of the Native," p. 4; November 25, 2001, Matt Wolf, "It's Sam's Grand Slam," p. 6.

Time, March 30, 1998, Richard Zoglin, review of *Cabaret,* p. 67; July 15, 2002, Richard Schickel, review of *Road to Perdition,* p. 62.

Times (London, England), June 20, 1991, Jeremy Kingston, review of *Troilus and Cressida;* September 13, 1995, Matt Wolf, "Is There a Rich Donor in the Donmar Tonight?," p. 36; February 28, 1997, Valerie Grove, "Theatre's Hot Ticket," p. 17; January 20, 2000, Matt Wolf, "Go West, Young Sam," p. 43; January 27, 2000, Adam Mars-Jones, review of *American Beauty,* p. 45; November 24, 2001, Benedict Nightingale, "A Hard Act to Follow as Donmar's Director," p. 23.

Variety, March 23, 1996, Chris Jones, review of *Cabaret,* p. 98; December 14, 1998, Charles Isherwood, review of *Blue Room,* p. 141; February 24, 2003, Matt Wolf, "Mendes Takes Home Olivier Trio," p. 84; May 5, 2003, Charles Isherwood, "Rose of a New Color," p. 31; May 26, 2003, Michaela Boland, "No-Shows Triumph at Aussie Legit Prizes," p. 48; October 4, 2004, Ellin Stein, "Brits in the Sticks," p. S36.

ONLINE

BBC Online, http;//www.bbc.co.uk/ (November 21, 2004), Jonathan Ross, "Sam Mendes, *Road to Perdition.*"*

Piet Mondrian

Personal

Born March 7, 1872, in Amersfoort, Netherlands; died of pneumonia February 1, 1944, in New York, NY; son of Pieter Cornelis Mondriaan (a schoolteacher and painter). *Education:* Attended Winterswijk schools; studied drawing with his father, painting with uncle, Frits Mondriaan; completed teachers training in drawing; attended Rijksakademie, Amsterdam, Netherlands, 1892-94; attended evening drawing classes, 1894-97.

Career

Painter. *Exhibitions:* Solo exhibitions: Stedelijk Museum, Amsterdam, Netherlands (retrospective), 1909, 1922; Rotterdam Kunststichting, 1924; Galerie Kuhl und Kuehn, Dresden, Germany, 1925; New York, NY (first American exhibition), 1926; Galerie Jeanne-Bucher, Paris, France, 1928; Museum of Modern Art, New York, NY, 1945, 1995; and National Gallery of Art, Washington, DC, 1995. Permanent collections: Stedelijk Museum; Tate Gallery, London; Museum of Modern Art; and Guggenheim Museum, New York, NY, among others.

Writings

Neo-Plasticism: The General Principle of Plastic Equivalence, [Paris, France], 1920.

The New Art—The New Life: The Collected Writings, edited by Harry Holtzman and Martin S. James, Da Capo Press (Cambridge, MA), 1993.

Piet Mondrian, 1872-1944, edited by Angelica Zander Rudenstine and Yve-Alain Bois, Bullfinch Press (Boston, MA), 1995.

Natural Reality and Abstract Reality: An Essay in Trialogue Form/ 1919-1920, George Braziler (New York, NY), 1995.

Contributed articles to journals, including *De Stijl* and *Abstraction, creation, art non-figuratif.*

Sidelights

A pioneer of modernism, Dutch painter Piet Mondrian made his revolutionary leap into geometrical paintings at age forty, after already establishing himself as a naturalist and symbolist painter. Together with Wassily Kandinsky and Kazmir Malevich, Mondrian is, as Eric Gibson and Stephen Goode noted in *Insight on the News,* "credited with the invention of the single most important development in 20th-century art—abstraction—a subjective, self-contained artistic language that makes no concessions to visible reality." The same authors went on to note that Mondrian "was one of the most prolific and important theorists of modern art." The artist's fame rests on the two hundred and fifty paintings he produced between 1917 and 1944. Though this is not a large oeuvre in terms of output, each of the canvases—seemingly simple geometric designs of rectangles of blue, red, or yellow separated by white or black vertical and perpendicular lines—was meticulously worked and reworked to obtain just the right surface, color, and form.

Mondrian dubbed his style "neoplasticism," a rough translation of the Dutch movement he helped found, called "Nieuwe Beelding"—"new form" or "new image." Such a style resulted from a mystical belief in the harmony of straight lines and primary colors that underlie the visible world. This style also laid the artist open to easy reproduction. Jed Perl, writing in the *New Republic,* commented that Mondrian "used the spare language of an ascetic to shape his overflowing romantic notions." However, Perl further explained that the Dutch artist's work "has inspired generations of dumbed-down graphic design, and the stuff lulls people into believing that they know Mondrian better than they do." Similarly, a contributor for the *Economist,* reviewing a 1995 retrospective exhibition at New York's Museum of Modern Art, observed that "among 20th-century path-breakers in art, Piet Mondrian suffers more than most from a false sense of familiarity. The work of this Dutch modernist is always in danger of vanishing behind its influence, and not just its influence on other painters." So ubiquitous had Mondrian's paintings become at the time of his death in 1944 that his asymmetrically arranged rectangles of blue, red, or yellow framed by black lines were as instantly "recognisable as a market brand," according to the *Economist* contributor. Such designs were thereafter used for everything from office building murals to shower curtain patterns.

This "supreme Platonist of modernism," as Robert Hughes described Mondrian in *Time,* believed that such basic patterns, "his grids, representing nothing but themselves and, as Plato said of his perfect solids, 'free from the itch of desire,' could demonstrate a universal order, an essence that underwrote the mere accidents of the world as it is." The irony of Mondrian's abstraction was, as Hughes also pointed out, that though the artist "may have wanted to transcend nature, . . . the Dutch landscape was in him like a DNA code." Hughes further explained that Mondrian "said there were not straight lines in nature, so that straight lines—the grid—were inherently more abstract than curves; and yet, as anyone can see in Holland, the flat horizons and punctuating verticals of mill and steeple must have affected him right from the start."

Dutch Beginnings

Mondrian's start was in the central Netherlands town of Amersfoort, where he was born on March 7, 1872. The second of five children, the artist's surname was originally spelled Mondriaan. Named after his father, the young boy was baptized in the Dutch Reformed Church and brought up in a strict religious atmosphere. His father was the head of the first Protestant primary school in Amersfoort and was an active member of the anti-revolutionary political party. Additionally, he was something of an artist, making lithographs of historical and biblical subjects. When Mondrian was eight years old the family moved to Winterswijk, where the elder Mondriaan became head of the Primary School for National Protestant Education. It was here, in his father's school, that Mondrian developed a love for drawing, aided by his father and also by his uncle, Frits Mondriaan, a professional landscape painter. Mondrian finished his formal schooling in 1886 and prepared to take an exam for a certificate to teach drawing in the primary school. In 1889 he earned this teacher's certificate, began teaching drawing in his father's school, and also began studying for a certificate to teach drawing and perspective in the secondary school.

By this time Mondrian had determined, against his father's wishes, to become a professional painter. In 1890 he exhibited two works at the Exhibition of Art by Living Masters in the Hague. Earning his secondary credential, he set off for Amsterdam and entrance to the National Academy of Art. He was age twenty when he entered the Academy; his years of study for teaching certificates exempted him from preparatory classes there. Two years later he added night classes in drawing to round out his artistic education. Frustrated with his studies and also short of cash, in 1895 he left the Academy for a time and worked as a freelance artist, painting mostly landscapes. He managed to earn his living by copying old masters, designing ex-libris, making bacteriological drawings, painting portraits, and giving drawing lessons.

For over a decade Mondrian continued to slowly make his way in the Amsterdam art scene. At this time he was hardly a revolutionary, but was influenced by the Hague school, Amsterdam impressionists, and symbolism. He was noted for his bucolic scenes of rural Holland with its windmills, churches, and wide, flat plains, and also painted flowers, often devoting an entire canvas to the finely detailed depiction of one blossom. Additionally, he joined several artistic societies in the city and exhibited with them regularly.

An exhibition of the works of Vincent Van Gogh in 1905 deeply influenced Mondrian, moving him away from symbolism to neo-impressionism. It is an indication of how cut off Mondrian was from modern art movements that into his thirties he was still unaware of the modernist revolution. Contact with Jan Toorop, a painter who was influenced by both Fauvism and art nouveau, nudged Mondrian away from the straight depiction of nature. He began spending summers along the Dutch coast, pushing his art in new directions. His *The Red Tree* from this time shows the influence of Fauvism on his work, as do dozens of other paintings and watercolors. Similarly, the 1908 *Mill in Sunlight* "explodes" with color, according to Hughes, the critic interpreting the work as an "orgiastic response to Van Gogh." Slowly his art was moving away from a careful representation of nature to a depiction of what Mondrian felt lay behind nature and above it.

Spiritual Awakening Leads to Abstraction

In 1908 Mondrian learned of the philosophies of Helena P. Blavatsky and Rudolf Steiner, theosophy and anthroposophy, and in 1909 he joined the Theosophical Society. This involvement with theosophy in particular—a movement based on a mystical insight into the divine nature—convinced Mondrian that his art could express the spiritual as well as the actual. An intensely spiritual man who felt that he himself had been reincarnated, Mondrian found in theosophy something that could not be found in Protestantism: a search for the ultimate good, a look at the underlying geometrical realities of eternity. Theosophy's reconciliation of science and religion, of Darwin and God, appealed to Mondrian's critical mind. It is interesting to note that other pioneers of abstraction were equally attracted to what might be considered nontraditional belief systems. Writing in the *New Criterion*, Hilton Kramer noted that "so prevalent was a steadfast belief in the occult among the pioneers of abstract art—not only Mondrian but also Kandinsky, Malevich, and a good many of their disciples—that we have no alternative but to regard such doctrine as a basic component of their artistic vision." Equally important in Mondrian's own development was the inclusion of modernist techniques into his pictorial style, blending pointillism with a symbolist feel for color to transform his Dutch landscapes into something wholly new.

Mondrian first visited Paris in 1911 and, after seeing an exhibition of works by Pablo Picasso and other cubists, he knew he had finally found his home. Now almost forty, Mondrian began to discover his own style, as witnessed in the cubist-influenced *Still Life with Gingerpot* of 1911. The following year he moved permanently to Paris and

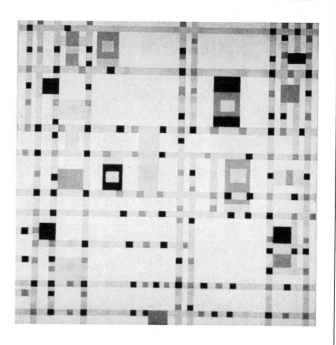

During the 1930s and 1940s Mondrian expressed his ideas through seemingly simple geometric designs composed of rectangles, straight lines, and primary colors.

imbibed the new art forms. His progress toward abstraction can be seen in a series of paintings of trees from 1912 to 1915. The tree motif itself became ever more simplified with branches becoming more and more altered and lattice like until finally they were actually a grid against a flat background rather than twisting, organic representations of actual branches.

In Paris as in Amsterdam, Mondrian avoided the nightlife and focused on his work. He made friends of fellow artists such as Ferdinand Leger and Mexican muralist Diego Rivera, but spent more time in his studio at work than in the cafés discussing the art scene. As early as 1912 he ceased to give individual titles to his paintings, instead labeling them "compositions." He did this in order to allow the viewer to make his or her own judgment of the work without his interference.

In 1914 World War I caught him visiting in Holland, and he remained there for the remainder of the hostilities, working out the ideas of his new art. There he met fellow artist Theo Van Doesburg with whom he began the artistic journal *De Stijl*, which spread the word of Mondrian's new aesthetic: abstraction, exactness, the idea that less is more in art, architecture and design. De Stijl as an art movement became a powerful influence on twentieth-century design.

A Life in Art

Slowly between 1912 and 1917, Mondrian's paintings lost their physical referents. Even curved lines were banished from his oeuvre as were those on the diagonal. His paintings of a pier and the ocean from 1915 to 1917 demonstrate a complete abstraction of form using vertical and horizontal lines only with blocks of color organized to his own secret harmony. Soon even these colors were reduced to the primaries: red, yellow, and blue. Meanwhile he was also sharing his thoughts about the new artistic principles in the journal *De Stijl*. As Henkels noted, these theories consisted primarily of the idea that "the painting of the future must be the expression of universal cosmic order." This could best be represented by line and color alone.

By the end of the war, Mondrian had become a guru of modernity. Returning to Paris, he published *Le Neo-plasticisme*, a further elucidation of his theories. Indeed, he would continue to write about art for the remainder of his life. As Yve-Alain Bois noted in *Artforum International*, "Like many of his peers in the first generation of abstract artists, Mondrian felt compelled to write in order to justify his then extremely enigmatic pictorial practice. However, his texts only exceptionally deal directly with the specifics of his painting: the theory of neo-plasticism covers all aspects of human activity, painting being only one." He would also paint, and write, about jazz; its music and dancing became his one non-painterly outlet. When the Charleston dance was banned in his native Holland, Mondrian vowed never to return.

If you enjoy the works of Piet Mondrian, you may also want to check out the following:

The abstract art of Wassily Kandinsky (1866-1944), Bart van der Leck (1876-1958), and Theo van Doesburg (1883-1931).

By 1925 Mondrian had broken with *De Stijl*, primarily because of a single line. Van Doesburg began to give the diagonal line a principal role in his paintings and design; Mondrian could not tolerate this. For him, the horizontal and vertical were the lines that revealed universal light and harmony. The following year he exhibited in the United States for the first time, and his name also became better known throughout Europe. His paintings began to fetch ever higher prices and Mondrian—who always lived simply and never married—continued to spread the word of abstraction. His black grid became bolder, defined by what may be the most archetypal of all his paintings, *Composition in Red, Yellow, and Blue* from 1930. Yet in abstraction, Mondrian also represented meaning. According to Perl, "there's nothing that Mondrian doesn't express between 1932 and 1944, whether it's serenity and delicacy, weight and speed, or mystery, anxiety, chaos. And he can at times include more than one of these qualities or emotions in the same ultra-pared-down painting."

With the advent of the Nazis in Germany, Mondrian left Paris, moving first to London in 1938. Once the war started and London was hit by air raids in 1940, Mondrian again moved, this time to New York. There he discovered a pulsing, vital city, alive with jazz and full of young painters eager to follow in his footsteps. This new generation would soon launch the art movement known as abstract expressionism. In Manhattan Mondrian began to tone down the heavy black grid lines of his paintings, emphasizing more the rectangles of primary colors. His *Broadway Boogie-Woogie*, from 1942-43, "evokes illuminated buildings, traffic lights, and jazz," according to a contributor for the *International Dictionary of Art and Artists*. Completed when Mondrian was seventy years old, *Broadway Boogie-Woogie* proved to be his final painting. He died in New York in 1944. The following year, the Museum of Modern Art in New York mounted a large retrospective in honor of this artist who helped revolutionize art. He influenced an entire generation of new artists, not only the abstract expressionists, but those who went on to found movements such as color-field abstraction, minimal art, and op art. Art theorist, pioneer of modern art—Mondrian was all of these. But first and foremost, he was a painter. Mondrian, as Hughes noted, "remains an artist of extreme importance, not only because of the historic inventiveness of his pictures and the daring leaps of consciousness they embody, but because of their beauty as art."

■ Biographical and Critical Sources

BOOKS

Bax, Marty, *Complete Mondrian*, Lund Humphries (London, England), 2002.
Blotkamp, Carel, *Mondrian: The Art of Destruction*, Abrams (New York, NY), 1995.

Faerna, Jose Maria, *Mondrian Cameo,* Abrams (New York, NY), 1997.

Gay, Peter, *Art and Act: On Causes in History—Manet, Gropius, Mondrian,* Harper (New York, NY), 1976.

International Dictionary of Art and Artists, St. James Press (Detroit, MI), 1990.

Jaffe, Hans Ludwig, *Piet Mondrian,* Thames and Hudson (London, England), 1970.

Jaffe, Hans Ludwig, *Masters of Art: Mondrian,* Abrams (New York, NY), 1986.

Janssen, Hans, and others, *Mondrian, 1892-1914: The Path to Abstraction,* B. V. Waanders Uitgeverji (Zwolle, Netherlands), 2003.

Joosten, Joop M., *Piet Mondrian,* Abrams (New York, NY), 1996.

Seuphor, Michel, *Piet Mondrian, Life and Work,* Abrams (New York, NY), 1957.

Welsh, Robert P., *Piet Mondrian's Early Career: The "Naturalistic" Periods,* Garland (New York, NY), 1977.

PERIODICALS

Artforum International, summer, 1995, Yve-Alain Bois, review of *Natural Reality and Abstract Reality: An Essay in Trialogue Form/ 1919-1920,* p. B30; October, 1995, Mel Bochner and Robert Rosenblum, "Plastic Made Perfect," p. 84, Dona Lydia, "Ascetic Esthetic," p. 90, David Sylvester, "Son of Cezanne," p. 92.

Economist, June 10, 1995, "To the Bare Lines: Piet Mondrian," p. 81.

Insight on the News, July 3, 1995, Eric Gibson and Stephen Goode, "Mondrian Art," p. 32.

New Criterion, September, 1995, Hilton Kramer, "Mondrian and Mysticism."

New Republic, July 31, 1995, Jed Perl, "Absolutely Mondrian," p. 27.

Newsweek, October 30, 1995, Peter Plagen, "When Less Was More," p. 76.

Telegraph, October 27, 2001, Richard Smith, "Piet Mondrian's *Broadway Boogie Woogie.*"

Time, October 23, 1995, Robert Hughes, "Purifying Nature," p. 91.

ONLINE

Artchive, http://www.artchive.com/ (November 17, 2004), "Piet Mondrian (1872-1944)."

Artmuseums, http://www.artmuseums.harvard.edu/ (November 17, 2004), "Piet Mondrian."

Mondriaanhuis Foundation, http://www.mondriaanhuis.nl/eng/ (November 18, 2004).*

Paul Robeson

■ Personal

Born April 9, 1898, in Princeton, NJ; died following a stroke January 23, 1976, in Philadelphia, PA; son of William Drew (a clergyman) and Maria Louisa (a schoolteacher; maiden name, Bustill) Robeson; married Eslanda Cardozo Goode, August 17, 1921 (died, December, 1965); children: Paul, Jr. *Education:* Rutgers College (now University), A.B., 1919; Columbia University, LL.B., 1923. *Politics:* Communist.

■ Career

Admitted to the Bar of New York State; employed in a law firm, 1923; actor in plays, including *Simon the Cyrenian,* 1921, *All God's Chillun Got Wings,* 1924, *Othello,* 1930 and 1943, and *Toussaint L'Ouverture,* 1936; actor in films, including *Body and Soul,* 1924, *The Emperor Jones,* 1933, *Sanders of the River,* 1935, and *Show Boat,* 1936; singer in concert performances, for recordings, and in musical productions, including *Show Boat,* 1928. Member, Council on African Affairs (co-founder), Joint Anti-Fascist Refugee Committee, and Committee to Aid China.

■ Member

National Maritime Union (honorary member), Phi Beta Kappa, Alpha Phi Alpha, Sigma Tau Delta.

■ Awards, Honors

Badge of Veterans of Abraham Lincoln Brigade, 1939; Donaldson Award for outstanding lead performance, 1944, for *Othello;* medal from American Academy of Arts and Letters, 1944, for good diction on the stage; Spingarn Medal, National Association for the Advancement of Colored People, 1944; Champion of African Freedom Award, National Church of Nigeria, 1950; Afro-American Newspapers Award, 1950; Stalin Peace Prize (U.S.S.R.), 1952; German Peace Medal (East Germany), 1960; Ira Aldridge Award, Association for the Study of Afro-American Life and History, 1970; Civil Liberties Award, American Civil Liberties Union, 1970; Duke Ellington Medal, Yale University, 1972; Whitney M. Young, Jr., National Memorial Award, Urban League of Greater New York, 1972. Honorary degrees from Rutgers University, 1932 and 1973, Hamilton College, 1940, Morehouse College, 1943, Howard University, 1945, Moscow State Conservatory, 1959, and Humboldt University, 1960.

■ Writings

Forge Negro-Labor Unity for Peace and Jobs, Harlem Trade Union Council, 1950.
Here I Stand (autobiography), Othello Associates (New York, NY), 1958.

Columnist for *People's Voice,* c. 1940s; editor and columnist for *Freedom,* c. 1951-55. Contributor to periodicals, including *African Observer, Afro-American,*

Robeson starred as an escaped prisoner who corrupts the natives of a small island in the 1933 film version of Eugene O'Neill's play *The Emperor Jones.*

American Dialog, American Scholar, Daily Worker, Freedomways, Jewish Life, Masses and Mainstream, Messenger, National Guardian, New Statesman and Nation, New World Review, New York Age, Opportunity, Spectator, and *Worker.* Created many sound recordings.

COLLECTIONS

(With others) *Paul Robeson: The Great Forerunner,* Freedomways, 1971, enlarged edition, Dodd (New York, NY), 1985.

Paul Robeson: Tributes, Selected Writings, compiled and edited by Roberta Yancy Dent with the assistance of Marilyn Robeson and Paul Robeson, Jr., The Archives (New York, NY), 1976.

Paul Robeson Speaks: Writings, Speeches, Interviews, 1918-1974, edited with an introduction by Philip S. Foner, Brunner, 1978.

■ **Sidelights**

Paul Robeson—civil rights activist, singer, actor, law school graduate, athlete, scholar, author—was per-

haps the best known and most widely respected black American of the first half of the twentieth century. Balancing his many accomplishments in the eyes of many, Robeson was also a Soviet apologist, and later in his life he was widely vilified and censured for his outspoken and unyielding views on issues to which American public opinion ran contrary. As a young man, Robeson was virile, charismatic, eloquent, and powerful; in his final decades he was defeated and unsure mentally, a mere remnant of his younger self. While Robeson learned to speak more than twenty languages in order to break down the barriers of race and ignorance throughout the world, as Sterling Stuckey pointed out in the *New York Times Book Review,* for the last twenty-five years of his life his name was "a great whisper and a greater silence in black America." Martin Baulm Duberman, in his 1989 biography, *Paul Robeson,* asserted that Robeson ultimately is a hero wrongly accused, that his story is an "American tragedy." Barry Gewen, writing in the *New Leader,* felt instead that Robeson was a great man tragically flawed, "an artist of unassailable gifts and achievement who was brought low through his own political obtuseness." Such divergent views of Robeson can only be reconciled by understanding the complexity of his life from the beginning.

Paul Leroy Robeson was born in Princeton, New Jersey, on April 9, 1898, the fifth and last child of Maria Louisa Bustill and William Drew Robeson. During these early years the Robesons experienced both family and financial losses. At the age of six Paul and his siblings, William, Reeve, Ben and Marian, suffered the death of their mother in a household fire. This was followed a few years later with their father's loss of his Princeton pastorate. After moving first to the town of Westfield, the family finally settled in Somerville, New Jersey, in 1909, where William Robeson was appointed pastor of St. Thomas AME Zion Church.

Driven to Success

Enrolling in Somerville High School as one of only two blacks, Robeson excelled academically while successfully competing in debate and oratorical contests and showing great promise as a football player. He got his first taste of acting in the title role of William Shakespeare's *Othello.* In his senior year he not only graduated with honors, but placed first in a competitive examination for scholarships to enter Rutgers University. Although his other male siblings chose all-black colleges, Robeson took the challenge of attending Rutgers, a predominantly white institution, in 1915.

In college from 1915 to 1919, Robeson experienced both fame and racism. In trying out for the varsity football team, where blacks were not wanted, he encountered physical brutality. In spite of this resistance, Robeson not only earned a place on the team but was named first on the roster for the All-American college team and went on to graduate with fifteen letters in sports. Academically he was equally successful, elected a member of the prestigious Phi Beta Kappa Society and the Cap and Skull Honor Society of Rutgers. Graduating in 1919 with the highest grade point average in his class, Robeson gave the class oration at the 153rd Rutgers commencement.

With college life behind him, Robeson moved to the Harlem section of New York City to attend law school, first at New York University, then transferring to Columbia University. He sang in the chorus of the 1921 musical *Shuffle Along* by Eubie Blake and Noble Sissle, and made his acting debut in 1920 playing the lead role in *Simon the Cyrenian* by poet Ridgely Torrence. Robeson's performance was so well received that he was congratulated not only by the Harlem Young Men's Christian Association audience but also by members of the Provincetown Players who were in the audience.

While working odd jobs and taking part in professional football to earn his college fees, Robeson met Eslanda "Essie" Cardozo Goode. The granddaughter of Francis L. Cardozo, South Carolina's secretary of state during the Reconstruction era following the U.S. Civil War, Goode was a graduate of Columbia University and was employed as a histological chemist, the first black staff person at Presbyterian Hospital in New York City. The couple married on August 17, 1921, and their son, Paul, Jr., was born on November 2, 1927.

To help support his family and fund his education while studying at Columbia Law School, Robeson played professional football for the Akron Pros from 1920-21 and the Milwaukee Badgers during the 1921-22 season. During the summer of 1922 he traveled to England to appear in a production of the play *Taboo*, which was renamed *Voodoo*. Graduating from Columbia in 1923 with a law degree, Robeson sought work in his new profession, all the while singing at the famed Cotton Club in Harlem. He obtained a position with a New York law firm, only to have his career halted when a stenographer, as Duberman related the incident, refused to take down a memorandum and stated, "I never take dictation from a nigger." Offered an acting role in 1923 in Eugene O'Neill's *All God's Chillun Got Wings,* Robeson quickly took this opportunity. "The stage," Harvey Klehr wrote in *Commentary*, "was an arena where his race, far from impeding his career, actually enabled him to capitalize on his talents much

Robeson takes a break during the filming of *Showboat,* the 1936 musical featuring his memorable performance of the classic song "Ol' Man River."

more quickly than would ordinarily have been the case." A *Nation* critic, reflecting on the traditional, stereotyped role for blacks then, posed this question and answer: "What if Paul Robeson had wanted to use his proven mental abilities to become a great lawyer instead of employing his magnificent voice and physical presence to become a brilliant performer? A comparable career would have been unlikely."

Although *All God's Chillun* brought threats by the Ku Klux Klan because of the play's interracial subject matter and the fact that a white woman was to kiss Robeson's hand, it proved to be an immediate theatrical success. Robeson soon found himself cast in a 1924 revival of *The Emperor Jones,* the play *Rosanne,* and the silent movie *Body and Soul,* the last under the direction of independent African-American filmmaker Oscar Micheaux. In 1925 Robeson debuted in a formal concert at Cape Cod's well-known Provincetown Playhouse. His performance, which consisted of Negro spirituals and folk songs, was so brilliant that he and his accompanist,

Lawrence Brown, were offered a contract with the Victor Talking Machine Company. Encouraged by this success, Robeson and Brown embarked on a tour of their own, but were sorely disappointed. Even though they received good reviews, crowds were small and they made very little money. What Robeson came to know was that his talents in acting and singing would serve as the combined focus of his career.

Acting and Singing Career

Robeson's acting career started to take off in 1928 when he accepted the role of Joe in a London production of *Show Boat*, a musical composed by Jerome Kern and Oscar Hammerstein. It was his singing of "Ol' Man River" that received most of the acclaim surrounding the show and earned him a great degree of attention from British socialites. Robeson gave concerts in London at Albert Hall and Sunday-afternoon performances at Drury Lane. In spite of all this attention, he still had to deal with racism, however. In 1929 Robeson was refused admission to a London hotel; because of the protest the actor then raised, major hotels in London soon announced that they would no longer refuse service to blacks.

Years later, Robeson recalled in his autobiography, *Here I Stand*, that in England he "learned that the essential character of a nation is determined not by the upper classes, but by the common people, and that the common people of all nations are truly brothers in the great family of mankind." Consequently he began singing spirituals and work songs to audiences of common men, and learning the languages and folk songs of other cultures, for "they, too, were close to my heart and expressed the same soulful quality that I knew in Negro music." Nathan Irvin Huggins, writing in the *Nation*, defined this pivotal moment: "He found the finest expression of his talent. His genuine awe of and love for the common people and their music flourished throughout his life and became his emotional and spiritual center."

Robeson was embraced by the media during the 1920s. In the *New Yorker* Mildred Gilman wrote during that decade that Robeson was "the promise of his race," "King of Harlem," and "Idol of his people." Respected by white audiences as well, Robeson returned briefly to the United States in 1929 to perform before a packed Carnegie Hall. In May of 1930, after establishing a permanent residence in England, he accepted the lead role in Shakespeare's *Othello*. This London production at the Savoy Theatre was the first time since the performance of well-known black actor Ira Aldridge in 1860 that a major production company cast a black in the part of the Moor. Robeson, a tall, strikingly handsome man with a deep, rich, baritone voice and a shy, almost boyish manner, so captivated the audience that the first performance included twenty curtain calls.

Robeson received many accolades for his outstanding acting and singing performances during the 1930s, but his personal and home life were surrounded by difficulties. His wife, Essie, who had published a book on her husband in 1930 titled *Paul Robeson, Negro*, sued for divorce in 1932. Her actions were encouraged by the fact that Robeson had fallen in love and planned to marry Yolande Jackson, a white Englishwoman. Jackson, whom Robeson called the love of his life, originally accepted the still-married actor's proposal, but later called the marriage off. It was thought by some who knew the Jackson family well that she was strongly influenced

Robeson became the first Black actor in more than a century to play the title role in William Shakespeare's *Othello*.

by her father, Tiger Jackson, who was less than tolerant of Robeson and people of color in general. With his marriage plans canceled, Robeson and Essie came to a new understanding regarding their relationship, and the divorce proceedings were canceled.

A Life of Activism

Robeson returned to New York briefly in 1933 to star in the film version of *Emperor Jones* before turning his attention to the study of singing and languages. His stay in the United States was a short one due to his racist treatment at the hands of the U.S. film industry and because of criticism he received from blacks upset over his role as a corrupt emperor. Upon returning to England, Robeson eagerly immersed himself in his language studies; along with Essie, he became an honorary member of the West African Students' Union and met students Kwame Nkrumah and Jomo Kenyatta, the future presidents of Ghana and Kenya, respectively. It was also during this time that Robeson performed at a benefit for Jewish refugees, an action that marked the beginning of his political activism.

Robeson's inclination to aid the less fortunate and the oppressed in their fight for freedom and equality was firmly rooted in his own family history. His father, William Drew Robeson, was an escaped slave who eventually graduated from Lincoln College in 1878, and his relative, Cyrus Bustill, was a slave who was freed by his second owner in 1769 and went on to become an active member of the African Free Society. Recognizing the heritage that brought him so many opportunities, Robeson chose roles in several films that present blacks in other than stereotypical ways: 1935's *Sanders of the River* and the 1937 film releases *King Solomon's Mines* and *Song of Freedom.*

In 1939 Robeson stated his intentions to retire from commercial entertainment and return to the United States. He gave his first American recital at Mother AME Zion Church Harlem, where his brother Benjamin was pastor. Later that same year he premiered the patriotic song "Ballad for Americans" on CBS radio as a preview of a play of the same title. The song was so well received that studio audiences cheered for twenty minutes after the performance, while the listening audience outnumbered that tuning in for actor Orson Welles's famous "War of the Worlds" broadcast. Robeson's popularity in the United States soared and he remained the most celebrated person in the country well into the 1940s. He was awarded the esteemed NAACP Spingarn

A vocal advocate of Communism, Robeson, here visiting with the wife of the Secretary to the Russian Ambassador, began to study Marxism and Socialism after a 1934 visit to the Soviet Union.

Medal in 1945 and received numerous other awards and recognitions from civic and professional groups. In the 1943 U.S. film production of *Othello* his performance placed him among the ranks of great Shakespearean actors. The production ran for 296 performances—over ten months—and toured both the United States and Canada.

Continued travels throughout Europe in the 1930s had brought Robeson in contact with members of politically leftist-leaning organizations, including socialists and African nationalists. Singing to and moving among the disadvantaged, the underprivileged, and the working classes, Robeson began viewing "himself and his art as serving the struggle for racial justice for nonwhites and economic justice for workers of the world," as Huggins noted. On a trip to the U.S.S.R. in 1934 to discuss the making of the film *Black Majesty*, he befriended Soviet film director Sergei Eisenstein and also became so impressed with the education Soviet school children received against racism that he began to study both Marxism and Socialism. He also decided to send his son, nine-year-old Paul Jr., to school in the U.S.S.R. so that Paul would not have to contend with the racism and discrimination his father had confronted in both Europe and the United States. Robeson was ecstatic with this new-found society, concluding, as *New York Times Book Review* contributor John Patrick Diggins explained, "that the country was entirely free of racial prejudice and that Afro-American spiritual music resonated to Russian folk traditions. 'Here, for the first time in my life . . . I walk in full human dignity,'" Robeson was quoted as saying. Noting Robeson's intellectual bent, Diggins went on to point out that Robeson's "attraction to Communism seemed at first more anthropological than ideological, more of a desire to discover old, lost cultures than to impose new political systems. . . . Robeson convinced himself that American blacks as descendants of slaves had a common culture with Russian workers as descendants of serfs."

Regardless of his desire to believe in a cultural genealogy, Robeson soon become a vocal advocate of communism and other politically left-wing causes. He returned to the United States in the late 1930s, Saal observed, as "a vigorous opponent of racism, picketing the White House, refusing to sing before segregated audiences, starting a crusade against lynching, and urging Congress to outlaw racial bars in baseball." After World War II, when relations between the United States and the U.S.S.R. dissolved into cold war hostility, many former advocates of communism backed away. When the many crimes of Soviet leader Josef Stalin became public—his forced famines, genocide, political purges, and death camps—still more advocates of communism left the ranks. Robeson, however, was not among them. Sobran explained why: "It didn't matter: he believed in the idea, regardless of how it might be abused. In 1946 the former All-American explained his loyalty to an investigating committee: 'The coach tells you what to do and you do it.' It was incidental that the coach was Stalin."

McCarthy-Era Backlash

Robeson's popularity soon plummeted in response to his increasing rhetoric. A violent riot prevented his appearing at a concert in Peekskill, New York, after he had urged black youths not to fight if the United States went to war against the Soviet Union. The State Department revoked Robeson's passport in 1950, ensuring that he would remain in the United States. "He was black-listed by concert managers—his income, which had been $104,000 in 1947, fell to [as little as] $2,000—and he was removed from the list of All-Americans," Saal observed. With no passport to travel abroad, Robeson continued to speak out in public forums in the United States and through his own monthly newspaper, *Freedom*. Barred from all other forms of media, his own newspaper became his primary platform from 1950 to 1955.

If you enjoy the works of Paul Robeson, you may also want to check out the following films:

To Kill a Mockingbird, starring Gregory Peck, 1962.
Glory, starring Denzel Washington, 1989.
Othello, starring Laurence Fishburne, 1995.

Robeson's passport was restored in 1958 after the U.S. Supreme Court ruled on a similar case, but it was of little consequence. By then he had become a nonentity. When his autobiography was published in that same year, leading newspapers, including the *New York Times* and the *New York Herald-Tribune*, refused to review it. Robeson traveled again to the Soviet Union, but his health began to fail. He tried twice to commit suicide. "Pariah status was utterly alien to the gregarious Robeson. He became depressed at the loss of contact with audiences and friends, and suffered a series of breakdowns that left him withdrawn and dependent on psychotropic drugs," Dennis Drabble explained in the *Smithsonian*. Slowly deteriorating and virtually unheard from in the 1960s and 1970s, Robeson died after suffering a stroke in 1976.

During his life, Robeson had thrilled thousands with his athletic achievements on the football field, had entertained thousands with his artistic presence on the stage and screen, and had inspired thousands with his voice raised in speech and song. But because of his singular support for communism and his inability to renounce Stalin, because his life in retrospect became "a pathetic tale of talent sacrificed, loyalty misplaced, and idealism betrayed," according to Jim Miller in *Newsweek*, Robeson went out in sadness and loneliness, "forced in the end to retreat into the wilderness with his ghosts," as Huggins asserted. Robeson's life, full of desire and achievement, passion and conviction, "the story of a man who did so much to break down the barriers of a racist society, only to be brought down by the controversies sparked by his own radical politics," Diggins explained, "is at once an American triumph and an American tragedy." On February 24, 1998, Robeson received a posthumous Grammy lifetime achievement award. On January 20, 2004, the U.S. Postal Service issued a stamp honoring the former actor in his hometown of Princeton, New Jersey. Writing in *Dynamic*, the official magazine of the Young Communist League, Brandon Slattery stated: "Robeson is perhaps the first U.S. communist to be so honored."

■ Biographical and Critical Sources

BOOKS

Boyle, Sheila Tully, and Andrew Bunie, *Paul Robeson: The Years of Promise and Achievement*, University of Massachusetts Press (Boston, MA), 2001.

Brown, Lloyd L., *The Young Paul Robeson*, Westview Press (Boulder, CO), 1997.

Davis, Lenwood G., *A Paul Robeson Research Guide: A Selected, Annotated Bibliography*, Greenwood Press (Westport, CT), 1982.

Dorinson, Joseph, and William Pencak, editors, *Paul Robeson: Essays on His Life and Legacy*, McFarland (Jefferson, NC), 2002.

Duberman, Martin Baulm, *Paul Robeson*, Knopf (New York, NY), 1988.

Editors of *Freedomways*, *Paul Robeson: The Great Forerunner*, enlarged edition, Dodd (New York, NY), 1985.

Gilliam, Dorothy Butler, *Paul Robeson: All-American*, New Republic Books, 1976.

Hoyt, Edwin P., *Paul Robeson: The American Othello*, World Publishing, 1967.

Robeson, Paul, Jr., *The Undiscovered Paul Robeson: An Artist's Journey, 1898-1939*, Wiley (New York, NY), 2001.

Robeson, Susan, *The Whole World in His Hands: A Pictorial Biography of Paul Robeson*, Citadel (New York, NY), 1981.

PERIODICALS

American Heritage, April, 1976; April, 1989.

Commentary, May, 1989, Harvey Klehr, review of *Paul Robeson*.

Dynamic, November, 2003, Brandon Slattery, "Paul Robeson Honored on U.S. Postage Stamp."

Journal of African American History, summer, 2002, Barbara J. Beeching, "Paul Robeson and the Black Press: The 1950 Passport Controversy," p. 339.

Nation, February 7, 1976; March 20, 1989, Nathan Irvin Huggins, "Paul Robeson," p. 383.

National Review, May 19, 1989, Joseph Sobran, review of *Paul Robeson*, p. 55.

New American, February 23, 2004, Warren Mass, "A Mockery of Black Heritage," p. 44.

New Leader, February 20, 1989, Barry Gewen, "The Robeson Record," p. 17.

Newsweek, February 13, 1989, review of *Paul Robeson*.

New York Review of Books, April 27, 1989, review of *Paul Robeson*.

New York Times, August 6, 1972; April 16, 1973; February 25, 1998, "Robeson Receives Posthumous Grammy."

New York Times Book Review, October 21, 1973; February 12, 1989, review of *Paul Robeson*.

Smithsonian, October, 1989, Dennis Drabble, review of *Paul Robeson*, p. 221.

■ Obituaries

PERIODICALS

Newsweek, February 2, 1976.
Time, February 2, 1976.*

Antoine de Saint-Exupery

■ Personal

Born June 29, 1900, in Lyon, France; shot down during reconnaissance flight over southern France and reported missing in action, July 31, 1944; son of Jean (some sources say Cesar) and Marie Boyer (de Fonscolombe) de Saint-Exupery; married Consuelo Gomez Carillo, 1931. *Education:* Attended École Bossuet and Lycée Saint-Louis (naval preparatory schools), 1917-19; attended school for air cadets at Avord, France, 1922.

■ Career

Aviator and writer. Worked as a tile manufacturer, flight instructor, and truck salesperson, c. 1920s; Latecoere Co. (became Air France), Toulouse, France, commercial pilot flying between France and western Africa, 1926-27; commander of airport at Cape Juby, Morocco, 1927-28; directed Argentinian subsidiary of company and established airmail route in South America from Brazil to Patagonia, 1929-31; test pilot of hydroplanes over Mediterranean Sea, Perpignan, France, 1933; publicity agent and magazine writer, 1934; pilot, late 1930s; foreign correspondent for newspapers, including *Paris Soir* and *Intransigeant,* beginning 1935; lecturer and freelance writer in the United States, 1940-43. *Military service:* Served in French Army Air Force, 1921-26 and during World War II; became captain in Air Corps Reserve, 1939; received Croix de Guerre for courage on reconnaissance flights, 1940; instructor for flying squadron in northern Africa, 1943; reconnaissance pilot between Algeria, Italy, and southern France, 1944.

■ Awards, Honors

Prix Femina (France), 1931, for *Vol de Nuit;* French Legion of Honor Award, 1929, for peaceful negotiations with Spaniards and Moors in Morocco; Grand Prix from Academie Française, 1939, for *Terre des Hommes* and other writings; Prix des Ambassadeurs (France), 1948, for *Citadelle; Wind, Sand, and Stars* named Best Adventure Book of the Last One Hundred Years, *Outside* magazine, 2002; the Lyon Saint-Exupery Airport is named in his honor.

■ Writings

FICTION

Courrier Sud (novel), Gallimard (Paris, France), 1929, translation by Stuart Gilbert published as *Southern Mail,* illustrations by Lynd Ward, H. Smith &

R. Haas (New York, NY), 1933, translation by Curtis Cate bound with *Night Flight,* Heinemann (London, England), 1971, published separately as *Southern Mail,* Harcourt (New York, NY), 1972.

Vol de nuit (novel), preface by André Gide, Gallimard (Paris, France), 1931, translation by Stuart Gilbert published as *Night Flight,* Century (New York, NY), 1932, translation by Curtis Cate bound with *Southern Mail,* Heinemann (London, England), 1971.

(And illustrator) *Le petit prince* (for children), Reynal & Hitchcock, 1943, translation by Katherine Woods published as *The Little Prince,* Harcourt (New York, NY), 1943, translated by Richard Howard, 2000.

ESSAYS

Terre des hommes, Gallimard (Paris, France), 1939, translation by Lewis Galantiere published as *Wind, Sand, and Stars,* Reynal & Hitchcock, 1939, with illustrations by John O. Cosgrave II, Harcourt (New York, NY), 1949, revised translation, Heinemann (London, England), 1970.

Pilote de guerre, Gallimard (Paris, France), 1942, translation by Lewis Galantiere published as *Flight to Arras,* illustrations by Bernard Lamotte, Harcourt (New York, NY), 1942, reprinted, 1985.

Citadelle, Gallimard (Paris, France), 1948, translation by Stuart Gilbert published as *The Wisdom of the Sands,* Harcourt (New York, NY), 1950, with introduction by Wallace Fowlie, University of Chicago Press (Chicago, IL), 1979.

Carnets, Gallimard (Paris, France), 1953, revised edition, introduction by Pierre Chevrier, 1975.

Saint-Exupery par lui-meme, illustrations by Luc Estang, Seuil (Paris, France), 1956.

Un sens a la vie, compiled and edited by Claude Reynal, Gallimard (Paris, France), 1956, translation by Adrienne Foulke published as *A Sense of Life,* Funk & Wagnalls (New York, NY), 1965.

Ecrits de guerre, 1939-1944 (includes *Lettre a un otage*), preface by Raymond Aron, Gallimard (Paris, France), 1982, translation by Norah Purcell published as *Wartime Writings, 1939-1944,* introduction by Anne Morrow Lindbergh, Harcourt (New York, NY), 1986.

LETTERS

Lettre a un otage (also see below), Brentano's (New York, NY), 1943, translation by Jacqueline Gerst published as *Letter to a Hostage,* Heinemann (London, England), 1950.

(Self-illustrated) *Lettres de jeunesse, 1923-1931* (also see below), introduction by Renée de Saussine, Gallimard (Paris, France), 1953, published as *Lettres a l'amie inventee,* Plon (Paris, France), 1953.

Lettres a sa mere (also see below), Gallimard (Paris, France), 1955, revised edition, 1984.

Lettres de Saint-Exupery: Lettres a sa mere, Lettres de jeunesse, Lettre a un otage, Club du Meilleur Livre, 1960.

COLLECTIONS

Airman's Odyssey (omnibus volume; contains *Wind, Sand, and Stars; Night Flight;* and *Flight to Arras*), Reynal & Hitchcock, 1943, with introduction by Richard Bach, Harcourt (New York, NY), 1984.

Oeuvres completes (complete works), illustrations by the author and others, Gallimard (Paris, France), 1950.

Pages choisies (selected works), introduction by Michel Quesnel, Gallimard (Paris, France), 1962.

Oeuvres completes de Saint-Exupery, Volume 1: *Courrier sud* [and] *Terre des hommes,* Volume 2: *Vol de nuit* [and] *Pilote de guerre,* Volume 3: *Lettre a un otage* [and] *Un sens a la vie,* Volume 4: *Lettres a sa mere* [and] *Le petit prince,* Volumes 5 and 6: *Citadelle,* Volume 7: *Carnets,* Club de l'Honnete Homme, 1985.

A Guide for Grown-ups: Essential Wisdom from the Collected Works of Antoine de Saint-Exupery, edited by Anna Marlis Burgard, Harcourt, 2002.

Saint-Exupery served as a French air force pilot in the early 1920s and in World War II.

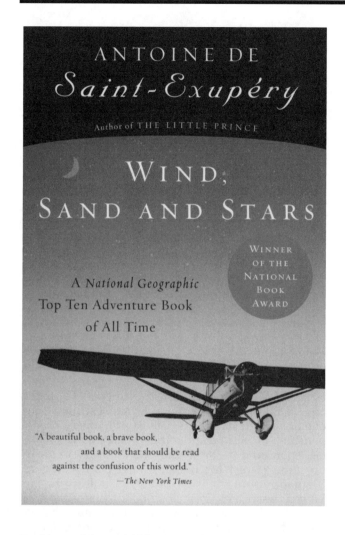

ANTOINE DE
Saint-Exupéry

Author of THE LITTLE PRINCE

WIND,
SAND AND STARS

WINNER
OF THE
NATIONAL
BOOK
AWARD

A *National Geographic*
Top Ten Adventure Book
of All Time

"A beautiful book, a brave book,
and a book that should be read
against the confusion of this world."
—*The New York Times*

In this autobiographical 1939 work, winner of the Grand
Prix of the Academie Francaise, Saint-Exupery conveys
the excitement and danger of flight.

OTHER

Courrier Sud (screenplay; adapted from author's
novel of the same title), released in France, 1937.

Contributor to periodicals, including *Harper's, New
York Times Magazine, Senior Scholastic,* and *Navire
d'Argent.*

■ **Adaptations**

Night Flight was adapted into a motion picture of
the same title, Metro-Goldwyn-Mayer, 1933; *The
Little Prince* was adapted into a motion picture of
the same title, Paramount, 1975, with a screenplay

and lyrics by Alan Jay Lerner published by Paramount, 1974. *The Little Prince* was read in English
by Peter Ustinov and recorded by Argo, 1972; *Le
Petit Prince* was read in French by Gerard Phillipe
and Georges Poujouly and recorded by Everest,
1973.

■ **Sidelights**

"There are certain rare individuals . . . who by the
mere fact of their existence put an edge on life, their
ceaseless astonishment before its possibilities awak-
ening our own latent sense of renewal and
expectation. No one ever stood out more conspicu-
ously in this respect than the French aviator and author Antoine de Saint-Exupery," extolled Nona Bal-
akian in the *New York Times Book Review.* A pilot
before and during World War II, Saint-Exupery was
praised for the lyricism with which he describes the
exhilaration of flight, the wonder of childhood, and
his visions of both personal and global peace.
Throughout his writings, which include two novels
and several essays, Saint-Exupery expresses the
"paradoxical truth," as noted French author André
Gide wrote in his preface to the pilot's novel *Vol de
Nuit—Night Flight—*that an individual's contentment "lies not in freedom but in his acceptance of a
duty." Even Saint-Exupery's children's tale, *Le Petit
Prince—The Little Prince—*for which he is probably
best known among English-language readers, depicts responsibility as a necessary element of love.

In both his personal and professional life, Saint-
Exupery lived according to the principles he es-
poused in his writings. Having developed a childhood interest in flying during family vacations near
the French airport at Bugey, he became a military
aviator soon after failing his exams at naval school—
perhaps intentionally, some biographers speculate.
Saint-Exupery combined his enthusiasm for flying
with a strong sense of duty to his country by serving as an air force pilot in the early 1920s and in
World War II, and as a pioneering long-distance airmail pilot in Africa and South America during the
interim. In 1929 he received the French Legion of
Honor Award for bringing about peaceful negotiations with feuding Spaniards and Moors during his
command of an airport in Morocco, and in 1940 he
was awarded the Croix de Guerre for the bravery
he demonstrated on reconnaissance flights during
the Battle of France. He insisted on serving in the
air force during World War II even when told he
was too old to fly, working as an instructor when
necessary and as a pilot when allowed. He began
his final mission—one of a series of reconnaissance
flights over northern Africa, southern Italy, and

The tools of the author's trade are displayed on his desk at the home of Bernard Lamotte, who illustrated the 1942 work *Flight to Arras*.

southern France—on July 29, 1944. He was reported missing two days later and was shot down over southern France. The search for his plane ended in 1998 when a bracelet engraved with the name of the author's wife was found off the coast of Marseille; the wreckage of his plane was discovered and retrieved in 2003.

Both Pilot and Writer from the First

Saint-Exupery began recording his piloting experiences during the 1920s, and he had his first book published in 1929. *Courrier sud—Southern Mail—*a semi-autobiographical novel about an airmail pilot's failed romance, describes the glory of flight, the potential sadness of love, and the comfort found in attending to one's responsibilities. *Night Flight*, a novel published two years later, concerns the director of a postal airline and includes descriptions of Saint-Exupery's pioneering—and often hazardous—night flights across South America. "For the most part," wrote M. Parry in *Modern Language Review*, Saint-Exupery "deals with individuals who are prepared to risk their lives for something which will endure beyond themselves."

In response to critics who accused Saint-Exupery of portraying aviators as unrealistically heroic, the author's admirers asserted that he considered pilots no better than any other people. Rather, he used his often mystical airborne experiences and the ideal qualities he saw in good pilots to illustrate the spiritual contentment people sought and the ideal qualities he believed everyone could possess. "Saint-Exupery's characters are not interested in the plane as machine," observed *Dictionary of Literary Biography* contributor Catharine Savage Brosman, "but in what it allows them to do." Similarly, Saint-Exupery was not interested in his characters and stories as simply pilots and events, but as metaphors to help him describe ideas he found otherwise indescribable. "The most significant passages" of *Southern Mail*, according to Parry, "deal indirectly with metaphysical ideas such as time, change and movement, and the desire to penetrate beyond the surface appearance of reality to discover an underlying essence."

In an essay in the *French Review*, Bonner Mitchell observed that Saint-Exupery "was venturing upon largely unbroken ground in choosing to write directly about 'man's fate' while remaining in the realm of belles-lettres. Like [French authors André] Malraux, [Jean-Paul] Sartre, and [Albert] Camus after him, he achieved his first successes in the novel, but his message fitted less and less well into that form." Saint-Exupery's writings after *Night Flight* took the form of essays and vignettes, this time frankly autobiographical. *Terre des hommes—Wind, Sand, and Stars—*conveys the joys and perils of flight and of life itself in its many anecdotes, including one of a desert crash in which Saint-Exupery nearly perished. In 1935 he and a friend had entered a contest sponsored by the French Air Ministry to break the time record for flying from Paris to Saigon, Vietnam. More than two hundred miles into the Libyan desert they crashed and, with almost no water or food, remained for three days before being rescued by a passing Bedouin. For its combination of realistic description and philosophic discussion, *Wind, Sand, and Stars* was awarded the Grand Prix from France's Academie Française.

Duty to Country and Humanity

Reviewers consider Saint-Exupery's essay collection *Pilote de guerre—Flight to Arras—*more cohesive than *Wind, Sand, and Stars*. The author based *Flight to Arras* on the 1940 reconnaissance mission over German territory for which he received the Croix de Guerre. The text begins by describing Saint-Exupery's preparations and contempt for the mission, which he considers needlessly dangerous. In the course of the flight, however, his contempt gradually transforms into an acceptance of his duty, and possible hazards concern him less as his acceptance strengthens. Brosman praised the lyricism with which Saint-Exupery camouflages potential dangers: "Literary transformations—that is, metaphors—by which he depicts the sky and earth in poetic terms disguise the treachery of the experience, in which a blue evening sky and peaceful countryside below conceal mortal danger." Saint-Exupery ultimately embraces the assignment, pointless and dangerous as the task may still be, as a selfless and patriotic act that he must perform for himself, for his countrymen, and for all of humanity, if only to demonstrate that such selflessness and loyalty are possible. "The pilot before the flight was only conscious of himself as an individual," explained Richard Rumbold and Margaret Stewart in their portrait *The Winged Life*, "but [he] achieves during it a new sense of 'belonging' which is expressed in almost mystical terms."

Some commentators have considered the author's conclusion in *Flight to Arras* almost unbelievably patriotic and self-sacrificing, while others have admired Saint-Exupery's ideals. Rumbold and Stewart, for example, described *Flight to Arras* as "a

record, sincere, passionate, heart-searching, of Saint-Exupery's own reactions to the disaster to his country which he sees, in a . . . theme fundamental to the book, as part of the deeper crisis of our times. . . . In the modern world, he believed, man has lost an essential quality, described variously as a common incentive, a sense of mutual brotherhood, and what he calls the life of the spirit as opposed to the life of the intellect." In dutifully performing his mission as a French military pilot, Rumbold and Stewart suggested, Saint-Exupery was attempting to help restore that "common incentive" among his fellow citizens. The author's success in his attempt was evidenced by the admiration and reverence with which he was regarded by his fellow pilots and compatriots.

The Little Prince

Soon after his flight over Germany, Saint-Exupery traveled to the United States, where he remained three years and wrote *The Little Prince*, his most popular work among English-language readers. Of all of Saint-Exupery's writings, *The Little Prince* is often said to provide the most accurate and personal portrait of its author. Philip A. Wadsworth, writing in *Modern Language Quarterly*, observed that the author frequently recalled his happy childhood in his other writings, though "he never turned to childhood as an escape; for him the past was not another world but was still alive as part of his present." The author was frequently known to doodle whimsical sketches of a small child, and at the urging of friends he drew more sketches and created a story about them. Maxwell A. Smith, writing in his *Knight of the Air: The Life and Works of Antoine de Saint-Exupery*, described the story *The Little Prince* as "a delicate and ethereal fairy tale apparently addressed to children," but he added that "its wide philosophical overtones as a parable will be understood only by adults."

The Little Prince is narrated by a pilot who has crashed in the desert—as Saint-Exupery had done in 1935—and is attempting to repair his plane before his provisions run out. Before him appears a child, the Little Prince, who has traveled to earth from his own tiny planet, and who immediately asks the pilot for a drawing of a sheep to take back home. He also requests a muzzle for the sheep, so it won't eat the beautiful rose he has cultivated and grown to love. The Little Prince tells the pilot that when he first arrived on earth he entered a garden containing hundreds of roses identical to his own, and he was filled with sadness as he suddenly realized that his rose was not unique. A fox he befriended, though, told the Little Prince that it was

This classic fable, first published in 1943, concerns an interplanetary traveler's search for love, friendship, truth, and beauty.

An image of Saint-Exupery, whose life and art was a source of pride to the French, appeared on the 50-Franc note.

the time he spent loving and caring for his rose, and his responsibility for keeping the rose alive, that would make his rose special to him. The Little Prince returns to his planet—with the sheep but without the muzzle, which he has forgotten—by asking a poisonous desert snake to bite him. The pilot hopes, as he gazes toward the sky and remembers the Little Prince, that the prince has been able to prevent the sheep from eating his beloved rose.

P. L. Travers believed *The Little Prince*'s interpretation of love and responsibility would "shine upon children with a sidewise gleam." As Travers explained in the *New York Herald Tribune Weekly Book Review:* "It will strike them in some place that is not the mind and glow there until the time comes for them to comprehend it." Praising *The Little Prince*'s "poetic charm, . . . its freshness of imagery, its whimsical fantasy, delicate irony and warm tenderness," Smith predicted in *Knight in the Air* that *The Little Prince* would "join that select company of books like [Jean de] La Fontaine's *Fables*, [Jonathan] Swift's *Gulliver's Travels*, [Lewis] Carroll's *Alice in Wonderland* and [Maurice] Maeterlinck's *Blue Bird*,

which have endeared themselves to children and grown-ups alike throughout the world." Book sales of *The Little Prince* over half a century after its initial publication more than substantiated Smith's prediction.

An Unfinished Masterwork

In 1943, after completing *The Little Prince*, Saint-Exupery returned to his old flying squadron as an instructor and pilot in northern Africa, southern Italy, and southern France. For several years he had been working on his lengthiest and most ambitious writing project, but he had not completed it by the time of his death in 1944. The book, *Citadelle—The Wisdom of the Sands*—was published in 1948 with few editorial revisions, and it received that year's Prix des Ambassadeurs for exemplifying the spirit of France. "A huge tapestry, woven across the years in hours of solitude and leisure," according to Wadsworth, *The Wisdom of the Sands* "incorporates every thread of [Saint-Exupery's] thought and serves as a mighty backdrop for his other works." Although the book encompasses Saint-Exupery's main themes, it never mentions flying or pilots; instead, it concerns a society of desert dwellers and the reminiscences and proclamations of their leader. The French title, which means "citadel" or city fortress, noted Brosman, refers simultaneously to "the desert city which is the [book's] geographical center . . . ; the city of God . . . ; and the fortress within each man." Saint-Exupery's intent is to depict the "responsibility and interdependency," in Brosman's words, of the city's chief and his people—his responsibility for them, theirs for him, and theirs for each other—just as he emphasized his own country's and all of humanity's responsibility and interdependency in his earlier writings.

If you enjoy the works of Antoine de St. Exupery, you may also want to check out the following books:

Peter S. Beagle, *The Last Unicorn*, 1968.
Clyde Edgerton, *The Floatplane Notebooks*, 1988.
Paulo Coelho, *The Alchemist*, 1993.

The Wisdom of the Sands has often been compared with the Christian Old Testament and Friedrich Nietzsche's *Thus Spake Zarathustra* because of its length and its weighty, majestic tone. Some critics, including Rumbold and Stewart, lamented the fact that Saint-Exupery could not revise *The Wisdom of the Sands* before the volume's publication, as he had done dozens of times with his other manuscripts. "It is perhaps unfair to judge a work which was never completed or revised," acknowledged Rumbold and Steward, "but, as it stands, it is little more than a series of rambling, disconnected notes, and consequently produces, particularly when taken as a whole, an impression of verbosity and even incoherence." Reviewers such as Wadsworth, however, felt that the book's "rough-draft form . . . displays the author's entire and intimate expression of thought before being revised to meet his high artistic standards. . . . If this book lacks the nervous quality, the charged meanings, to which we are accustomed in Saint Exupery," Wadsworth declared, "it has the merit of showing us the author, pen in hand, in the act of baring his soul on paper."

For Brosman, *The Wisdom of the Sands* constitutes a fitting conclusion to Saint-Exupery's body of work. "The unity of Saint-Exupery's work derives from his style, his poetic vision of the world, and his moral concern," asserted Brosman, "which begins in *Courrier sud* by focusing on the quality of the individual, seen in relation to his tasks, and ends in *Citadelle* by posing the principles for the city of man." Wadsworth likewise found the themes of morality and responsibility permeating Saint-Exupery's writings and his life. Saint-Exupery's "gift," Wadsworth declared, "was that he saw no frontier between art and life, that he identified in his personality and in all his writing the artist, the thinker, and the man of action."

■ Biographical and Critical Sources

BOOKS

Breaux, Adele, *Saint-Exupery in America, 1942-1943: A Memoir,* Fairleigh Dickinson University Press (Rutherford, NJ), 1971.

Chadeau, Emmanuel, *Sainte-Exupery,* Plon (Paris, France), 1994.

Children's Literature Review, Volume 10, Gale (Detroit, MI), 1986.

DeRamus, Barnett, *From Juby to Arras: Engagement in Saint-Exupery,* University Press of America (Lanham, MD), 1990.

Des Vallieres, Nathalie, and Roselyne de Ayala, *Saint Exupery: Art, Writings, and Musings,* translated by Anthony Zielonka, Rizolli (New York, NY), 2004.

Dictionary of Literary Biography, Volume 72: *French Novelists, 1930-1960,* Gale (Detroit, MI), 1988.

Drewermann, Eugen, *Discovering the Royal Child Within: A Spiritual Psychology of the Little Prince,* Crossroad Publishing, 1993.

Forsberg, Roberta J., *Antoine de Saint-Exupery and David Beaty: Poets of a New Dimension,* Astra Books (New York, NY), 1974.

Harris, John R., *Chaos, Cosmos, and Saint-Exupery's Pilot-Hero: A Study in Mythopoeia,* University of Scranton Press (Scranton, PA), 1999.

Higgins, James E., *The Little Prince: A Reverie of Substance,* Twayne (Boston, MA), 1996.

Masters, Brian, *A Student's Guide to Saint-Exupery,* Heinemann (London, England), 1972.

Migeo, Marcel, *Saint-Exupery: A Biography,* Macdonald (London, England), 1961.

Robinson, Joy D. Marie, *Antoine de Saint-Exupery,* Twayne (Boston, MA), 1984.

Rumbold, Richard, and Margaret Stewart, *The Winged Life: A Portrait of Antoine de Saint-Exupery, Poet and Airman,* Weidenfeld & Nicolson (London, England), 1953.

Saint-Exupery, Consuelo de, *The Tale of the Rose: The Passion That Inspired "The Little Prince,"* Random House (New York, NY), 2001.

Schiff, Stacy, *Saint-Exupery: A Biography,* Knopf (New York, NY), 1994.

Smith, Maxwell A., *Knight of the Air: The Life and Works of Antoine de Saint-Exupery,* Pageant Press, 1956.

PERIODICALS

Atlantic Monthly, November, 1995, Nancy Caldwell Sorel, "Anne Morrow Lindbergh and Antoine de Saint-Exupery," p. 121.

Economist, December 5, 1998, "Hunting for Saint-Exupery: France's Superboy," p. 104.

French Review, April, 1960.

Horn Book, January-February, 1994, p. 95; July, 2000, review of *The Little Prince,* p. 429.

Insight on the News, February 6, 1995, p. 27.

Modern Language Quarterly, March, 1951.

Modern Language Review, April, 1974.

New York Herald Tribune Weekly Book Review, April 11, 1943.

New York Times Book Review, August 31, 1986.

School Library Journal, September, 2000, Molly Connally, review of *The Little Prince,* p. 259.

Time, August 4, 1986.

Washington Post Book World, July 27, 1986.*

Upton Sinclair

Senate from California, 1922, and for governor of California, 1926 and 1930; Democratic candidate for governor of California, 1934. Occasional lecturer.

■ Personal

Born September 20, 1878, in Baltimore, MD; died November 25, 1968, in Bound Brook, NJ; son of Upton Beall (a traveling salesman) and Priscilla (Harden) Sinclair; married Meta H. Fuller, 1900 (divorced, 1913); married Mary Craig Kimbrough (a poet), April 21, 1913 (died April 26, 1961); married Mary Elizabeth Willis, October 14, 1961 (died December 18, 1967); children: (first marriage) David. *Education:* City College (now City College of the City University of New York), A.B., 1897; graduate studies at Columbia University, 1897-1901. *Politics:* Formerly Socialist, then left-wing Democrat.

■ Career

Full-time writer, 1898-1962. Founder, Intercollegiate Socialist Society (now League for Industrial Democracy), Helicon Home Colony, Englewood, NJ, 1906, and EPIC (End Poverty in California) League, 1934; assisted U.S. Government in investigation of Chicago stock yards, 1906; established theater company for performance of socialist plays, 1908. Socialist candidate for U.S. House of Representatives from New Jersey, 1906, and from California, 1920, for U.S.

■ Member

Authors League of America (founder), American Institute of Arts and Letters, American Civil Liberties Union (founder of Southern California chapter).

■ Awards, Honors

Nobel Prize for literature nomination, 1932; Pulitzer Prize, 1943, for *Dragon's Teeth;* Page One Award, New York Newspaper Guild, 1962; Social Justice Award, United Auto Workers, 1962.

■ Writings

NOVELS

Springtime and Harvest: A Romance, Sinclair Press, 1901, published as *King Midas,* Funk (New York, NY), 1901, 2nd edition, Heinemann (London, England), 1906.

The Journal of Arthur Stirling, revised and condensed edition, Appleton (New York, NY), 1903, new edition, Heinemann (London, England), 1907.

Prince Hagen: A Phantasy, L. C. Page and Co., 1903, reprinted, Arno (New York, NY), 1978.

Manassas: A Novel of the War, Macmillan (New York, NY), 1904, revised edition published as *Theirs Be the Guilt: A Novel of the War between the States,* Twayne (Boston, MA), 1959, original edition, introduction by Kent Gramm, University of Alabama Press (Tuscaloosa, AL), 2000.

The Jungle, Doubleday (New York, NY), 1906, reprinted, See Sharp Press (Tucson, AZ), 2003.

A Captain of Industry, Being the Story of a Civilized Man, The Appeal to Reason, 1906, reprinted, Haldeman-Julius (Girard, KS), 1924.

The Overman, Doubleday, Page and Co. (New York, NY), 1907.

The Moneychangers, B. W. Dodge and Co. (New York, NY), 1908, reprinted, Classic Books (Murrieta, CA), 2000.

The Metropolis, Moffat, Yard and Co., 1908.

Samuel the Seeker, B. W. Dodge and Co., 1910.

Love's Pilgrimage, M. Kennerley (New York, NY), 1911, reprinted, Classic Books (Murrieta, CA), 2000.

The Millennium: A Comedy of the Year 2000, Laurie (London, England), 1912, reprinted, Seven Stories Press (New York, NY), 2000.

Damaged Goods (novelization of play "Les Avaries" by Eugene Brieux), Winston, 1913, reprinted, Laurie (London, England), 1931, published as *Damaged Goods: A Novel about the Victims of Syphilis,* Haldeman-Julius (Girard, KS), 1948.

Sylvia, Winston, 1913, reprinted, Scholarly Press, 1970.

Sylvia's Marriage, Winston, 1914.

King Coal, Macmillan (New York, NY), 1917, reprinted, AMS Press (New York, NY), 1980.

Jimmie Higgins, Boni & Liveright (New York, NY), 1919, reprinted, University Press of Kentucky, 1970.

100 Percent: The Story of a Patriot (also see below), privately printed, 1920, published as *The Spy,* Laurie (London, England), 1920.

They Call Me Carpenter: A Tale of the Second Coming, Boni & Liveright (New York, NY), 1922, reprinted, Chivers, 1971.

Oil!, A. C. Boni (New York, NY), 1927, reprinted, University of California Press (Berkeley, CA), 1997.

Boston: A Documentary Novel of the Sacco-Vanzetti Case, A. C. Boni (New York, NY), 1928, published as *Boston: A Novel,* Laurie (London, England), 1929, reprinted, Robert Bentley, 1978, condensed edition published as *August 22,* Award Books, reprinted, Classic Books (Murietta, CA), 1998.

Mountain City, A. C. Boni (New York, NY), 1930.

Peter Gudge Becomes a Secret Agent (excerpted from *100 Percent*), State Publishing House, 1930.

Roman Holiday, Farrar & Rinehart (New York, NY), 1931.

The Wet Parade, Farrar & Rinehart (New York, NY), 1931.

Co-op: A Novel of Living Together, Farrar & Rinehart (New York, NY), 1936.

The Gnomobile: A Gnice Gnew Gnarrative with Gnonsense, but Gnothing Gnaughty (juvenile), illustrated by John O'Hara Cosgrave, Farrar & Rinehart (New York, NY), 1936, reprinted, Bobbs-Merrill (Indianapolis, IN), 1962.

No Pasaran! (They Shall Not Pass): A Story of the Battle of Madrid, Laurie (London, England), 1937.

Little Steel, Farrar & Rinehart (New York, NY), 1938, reprinted, AMS Press (New York, NY), 1976.

Our Lady, Rodale Press (Emaus, PA), 1938.

Limbo on the Loose: A Midsummer Night's Dream, Haldeman-Julius (Girard, KS), 1948.

Marie and Her Lover, Haldeman-Julius (Girard, KS), 1948.

Another Pamela; or, Virtue Still Rewarded, Viking (New York, NY), 1950.

What Didymus Did, Wingate (London, England), 1954, published as *It Happened to Didymus,* Sagamore Press (New York, NY), 1958.

Cicero: A Tragedy of Ancient Rome, privately printed, 1960.

Affectionately Eve, Twayne (Boston, MA), 1961.

The Coal War: A Sequel to King Coal, edited by John Graham, Colorado Associated University Press (Boulder, CO), 1976.

POLITICAL, SOCIAL, AND ECONOMIC STUDIES

The Industrial Republic: A Study of the America of Ten Years Hence, Doubleday, Page and Co. (New York, NY), 1907, reprinted, Hyperion Press (New York, NY), 1976.

(With Michael Williams) *Good Health and How We Won It, with an Account of the New Hygiene,* F. A. Stokes (New York, NY), 1909.

The Fasting Cure, M. Kennerley (New York, NY), 1911.

The Profits of Religion: An Essay in Economic Interpretation, privately printed, 1918, Vanguard (New York, NY), 1927, reprinted, Prometheus Books (Amherst, NY), 2000.

The Brass Check: A Study of American Journalism, privately printed, 1919, 11th edition, 1936, with an introduction by Robert W. McChesney and Ben Scott, University of Illinois Press (Urbana, IL), 2003.

The Book of Life, Mind and Body, Macmillan (New York, NY), 1921, 4th edition, privately printed, 1926.

The Goose-step: A Study of American Education, privately printed, 1923, revised edition, Haldeman-Julius (Girard, KS), 1923, reprinted, AMS Press (New York, NY), 1970.

The Goslings: A Study of the American Schools, privately printed, 1924, reprinted, AMS Press (New York, NY), 1970.

Mammonart: An Essay in Economic Interpretation, privately printed, 1925, reprinted, Simon Publications (San Diego, CA), 2003.

Letters to Judd, An American Workingman, privately printed, 1926, revised edition published as *This World of 1949 and What to Do about It: Revised Letters to a Workingman on the Economic and Political Situation*, Haldeman-Julius (Girard, KS), 1949.

The Spokesman's Secretary, Being the Letters of Mame to Mom, privately printed, 1926.

Money Writes!, A. C. Boni (New York, NY), 1927, reprinted, Scholarly Press, 1970.

Upton Sinclair Presents William Fox, privately printed, 1933, reprinted, Arno (New York, NY), 1970.

The Way Out: What Lies Ahead for America, Farrar & Rinehart (New York, NY), 1933.

I, Governor of California, and How I Ended Poverty: A True Story of the Future, Farrar & Rinehart (New York, NY), 1933.

The Lie Factory Starts, End Poverty League, 1934.

The EPIC Plan for California, Farrar & Rinehart (New York, NY), 1934.

EPIC Answers: How to End Poverty in California, End Poverty League, 1934, 2nd edition, 1935.

I, Candidate for Governor, and How I Got Licked, Farrar & Rinehart (New York, NY), 1935, introduction by James N. Gregory, University of California Press (Berkeley, CA), 1994, published as *How I Got Licked and Why*, Laurie (London, England), 1935.

We, People of America, and How We Ended Poverty: A True Story of the Future, National EPIC League, 1935, republished, University of California Press (Berkeley, CA), 1994.

The Flivver King: A Story of Ford-America, Haldeman-Julius (Girard, KS), 1937, published as *The Flivver King: A Novel of Ford-America*, Laurie (London, England), 1938, reprinted, Chivers, 1971.

(With Eugene Lyons) *Terror in Russia?: Two Views*, Richard R. Smith, 1938.

Your Million Dollars, privately printed, 1939, published as *Letters to a Millionaire*, Laurie (London, England), 1939.

Expect No Peace!, Haldeman-Julius (Girard, KS), 1939.

What Can Be Done about America's Economic Troubles, privately printed, 1939.

Telling the World, Laurie (London, England), 1940.
The Cup of Fury, Channel Press, 1956.

PLAYS

Plays of Protest (includes *The Naturewoman, The Machine, The Second-story Man*, and *Prince Hagen*), M. Kennerley (New York, NY), 1912, reprinted, Scholarly Press, 1970.

Hell: A Verse Drama and Photo-play, privately printed, 1923.

Singing Jailbirds: A Drama in Four Acts, privately printed, 1924.

Bill Porter: A Drama of O. Henry in Prison, privately printed, 1925.

Oil! (four-act play; adaptation of his novel), privately printed, 1929.

Depression Island, Laurie (London, England), 1935.

Wally for Queen!: The Private Life of Royalty, privately printed, 1936.

Marie Antoinette, Vanguard (New York, NY), 1939.

A Giant's Strength, Laurie (London, England), 1948.

The Enemy Had It Too (three-act), Viking (New York, NY), 1950.

JUVENILE NOVELS; UNDER PSEUDONYM CLARKE FITCH

Courtmartialed, Street Smith, 1898.
Saved by the Enemy, Street Smith, 1898.
Wolves of the Navy; or, Clif Faraday's Search for a Traitor, Street Smith, 1899.
A Soldier Monk, Street Smith, 1899.
A Soldier's Pledge, Street Smith, 1899.
Clif, the Naval Cadet; or, Exciting Days at Annapolis, Street Smith, 1903.
From Port to Port; or, Clif Faraday in Many Waters, Street Smith, 1903.
The Cruise of the Training Ship; or, Clif Faraday's Pluck, Street Smith, 1903.
A Strange Cruise; or, Clif Faraday's Yacht Chase, Street Smith, 1903.

"LANNY BUDD" SERIES; NOVELS

World's End, Viking (New York, NY), 1940, reprinted, Curtis Books, 1968.
Between Two Worlds, Viking (New York, NY), 1941, reprinted, Curtis Books, 1968.
Dragon's Teeth, Viking (New York, NY), 1942, reprinted, New American Library (New York, NY), 1968.
Wide Is the Gate, Viking (New York, NY), 1943.
Presidential Agent, Viking (New York, NY), 1944.
Dragon Harvest, Viking (New York, NY), 1945.

THE JUNGLE

UPTON SINCLAIR

An international best-seller, this 1906 work exposed the wretched conditions in Chicago's meat-packing plants.

A World to Win, 1940-1942, Viking (New York, NY), 1946.

Presidential Mission, Viking (New York, NY), 1947.

One Clear Call, Viking (New York, NY), 1948.

O Shepherd, Speak, Viking (New York, NY), 1949.

The Return of Lanny Budd, Viking (New York, NY), 1953.

OTHER

(Under pseudonym Frederick Garrison) *Off for West Point; or, Mark Mallory's Struggle,* Street Smith, 1903.

(Under Garrison pseudonym) *On Guard; or, Mark Mallory's Celebration,* Street Smith, 1903.

(Editor) *The Cry for Justice: An Anthology of the Literature of Social Protest,* Winston, 1915, 2nd revised edition, Barricade Books (New York, NY), 1996.

Mental Radio, A. C. Boni (New York, NY), 1930, published as *Mental Radio: Does It Work, and How?,* Laurie (London, England), 1930, revised edition, C. C. Thomas, 1962, original edition reprinted, Hampton Roads (Charlottesville, VA), 2001.

American Outpost: A Book of Reminiscences, Farrar & Rinehart (New York, NY), 1932, published as *Candid Reminiscences: My First Thirty Years,* Laurie (London, England), 1932), reprinted, Kennikat Press, 1969.

The Book of Love, Laurie (London, England), 1934.

An Upton Sinclair Anthology, compiled by I. O. Evans, Farrar & Rinehart (New York, NY), 1934, revised edition, Murray Gee, 1947.

What God Means to Me: An Attempt at a Working Religion, privately printed, 1935, Farrar & Rinehart (New York, NY), 1936.

A Personal Jesus: Portrait and Interpretation, Evans Publishing Co., 1952, 2nd edition published as *The Secret Life of Jesus,* Mercury Books, 1962.

My Lifetime in Letters, University of Missouri Press (Columbia, MO), 1960.

Autobiography, Harcourt (New York, NY), 1962.

(Author of foreword) Morton T. Kelsey, *Tongue Speaking,* Doubleday (New York, NY), 1964.

The Land of Orange Groves and Jails: Upton Sinclair's California, edited by Lauren Coodley, Heyday Books (Berkeley, CA), 2004.

Sinclair's personal papers, books, manuscripts, and other materials are housed in the Lilly Library at Indiana University.

■ Adaptations

Sinclair's works adapted for film include *The Adventurer,* U.S. Amusement Corp., 1917; *The Money Changers,* Pathé Exchange, 1920; *Marriage Forbidden,* Criterion, 1938; and *The Gnome-Mobile,* Walt Disney Productions, 1967. *The Jungle* was adapted as a graphic novel by Peter Kuper and Emily Russell, ComicsLit (New York, NY), 2004.

■ Sidelights

"He was a man with a cause, and his weapon was an impassioned pen." With these words, a *National Observer* reporter summed up the life of Upton Sinclair, one of the twentieth century's foremost novelists, journalists, and pamphleteers. A "muckraker" whose motto, like that of American reformer Wendell Phillips, was "If anything can't stand the truth, let it crack," Sinclair spent most of his ninety years engaged in what William A. Bloodworth, Jr., in the *Dictionary of Literary Biography* called "idealistic opposition to an unjust society." Time and time again, in books like his international best-seller *The Jungle*—a graphic portrayal of the wretched lives of workers in Chicago's meat-packing plants—the socialist crusader set out to reveal what he described as "the breaking of human hearts by a system which exploits the labor of men and women for profits."

A Reaction to a Morally Fragmented Age

According to Bloodworth, Sinclair pursued his theme of social justice for all with "single-minded intensity." He regarded all art as propaganda, continues the critic, using the novel not only to denounce wealth, corruption, and "loose morals"—alcohol and promiscuity were favorite targets—with puritanical fierceness, but also "to publicize and interpret contemporary events that he felt had not been adequately covered by the news media." And because Sinclair believed that the primary purpose of his books was to bring about improvement in the human condition, he placed more emphasis on content than on form, a major factor in the development of his reputation as a writer who displayed more zeal than style.

In addition to zeal, Sinclair was noted for his morally simple view of history, a view that is especially evident in his "Lanny Budd" novels. This eleven-volume series, begun in 1940 and completed in 1953, traces the political history of the Western world from 1913 to 1950. It describes historical change in terms of international conspiracy and conflict, primarily between the forces of progress—socialism and communism—and the forces of oppression—fascism. As the series moves forward in time, however, America of the 1930s and 1940s takes up the cause of progress to do battle with both fascism and Soviet-style communism. Sinclair, who took pleasure in responding to his critics, had a simple explanation for his commonplace style and tendency toward oversimplification. "Somebody has to write for the masses and not just the Harvard professors," he once remarked. "I have tried to make my meaning plain so that the humblest can understand me."

Sinclair enthusiastically supported U.S. President Franklin Roosevelt and abhorred Soviet Stalinism, and his equally simple view of human nature is evident in his characterization. Virtually all of his figures are two-dimensional, more symbolic than real. His typical hero is a young and noble paragon of socialism; his typical villain is usually the personification of a specific trait such as greediness or corruption. Explained V. F. Calverton in the *Nation*: Sinclair's "characters are rational—or cerebral if

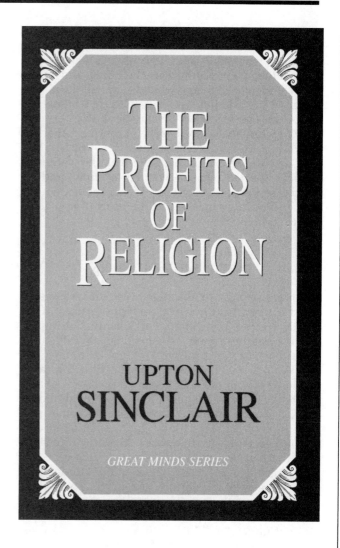

Sinclair presents his views on the hypocrisies of organized religion in this 1918 book.

you will—rather than emotive creations. One can see them but not experience them. This is partly due to the fact that, in the main, they are types instead of individuals, types that you know. . . . Sinclair tends to portray his characters in terms of straight lines instead of in terms of all those zigzags of personality, those intricate and irrational contradictions of self, which create individuality in life as well as in fiction."

In his book *Sketches in Criticism*, Van Wyck Brooks presented a more pointed assessment of Sinclair's characters. It is hardly surprising, he noted, that "Sinclair should be popular with the dispossessed: they who are so seldom flattered find in his pages a land of milk and honey. Here all the workers wear haloes of pure golden sunlight and all the capitalists have horns and tails; socialists with fashionable

English wives invariably turn yellow at the appropriate moment, and rich men's sons are humbled in the dust, winsome lasses are always true unless their fathers have money in the bank, and wives never understand their husbands, and all those who are good are also martyrs, and all those who are patriots are also base. Mr. Sinclair says that the incidents in his books are based on fact and that his characters are studied from life. . . . But Mr. Sinclair, like the rest of us, has seen what he wanted to see and studied what he wanted to study; and his special simplification of the social scene is one that almost inevitably makes glad the heart of the victim of our system."

A Childhood of Hardship

Sinclair's strong identification with "the masses" is most often attributed to the circumstances of his youth. He was born into an aristocratic but impoverished Southern family whose financial difficulties dated back to the U.S. Civil War era. His father, Upton Beall, a traveling salesman who turned to alcohol to cope with the unaccustomed pressures of having to work for a living, rarely made enough money to provide Upton and his mother with some measure of comfort. This life of genteel hardship contrasted sharply with that of Priscilla Sinclair's wealthy Baltimore relatives; it was a difference that disturbed young Sinclair, who could not understand why some people were rich and others poor. Many years later, at the age of eighty-five, he would remark at a gathering held in his honor that he still did not understand.

A sickly but precocious child, Sinclair entered New York's City College at the age of fourteen. Determined to become financially independent from his unreliable father, he immediately began submitting jokes, riddles, poems, and short stories to popular magazines; by the time he graduated, Sinclair was selling full-length adventure novels published under various pseudonyms to Street Smith, one of the day's foremost publishers of pulp fiction. During this period, the teenager learned to write quickly, prolifically, and with a minimum of effort, turning out an average of six to eight thousand words per day, seven days per week.

After receiving his degree from City College, Sinclair went on to graduate school at Columbia University, where he was attracted to the romantic poets and their belief in the power of literature to make an appreciable difference in the world. The thought of being able to influence the course of human events was so appealing to the young student that he decided to give up hack writing and concentrate on "real" writing instead.

The next few years were filled with nothing but misery for Sinclair, his wife, and their infant son as the writer watched his first three highly idealistic, semi-autobiographical novels fade into oblivion soon after being published. Increasingly bitter, depressed, and even physically ill from his life of deprivation, Sinclair decided to make one last attempt to write a popular romantic work. His dream of a Civil War trilogy never went beyond the first volume, *Manassas*, but this single novel proved to be the turning point in his career. With its theme of a rich young Southerner who rejects plantation life to join the abolitionist movement, *Manassas* demonstrated the author's growing interest in radical politics and eventually brought him to the attention of the American Socialists.

Embraced by Socialist Press

Once in contact with members of the socialist movement, Sinclair began studying philosophy and theoretics in earnest and was soon invited to contribute articles to major socialist publications. In late 1904, Fred D. Warren, editor of the magazine *Appeal to Reason,* approached Sinclair and challenged him to write about the "wage slaves" of industry in the same way he had written about the "chattel slaves" on the Southern plantations of *Manassas.* Encouraged by his editor at Macmillan, Sinclair accepted Warren's challenge and took as his starting point an article he had worked on that very summer dealing with an unsuccessful strike in the Chicago meatpacking industry. Thus in November 1904, having moved his wife and son to a small New Jersey farm he had bought with the five-hundred-dollar advance he received for his novel-to-be, *The Jungle,* Sinclair set out for Chicago, promising to "shake the popular heart and blow the roof off of the industrial tea-kettle." It was, noted Bloodworth in his study *Upton Sinclair,* a trip that "made a traumatic, life-long impression on him." Explained the critic: "What World War I meant to Ernest Hemingway, what the experiences of poverty and crime meant to Jack London, the combination of visible oppression and underlying corruption in Chicago in 1904 meant to Upton Sinclair. *This* kind of evidence, *this* kind of commitment to social justice became the primal experience of his fiction. For at least the next four decades, . . . Sinclair would continually retell the story of what happened to him in Chicago."

Sinclair's investigative work for *The Jungle* took seven weeks, during which time the young man talked with workers and visited packing plants, both on an official basis and in disguise. "I sat at night in the homes of the workers, foreign-born and native, and they told me their stories, one after one,

"Sinclair" dollars were used to discredit the author's gubernatorial campaign in California.

and I made notes of everything," he once recalled. "In the daytime I would wander about the yards, and their friends would risk their jobs to show me what I wanted to see."

Returning to New Jersey in December 1904, Sinclair began writing with his customary compulsiveness. "For three months," he said, "I worked incessantly. I wrote with tears and anguish, pouring into the pages all that pain which life had meant to me. Externally, the story had to do with a family of stockyards workers, but internally it was the story of my own family. Did I wish to know how the poor suffered in winter time in Chicago? I had only to recall the previous winter in the cabin, where we had only cotton blankets, and had to put rugs on top of us, and cowered shivering in our separate beds. It was the same with hunger, with illness, with fear."

Sinclair fashioned his story around the experiences of Jurgis Rudkus, a fictional Lithuanian immigrant who arrives in Chicago with his family "expecting to achieve the American dream," Bloodworth wrote. "Instead," the critic continued, "their life becomes a nightmare of toil, poverty, and death. . . . [Rudkus] not only sees his father, wife, and son die, but he is also brutalized by working conditions in the Chicago packing houses and exploited by corrupt politics." To dramatize his story of pain and oppression, Sinclair included some unpleasant passages on the meat-packing process itself, focusing on the dis-

eased and chemically tainted condition of the products manufacturers were offering to the American public.

Having spent most of his novel chronicling the tragedy of life in Packingtown, Sinclair was left with the problem of ending *The Jungle* on a note of socialist hope. It was not enough to show that capitalism crushed the lives of workers, he decided; he had to prove that socialism was the best way to overcome capitalist exploitation. Though Sinclair wanted to avoid sermonizing, he saw no alternative: his hero, devastated by his brutal experiences, was in no condition to lead a revolution. Thus, the author has the despondent Rudkus stumble into a political meeting where he undergoes what most critics have likened to a religious conversion, won to socialism as he listens to the words of various orators. Explained Bloodworth: "Sinclair finally presents Socialistic concepts in the closing chapters of [*The Jungle*] as part of a radical morality play in which the hero comes to accept as sinful the way in which he has worked unresistingly and individualistically within the capitalist system."

Sinclair completed *The Jungle* in late 1905. Though a serialized version in *Appeal to Reason* had begun to attract attention as early as the summer of that year, the book version caused officials at Macmillan and four other companies the author approached to balk at the idea of publishing potentially libelous material. Eventually, however, after sending investigators to Chicago to check out Sinclair's facts, the firm of Doubleday, Page and Company agreed to bring out *The Jungle*.

The Jungle Produces Public Outcry

The book appeared early in 1906 and, in an ironic twist of fate, was promoted not as a socialist novel, but as an exposé of "the flagrant violations of all hygienic laws in the slaughter of diseased cattle . . . and in the whole machinery of feeding a nation." Published at a time of growing public outcry against contaminated food, *The Jungle* shocked and infuriated Americans; it was, in fact, this widespread revulsion that made the book a best seller and its author a world-famous writer. Well aware of the real reason for *The Jungle*'s success, Sinclair once remarked, "I aimed at the public's heart, and by accident I hit it in the stomach."

Observed Alfred Kazin in his *On Native Grounds:* "*The Jungle* attracted attention because it was obviously the most authentic and most powerful of the muckraking novels. The romantic indignation of the book gave it its fierce honesty, but the facts in it gave Sinclair his reputation, for he had suddenly given an unprecedented social importance to muckraking. The sales of meat dropped, the Germans cited the book as an argument for higher import duties on American meat, Sinclair became a leading exponent of the muckraking spirit to thousands in America and Europe, and met with the president of the United States. No one could doubt it, the evidence was overwhelming: here in *The Jungle* was the great news story of a decade written out in letters of fire."

While few reviewers dispute the remarkable emotional impact of *The Jungle,* many believe its "letters of fire" do not constitute great literature. Its plot and characterization have come under increasingly heavy fire in the years since 1906. *Bookman*'s Edward Clark Marsh, for instance, found it "impossible to withhold admiration of Mr. Sinclair's enthusiasm" as he describes the "intolerable" conditions in Packingtown. But "when [the author] betakes

During his final, unsuccessful run for governor of California in 1934, Sinclair made the cover of *Time* magazine.

himself to other scenes, and attempts to let his characters breathe the air of a more familiar life," continues the critic, "it is impossible not to recognize his ignorance." Furthermore, declared Marsh, "we do not need to be told that thievery, and prostitution, and political jobbery, and economic slavery exist in Chicago. So long as these truths are before us only as abstractions they are meaningless."

Several reviewers expressed disappointment with the book's ending, especially the abrupt switch from fiction to political rhetoric that occurs when Jurgis is converted to socialism. Writing in *The Strenuous Age in American Literature,* Grant C. Knight observed that the final section "is uplifting but it is also artificial, an arbitrary re-channelling of the narrative flow, a piece of rhetoric instead of a logical continuation of story." In his *The Radical Novel in the United States, 1900-1954,* Walter Rideout accepted the notion of a religious-like conversion to socialism as being "probable enough," but declared that from that point onward *The Jungle* becomes "intellectualized" as political philosophy supplants Jurgis as the novel's focus. In short, noted Bloodworth, Sinclair failed to "carry out his intentions of a heart-breaking story with imminent Socialism. Instead, he settled for an uneven story dealing mainly with proletarian experience until the last four chapters, which switch disturbingly to the Socialist movement, its leaders, and its ideas."

Some critics have regarded this ending not so much as a demonstration of Sinclair's lack of literary skill as a confirmation of his elitism and essentially nineteenth-century liberal—rather than socialist—bent. Like several of his colleagues, Rideout maintained that Sinclair has more in common with someone like Charles Dickens than with most other socialist writers, observing that the two men champion not "blood and barricades, but . . . humanitarianism and brotherly love." Granville Hicks, commenting in his book *The Great Tradition,* maintained that Sinclair's socialism was "of the emotional sort, a direct response to his own environment, and, as a result of his failure to undergo an intense intellectual discipline, . . . his bourgeois upbringing. Though his aim has been socialistic, his psychology has remained that of the liberal. Therefore, whether he realizes it or not, he is always writing for the middle class, trying to persuade his fellows to take their share of the burden of humanity's future, to pity the poor worker and strive for his betterment." Bloodworth also believed that Sinclair's socialism "had an obvious middle-class bias to it. Although he spoke *for* the lowest working classes, he spoke *to* a much wider audience in *The Jungle.* . . . [In the last few chapters of the novel] Sinclair's attitudes towards his protagonist and the lower social class he represents seem to take on qualities of paternalism and condescension. . . . The overcoming of capitalism that the orator speaks of does not really seem to be the task of the working class. The responsibilities fall mainly on the shoulders of men like himself—articulate, educated, even wealthy spokesmen." Brooks, noting that Sinclair fosters "the emotion of self-pity" among members of the working class because he chooses to depict "the helplessness, the benightedness, [and] the naivete of the American workers' movement," wondered how the author expects such an inept group to master their own fate and advance the cause of socialism.

Literature or Polemic?

To most critics, questions regarding the amount of literary skill or philosophical consistency in *The Jungle* remain beside the point; what does count, they say, is the book's undeniably strong emotional impact. Wrote Bloodworth: "As a work of modern fiction measured against the aesthetic achievements of a Henry James or a William Faulkner or a James Joyce, *The Jungle* hardly merits any discussion at all. Psychological complexity is alien to Sinclair's characterization, style is a matter of piling up details and modifiers, and structure is confused after the first twenty-one chapters." Nevertheless, the reviewer continued, "while such criticisms are common as well as obvious, they seem out of place, almost completely unrelated to the features of *The Jungle* that contribute to or detract from its significance and power. . . . In [simple] terms, *The Jungle* is a muckraking novel directed at documenting conditions and striving for an emotional response on the part of readers. In his novel Sinclair attacks traditional distinctions between literature and life. With *The Jungle* literature is less a way of ordering and interpreting experience—less the imposition of a particular artistic vision—than a way of simply presenting life and, in the subjective way that Sinclair does this, responding to it with regret, shame, and anger."

Writing in the *New Republic,* Robert Herrick presented an emphatic defense of Sinclair. "Sophisticated readers, professors and critics, hold that Mr. Sinclair's novels are not 'literature'—whatever that may mean," the critic noted. "If a passionate interest in the substance of all great literature—life, if a wide acquaintance with its special manifestations of the writer's own day, if a deep conviction about the values underlying its varied phenomena and the ability to set them forth, count in the making of enduring literature, all these Mr. Sinclair has demonstrated again and again that he possesses."

Never again did Sinclair write a novel with quite the impact of *The Jungle.* In fact, Bloodworth contended, the success of this one book "virtually guar-

During his career, the muckraking novelist and journalist received a Pulitzer Prize as well as a Nobel Prize nomination.

anteed that the rest of [Sinclair's] career would be anticlimactic." In the book *Sixteen to One,* David Karsner expanded on this idea, stating: "I cannot help but feel that *The Jungle* gave Sinclair a bad start by making him famous before he had reached his maturity as an artist. It chained him to propaganda and placed him in the literary pulpit where [he continued to preside] over our social morals and economic manners. . . . The true artist does not address his readers from a rostrum."

Because of his many highly publicized failures and eccentricities, as well as his tendency to polarize readers and critics, Sinclair has proven to be somewhat of a problem for those attempting to determine his place in American literature. As Bloodworth pointed out in his study of the author: "Sympathetic critics have generally seen him as a passionate crusader who selflessly attacked injustice whenever it reared its ugly head in American life and who shied away from few subjects, however unpopular they were at the time. . . . On the other hand, detractors have always found Sinclair an easy target. Politically, he is not only open to attacks from conservative critics, but his liberal ideas are often inconsistent, his radicalism often naive. His support of such quackish causes as fasting and psychic healing has often been an embarrassment to readers who might agree with him politically. Recent radical critics, those with a New Left orientation, have found little inspiration in Sinclair. Above all, he has been scorned by literary critics and scholars who find him simple-minded and shallow beside the

If you enjoy the works of Upton Sinclair, you may also want to check out the following books:

Lincoln Steffens, *The Shame of the Cities*, 1904.
Jack London, *War of the Classes*, 1905.
John Steinbeck, *The Grapes of Wrath*, 1939.

great twentieth-century writers who were, after all, his competitors in the race for reputation and recognition."

Noting that Sinclair was "never a great writer in the terms of style and structure, never a symbolist or a modernist, interested in the external affairs of society and politics rather than in the internal affairs of human consciousness, journalistic and populistic rather than poetic and eloquent," Bloodworth went on to characterize the author as "a nineteenth century moral idealist somewhat ill at ease in the twentieth century but almost totally committed to the exploration and, where possible, reform of the world around him. . . . No writer ever made [this subject] so exclusively his or her *raison d' etre* as Sinclair did. Even within a larger realization of his literary weaknesses and intellectual ambivalences, and taking into account even his blindness to racial oppression, Sinclair's commitment to social justice commands respect. . . . [His works have] survived to be read and to produce often striking effects." In short, concluded the critic, "no picture of twentieth century American life could pretend to be complete without him."

"Sinclair originated *none* of the ideas for which he propagandized, nor did he claim to have," observed Leon Harris in his book *Upton Sinclair: American Rebel*. "But he convinced millions of people all over the world of them. Other of his contemporary muckrakers played a greater role than he in effecting particular social change. But not one of them approached his total influence in regard to all the ideas he advocated. In the variety of his work and in his incomparable success in having it widely reprinted, discussed, attacked, and kept in print, Sinclair outweighed all other individual muckrakers."

These sentiments were echoed by Arthur Koestler in his eightieth-birthday tribute to Sinclair, as recorded in the *Dictionary of Literary Biography*: "Perhaps a writer is judged by posterity not so much by the actual text of his work as by the size of the hole that would be left in the fabric of history had he

never lived. Other authors in our age outshone Sinclair in artistic quality, subtlety of characterization, and so on, but I can think of no contemporary writers whose non-existence would leave such a gaping hole in the face of the twentieth century than Upton Sinclair's."

■ Biographical and Critical Sources

BOOKS

American Writers, Scribner (New York, NY), 2000.
Blinderman, Abraham, editor, *Critics on Upton Sinclair*, University of Miami Press (Miami, FL), 1975.
Bloodworth, William A., Jr., *Upton Sinclair*, Twayne (Boston, MA), 1977.
Brooks, Van Wyck, *Sketches in Criticism*, Dutton (New York, NY), 1932.
Brooks, Van Wyck, *The Confident Years*, Dutton (New York, NY), 1952.
Contemporary Literary Criticism, Gale (Detroit, MI), Volume 1, 1973, Volume 9, 1979, Volume 15, 1980, Volume 63, 1991.
Cowley, Malcolm, editor, *After the Genteel Tradition: American Writers since 1910*, Norton (New York, NY), 1937, published as *After the Genteel Tradition: American Writers 1910-1930*, Southern Illinois University Press (Carbondale, IL), 1964.
Dekle, Bernard, *Profiles of Modern American Authors*, Tuttle, 1969.
Dell, Floyd, *Upton Sinclair: A Study in Social Protest*, Doubleday (New York, NY), 1927, reprinted, AMS Press (New York, NY), 1970.
Dictionary of Literary Biography, Volume 9: *American Novelists, 1910-1945*, Gale (Detroit, MI), 1981.
Evans, I. O., compiler, *An Upton Sinclair Anthology*, Farrar & Rinehart (New York, NY), 1934.
Gaer, Joseph, *Upton Sinclair: Bibliography and Biographical Data*, B. Franklin (New York, NY), 1971.
Gottesman, Ronald, *Upton Sinclair: An Annotated Checklist*, Kent State University Press (Kent, OH), 1973.
Harris, Leon, *Upton Sinclair: American Rebel*, Crowell (New York, NY), 1975.
Harte, James Lambert, *This Is Upton Sinclair*, Rodale Press (Emaus, PA), 1938.
Hicks, Granville, *The Great Tradition*, revised edition, Biblo Tannen, 1967.
Karsner, David, *Sixteen Authors to One*, Books for Libraries, 1968.
Kazin, Alfred, *On Native Grounds: An Interpretation of Modern American Prose Literature*, Harcourt (New York, NY), 1942.

Knight, Grant C., *The Strenuous Age in American Literature*, University of North Carolina Press (Durham, NC), 1954.

Loggins, Vernon, *I Hear America . . .*, Crowell (New York, NY), 1937.

Millgate, Michael, *American Social Fiction*, Oliver & Boyd (London, England), 1964, Barnes & Noble (New York, NY), 1967.

Mitchell, Greg, *The Campaign of the Century: Upton Sinclair's Race for Governor of California and the Birth of Media Politics*, Random House (New York, NY), 1992.

Mookerjee, R.N., *Art for Social Justice: The Major Novels of Upton Sinclair*, Scarecrow Press (Metuchen, NJ), 1988.

Reference Guide to American Literature, 4th edition, St. James Press (Detroit, MI), 2000.

Rideout, Walter, *The Radical Novel in the United States 1900-1954: Some Interrelations of Literature and Society*, Harvard University Press (Cambridge, MA), 1956.

St. James Guide to Young Adult Writers, 2nd edition, St. James Press (Detroit, MI), 1999.

Schreiber, Georges, editor, *Portraits and Self-Portraits*, Houghton (Boston, MA), 1936.

Scott, Ivan, *Upton Sinclair: The Forgotten Socialist*, University Press of America (Lanham, MD), 1996.

Sinclair, Upton, *American Outpost* (autobiography), Farrar & Rinehart (New York, NY), 1934.

Sinclair, Upton, *The Autobiography of Upton Sinclair*, Harcourt (New York, NY), 1962.

Yoder, John A., *Upton Sinclair*, Ungar (New York, NY), 1975.

PERIODICALS

American Book Collector, Volume 20, number 8, 1970, Justin G. Turner, "Conversation with Upton Sinclair," pp. 7-10.

American Heritage, September-October, 1988, p. 34.

Atlantic, August, 1946; July-August, 2002, Christopher Hitchens, "A Capitalist Primer: Upton Sinclair's Realism Got the Better of His Socialism," p. 176.

Bookman, April, 1906.

Canadian Dimension, July-August, 1997, Fraser Bell, "The Other History," p. 35.

Chicago Tribune, April 16, 1932.

Christian Century, October 19, 1932.

College English, January, 1943; December, 1959.

Columbia Journalism Review, September-October, 1992, Curt Gentry, "Right Back Where We Started From," p. 60; March-April, 2003, James Boylan, review of *The Brass Check*, p. 57.

Critic, December, 1962-January, 1963.

Harper's, March, 1961.

Library Journal, April 15, 2003, Michael Rogers, review of *The Jungle*, p. 132.

Monthly Review, December, 1991, Christopher Phelps, review of *The Jungle*, p. 58; May, 2002, Robert W. McChesney and Ben Scott, "Upton Sinclair and the Contradictions of Capitalist Journalism," p. 1.

Nation, February 4, 1931; April 13, 1932.

New Republic, October 7, 1931; June 22, 1932, February 24, 1937; June 24, 1940; January 11, 1943; September 29, 1958; December 1, 1962; December 1, 1997, Richard White, review of *Oil!*, p. 38.

New Yorker, June 26, 1995, p. 66.

New York Herald Tribune, February 11, 1960.

New York Herald Tribune Books, December 9, 1962.

New York Times, March 3, 1906; June 16, 1906, August 22, 1988.

New York Times Book Review, May 13, 1962.

Publishers Weekly, December 13, 2004, review of *The Jungle*, p. 47.

Saturday Review, March 3, 1928; August 28, 1948.

Saturday Review of Literature, May 7, 1932.

Spectator, July 9, 1932.

Studies in American Fiction, spring, 1995, Scott Derrick, "What a Beating Feels Like: Authorship, Dissolution, and Masculinity in Sinclair's *The Jungle*," p. 85.

Time, December 14, 1962.

Utopian Studies, spring, 2001, Arthur O. Lewis, review of *The Millennium, a Comedy of the Year 2000*, p. 385.

Vanity Fair, August, 1991, p. 176.

■ Obituaries

PERIODICALS

Detroit Free Press, November 26, 1968.

Nation, December 9, 1968.

National Observer, December 2, 1968.

New York Times, November 27, 1968.

Publishers Weekly, December 9, 1968.

Time, December 6, 1968.

Times (London, England), November 27, 1968.

Washington Post, November 27, 1968.*

Tom Stoppard

1958-60; freelance reporter, 1960-63. Director of play *Born Yesterday*, London, England, 1973; director of film *Rosencrantz and Guildenstern Are Dead*, 1991. Member of Royal National Theatre Board, 1989—.

■ Personal

Born Tomas Straussler, July 3, 1937, in Zlin, Czechoslovakia; naturalized British citizen; son of Eugene Straussler (a physician) and Martha Stoppard; married Jose Ingle, 1965 (divorced, 1972); married Miriam Moore-Robinson (a physician), 1972 (separated); children: (first marriage) Oliver, Barnaby; (second marriage) Ed, one other son. *Education:* Educated in England and Continental Europe.

■ Addresses

Home—Chelsea Harbor, London, England. *Agent*—Peters, Fraser & Dunlop, The Chambers, 5th Floor, Chelsea Harbor, Lots Road, London SW10 0XF, England.

■ Career

Playwright, novelist, and radio and television script writer. *Western Daily Press*, Bristol, England, reporter and critic, 1954-58; *Evening World*, Bristol, reporter,

■ Member

Royal Society of Literature (fellow).

■ Awards, Honors

Ford Foundation grant to Berlin, 1964; John Whiting Award, Arts Council of Great Britain, 1967; London *Evening Standard* Drama Awards, 1967, for most promising playwright, 1972, for best play *Jumpers*, 1974, for best comedy *Travesties*, 1978, for *Night and Day*, and 1983, for best play *The Real Thing*; *Plays and Players* Awards for best new play, 1967, for *Rosencrantz and Guildenstern Are Dead*, and 1972, for *Jumpers*; Prix Italia, 1968, for *Albert's Bridge*; Antoinette Perry ("Tony") Awards for best play, 1968, for *Rosencrantz and Guildenstern Are Dead*, 1976, for *Travesties*, and 1984, for *The Real Thing*; New York Drama Critics Circle Awards, 1968, for best play, for *Rosencrantz and Guildenstern Are Dead*, 1976, for best play, for *Travesties*, and 1984, for best foreign play, for *The Real Thing*; Commander, Order of the British Empire, 1978; Shakespeare Prize (Hamburg, Germany), 1979; Academy Award nomination, and Los Angeles Critics Circle Award for best original screenplay (with Terry Gilliam and Charles McKeown), both 1985, both for *Brazil*; Golden Lion, Venice Film Festival, and Directors' Week award, Fantasporto, both 1990, both for *Rosencrantz and Guildenstern Are Dead*; Tony Award nomination for best play, 1995, for *Arcadia*; Academy Award, Golden Globe award, Chicago Film Critics Association award, Broadcast Film Critics Association award, London *Evening Standard* British Film award, Florida Film Critics Circle award, New York Film Critics Circle award, Southeastern Film Critics Association award, Writers Guild of America award, and Las Vegas Film Critics Society award (all with Marc Norman), all 1998, all for best original screenplay, for *Shakespeare in Love*; Silver Berlin Bear for outstanding single achievement, Berlin International Film Festival, 1998, for *Shakespeare in Love*; knighted, 1997; Order of Merit, 2000; inducted into Theater Hall of Fame, 2000. Honorary degrees include M.Lit. from University of Bristol, 1976, Brunel University, 1979, and University of Sussex, 1980, and degrees from University of London, 1982, Kenyon College, 1984, and University of York, 1984.

■ **Writings**

PLAYS

The Gamblers, produced in Bristol, England, 1965.

Tango (based on the play by Slawomir Mrozek; produced in London, England, 1966; produced on the West End, 1968), J. Cape (London, England), 1968.

Rosencrantz and Guildenstern Are Dead (three-act; also see below; first produced at Edinburgh Festival, 1966; produced on the West End, 1967; produced on Broadway, 1967), Grove (New York, NY), 1967.

Enter a Free Man (based on his teleplay *A Walk on the Water*; also see below; first produced on the West End, 1968; produced Off-Broadway, 1974), Faber (Boston, MA), 1968.

The Real Inspector Hound (one-act; first produced on the West End, 1968; produced Off-Broadway with *After Magritte*, 1972), Faber (London, England), 1968, Grove (New York, NY), 1969.

Albert's Bridge [and] If You're Glad I'll Be Frank (based on his radio plays; also see below; produced in Edinburgh, Scotland, 1969, produced in New York, NY, 1987), Faber (London, England), 1969.

Albert's Bridge, French (New York, NY), 1969.

After Magritte (one-act; first produced in London, England, 1970; produced Off-Broadway with *The Real Inspector Hound*, 1972), Faber (London, England), 1971, Grove (New York, NY), 1972.

Dogg's Our Pet (also see below; produced in London, England, 1971), published in *Six of the Best*, Inter-Action Imprint, 1976.

Jumpers (first produced on the West End, 1972; produced in Washington, DC, 1974; produced on Broadway, 1974, 2004), Grove (New York, NY), 1972, revised edition, Faber (Boston, MA), 1986.

Artist Descending a Staircase [and] Where Are They Now?, Faber (London, England), 1973.

The House of Bernarda Alba (based on the play by Federico García Lorca), produced in London, England, 1973.

Travesties (produced on the West End, 1974; produced on Broadway, 1974), Grove (New York, NY), 1975.

The Fifteen-Minute Hamlet, French (New York, NY), 1976.

Dirty Linen and New-Found-Land (produced in London, England, 1976; produced on Broadway, 1977), Grove (New York, NY), 1976.

Every Good Boy Deserves Favor (first produced in London, England, 1977, produced on the West End, 1978, produced at the Metropolitan Opera House, 1979), music by Andre Previn, Edition Wilhelm Hansen (New York, NY), 1982.

Night and Day (produced on the West End, 1978; produced on Broadway, 1979), Faber (Boston, MA), 1978, revised edition, French (New York, NY), 1980.

Dogg's Hamlet, Cahoot's Macbeth (one-act plays; *Dogg's Hamlet* based on his play *Dogg's Our Pet*; produced in New York, 1979), Inter-Action Inprint (London, England), 1979, Faber (Boston, MA), 1980.

Undiscovered Country (adapted from Arthur Schnitzler's *Das Weite Land*; produced on the West End, 1979; produced in Hartford, CT, 1981), Faber (Boston, MA), 1980.

On the Razzle (adapted from Johann Nestroy's *Einen Jux will er sich machen*; produced on the West End, 1981; produced in Los Angeles, CA, 1985), Faber (Boston, MA), 1981.

The Real Thing (produced on the West End, 1982; produced on Broadway, 1984, 2000), Faber (London, England), 1982, revised edition, Faber (Boston, MA), 1983.

Rough Crossing (adaptation of Ferenc Molnár's *The Play's the Thing*; produced in London, England, 1984; produced in New York, NY, 1990), Faber (Boston, MA), 1985.

Dalliance (adapted from Arthur Schnitzler's *Liebelei*), produced in London, England, 1986.

(Translator) Vaclav Havel, *Largo Desolato*, Faber (Boston, MA), 1987.

Hapgood (produced in London, England, then New York, NY, 1988), Faber (Boston, MA), 1988.

Artist Descending a Staircase (based on his radio play [also see below]; produced on the West End, 1988; produced on Broadway, 1989), Faber (Boston, MA), 1988.

(With Clive Exton) *The Boundary,* French (New York, NY), 1991.

Arcadia (produced in London, England, 1994; produced on Broadway, 1995), Faber (Boston, MA), 1993.

The Invention of Love (produced on Broadway, 2001), Grove (New York, NY), 1998.

Doing It: Five Performing Arts, edited by Robert B. Silvers, New York Review of Books (New York, NY), 2001.

(Translator) Anton Chekhov, *The Seagull,* Faber (New York, NY), 2001.

The Coast of Utopia, (trilogy of plays; contains *Voyage, Shipwreck,* and *Salvage*), produced in London, England, 2002), published individually, Grove (New York, NY), 2003.

Also author of *Home and Dry* and *Riley.*

SCREENPLAYS

(With Thomas Wiseman) *The Romantic Englishwoman,* New World Pictures, 1975.

Despair (adapted from the novel by Vladimir Nabokov), New Line Cinema, 1978.

The Human Factor (adapted from the novel by Graham Greene), Metro-Goldwyn-Mayer (MGM), 1980.

(With Terry Gilliam and Charles McKeown) *Brazil,* Universal, 1985.

Empire of the Sun (adapted from the novel by J. G. Ballard), Warner Brothers, 1987.

The Russia House (adapted from the novel by John le Carré), MGM/United Artists, 1989.

(And director) *Rosencrantz and Guildenstern Are Dead* (adapted from his play), Cinecom, 1991, published as *Rosencrantz and Guildenstern Are Dead: The Film,* Faber (Boston, MA), 1991.

Billy Bathgate (adapted from the novel by E. L. Doctorow), Touchstone, 1991.

(With Marc Norman) *Shakespeare in Love* (Miramax, 1998), Hyperion (New York, NY), 1998.

(Adaptor in English) *Vatel,* 2000.

Enigma (adapted from the novel by Robert Harris), Manhattan Pictures, 2001.

FOR TELEVISION

A Walk on the Water, ITV Television, 1963, broadcast as *The Preservation of George Riley,* British Broadcasting Corporation (BBC-TV), 1964.

A Separate Peace (based on the novel by John Knowles; BBC-TV, 1966), Samuel French (London, England), 1977.

Teeth, BBC-TV, 1967.

Another Moon Called Earth, BBC-TV, 1967.

Neutral Ground, Thames Television, 1968.

The Engagement (based on his radio play *The Dissolution of Dominic Boot;* also see below), NBC-TV, 1970.

One Pair of Eyes, BBC-TV, 1972.

(With Clive Exton) *Eleventh House,* BBC-TV, 1975.

(With Clive Exton) *Boundaries,* BBC-TV, 1975.

Three Men in a Boat (based on the novel by Jerome K. Jerome), BBC-TV, 1975.

Professional Foul, BBC-TV, 1977, Public Broadcasting Service (PBS-TV), 1978.

Squaring the Circle: Poland, 1980-81 (BBC-TV, 1985), Faber (Boston, MA), 1985.

FOR RADIO

The Dissolution of Dominic Boot, BBC, 1964.

"M" Is for Moon among Other Things, BBC, 1964.

If You're Glad I'll Be Frank (BBC, 1966), Faber (London, England), 1969, revised edition, Samuel French (New York, NY), 1978.

Albert's Bridge, BBC, 1967.

Where Are They Now?, BBC, 1970.

Artist Descending a Staircase, BBC, 1972.

The Dog It Was That Died, BBC, 1982.

In the Native State (BBC, 1991), Faber (Boston, MA), 1991, revised edition published as *Indian Ink,* Faber (Boston, MA), 1995.

Also author of episodes of radio serials *The Dales,* 1964, and *A Student's Diary,* 1965.

OMNIBUS VOLUMES

The Real Inspector Hound [and] *After Magritte,* Grove (New York, NY), 1970.

Artist Descending a Staircase and Where Are They Now?: Two Plays for Radio, Faber (London, England), 1973.

Albert's Bridge and Other Plays (contains *Albert's Bridge, If You're Glad I'll Be Frank, Artist Descending a Staircase, Where Are They Now?,* and *A Separate Peace*), Grove (New York, NY), 1977.

Every Good Boy Deserves Favor [and] *Professional Foul,* Grove (New York, NY), 1978.

The Dog It Was That Died, and Other Plays (contains *Teeth, Another Moon Called Earth, Neutral Ground, A Separate Peace, "M" Is for Moon among Other Things,* and *The Dissolution of Dominic Boot*), Faber (Boston, MA), 1983.

Four Plays for Radio, Faber (Boston, MA), 1984.

Squaring the Circle; Every Good Boy Deserves Favor; Professional Foul, Faber (Boston, MA), 1984.

Dalliance [and] *Undiscovered Country,* Faber (Boston, MA), 1986.

Stoppard: The Radio Plays, 1964-1983, Faber (Boston, MA), 1991.

Rough Crossing [and] *On the Razzle,* Faber (Boston, MA), 1991.

The Television Plays, 1965-1984, Faber (Boston, MA), 1993.

The Real Inspector Hound and Other Entertainments, Faber (Boston, MA), 1993, published as *The Real Inspector Hound and Other Plays,* Grove (New York, NY), 1996.

Tom Stoppard Plays (multivolume series), Faber (London, England), 1996—.

OTHER

Lord Malquist and Mr. Moon (novel), Anthony Blond (London, England), 1966, Knopf (New York, NY), 1968.

(With Paul Delaney), *Tom Stoppard in Conversation,* University of Michigan Press (Ann Arbor, MI), 1994.

(With Mel Gussow), *Conversations with Stoppard,* Limelight Editions (New York, NY), 1995.

(Author of introduction) Duchess of Devonshire, *Counting My Chickens: And Other Home Thoughts,* Farrar, Straus (New York, NY), 2002.

Contributor of short stories to *Introduction 2,* 1964; contributor of essay to *Anthony Fry,* Umbrage Editions, 2002. Reviewer, sometimes under pseudonym William Boot, for *Scene,* 1962.

■ Work in Progress

The screenplay adaptations of *His Dark Materials: The Golden Compass* by Philip Pullman, and *Tulip Fever,* by Deborah Moggach.

■ Sidelights

The plays of multi-award-winning British playwright Tom Stoppard have revolutionized twentieth-century theatre with their uniquely comic combinations of verbal intricacy, complex structure, and philosophical themes. With such works as *Rosencrantz and Guildenstern Are Dead, Jumpers, Trav-* *esties,* and *The Real Thing* to his credit, Stoppard compares with "the masters of the comic tradition," Joan Fitzpatrick Dean wrote in *Tom Stoppard: Comedy as a Moral Matrix.* "Like the best comic dramatists, his gift for language and physical comedy fuses with an active perception of the excesses, eccentricities, and foibles of man." "Stoppard is that peculiar anomaly—a serious comic writer born in an age of tragicomedy and a renewed interest in theatrical realism," Enoch Brater summarized in *Essays on Contemporary British Drama.* "Such deviation from dramatic norms . . . marks his original signature on the contemporary English stage," the critic continued, for his "'high comedy of ideas' is a refreshing exception to the rule."

Born Tomas Straussler in Czechoslovakia in 1937, Stoppard and his parents emigrated to England when he was young. Because his family was relatively affluent—his father was a physician—Stoppard was able to attend good schools in both Europe and England. After college, he began a career as a journalist, beginning as a reporter for Bristol, England's *Western Daily Press* and soon graduating to critic. Although he continued to work as a jour-

Rosencrantz and Guildenstern Are Dead, **which uses text and characters from William Shakespeare's** *Hamlet* **as a dramatic framework, was Stoppard's first major theatrical success.**

nalist throughout much of the 1950s and 1960s, Stoppard also began to develop his talents as a playwright, and in 1963 left journalism for good. The reason: his first teleplay, *Walk on the Water,* was produced by British television, and with several radio plays also in production, Stoppard decided to devote his full attention to his ultimate goal: writing for the stage. In 1965 his first play, *The Gamblers,* was produced in Bristol; his first play to reach the London stage was 1966's *Tango.*

From Journalist to Dramatist

"Stoppard's virtuosity was immediately apparent" in his first major dramatic work, *Rosencrantz and Guildenstern Are Dead,* Mel Gussow wrote in the *New York Times.* The play, which won the London *Evening Standard* award for best new play in 1967, revisits Shakespeare's *Hamlet* through the eyes of the two players whose task of delivering Hamlet's death sentence prompts their own execution instead. Vaguely aware of the scheming at Elsinore and their own irrelevance to it, Rosencrantz and Guildenstern meander through the drama playing games of language and chance until, circumscribed by Shakespeare's script, they cease to exist. By turning *Hamlet* "inside out" in this way, the play is able "to be simultaneously frivolous in conception but dead serious in execution," Brater stated, and it addresses issues of existentialism reminiscent of Samuel Beckett's drama *Waiting for Godot.* The result, the critic added, "is not only a relaxed view of *Hamlet,* but a new kind of comic writing halfway between parody and travesty."

Also notable is the play's innovative use of language and Shakespeare's actual text. *Rosencrantz and Guildenstern* is interwoven with references to *Hamlet* as well as actual lines of the bard's verse; in addition, Stoppard packs the drama with "intricate word plays, colliding contradictions and verbal and visual puns," as Gussow described it. "Stoppard's lines pant with inner panic," a *Time* reviewer noted, as the title characters, according to *Village Voice*'s Michael Smith, ultimately "talk themselves out of existence." The play, one of his earliest works, has also become one of Stoppard's most popular and acclaimed works, and in 1991 the playwright directed a film adaptation of the stage drama. "With its dazzling feel for the duplicities and delights of language and its sense that modern consciousness is a gummed-up kaleidoscope that needs to be given a severe shake," Jack Kroll of *Newsweek* contended, *Rosencrantz and Guildenstern* established "the characteristic Stoppard effect."

Stoppard makes use of another dramatic "adaptation" in his second Tony Award-winner, *Travesties.* The play takes as its starting point the historical fact

Adrian Scarborough (left) and Simon Russell Beale starred in a 1995 revival of Stoppard's multi-award-winning play *Rosencrantz and Guildenstern Are Dead.*

that Zurich of 1917 was inhabited by three revolutionaries: the Communist leader Lenin, modernist writer James Joyce, and dadaist poet-critic Tristan Tzara. Their interactions are related through the recollections of Henry Carr, a minor British official who meets Lenin at the local library and the others during a production of Oscar Wilde's *The Importance of Being Earnest.* In a manner similar to that of *Rosencrantz and Guildenstern Are Dead,* Stoppard uses plot line and characterization from Wilde's play to parallel and emphasize events and characters in his own work; the play "races forward on Mr. Stoppard's verbal roller coaster, leaving one dizzy yet exhilarated by its sudden semantic twists, turns, dips, and loops," Wilborn Hampton remarked in the *New York Times.* The result, Anne Wright wrote in her *Dictionary of Literary Biography* essay, is "a virtuoso piece, a 'travesty' of the style of each of its masters, including Joycean narrative and dadaist verse as well as Wildean wit. The parody extends to the discourse appropriate to Lenin, as the play incorporates lectures and polemical sequences."

Political Satire Set to Music

Stoppard's political concerns come to the fore in *Every Good Boy Deserves Favor,* a piece for actors and orchestra set to the music of Andre Previn. Set in a prison hospital inhabited by lunatics and dissidents, *Every Good Boy Deserves Favor* "has the witty dialogue and clever plot that we associate with Stoppard's plays, and a sense of social concern that we didn't," *Los Angeles Times* critic Dan Sullivan recounted. Stoppard brings the musicians into the action of the play through the character of a mad-

Travesties juxtaposes the politics and aesthetics of Communist leader Vladimir Lenin, modenist writer James Joyce, and dadaist poet Tristan Tzara, who all lived in Zurich, Switzerland, during World War I.

man who believes he conducts an imaginary orchestra; not only does the group respond to his direction, but one of the violinists doubles as his psychiatrist. The play's use of "irony, mixed identities, outrageous conceits (not to mention a full-scale symphony orchestra)," observed *Washington Post* contributor Michael Billington, distinguishes it as "the work of a dazzling high-wire performer." In addition, the critic noted, *Every Good Boy* is "a profoundly moral play about the brainwashing of political dissidents in Soviet mental hospitals."

John Simon of *New York,* however, faulted the play for being "too clever by half," and added that the concept of a play for full orchestra seems forced and contrived. But Gussow, in his review of the Metropolitan Opera production, thought that "the full orchestra and the enormous stage give the play a richness and even an opulence that embellishes the author's comic point of view." He continued: "So much of the comedy comes from the contrast between the small reality—two men in a tiny cell—

and the enormity of the delusion." "Nothing if not imaginative, Stoppard's plot makes the orchestra an active, provocative participant in the story," Richard Christiansen of the *Chicago Tribune* similarly declared. Nevertheless, the critic advised, the play also stands "on its own as a moving and eloquent work, an occasional piece of quick wit and deep thoughtfulness."

With *Night and Day* former journalist Stoppard broaches another "public issue—the role of the press in what is commonly called the Western World," as James Lardner described it in the *Washington Post.* Set in an African nation beset by revolution, *Night and Day* looks at issues of censorship, politics, colonialism, and journalistic ethics through the character of a young, idealistic reporter. "There are theatergoers who will not sit still for a play that encompasses an intellectual debate, no matter how gracefully rendered," Lardner commented, and indeed, some observers have criticized the play for emphasizing ideas over characters. *New York Times* reviewer Walter Kerr, for instance, said that "virtually no effort is made during the evening to link up thought and events, arguments and action. The debate really takes place in a void." In contrast, Judith Martin thought that in *Night and Day* "it even seems as if the good lines were written for the play, rather than the play's having been written to display unrelated good cracks," as she wrote in the *Washington Post Weekend*. "This is a taut drama, dealing intelligently and with a degree of moral passion with a range of difficult issues," Wright concluded. "Moreover, despite its clear plea for freedom of speech and action, the play does not oversimplify the issues: *Night and Day* presents a genuine dramatic debate which confronts divergent and often contradictory attitudes."

Heady Themes Sparked by "Verbal Pyrotechnics"

In the double-bill *Dogg's Hamlet, Cahoot's Macbeth*, Stoppard "brilliantly harnesses his linguistic ingenuity to his passion for the cause of artistic freedom," Gerald M. Berkowitz noted in *Theatre Journal*. In the first half, *Dogg's Hamlet*, a group of schoolboys contort the English language by giving entirely new meanings to familiar words; their interactions with puzzled outsiders culminate in an abbreviated performance of *Hamlet*. The second play, *Cahoot's Macbeth*, presents an underground performance of Shakespeare which is interrupted by government censors; only by switching to "Dogg," the language of the first play, do the actors avoid arrest. Critics have split over the effectiveness of this double-bill. *Chicago Tribune* writer Sid Smith, for instance, found that the second play "promises more than it delivers, certainly more than a rehash of the first play's comedy." Berkowitz, however, thought that "Stoppard knows what he's doing," for instead of reducing "this serious play to the farcical level of the first" the switch to Dogg reinforces his message, which "strikes us with tremendous power: repressive societies fear artistic expression because it is a 'language' they don't share and thus can't control." As a result, the critic concluded, *Dogg's Hamlet, Cahoot's Macbeth* "may well be [Stoppard's] most important play so far, and a harbinger of major works to come."

Berkowitz's words were prophetic, for in 1982 Stoppard premiered one of his most highly acclaimed dramas, *The Real Thing*. While the playwright returned to a favorite form—that of the play-within-a-play—his subject—"an imaginatively and uniquely theatrical exploration of the pain and the power of love," as Christiansen characterized it—surprised many critics. The opening reveals a man confronting his wife with evidence of her adultery;

it soon becomes clear, however, that this encounter is only a scene in a play. "Reality" is much more complex, for the actors in the first scene are being betrayed by their spouses—the playwright and his mistress Annie, another actress. Henry is the successful author of witty, cerebral dramas of infidelity, but his own struggles with love, especially those in his sometimes-troubled marriage to Annie, prove more difficult and painful. Annie's romantic involvement with a young actor and professional involvement with the young revolutionary Brodie cause Henry to not only question his assumptions about love, but his opinions about the significance of writing. While the meaning of the "real thing" might seem a commonplace theme for Stoppard to examine, "home truths can be banal," Sullivan observed. "All that an author can do is to write a non-banal play around them, and this Stoppard has done."

While many of Stoppard's plays have captured public attention despite their serious themes, some have proved to be more challenging than the average theatregoer might desire. His play *Arcadia* juxtaposes three different time periods on one stage—the years 1809 and 1812 as well as the present day—and combines such topics as mathematics and chaos theory, landscape gardening, and Lord Byron. In addition, Anne Barton noted in the *New York Review of Books*, "*Arcadia* constantly engages the imaginary in a dialogue with the historically true." Several reviewers noted the need for playgoers to review the printed text before seeing the play, see the play twice, or utilize both methods to yield a better understanding of the complex story. *The Coast of Utopia* is also a demanding work, and not just because the trilogy of plays is over nine hours long. The three works, *Voyage, Shipwreck*, and *Salvage*, cover thirty-five tumultuous years in the history of Russia, from 1833 to 1868, through the eyes of three radicals: Michael Bakunin, Vassarion Belinsky, and Alexander Herzen. Most of the major thinkers of the nineteenth century Russian intelligentsia make an appearance, as does Marx (in a dream), the German thinker who inspired the Communist movement. To Toby Young of the *Spectator*, the trilogy is "such heavy going that for several hours at a stretch it feels like watching history unfold in real time," but the *Nation*'s Carol Rocamora was more impressed. To her, *The Coast of Utopia* is "both a mesmerizing history lesson and a theatergoing discovery, leaving you dazzled, dazed and off to the theater bookstore to delve into this period of history."

Pens Film *Shakespeare in Love*

Stoppard's talents extend beyond writing for the stage; he is also noted for his radio plays, as well as for such highly literate screenplay adaptations as *Empire of the Sun, The Russia House, Tulip Fever,* and his own *Rosencrantz and Guildenstern Are Dead.* His most notable screenplay, however, is an original one: *Shakespeare in Love,* which won Stoppard and his collaborator Marc Norman both an Academy Award and a Golden Globe. The film lightheartedly imagines Shakespeare (played by Joseph Fiennes) as a struggling young writer, searching for inspiration for his current play, *Romeo and Ethel the Pirate's Daughter.* He finds it in the person of Lady Viola de Lesseps (played by Gwyneth Paltrow), who, disguised as a boy, takes a role in one of Shakespeare's plays. To truly understand the film, Lisa Schwarzbaum commented in *Entertainment Weekly,* the viewer needs "an adult appreciation of mistaken-identity plot devices and the Elizabethan tradition of men performing as women." Stoppard and Norman also weave quotations from various Shakespearean works into the dialogue, rewarding audience members who are familiar with the Shakespearean canon. In order to make those quotations work, throughout the film Stoppard and Norman "provide a modernization of Elizabethan language sleek enough to speed the action along but also 'period' enough for the several excerpts from *Romeo* not to seem too archaic by contrast," Richard Alleva noted in *Commonweal.*

Stoppard's use of various dramatic techniques, intricately worked into innovative forms, contribute much to the vitality of his plays, as well as for his film. "He is a skilled craftsman," Wright said, "handling with great dexterity and precision plots of extreme ingenuity and intricacy. The plays are steeped in theatrical convention and stock comic situations, with mistaken identity, verbal misunderstandings, innuendo, and farcical incongruity." The playwright's use of traditional dramatic elements, contended Dean, reveals his "penchant for and skill in parodying popular dramatic genres. Like most contemporary playwrights, he has not contented him-

Stoppard in conversation with Uta Hagen at the opening party for his play *The Invention of Love.*

If you enjoy the works of Tom Stoppard, you may also want to check out the following plays:

Samuel Beckett, *Waiting for Godot*, 1952.
N. F. Simpson, *A Resounding Tinkle*, 1957.
Eugène Ionesco, *Exit the King*, 1962.

self with the confines of representational drama but has broken out of those constraints by [reviving use] . . . of the soliloquy, aside, song, and interior monologue." Despite his "free" use of various dramatic forms, Stoppard is able to superimpose an overall structure on his plays, Victor Cahn declared in his *Beyond Absurdity: The Plays of Tom Stoppard:* "Amid all the clutter and episodic action, a structure emerges, a tribute to the organizing powers of the playwright's rationality and his expectations of the audience's ability to grasp that structure." As the author related to Kroll, "Theater is an event, not a text. I respond to spectacle. Ambushing the audience is what theater is all about."

Part of Stoppard's "ambush" involves the way he shrewdly infuses his plays with sophisticated concepts. As Billington described, Stoppard "can take a complex idea, deck it out in fancy dress and send it skipping and gambolling in front of large numbers of people," for the playwright has "a matchless ability to weave into a serious debate boffo laughs and knockdown zingers." This combination has led some critics to attempt to classify his works as either humorous or philosophical. Stoppard himself, however, believes that questions concerning the comic intent of his works are superfluous; "All along I thought of myself as writing entertainments, like *The Real Inspector Hound*, and plays of ideas . . . ," the author told Gussow. "The confusion arises because I treat plays of ideas in just about the same knockabout way as I treat the entertainments." He further explained to *Washington Post* contributor Joseph McLellan: "The stuff I write tends to work itself out in comedy terms most of the time." But whatever degree of comedy or seriousness in Stoppard's approach, Nightingale concluded in the *New York Times*, he has been consistent in the themes he examines: "All along he's confronted dauntingly large subjects, all along he's asked dauntingly intricate questions about them, and all along he's sought to touch the laugh glands as well as the intellect."

■ Biographical and Critical Sources

BOOKS

Bigsby, Christopher William Edgar, editor, *Writers and Their Work*, Longman (London, England), 1976.

Bock, Hedwig, and Albert Wetheim, editors, *Essays on Contemporary British Drama*, Hueber, 1981.

Brustein, Robert, *The Third Theatre*, Knopf (New York, NY), 1969.

Cahn, Victor L., *Beyond Absurdity: The Plays of Tom Stoppard*, Associated University Presses (Cranbury, NJ), 1979.

Concise Dictionary of British Literary Biography, Volume 8: *Contemporary Writers, 1960-Present*, Gale (Detroit, MI), 1992.

Contemporary Dramatists, sixth edition, St. James Press (Detroit, MI), 1999.

Contemporary Literary Criticism, Gale (Detroit, MI), Volume 1, 1973, Volume 3, 1975, Volume 4, 1975, Volume 5, 1976, Volume 8, 1978, Volume 15, 1980, Volume 29, 1984, Volume 34, 1985, Volume 63, 1991, Volume 91, 1996.

Dean, Joan Fitzpatrick, *Tom Stoppard: Comedy as a Moral Matrix*, University of Missouri Press (Columbia, MO), 1981.

Dictionary of Literary Biography, Gale (Detroit, MI), Volume 13: *British Dramatists since World War II*, 1982, Volume 233: *British and Irish Dramatists since World War II, Second Series*, 2001.

Dictionary of Literary Biography Yearbook: 1985, Gale (Detroit, MI), 1985.

International Directory of Theatre, Volume 2: *Playwrights*, St. James Press (Detroit, MI), 1993.

Nadel, Ira, *Double Act: A Life of Tom Stoppard*, Methuen (London, England), 2002, published as *Tom Stoppard: A Life*, Palgrave Macmillan, 2003.

Newsmakers 1995, Issue 4, Gale (Detroit, MI), 1995.

Reference Guide to English Literature, second edition, St. James Press (Detroit, MI), 1991.

Schlueter, June, *Dramatic Closure: Reading the End*, Fairleigh Dickinson University Press (Madison, NJ), 1995.

Taylor, John Russell, *The Second Wave: British Drama for the Seventies*, Hill & Wang (New York, NY), 1971.

PERIODICALS

Advocate, May 8, 2001, Gerard Raymond, interview with Stoppard, p. 69.

America, February 18, 1984; January 29, 1994, p. 23; April 22, 1995, James S. Torrens, review of *Arcadia*, p. 23; September 23, 2000, Frederick P. Tollini, review of *The Real Thing*, p. 24.

American Scientist, November-December, 2002, Harry Lustig and Kirsten Shepherd-Barr, "Science as Theater: From Physics to Biology, Science is Offering Playwrights Innovative Ways of Exploring the Intersections of Science, History, Art and Modern Life," pp. 550-555.

American Theatre, December, 1995, Mel Gussow, interview with Stoppard, pp. 22-28; September, 2001, Bab Mondello, review of *The Invention of Love*, p. 76; November, 2002, Matt Wolf, Celia Wren, and Julia M. Klein, review of *The Coast of Utopia* and *Every Good Boy Deserves Favor*, pp. 40-43.

Antioch Review, spring, 1996, David Guaspari, review of *Arcadia*, pp. 222-238.

Atlantic, May, 1968; December, 2002, review of *The Coast of Utopia*, pp. 141-146.

Back Stage, April 7, 1995, David Sheward, review of *Arcadia*, p. 56; August 29, 1997, Eric Grode, review of *Rough Crossing*, p. 48; September 17, 1999, Irene Backalenick, review of *On the Razzle*, p. 96; November 19, 1999, May 19, 2000, Roger Armbrust, "Tom Stoppard Receives England's Highest Honor," p. 2; December 8, 2000, review of *The Invention of Love*, p. 15; April 13, 2001, David A. Rosenberg, review of *The Invention of Love*, p. 56; November 22, 2002, J. Cooper Robb, review of *Every Good Boy Deserves Favor*, p. 7.

Back Stage West, August 3, 2000, John Angell Grant, review of *Rosencrantz and Guildenstern Are Dead*, p. 18; June 12, 2003, Kristina Mannion, review of *The Real Thing*, p. 11; September 25, 2003, Emily Parker, review of *Rough Crossing*, p. 15.

Chicago Tribune, April 24, 1985; June 3, 1985; September 20, 1985; March 17, 1991.

Christian Science Monitor, April 25, 1974; November 6, 1975; December 6, 1982; January 11, 1984, John Beaufort, review of *The Real Thing*, p. 21.

Commentary, December, 1967; June, 1974.

Commonweal, November 10, 1967; February 12, 1999, Richard Alleva, review of *Shakespeare in Love*, pp. 16-17; June 16, 2000, Celia Wren, review of *The Real Thing*, p. 17.

Contemporary Literature, summer, 1979.

Contemporary Review, March, 2003, Michael Karwowski, "All Right: An Assessment of Tom Stoppard's Plays," pp. 161-166.

Daily Variety, November 26, 2002, Toby Zinman, review of *Every Good Boy Deserves Favor*, p. 22.

Drama, summer, 1968; fall, 1969; summer, 1972; winter, 1973; autumn, 1974.

East European Quarterly, fall, 2004, Ileana Alexandra Orlich, "Tom Stoppard's Travesties and the Politics of Earnestness," p. 371.

Economist, February 6, 1999, review of *Shakespeare in Love*, p. 91; August 10, 2002, review of *The Coast of Utopia*.

Encounter, September, 1974; November, 1975; February, 1983.

Entertainment Weekly, December 11, 1998, review of *Shakespeare in Love*, p. 43; August 13, 1999, Lisa Schwarzbaum, review of *Shakespeare in Love*; April 13, 2001, Lawrence Frascella, review of *The Invention of Love*, p. 67.

Europe Intelligence Wire, October 23, 2002, Lyn Gardiner, review of *Arcadia*; May 7, 2003, review of *Travesties*; August 22, 2003, "Stoppard Pays a Visit to 'Utopia.'"

Explicator, winter, 2000, Christopher S. Nassaar, review of *Rosencrantz and Guildenstern Are Dead*, p. 91.

Financial Times, June 4, 1999, Alastair Macaulay, review of "Thrilling Display of the Heart," p. 18; June 6, 2001, Alastair Macaulay, review of *On the Razzle*, p. 18; August 5, 2002, Alastair Macaulay, review of *The Coast of Utopia*, p. 14; June 16, 2003, Alastair Macaulay, interview with Stoppard, p. 17; September 6, 2003, Arkady Ostrovsky, interview with Stoppard, p. 33.

Gay and Lesbian Review Worldwide, September, 2001, Allen Ellenzweig, review of *The Invention of Love*, p. 49.

Harper's Bazaar, March, 1995, p. 126.

Hollywood Reporter, July 1, 2003, Ray Bennett, review of *Jumpers*, p. 63.

Hudson Review, winter, 1967-68; summer, 1968.

Insight on the News, May 21, 2001, Rex Roberts, review of *The Invention of Love*, p. 26.

Journal of Modern Literature, winter, 2000, Carrie Ryan, "Translating *The Invention of Love*: The Journey from Page to Stage for Tom Stoppard's Latest Play," pp. 197-206.

Knight Ridder/Tribune News Service, December 5, 1994, Clifford A. Ridley, review of *Hapgood*, p. 1205K5825; December 30, 1998, Larry Swindell, review of *The Invention of Love*, p. K2956; April 2, 2001, Graham Fuller, interview with Stoppard, p. K7157.

Life, February 9, 1968.

Listener, April 11, 1968; April 18, 1968; June 20, 1974.

London Magazine, August, 1968; August-September, 1976.

Long Island Business News, June 30, 2000, Richard Scholem, review of *The Real Thing*, p. 39A.

Look, December 26, 1967; February 9, 1968.

Los Angeles Times, June 6, 1986; December 20, 1986; February 20, 1991; December 12, 1998, Patrick Pacheco, interview with Stoppard, p. F1; April 17, 2001, Michael Phillips, review of *The Invention of Love*, p. F4.

Modern Drama, winter, 1997, Susanne Arndt, "'We're All Free to Do as We're Told': Gender and Ideology in Tom Stoppard's *The Real Thing,*" pp. 489-501; spring, 1997, Prapassaree Kramer and Jeffrey Kramer, "Stoppard's *Arcadia:* Research, Time, Loss," pp. 1-10; fall, 1998, Laurie Kaplan, "In the Native State: *Indian Ink:* Footnoting the Footnotes on Empire," p. 337; winter, 1998, Lucy Melbourne, "'Plotting the Apple of Knowledge': Tom Stoppard's Arcadia as Iterated Theatrical Algorithm," p. 557; fall, 1999, Susanne Vees-Gulani, "Hidden Order in the 'Stoppard Set': Chaos Theory in the Content and Structure of Tom Stoppard's *Arcadia,*" p. 411; summer, 2000, Ira B. Nadel, "Tom Stoppard and the Invention of Biography," p. 157.

Nation, November 6, 1967; May 11, 1974; May 18, 1974; May 1, 1995, Tim Appelo, review of *Arcadia,* pp. 612-613; February 22, 1999, Stuart Klawans, review of *Shakespeare in Love,* p. 34; September 3, 2001, Carol Rocamora, review of *The Seagull,* p. 47; May 15, 2000, Elizabeth Pochoda, review of *The Invention of Love,* p. 33; December 9, 2002, Carol Rocamora, review of *The Coast of Utopia,* p. 34.

National Observer, October 23, 1967.

National Review, December 12, 1967; November 29, 1993, p. 71; January 25, 1999, John Simon, review of *Shakespeare in Love,* p. 54.

New Criterion, September, 2002, Mark Steyn, review of *The Coast of Utopia,* pp. 46-50.

New Leader, September 21, 1992, p. 21; March 13, 1995, Stefan Kanfer, review of *Arcadia,* p. 23; May, 2001, Stefan Kanfer, review of *The Invention of Love,* p. 57.

New Republic, June 15, 1968; May 18, 1974; November 22, 1975; January 30, 1984; January 30, 1995, Robert Brustein, review of *Hapgood,* p. 31; July 17, 1995, Robert Brustein, review of *Arcadia,* pp. 36-37; May 14, 2001, Robert Brustein, review of *The Invention of Love,* p. 29; May 13, 2002, Stanley Kauffmann, review of *Enigma,* p. 24.

New Statesman, June 14, 1974; October 10, 1997, Kate Kellaway, review of *The Invention of Love,* pp. 37-38; January 29, 1999, David Jays, review of *Shakespeare in Love,* p. 39; September 17, 2001, Philip Kerr, review of *Enigma,* p. 44; July 8, 2002, Mary Riddell, interview with Stoppard, pp. 22-23; August 26, 2002, Katherine Duncan-Jones, review of *The Coast of Utopia,* pp. 26-27.

Newsweek, August 7, 1967; August 31, 1970; March 4, 1974; January 8, 1975; November 10, 1975; January 16, 1984; April 3, 1995, Jack Kroll, "Mind over Matter," pp. 64-66; December 14, 1998, David Ansen, interview with Stoppard, p. 78; August 26, 2002, Carla Power, review of *The Coast of Utopia,* p. 50.

New York, March 11, 1974; May 13, 1974; August 26, 1974; November 17, 1975; August 13-20, 1979; July 26, 1993, p. 51; January 9, 1995, p. 36.

New Yorker, May 6, 1967; October 28, 1967; May 4, 1968; May 6, 1972; March 4, 1974; May 6, 1974; January 6, 1975; January 24, 1977; September 23, 2002, John Lahr, review of *The Coast of Utopia.*

New York Post, April 23, 1974; January 6, 1984.

New York Review of Books, June 8, 1995, p. 28.

New York Times, October 18, 1967; October 29, 1967; March 24, 1968; May 8, 1968; June 19, 1968; July 8, 1968; October 15, 1968; April 23, 1974; July 29, 1979; August 1, 1979; October 4, 1979; November 25, 1979; November 28, 1979; June 23, 1983, Frank Rich, review of *The Real Thing,* pp. 21, C15; November 22, 1983, Leslie Bennetts, review of *The Real Thing,* p. 20; January 6, 1984, Frank Rich, review of *The Real Thing,* p. 13; January 15, 1984; February 20, 1984; August 1, 1984, Frank Rich, review of *The Real Thing,* p. 17; May 17, 1987, Benedict Nightingale and Mervyn Rothstein, review of *Rosencrantz and Guildenstern Are Dead,* p. H5; May 18, 1987, Mel Gussow, review of *Rosencrantz and Guildenstern Are Dead,* p. 21; November 22, 1987; November 3, 1989; November 26, 1989; December 26, 1989; February 8, 1991; August 14, 1992, Mel Gussow, review of *The Real Inspector Hound,* p. B2; August 28, 1992, Mel Gussow, review of *The Fifteen-Minute Hamlet* and *On the Razzle,* p. B5; July 8, 1993, Frank Rich, review of *Arcadia,* p. B1; November 6, 1994, Vincent Canby, review of *Rough Crossing,* p. H32; December 5, 1994, David Richards, review of *Hapgood,* p. B11; December 11, 1994, Vincent Canby, review of *Hapgood,* p. H5; February 17, 1995, Donald G. McNeil, Jr., review of *Hapgood* and *Arcadia,* p. B2; March 19, 1995, Benedict Nightingale, review of *Arcadia,* p. H7; March 31, 1995, Vincent Canby, review of *Arcadia,* p. B1; April 9, 1995, Margo Jefferson, review of *Arcadia,* p. H5; April 20, 1995, Vincent Canby, review of *Indian Ink,* p. B1; November 26, 1995, Matt Wolf, review of *Taking Sides,* p. H4; August 22, 1997, Wilborn Hampton, review of *Rough Crossing,* p. B2; October 19, 1997, Benedict Nightingale, review of *The Invention of Love,* p. AR5; December 14, 1997, Vincent Canby, review of *The Invention of Love,* p. AR4; June 3, 1998, Peter Marks, review of *The Sea Gull,* p. B5; July 24, 1998, Will Joyner, review of *Poodle Springs,* p. B30; December 11, 1998, Janet Maslin, review of *Shakespeare in Love,* p. E16; December 13, 1998, Sarah Lyall, review of *Shakespeare in Love,* p. 17; January 12, 1999, Mel Gussow, review of *Shakespeare in Love,* p. E1; November 12, 1999, Jesse McKinley, review of *The Real Thing,* p. B2; January 29, 2000, Ben Brantley, review of *The Invention of Love,* p. A17; February 2, 2000, Bernard Weinraub, review of *The Invention of Love,* p. B1; April 18, 2000, Ben Brantley, review of *The Real Thing,* p. B1; December 25, 2000, Elvis Mitchell, review of *Vatel,* p. B5; January 25, 2001, Wilborn Hampton, review of *Night and Day,* p. B5;

March 18, 2001, Mel Gussow and Robin Pogrebin, reviews of *The Invention of Love*, p. AR7; March 30, 2001, Ben Brantley, review of *The Invention of Love*, p. B1; April 29, 2001, Margo Jefferson, review of *The Invention of Love*, p. AR11; May 20, 2001, Matt Wolf, review of *The Invention of Love*, p. AR11; March 17, 2002, Benedict Nightingale, "In London, Stoppard Joins the Americans," p. TR11; August 4, 2002, Benedict Nightingale, review of *The Coast of Utopia*, p. AR7; August 21, 2002, Ben Brantley, review of *The Coast of Utopia*, p. B1; October 22, 2002, Adam Cohen, review of *The Coast of Utopia*, p. A30; June 23, 2003, Ben Brantley, review of *Jumpers*, p. E1.

New York Times Book Review, August 25, 1968; March 3, 1996, p. 19.

New York Times Magazine, January 1, 1984, Mel Gussow, "The Real Tom Stoppard," pp. 18-24; May 20, 2001, Amy Barrett, interview with Stoppard, p. 23.

North American Review, May-August, 1998, Robert L. King, review of *The Invention of Love*, pp. 72-77; May-August, 2003, Robert L. King, review of *The Coast of Utopia*, pp. 71-76.

Observer (London, England), August 1, 1993.

Observer Review, April 16, 1967; December 17, 1967; June 23, 1968.

Papers on Language and Literature, fall, 2000, Derek B. Alwes, "'Oh, Phooey to Death!': Boethian Consolation in Tom Stoppard's *Arcadia*," p. 392.

Playboy, May, 1968.

Plays and Players, July, 1970.

Publishers Weekly, February 12, 1996, p. 24.

Punch, April 19, 1967.

Reporter, November 16, 1967.

Sarasota Herald Tribune, May 24, 2002, review of *Enigma*, p. 19; July 13, 2003, Charlie Huisking, review of *Rough Crossing*, p. G1; July 22, 2003, Jay Handelman, review of *Rough Crossing*, p. E3.

Saturday Review, January 8, 1977.

Saturday Review of the Society, August 26, 1972.

Show Business, April 25, 1974.

Spectator, June 22, 1974; April 7, 2001, "Setting Standards," p. 44; March 16, 2002, John McEwen, review of *Anthony Fry*, p. 52; August 10, 2002, Toby Young, review of *The Coast of Utopia*, pp. 43-44; July 19, 2003, Toby Young, review of *Jumpers*, pp. 41-42.

Stage, February 10, 1972.

Sunday Times Review, April 21, 1991.

Theatre Journal, March, 1980.

Time, October 27, 1967; August 9, 1968; March 11, 1974; May 6, 1974; June 20, 1983; August 24, 1992, p. 69; July 19, 1993, p. 60; March 27, 1995, Christopher Porterfield, review of *Indian Ink*, pp. 74-75; December 14, 1998, Richard Corliss, review of *Shakespeare in Love*, p. 99; January 25, 1999, Elizabeth Gleick, interview with Stoppard, p. 70; March 13, 2000, William Tynan, review of *The Invention of Love*, p. 90; May 8, 2000, Richard Zoglin, review of *The Real Thing*, p. 97; May 6, 2002, Richard Schickel, review of *Enigma*, p. 66.

Times (London, England), November 18, 1982; April 3, 1985; April 13, 1993, Nigel Hawkes, interview with Stoppard, p. 29.

Times Literary Supplement, March 21, 1968; December 29, 1972; November 26, 1982; December 24, 1982; April 23, 1993, Marilyn Butler, review of *Arcadia*, p. 18; October 1, 1993, Frank Whitford, review of *Travesties*, p. 19; March 17, 1995, Peter Kemp, review of *Indian Ink*, p. 17; September 29, 1995, p. 23; October 10, 1997, Jeremy Treglown, review of *The Invention of Love*, p. 20; February 5, 1999, Katherine Duncan-Jones, review of *Shakespeare in Love*, p. 18; April 19, 2002, Robert Douglas-Fairhurst, review of *The Inland Sea*, p. 19; August 9, 2002, Peter Kemp, review of *The Coast of Utopia*, pp. 3-4.

Times Saturday Review (London, England), June 29, 1991.

Transatlantic Review, summer, 1968.

TriQuarterly, summer, 2003, John Bull, "From Illyria to Arcadia: Uses of Pastoral in Modern English Theater," pp. 57-73.

Twentieth Century Literature, fall, 1999, Natalie Crohn, review of *Artist Descending a Staircase*, p. 385.

United Press International, April 9, 2001, review of *The Invention of Love*; August 27, 2002, Stephen Brown, review of *The Coast of Utopia*.

Variety, May 25, 1998, Matt Wolf, review of *The Real Inspector Hound*, pp. 68-69; December 7, 1998, Lael Loewenstein, review of *Shakespeare in Love*, p. 53; March 8, 1999, Dennis Harvey, review of *Indian Ink*, p. 74; July 12, 1999, Markland Taylor, review of *Rosencrantz and Guildenstern Are Dead*, p. 48; December 13, 1999, Christopher Stern, review of *Indian Ink*, p. 114; January 24, 2000, Dennis Harvey, review of *The Invention of Love*, p. 68; January 29, 2001, Joe Leydon, review of *Enigma*, p. 47; April 2, 2001, Charles Isherwood, review of *The Invention of Love*, p. 28; August 12, 2002, Matt Wolf, review of *The Coast of Utopia*, pp. 21-22; June 30, 2003, Matt Wolf, review of *Jumpers*, pp. 34-35; July 14, 2003, Charles Isherwood, review of *Jumpers*, pp. 48-49; September 9, 2002, Toby Zinman, review of *Every Good Boy Deserves Favor*, p. 62; October 14, 2002, Dennis Harvey, review of *Night and Day*, p. 39.

Village Voice, May 4, 1967; October 26, 1967; May 2, 1974.

Virginia Quarterly Review, autumn, 1995, p. 642.

Vogue, November 15, 1967; April 15, 1968; December, 1994, p. 180.

Wall Street Journal, March 11, 1974; November 3, 1975; January 6, 1984, Edwin Wilson, review of *The Real Thing,* p. 18; March 31, 1995, Donald Lyons, review of *Arcadia,* p. A10; August 2, 1995, David Lyons, review of *The Play's the Thing* and *Arcadia,* p. A9; August 15, 1997, Donald Lyons, review of *Rough Crossing,* p. A14; October 27, 1997, Paul Levy, review of *The Invention of Love,* p. A20; March 10, 1999, David Littlejohn, review of *India Ink,* p. A22; January 20, 2000, David Littlejohn, review of *The Invention of Love,* p. A20; April 19, 2000, Amy Gamerman, review of *The Real Thing,* p. A28; April 4, 2001, Amy Gamerman, review of *The Invention of Love,* p. A18.

Washington Post, May 11, 1969; June 25, 1969; July 9, 1969; August 29, 1978; November 26, 1978; January 12, 1984; May 23, 1985.

Washington Post Weekend, October 19, 1979.

Women's Wear Daily, April 24, 1974.

World and I, May, 2003, Herb Greer, review of *The Coast of Utopia,* p. 228.

World Literature Today, winter, 1978; summer, 1986; spring, 1995, p. 369; winter, 1996, p. 193.*

Chris Trottier

■ Personal

Female; married. *Education:* University of Utah, B.A.; University of Delaware, M.A. (in early childhood education). *Hobbies and other interests:* Skiing, painting, biking, spending time with husband and dog.

■ Addresses

Office—Electronic Arts, Redwood Shores Studio, 209 Redwood Shores Parkway, Redwood City, CA 94065.

■ Career

Game designer and producer. Worked for Theatrix Interactive (children's software company); Maxis Software/Electronic Arts Inc., associate producer, designer, and lead designer on various *Sims* products, including translation of the original game to computer and for the online version, 1999—.

■ Writings

GAME DESIGNER; WITH OTHERS

SimIsle: Missions in the Rainforest, Maxis Software Inc., 1995.

SimSafari, Electronic Arts Inc. (Redwood City, CA), 1998.

SimCity 3000, Electronic Arts Inc. (Redwood City, CA), 1999.

The Sims, Electronic Arts Inc. (Redwood City, CA), 2000.

The Sims Online, Electronic Arts Inc. (Redwood City, CA), 2002.

The Sims: Deluxe Edition, Electronic Arts Inc. (Redwood City, CA), 2002.

The Sims 2, Electronic Arts Inc. (Redwood City, CA), 2004.

■ Work in Progress

Further upgrades of *The Sims.*

■ Sidelights

"The goal has always been to facilitate players entertaining each other," Chris Trottier, lead designer for *The Sims Online* told David Becker of *CNET News.com.* That one small sentence speaks volumes about the difference between the entire *Sims* video/computer games and their more testosterone-charged competition. As Dawn C. Chmielewski noted in *SiliconValley.com,* "The bestselling computer game of all time isn't about winning the Super

Bowl, repelling an invading force or indulging any other adolescent-boy fantasy. 'The Sims' is electronic entertainment's version of 'Seinfeld': It's a game about simply existing." Instead of destroying worlds, players of any of the myriad *Sims* products create them. And in doing so, they have attracted an entirely new demographic to gaming: women, many of whom are over age twenty-four.

The formula has been a winning one, with over thirty-six million copies of *The Sims* and its various incarnations sold worldwide. "We had a feeling when developing it that it would either be a colossal success or a colossal failure," Trottier recalled in an interview with *Sims Online News Interview.* "We had our hopes that gamers would be intrigued by a different kind of game. But I don't think anyone anticipated how many non-gamers would not only play *Sims* but become incredibly hardcore and loyal about it."

From Education to Gaming

Trottier is part of a new generation of game designers who are leading the industry in a new direction: toward more cooperative play with an emphasis on social interaction. Earning a master's degree in early childhood education, she initially worked for a children's software company. By the late 1990s she had joined the California-based Maxis Software and its *Sims* team. "I came to Maxis . . . when they were still doing kids products," Trottier told Libe Goad in a *GameGal.com* interview, "and then it was probably two months after I started that they canceled the kids' line and said, 'You're going to go to work on *The Sims.*'"

These were still early days for the game created by Will Wright, who began conceptualizing a simulated life game idea in 1984. It wasn't until 1987 that Wright cofounded Maxis Software and two years later he released *SimCity* for the Mac and PC. This game simulates building a city, and for the next decade Wright and his production team turned out numerous titles featuring this simulated world: *SimEarth, SimAnt, SimFarm, SimCity 2000,* and *Sim-City 3000.* Maxis was bought out by Electronic Arts Inc. in 1997, but Wright stayed on, and by the time Trottier joined the team work was already underway on *The Sims.* Whereas earlier titles had been about building and constructing and then managing various structures, *The Sims* took the concept one step forward and featured the construction of characters or Sim people.

At the time Trottier was assigned to Wright's team, *The Sims* was "a bastard product that nobody wanted to be on," the game designer told Goad.

"Nobody really understood it and they thought it was a game about going to the bathroom. It was kind of this secret project that Will was doing now and then. . . . I fell in love with it and I've been doing *Sims* stuff ever since." In 2000 *The Sims* was released, and what had been a suspect project quickly became a crowd pleaser.

The World of *Sims*

As a writer for *VirtualGamerz.com* noted of the 2000 release, *The Sims* is the "very first family simulation in the world.. . . . First [it] proposes that you create your family. Depending on your feelings, you have the opportunity to begin with a single character or with the whole family (little baby crying included)." The personalities of such characters are determined by a limited number of factors, such as character, cleanliness, love of fun, ease, and dynamism. Gender, race, clothing style and more can also be determined by the player. Once the character or characters are chosen and programmed, life begins. Abilities and skills are added and then the Sim is free to begin working his or her way up the social ladder, for that is the point of the game. Consumption is built in from the start with a base amount of money (Simolians) provided for each Sim to purchase and decorate a home. Possessions can be added by earning more money, and there are catalogs from which to choose things such as furniture, clothing, and cars.

Once set up, these characters take on their own character, depending on the parameters entered. Untended, they will simply fall over of exhaustion if they miss their sleep, or run to the bathroom, or interact with each other. According to the *VirtualGamerz.com* critic, "the most phenomenal thing in this game is without any doubt, the interactions between the characters." They babble to one another in Simlish, a blend of English and Romance languages. Similarly, the reviewer for *Armchair Empire* felt that the "most intriguing part of the game is making friendships. The character traits that were assigned to the Sim at the creation stage come into play. If your Sim is very outgoing it may be easier to make friends."

A reviewer for *Armchair Empire* noted that the goal of the game "is to make your Sim happy. This is accomplished by initiating friendships with people in the neighborhood, acquiring bigger and better things, and earning more money. No spiritual enlightenment here, folks! A diamond over the head of each Sim displays their general psychological condition." Along those same lines, J. C. Herz, reviewing the game in the *New York Times* commented that *The Sims* "is disturbing in its crudeness," especially in its emphasis on consumerism. "But it's also disturbing in its accuracy," the critic added, "to the extent that getting and spending is the modus operandi for a lot of folks." Herz concluded that *The Sims* "succeeds as art, or as modern architecture," for "by building a window into Sims' souls, it prompts us to consider our own."

Writing in the *Houston Chronicle*, Dwight Silverman found *The Sims* "easily the most addictively enjoyable game . . . since the first *SimCity.*" Similarly, Aubrey Hovey noted in the *Albuquerque Tribune* that *The Sims* "sucks in even the most casual computer gamer, [and] is turning everyday living into addiction." The fascination was not uniquely American. Tim Wapshott, writing in the London *Times*, dubbed it a "soaraway success." Writing in *GameSpot.com*, Andrew Seyoon Park noted that *The Sims* "is about creating, managing, and controlling the lives of tiny computerized people who dwell in miniature homes." However, Park also noted that the "actual gameplay is rather limited in some respects—either by odd inconsistencies or by actual restrictions placed on your actions."

Online and AI Versions

Such initial restrictions were addressed in more recent evolutions of the game, including *The Sims Online* from 2002, and *The Sims 2* from 2004, which pushed artificial intelligence to new levels. Going online with *The Sims* was, as Trottier, who was lead designer for the online model, a "no-brainer." Speaking with John Callaham on *Sims Online Stratics*, Trottier further noted that "the minute people started playing *The Sims,* they wished they could have their friends come over to the houses they were building. . . . Also, Sim to Sim interactions were one of the most fun and challenging things in *The Sims.* But AI (artificial intelligence) we put in for other Sims could only begin to scratch the surface of real human behavior which can be unbelievably complex and contradictory. Having real humans driving the other Sims makes for a much richer experience." Trottier further commented to Callaham on the development and testing of the online version: "It's been amazing to watch the nesting instinct of initial players. We've put incredible incentives on grouping in-game, whether it's owning a property together or just hanging out together." Speaking with Bob Simon of *CBSNews.com*, Trottier observed some of the appeal of the game. "You're completely anonymous and temporary, if you wish," she said. Also, the reality of the environment becomes a natural draw to the player. "If they

tickle you, you feel like you just got tickled," Trottier explained. "If you kiss someone, it's like, 'I just kissed this other someone.' It's pretty amazing how much you end up putting yourself into that Sim. It feels like you're really doing it."

If you enjoy the works of Chris Trottier, you may also want to check out the following computer games:

Immortal Cities, designed by Chris Beatrice.
Railroad Tycoon, created by Sid Meier.
Rise of Nations, designed by Brian Reynolds.

Such virtual reality is also strong in *The Sims 2* which is much richer than earlier editions in terms of choices. For example, there are 13,000 different animations that illustrate the outcomes of "choices" made by the Sims. The AI element takes the game beyond the merely Pavlovian reactions which motivated characters in the 2000 edition of *The Sims.* It also includes 3-D graphics animation. For Takahashi, "what's remarkable about this computer game . . . is that the domestic drama is not scripted. The characters act the way they do because that is what naturally unfolds. It's a quality dubbed 'emergence,' based on the history of the characters' relationships and their own artificial, or preprogrammed intelligence." A reviewer for *Computer Gaming World* called *The Sims 2* "hypnotically addictive" and a "masterpiece."

Sims games have attracted female players to a much larger degree than have other games. Almost half the players of *The Sims* are female, and this is in large part due to the influence of female designers such as Trottier. Speaking with Lee Cieniawa of *Armchair Empire*, she noted that "there are several untraditional forms of game-play in *The Sims.* For instance, there are many people who spend most of their time decorating and redecorating their homes. . . . There are a lot of people who enjoy having a fantasy life where they get to call the shots." The noncompetitive, relation-based nature of the game is a definite draw for female gamers. And the game is not judgmental. All sorts of relationships are possible in *The Sims.* As Trottier noted in *Advocate Online*, the game "isn't themed to appeal to gaming geeks alone. . . . It allows the player to pursue a fantasy life in a contemporary, campy setting." This means that there are gay and lesbian relationships programmed as well. "We're here to make games," Trottier explained, "not to push any moral agenda."

■ Biographical and Critical Sources

PERIODICALS

Albuquerque Tribune (Albuquerque, NM), February 13, 2001, Aubrey Hovey, "Home Simulated Home," p. A1.

Computer Gaming World, Jun 1, 2003, review of *The Sims Online;* November 1, 2004, "Real Child of Hell," "Is It Even a Game?," and "Take Your Sims from the Cradle to the Grave in *The Sims 2.*"

Daily Mail (London, England), April 29, 2004, "A Simple Way of Life," p. 64.

Daily Variety, November 26, 2002, David Bloom, "Reality, Virtuality Blur at Sims' Soiree," p. 28.

Electronic Gaming Monthly, May, 2003, review of *The Sims.*

Houston Chronicle, March 3, 2001, Dwight Silverman, "Sims Game's Allure Is That It's like Life," p. 1.

Network World, March 20, 2000, Keith Shaw, "Reality vs. Virtual Reality."

New Media Age, June 26, 2003, "Electronic Arts to Increase Use of Mobile Marketing," p. 7.

New York Times, February 10, 2000, J. C. Herz, "The Sims Who Die with the Most Toys Win," p. G10.

PC, October 19, 2004, Troy Dreier, "*The Sims 2* Proves Grown-up Games Still Live," p. 42.

San Jose Mercury News (San Jose, CA), September 13, 2004, Dean Takahashi, "New *Sims* Computer Game Takes a Big Leap Forward in Artificial Intelligence."

Times (London, England), February 26, 2000, Tim Wapshott, "Computer Games and Pastimes," p. 39.

ONLINE

Advocate Online, http://www.advocate.com/ (February 4, 2003), Gretchen Dukowitz, "Virtually Gay."

Armchair Empire, http://www.armchairempire.com/ (February 27, 2003), Lee Cieniawa, "Chris Trottier (Sims Online) Q & A"; (November 22, 2004) review of *The Sims.*

CBSNews Online, http://www.cbsnews.com/ (August 6, 2003), Bob Simon, "Sex, Lies and Video Games."

CNET News.com, http://att.com/ (December 14, 2002, David Becker, "Will *Sims Online* Alter Gaming World?"

Discovery Channel Online, http://exn.net/ (February 24, 2003), "Cable in the Classroom: Simulation Station."

Electronic Arts, http://www.ea.com/home/home.jsp/ (April 24, 2005).

GameGal.com, http://www.gamegal.com/ (November 22, 2004), Libe Goad, interview with Trottier.

GameSpot.com, http://www.gamespot.com/ (February 11, 2000), Andrew Seyoon Park, review of *The Sims.*

Maxis, http://www.maxis.com/ (November 22, 2004).

MobyGames.com, http://www.mobygames.com/ (November 22, 2004), "Chris Trottier."

SiliconValley.com, http://www.silconvalley.com/ (December 15, 2002), Dawn C. Chmielewski, *Online Play to Added New Wrinkle to Curiously Compelling 'Sims.'*

Sims Online, http://www.eagames.com/ (November 22, 2004), Jerry Chantemsin, "Meet Some Real Sims."

Sims Online News Interview, http://www.gamegossip.com/ (December 15, 2002), "Chris Trottier."

Sims Online Stratics, http://sims.stratics.com/ (October 17, 2002), John Callaham, "Sims Online Q & A at HomeLAN."

VirtualGamerz.com, http://www.virtualgamerz.com/ (November 24, 2004), review of *The Sims.**

Bill Watterson

■ Personal

Born July 5, 1958, in Washington, DC; son of James (a patent attorney) and Kathryn Watterson; married; wife's name, Melissa (an artist). *Education:* Kenyon College, B.A., 1980.

■ Addresses

Home—Chagrin Falls, OH. *Office*—c/o Universal Press Syndicate, 4900 Main St., Kansas City, MO 64112.

■ Career

Cartoonist. *Cincinnati Post,* Cincinnati, OH, editorial cartoonist, 1980; creator of comic strip "Calvin and Hobbes," syndicated with Universal Press Syndicate, 1985-95.

■ Awards, Honors

National Cartoonists Society's Reuben Awards, for outstanding cartoonist of the year, 1986 and 1988, and for outstanding humor strip, 1988.

■ Writings

COMIC-STRIP COLLECTIONS; SELF-ILLUSTRATED

Calvin and Hobbes, Andrews, McMeel & Parker (Kansas City, MO), 1987.

The Essential Calvin and Hobbes: A Calvin and Hobbes Treasury, Andrews & McMeel (Kansas City, MO), 1988.

Something under the Bed Is Drooling: A Calvin and Hobbes Collection, Andrews & McMeel (Kansas City, MO), 1988.

Yukon Ho!, Andrews & McMeel (Kansas City, MO), 1989.

The Calvin & Hobbes Lazy Sunday Book, Andrews & McMeel (Kansas City, MO), 1989.

The Authoritative Calvin and Hobbes, Andrews & McMeel (Kansas City, MO), 1990.

Weirdos from Another Planet!, Andrews & McMeel (Kansas City, MO), 1990.

The Revenge of the Baby-Sat, Andrews & McMeel (Kansas City, MO), 1991.

Scientific Progress Goes "Boink," Andrews & McMeel (Kansas City, MO), 1991.

Attack of the Deranged Mutant Killer Monster Snow Goons, Andrews & McMeel (Kansas City, MO), 1992.

The Indispensable Calvin and Hobbes, Andrews & McMeel (Kansas City, MO), 1992.

The Days Are Just Packed, Andrews & McMeel (Kansas City, MO), 1993.

Homicidal Psycho Jungle Cat, Andrews & McMeel (Kansas City, MO), 1994.

The Calvin and Hobbes Tenth Anniversary Book, Andrews & McMeel (Kansas City, MO), 1995.

There's Treasure Everywhere: A Calvin and Hobbes Collection, Andrews & McMeel (Kansas City, MO), 1996.

It's a Magical World, Andrews & McMeel (Kansas City, MO), 1996.

Calvin and Hobbes Sunday Pages: 1985-1995, Andrews & McMeel (Kansas City, MO), 2001.

The Complete Calvin and Hobbes, Andrews & McMeel (Kansas City, MO), 2005.

Contributor to *Tribute to Sparky: Cartoon Artists Honor Charles M. Schulz,* Charles M. Schulz Museum and Research Center (Santa Rosa, CA), 2003. Contributor to *Target.*

■ Sidelights

Bill Watterson's comic strip "Calvin and Hobbes" became one of the most popular series in syndication shortly after it made its debut in 1985. For ten years, readers avidly followed the adventures of Calvin, a precocious and outrageously brash six year old, and Hobbes, the tiger that appears as a stuffed animal to everyone but Calvin. Calvin's active imagination and unique outlook on life led the pair into conflicts with parents, school officials, babysitters, other children, and sometimes with reality itself. Watterson's entertaining storylines, fully developed characters, and distinctive illustrations have led some critics to rate him as one of the most imaginative cartoonists of modern America. Yet at the height of his fame and popularity, Watterson ended the strip and did his best to disappear from the public eye altogether.

Origin of "Calvin and Hobbes"

Some of Watterson's earliest cartoons were drawn for his high school newspaper and the weekly newspaper in his home town of Chagrin Falls, Ohio. In college, he contributed to the *Kenyon Collegian,* the campus paper at Kenyon College. Most of his work for the *Collegian* lampooned college life. Following graduation, he found a job as a political cartoonist at the *Cincinnati Post,* but he was fired after a six-month trial period. Watterson began submitting several strip ideas to syndicates, including one called "Spaceman Spiff," an animal comic, and a cartoon about a young man of his own age in his first job and apartment. One of the ideas Watterson submitted included the minor characters of Calvin and Hobbes, a little boy and his stuffed tiger playmate. The characters of Calvin and Hobbes caught the attention of a staffer at United Features Syndicate, who proposed that Watterson build a series focusing on the duo. Watterson agreed.

Oddly enough, United Features turned down the new strip once the author developed it. Instead, they offered syndication to Watterson only if he agreed to include a character called "Robotman," which had been created to merchandise a range of products. "Not knowing if 'Calvin and Hobbes' would ever go anywhere, it was difficult to turn down another chance at syndication," Watterson related to Andrew Christie in a *Honk!* interview. "But I really recoiled at the idea of drawing somebody else's character. It's cartooning by committee, and I have a moral problem with that. It's not art then." Once again unemployed as a cartoonist, Watterson returned to sending around "Calvin and Hobbes." Universal Press Syndicate eventually accepted it, and the strip was formally introduced on November 18, 1985. Less than three years later, "Calvin and Hobbes" was appearing in more than six hundred newspapers, and *Something under the Bed Is Drooling: A Calvin and Hobbes Collection* stayed on best-seller lists for almost a year.

"Calvin and Hobbes" deals with the well-covered ground of family and relationships, but focuses mainly on the deep friendship between the hyperactive Calvin and the much calmer Hobbes. Calvin "is the personification of kid-dom," as one writer described him in *Comics Journal.* "He's entirely self-centered, devoted wholly to his own self-gratification. In pursuit of this completely understandable childhood goal, Calvin acknowledges no obstacle, no restraint. His desire and its satisfaction are all that matter to him." The more relaxed and cautious Hobbes often warns Calvin against causing trouble, but even if the tiger seems to resist Calvin's schemes, he always remains the boy's best friend.

An extraordinary imagination isn't the only thing that distinguishes Calvin from other children. "I've never sat down to spell it out," noted Watterson in a *Los Angeles Times* interview, "but I guess [Calvin's] a little too intelligent for his age. The thing that I really enjoy about him is that he has no sense of restraint, he doesn't have the experience yet to know the things that you shouldn't do." Hobbes "is a little more restrained, a little more knowledgeable," the author continued, because he has "a little bit of that sense of consequence that Calvin lacks entirely." Together, Calvin and Hobbes "are more than the sum of their parts," the author told a contributor to *Comics Journal.* "Each ticks because the other is around

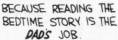

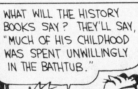

In the *Calvin and Hobbes* strips Watterson features the adventures of a hyper-imaginative six-year-old and his stuffed tiger playmate. (CALVIN AND HOBBES © 1992 Watterson. Dist. By UNIVERSAL PRESS SYNDICATE. Reprinted with permission. All rights reserved.)

to share in the little conspiracies, or to argue and fight with. . . . Each is funnier in contrast to the other than they would be by themselves."

Bright youngsters are common in the comics and can lead to stale, overused storylines. "But rather than follow the easy formula of keeping Calvin an obnoxious but funny little kid, Watterson takes chances and explores other facets of his character," a *Los Angeles Times* writer declared. For instance, in one comic series Calvin tries to save a baby raccoon that has been injured and is left bewildered and hurt when it dies. Another sequence shows a scared Calvin turning to his parents for help in finding Hobbes, who has been lost. "I'll have a slapstick joke one day, a fantasy another day, a friendship, a sadness," Watterson stated in *Comics Journal.* He

elaborated: "My main concern really is to keep the reader on his toes, or to keep the strip unpredictable. I try to achieve some sort of balance . . . that keeps the reader wondering what's going to happen next and be surprised."

Another unique feature of "Calvin and Hobbes" is the quality of Watterson's artwork. "Watterson draws comic strips the way they should be drawn," according to the *Comics Journal* writer. "Much of his humor lies in the pictures. And in many of the individual strips, the words alone make no sense at all without the pictures." In addition, said the essayist, "not only does the humor usually arise from the words and pictures in tandem, the pictures alone, without words, are funny. Their energy makes them funny. Watterson's action sequences, particularly,

A strip published in the 1994 volume *Homicidal Psycho Jungle Cat* in which Watterson offers selections from his wildly popular, award-winning comic strip *Calvin and Hobbes.* (CALVIN AND HOBBES © 1994 Watterson. Dist. By UNIVERSAL PRESS SYNDICATE. Reprinted with permission. All rights reserved.)

are comically imaginative and inventive. . . . With increasing mastery of his supple brush, Watterson makes credible even the most fantastic of Calvin's daydreams." The *Los Angeles Times* writer concurred with this assessment, noting that the "Calvin and Hobbes" strip "continues the strongly pictorial tradition" of classic comics such as George Herriman's "Krazy Kat" and Watterson's childhood favorite, Walt Kelly's "Pogo." "Watterson's vivid drawings often don't require captions, as the characters' expressions and poses are all that's needed," the writer added.

Fighting against Commercialism

Throughout his career, Watterson maintained a somewhat tense relationship with the world of comic-strip syndication. In 1987, when the first book-length collection of his comics was published, he refused to tour in order to promote the book, believing that the strip should stand on its own. Upon twice winning the top award in cartooning, the Reuben, he refused to show up at the ceremony to accept it. He also took a steadfast stand against allowing licensing of the characters, so that Calvin and Hobbes tee shirts, toys, and greeting cards could not be manufactured. In a rare public appearance, Watterson made a speech at the Festival of Cartoon Art in 1989, a transcription of which was published on the *Planet Cartoonist* Web site. He explained the reasons for his opposition to merchandising: "Licensed products, of course, are incapable of capturing the subtleties of the original strip, and the merchandise can alter the public perception of the strip, especially when the merchandise is aimed at a younger audience than the strip is. The deeper concerns of some strips are ignored or condensed to fit the simple gag requirements of mugs and T-shirts. In addition, no one cartoonist has the time to write and draw a daily strip and do all the work of a licensing program. Inevitably, extra assistants and business people are required." Most major cartoonists do hire assistants to help with their strips, but Watterson always took pride in doing every bit of the work on "Calvin and Hobbes" by himself.

Watterson's speech continued: "Characters lose their believability as they start endorsing major companies and lend their faces to bedsheets and boxer shorts. The appealing innocence and sincerity of cartoon characters is corrupted when they use those qualities to peddle products. One starts to question whether characters say things because they mean it or because their sentiments sell T-shirts and greeting cards. Licensing has made some cartoonists extremely wealthy, but at a considerable loss to the precious little world they created." Despite a huge

loss of income, Watterson never budged on his refusal to merchandise "Calvin and Hobbes." As a *Los Angeles Times* writer remarked: "This dedication and integrity seem sadly out of place in an era that exalts hype over substance, but his readers and the art of the newspaper comic strip are richer for it."

If you enjoy the works of Bill Watterson, you may also want to check out the following comic strips:

The Far Side by Gary Larson.
FoxTrot by Bill Amend.
Get Fuzzy by Darby Conley.

Another battle Watterson fought was against the shrinking space allotted to comic strips in the newspaper. Newspaper circulation dropped dramatically in the last decades of the twentieth century, while printing costs rose. As a result, newspaper editors often limited the amount of space given over to comic strips. Cartoonists were forced, in turn, to adopt a simpler style so that words and drawings could be reproduced in this greatly reduced framework. Using his clout as a top cartoonist, Watterson gave newspapers an ultimatum: Give "Calvin and Hobbes" enough page space, or he would not allow the strip to be run. For the most part, newspapers complied with his wishes.

Although he was able to get the upper hand in most of his conflicts with the syndicates, Watterson still felt burdened by the constant pressures to be creative and to give up his resistance to the lucrative prospects of marketing. In 1991, he took a sabbatical from drawing his strip, and did so again in 1994. Each time, readers had to be satisfied with reruns of old strips. Then, on Christmas Day, 1995, the newspapers that published "Calvin and Hobbes" received a letter from Watterson, saying he felt he had contributed what he could within the constraints of daily deadlines and small panels. On December 31, 1995, the strip made its last appearance, with Calvin and Hobbes sledding down a hill in search of new adventure. Watterson and his wife returned to his home town in Ohio, where he now spends his time painting landscapes in oils and avoiding the limelight.

■ Biographical and Critical Sources

BOOKS

Holmen, Linda, *Teaching with Calvin and Hobbes*, Playground Publications (Fargo, ND), 1993.
Newsmakers 1990, Issue 3, Gale (Detroit, MI), 1990.

PERIODICALS

American Spectator, December, 1991, review of *Scientific Progress Goes Boink*, p. 14.
Booklist, June 15, 1988, review of *Something under the Bed Is Drooling*, p. 1701; December 15, 1988, review of *The Essential Calvin and Hobbes*, p. 675; December 1, 1989, review of *The Calvin and Hobbes Lazy Sunday Book*, p. 718; June 1, 1990, review of *Weirdos from Another Planet!*, p. 1865; November 15, 1992, review of *The Indispensable Calvin and Hobbes*, p. 570.
Bookwatch, December, 1989, review of *The Calvin and Hobbes Lazy Sunday Book*, p. 1; June, 1990, review of *Weirdos from Another Planet!*, p. 1; March, 1991, review of *The Authoritative Calvin and Hobbes*, p. 1; March, 1992, review of *Scientific Progress Goes Boink*, p. 1; July, 1992, review of *Attack of the Deranged Mutant Killer Monster Snow Goons*, p. 1; March, 1993, review of *The Indispensable Calvin and Hobbes*, p. 1; January, 1994, review of *The Days Are Just Packed*, p. 5; November, 1996, review of *It's a Magical World*, p. 11.
Boy's Life, September, 1993, p. 46.
Buffalo News (Buffalo, NY), December 22, 1998, "Where's Calvin Now?," p. C2.
Charlotte Observer (Charlotte, NC), July 29, 2003, Jeff Elder, "Where Have You Gone, Calvin, Opus and Cow?"
Christian Science Monitor, June 11, 1998, "Calvin Creator Says: 'I'd Rather Be Painting,'" p. 10.
Comics Journal, March, 1989.
Editor & Publisher, February 8, 1986; December 3, 1988; May 27, 1989; November 4, 1989; March 19, 1994, David Astor, "Watterson to Take Second Break from 'Calvin and Hobbes' Strip," p. 59; March 26, 1994, David Astor, "Mixed Response to Second Sabbatical," p. 30; November 18, 1995, "Strong Reaction to End of Comic Strip," p. 38; November 5, 2001, Dave Astor, "'Calvin' Book Is the First One in Half-Decade," p. 24.
Entertainment Weekly, November 24, 1995, p. 16.
Gazette (Colorado Springs, CO), March 21, 2004, Dave Philipps, "Whiz Kid: Cartoon Image Co-opted as a Symbol for All Sorts of Social Commentary," p. L1.

Honk!, January, 1987, Andrew Christie, interview with Watterson.
Investor's Business Daily, January 16, 2002, Jonah Keri, "Cartoonist Drew from the Well of Integrity," p. A3.
Kenyon College Alumni Bulletin, spring, 1988.
Knight Ridder/Tribune News Service, November 14, 1995, John Barry, "Comic Strips' Demise Is No Laughing Matter for Fans."
Library Journal, May 1, 1989, review of *The Calvin and Hobbes Lazy Sunday Book*, p. 69.
Los Angeles Times, April 1, 1987; April 17, 1988, review of *Something under the Bed Is Drooling*, p. 15; December 18, 1988, review of *The Essential Calvin and Hobbes*, p. 6; November 26, 1989, review of *The Calvin and Hobbes Lazy Sunday Book*, p. 34; April 8, 1990, review of *Weirdos from Another Planet!*, p. 10; April 28, 1991, review of *The Revenge of the Baby-Sat*, p. 14; December 1, 1991, review of *Scientific Progress Goes Boink*, p. 31; April 5, 1992, review of *Attack of the Deranged Mutant Killer Monster Snow Goons*, p. 10; December 6, 1992, review of *The Indispensable Calvin and Hobbes*, p. 39; November 19, 1995, review of *The Calvin and Hobbes Tenth Anniversary Book*, p. 6.
Mediaweek, December 4, 1995, Lewis Grossberger, "Hold That Tiger," p. 30.
Newsweek, December 7, 1992, review of *The Indispensable Calvin and Hobbes*, p. 71.
Philadelphia Inquirer, December 26, 1995, Joe Logan, "'Calvin and Hobbes' Is Latest Comic Strip to Be Killed by Creator."
Plain Dealer (Cleveland, OH), August 30, 1987, Gene Williams, "Watterson: Calvin's Other Alter Ego;" December 20, 1998, "Cartoonist Bill Watterson Returns to a Cloistered Life."
Rolling Stone, May 19, 1988.
San Francisco Chronicle, April 13, 1987.
School Library Journal, September, 1990, review of *Weirdos from Another Planet!*, p. 271.
Time, November 20, 1995, p. 123.
Wall Street Journal, November 3, 1988, David Brooks, review of *The Essential Calvin and Hobbes*, p. A18.

ONLINE

Cleveland Scene Online, http://www.clevescene.com/ (November 26, 2003), James Renner, "Missing!"
In Search of Bill Watterson, http://www.kerzap.com/calvin/billw.html/ (April 24, 2005).
PlanetCartoonist.com, http://www.planetcartoonist.com/ (January 14, 2005), "The State of Cartooning" (transcript of speech by Watterson).*

Meg Wolitzer

■ Personal

Born May 28, 1959, in New York, NY; daughter of Morton (a psychologist) and Hilma (a novelist; maiden name, Liebman) Wolitzer; married Richard Panek (an author); children: two sons. *Education:* Attended Smith College, 1977-79; Brown University, B.A., 1981.

■ Addresses

Home—New York, NY. *Agent*—Peter Matson, Literistic Ltd., 264 5th Ave., New York, NY.

■ Career

Writer. Skidmore College and Iowa Writer's Workshop, University of Iowa, writing instructor.

■ Awards, Honors

Winner of *Ms.* fiction contest, 1979, for "Diversions"; MacDowell Colony fellowship, 1981; Yaddo residency, 1983; National Endowment for the Arts grant, 1994; Pushcart Prize, 1998.

■ Writings

Sleepwalking (novel), Random House, 1982.
Caribou (juvenile), Greenwillow, 1984.
Sparks, Houghton, 1985.
Hidden Pictures, Houghton, 1986.
The Dream Book, Greenwillow (New York, NY), 1986.
This Is Your Life, Crown (New York, NY), 1988.
(With Jesse Green) *Nutcrackers: Devilishly Addictive Mind Twisters for the Insatiably Verbivorous,* Grove & Weidenfeld (New York, NY), 1991.
Tuesday Night Pie, Avon (New York, NY), 1993.
Wednesday Night Match, Avon (New York, NY), 1993.
Saturday Night Toast, Avon (New York, NY), 1993.
Friends for Life, Crown (New York, NY), 1994.
Fitzgerald Did It: The Writer's Guide to Mastering the Screenplay, Penguin (New York, NY), 1999.
Surrender, Dorothy, Scribner (New York, NY), 1999.
The Wife, Scribner (New York, NY), 2003.
The Position, Scribner (New York, NY), 2005.

Contributor to *New York Times* and *Ms.* Contributor of short stories to periodicals and anthologies, including *Best American Short Stories,* 1998; author of screenplays and radio plays.

■ Adaptations

This Is Your Life was adapted for the 1992 movie *This Is My Life,* directed by Nora Ephron; *The Wife* was optioned for a film to be written and directed by Jane Anderson.

■ Sidelights

"Humor is very important to me in life and work," author Meg Wolitzer revealed in an interview for *Barnes and Noble* Web site. "I take pleasure from laughing at movies, and crying at books, and sometimes vice versa." Such humor comes in handy, for Wolitzer tackles difficult themes in her novels. Susan Lotempio, writing in the *Buffalo News*, listed such themes: "Family. Death. Men and women. Relationships. These are the topics that Meg Wolitzer plumbs in her novels." Wolitzer's debut book, *Sleepwalking*, follows the stressed-out lives of three college women who make their way in the world. *Hidden Pictures*, from 1986, examines a lesbian relationship. *This Is Your Life* looks at dysfunction in the family, while *Friends for Life* is played more for laughs, the story of three girls/women, friends and rivals since they were five, who are now tested in their friendship at age thirty. Family problems, death, and homosexual relationships are mixed in Wolitzer's fifth novel, *Surrender, Dorothy*, and the frustration of the "better half" in a marriage goes under the Wolitzer lens in *The Wife*. With her 2004 novel, *The Position*, Wolitzer details another family whose lives have been forever altered in both comic and serious ways by a bestselling sex manual authored by the parents. Donna Seaman, writing in *Booklist*, affirmed Wolitzer's own judgment, noting that the author is "a warm, brisk, and extremely funny novelist." Seaman further noted, "Her light touch eschews pretension or false piety, enabling her to write about emotionally charged issues with insight and sophistication." Wolitzer's themes appeal to adult and young adult readers alike; for younger readers she has also penned several light novels.

Novelist at an Early Age

Born in Brooklyn, in 1959, Wolitzer was raised in Syosset, Long Island. In a way, she really never had a chance: writing and reading were pre-ordained. Her mother, Hilma, was an author whose novels were being published when her daughter was in high school and college. Equally interested in human stories was her father, Morton, a psychologist. "Stories," wrote Dan Cryer in *Newsday Online*, "were a staple in the Wolitzer household." Friday evenings after dinner the entire family went to the local library, with young Wolitzer seeking out the fiction shelves. "It's not surprising," Cryer added, "that Wolitzer's sights were set on writing early on." In both junior high and high school she edited literary magazines, and while other kids were involved in school athletics and social clubs, Wolitzer began making solo trips into New York City to visit museums, see first-run movies, and indulge in foreign restaurants.

Wolitzer attended Smith College from 1977 to 1979 and finished her undergraduate degree at Brown University in 1981. Coming of age in the 1970s, she was greatly affected by Sylvia Plath's novel *The Bell Jar*, and like Plath, was a guest editor at *Mademoiselle* magazine. Other books that influenced her include *The Dubliners* by James Joyce, *To the Lighthouse* by Virginia Woolf, J.D. Salinger's *Nine Stories*, Evelyn Waugh's *Brideshead Revisited*, and F. Scott Fitzgerald's *The Great Gatsby*. Even as she was in college, Wolitzer was working on her first novel. Her debut novel, *Sleepwalking*, appeared the year after she graduated from Brown.

Wolitzer's critically acclaimed first novel explores the often cold world of adolescents. By magnifying the rites of passage of three anorexic college girls, *Sleepwalking* "captures the very real unhappiness of growing up sensitive and misunderstood," wrote Deirdre M. Donahue in the *Washington Post Book World*. Called "death girls" by their peers because "they talked about death as if it were a country in Europe," these "high-strung, over-enriched, self-conscious" young ladies are preoccupied with suicidal poets. Laura identifies with the whiskey-voiced Anne Sexton; Naomi dyes her hair blonde in the Sylvia Plath tradition; and Claire, the focus of the novel, surrounds her eyes with kohl, covers her lips with dark gloss, and scents her wrists with ambergris like the fictional Lucy Ascher.

Overcome by the death of a beloved brother, Claire finds in Ascher's poetry the grief and the resentment of adulthood she feels. Claire's acceptance of life and the question of her survival occupy most of *Sleepwalking*, thus making the novel, Elaine Kendall wrote in the *Los Angeles Times Book Review*, "a remarkably sophisticated inquiry into the nature of such adolescent identity crises." Sara Blackburn noted in the *New York Times Book Review* that "Wolitzer quickly shows us, with empathy and wit, that these young women are so terrified of maturing that they'll do almost anything to paralyze themselves safely inside the lives of 'their' respective dead poets." "Wolitzer is so intelligent about adolescence," Laurie Stone stated in the *Village Voice Literary Supplement*. "She depicts it as a plague-ridden country to which children are summarily exiled and where they must wait, hoping for an exit visa or a rescue ship approaching through fog." "Wolitzer's gift," concluded Blackburn, "is being able to sense the tragicomic aspects of both childhood and adulthood and to describe them to us in a voice that is always lucid, insightful and, most of all, tempered with the hard-won wisdom of compassion."

Wolitzer was only twenty-three years old when she published *Sleepwalking*. Merryl Maleska of the *Chicago Tribune Book World*, noting the writer's youth,

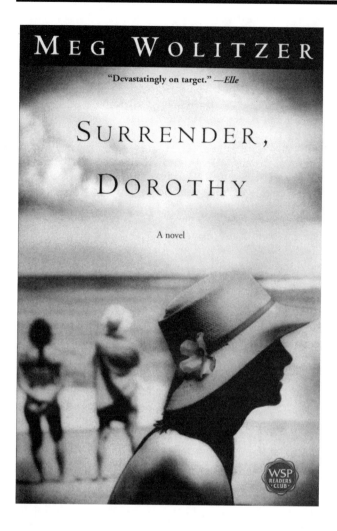

After a young woman is killed in a car accident, her friends and family are left to cope with her loss in this 1999 novel.

lationship, attempting, as Richard Eder noted in the *Los Angeles Times Book Review,* to "write about lesbian love, not as part of a separate culture, but trying to fit into mainstream life," and to make it seem as "normal and American as apple pie." Eder, however, was not impressed with this effort, complaining that the author does not give her characters "individuality" and that the book is "full of . . . authorial chaperoning." A more positive assessment came from Isabel Raphael, reviewing the novel in the London *Times.* Raphael felt that the book "has a depth, poise, and serenity that belie the author's own youth; for a second novel it is astonishingly confident."

After writing several books for younger readers, Wolitzer returned to adult fiction with the novel *This Is Your Life,* featuring two adolescent sisters, Opal and Erica, who try to work out a love-hate relationship between themselves and their famously overweight mother, Dottie. Dottie has made her weight into a profession, becoming a famous comedienne by telling fat jokes; however, such fame does not sit well with the daughters. Opal is as strong as her mom, but not overweight, while the older daughter, Erica, is both overweight and deadly serious. Penny Perrick, writing in the *Sunday Times,* noted that "the lives of Dottie and her daughters change when fat becomes a feminist issue." Perrick went on to comment, "This perceptive book charts the enormous, inescapable importance of personal appearance with a grim lack of pity." Jane DeLynn, reviewing the novel in the *Los Angeles Times Book Review,* felt that "many of these individual scenes, written in Wolitzer's usual pellucid style, are effective." However, DeLynn also thought that "much of the story is unconvincing and unbelievable." Adapted for a feature film, Wolitzer's novel appeared on the big screen in 1992 as *This Is My Life.*

concluded that *Sleepwalking* is an "astonishingly mature first novel. . . . The wisdom and sensibility of this novel and of its author—who can know so much at such a young age—leave one genuinely in awe."

Wolitzer's fourth novel, *Friends for Life,* appeared in 1994. Protagonists Meredith, Lisa, and Ann, have known each other since the fifth grade. Now nearing thirty, they live in Manhattan and meet for lunch regularly. While Meredith is a beautiful and successful television commentator, her friendly enemy Ann works at a publishing house for low wages. Lisa, a medical student, remains the go-between who keeps the three together. Personal crises strike the three and strain their relationship. A contributor for *Publishers Weekly* praised Wolitzer's "snappy dialogue and nicely captured trendy detail," but also criticized the main characters as "shallow, silly and superficial." Donna Seaman, writing in *Booklist,* found more to like in this novel, commending scenes "that sparkle with wit."

Fulfills Expectations of Promising Debut

Wolitzer's 1986 novel, *Hidden Pictures,* focuses on Laura Giovanni, who illustrates children's books, is married to a lawyer, and has a sensitive, bright boy. Her life in Manhattan seems perfect, but she is not close to her husband. After they go their separate ways, Laura is free to finally discover her lesbian identity, and finds a lover, Jane, to share her life with. Wolitzer examines the difficulties of such a re-

Of Death and Vengeful Wives

Wolitzer's fifth novel combines several of the themes from her earlier novels, such as family relations and homosexuality, adding the grieving process into the mix. *Surrender, Dorothy* is an "exquisitely wrought story about the sudden death of a charming 30-year-old woman," according to a *Publishes Weekly* contributor, who also praised Wolitzer's "seamless prose and light touch" in the book. Writing in the *New York Times*, Richard Bernstein noted that "Sara Swerdlow is the kind of person you do not expect to die young." When she dies in a traffic accident, her friends and relations are left to try to figure out how to carry on without her. The novel thus details what happens after Sara dies: Sara's mother, lover, and close friends come to understand that there are bonds between them, as well. Bernstein went on to call Wolitzer a "witty and likable

writer with a tenderhearted, critical awareness of the lighter-than-air quality of her characters." However, he also found that Wolitzer's novel "incarnates the very weightlessness it describes.... It is a divertimento, not a symphony." Further criticism came from Sylvia Brownrigg in the *New York Times Book Review*. Brownrigg felt that Wolitzer's "amiability proves something of a liability" in this novel with its "somber theme." The *Publishers Weekly* contributor, on the other hand, concluded that the author "enchants with wholly realized characters and a sly narrative voice that floats just above the angst and searing grief."

Marital relations move into the spotlight with the 2003 novel *The Wife*. Joan, forty years married to her novelist husband, Joe, is on a flight with him to Finland, where he will receive a major literary award, when she decides that enough is enough. A one-time writer herself, Joan has put her ambitions on the shelf to support Joe, who was her college English professor. Indeed, the story of their affair, translated to a novel, launched Joe's literary career. But Joe is less than grateful, carrying on with other women and being inattentive to his children by Joan. Now Joan decides that it is her turn: she will live the rest of her life for her, and not for her husband. To accomplish this mission, she threatens to reveal a nasty family secret: she has actually authored the books that have made Joe famous.

Reviewing this sixth title in the *New York Review of Books*, Claire Dederer found it a "light-stepping, streamlined" work, both a "puzzle and an entertainment," but also a "near heart-breaking document of feminist realpolitik." Other reviewers joined in the praise. A critic for London's *Mail on Sunday* called it a "smart, sad, funny and subtle novel," while Kera Bolonik, writing in the *Washington Post Book World*, felt that to dub *The Wife* Wolitzer's "most ambitious novel to date is an understatement." Bolonik further noted that "this important book introduces another side of a writer we thought we knew: Never before has she written so feverishly, so courageously." For Laurie Stone, reviewing *The Wife* in the *Los Angeles Times Book Review*, Wolitzer created a "rollicking, perfectly pitched triumph." Stone went on to note that "Wolitzer's unqualified achievement is creating satire that's purged of sentimentality and that seeks to protect nothing." Emma Hagestadt wrote in London's *Independent* that the novel is both "funny [and] angry," further observing that the author "does a wonderful job of satirizing the East Coast intelligentsia, while gleefully taking the lid off marriage, sexual politics and the creative ego." A contributor for *Publishers Weekly* similarly commented that "crisp pacing and dry wit carry us headlong into a devastating message about the price of love and fame," and

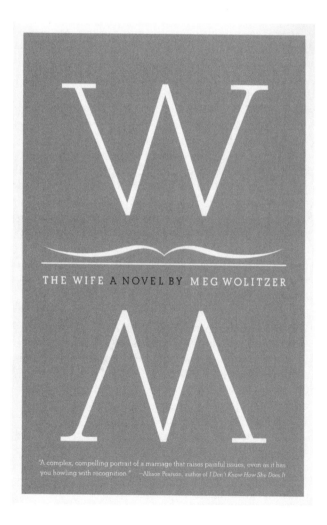

THE WIFE A NOVEL BY MEG WOLITZER

"A complex, compelling portrait of a marriage that raises painful issues, even as it has you howling with recognition." —Allison Pearson, author of *I Don't Know How She Does It*

The disintegration of a forty-year marriage is the subject of this 2003 work.

Entertainment Weekly's Nancy Miller called *The Wife* "an eviscerating and acerbically funny novel."

If you enjoy the works of Meg Wolitzer, you may also want to check out the following books:

Anne Tyler, *Breathing Lessons*, 1988.
Alice Sebold, *The Lovely Bones*, 2002.
Karen Joy Fowler, *The Jane Austen Book Club*, 2004.

More family and marital relations are served up in Wolitzer's 2004 novel, *The Position*. Paul and Roz Mellow co-authored a 1975 sex manual with illustrations of themselves in various intimate positions. The book became a huge hit, on the order of *The Joy of Sex*. Now several decades later, the Mellow children confront their parents, for they were traumatized as youngsters when they found and read their parents' book. Since then, the parents have divorced, Roz has married the book's illustrator, and now the publisher is about to re-issue their manual. As Nora Seton remarked in the *Houston Chronicle*, "Paul and Roz have neglected to imagine one remaining position, however: the position they've put their children in." On the eve of publication, the four children reassess the wreckage of their lives. Holly has recurrent drug problems, while Michael battles depression. All the children have troubled relationships and are unable to confront their feelings. Andrea Simakis in the *Plain Dealer* found that "Wolitzer's dead-on observations about sex, marriage and the family ties that strangle and bind are darkly funny and poignant without ever being mawkish." The critic for *Kirkus Reviews* claimed that "Wolitzer is best when she stirs the pot of familial and generational tensions." Beth E. Andersen, reviewing the novel for *Library Journal*, called it a "droll, often poignant tale."

In her *Barnes and Noble* Web site interview, Wolitzer concluded with some words of advice to young writers. A professional career in literature "is a protracted process, and . . . you have to be in it for the long run, and . . . you have to actually love writing, because the gratifications can be few and far between. But when they do come, these gratifications, they are . . . gratifying! You need to love the work itself, and to be really excited about writing, and comfortable being alone all day, and trusting your own instincts."

■ **Biographical and Critical Sources**

PERIODICALS

Booklist, March 1, 1994, Donna Seaman, review of *Friends for Life*, p. 1182; May 15, 1999, Ron Kaplan, review of *Fitzgerald Did It: The Writer's Guide to Mastering the Screenplay*, p. 1662; March 1, 2003, Donna Seaman, review of *The Wife*, p. 1143; December 15, 2004, Donna Seaman, review of *The Position*, p. 710.

Buffalo News (Buffalo, NY), September 7, 2004, Susan Lotempio, "Meg Wolitzer, Engaging in Life and Fiction," p. C1.

Chicago Tribune Book World, August 22, 1982, Merryl Maleska, review of *Sleepwalking*.

Daily Telegraph (London, England), September 25, 2004, Mary Wakefield, review of *The Wife*.

Entertainment Weekly, April 11, 2003, Nancy Miller, review of *The Wife*, p. 82.

Houston Chronicle, April 10, 2005, Nora Seton, review of *The Position*, p. 20.

Independent (London, England), July 30, 2004, Emma Hagestadt, review of *The Wife*, p. 27.

Kirkus Reviews, January 1, 2003, review of *The Wife*, p. 26; December 1, 2004, review of *The Position*, p. 1116.

Library Journal, February 1, 1982; March 1, 2003, Beth Gibbs, review of *The Wife*, p. 121; December 1, 2004, Beth E. Andersen, review of *The Position*, p. 106.

Los Angeles Times Book Review, July 1, 1982, Elaine Kendall, review of *Sleepwalking*; May 11, 1986, Richard Eder, review of *Hidden Pictures*, p. 3; October 9, 1988, Jane DeLynn, review of *This Is Your Life*, p. 8; April 11, 1999, Susan Salter Reynolds, review of *Surrender, Dorothy*, p. 11; July 27, 2003, Laurie Stone, review of *The Wife*, p. 11.

Mail on Sunday (London, England), October 3, 2004, review of *The Wife*, p. 87.

New York Times, April 7, 1999, Richard Bernstein, review of *Surrender, Dorothy*, p. E9; June 27, 2004, Meg Wolitzer, "Chapter II: The Park Bench," Section 14, p. 3.

New York Times Book Review, August 8, 1982, Sara Blackburn, review of *Sleepwalking*; March 3, 1985; June 8, 1986, Gloria Naylor, review of *Hidden Pictures*, p. 12; December 11, 1988, Kit Reed, review of *This Is Your Life*, p. 9; April 10, 1994, Linda Gray Sexton, review of *Friends for Life*, p. 716; April 25, 1999, Sylvia Brownrigg, review of *Surrender, Dorothy*, p. 22; April 20, 2003, Claire Dederer, review of *The Wife*, p. 11.

Organic Style, April, 2004, Barbara Jones, review of *The Wife*, p. 22.

People, April 7, 2003, John Freeman, review of *The Wife*, p. 45; April 4, 2005, Moira Bailey, review of *The Position*, p. 46.

Plain Dealer (Cleveland, OH), March 4, 2005, Andrea Simakis, review of *The Position*, p. E1.

Publishers Weekly, March 15, 1993, review of *Tuesday Night Pie*, p. 89; February 14, 1994, review of *Friends for Life*, p. 81; February 1, 1999, review of *Surrender, Dorothy*, p. 72; February 3, 2003, review of *The Wife*, p. 53; November 8, 2004, review of *The Position*, p. 32.

Star-Ledger (Newark, NJ), May 11, 2004, Roger Harris, review of *The Wife*, p. 5.

Sunday Times (London, England), April 30, 1989, Penny Perrick, review of *This Is Your Life.*

Times (London, England), November 6, 1986, Isabel Raphael, review of *Hidden Pictures.*

Times Literary Supplement, April 1, 1983.

Village Voice Literary Supplement, June, 1982, Laurie Stone, review of *Sleepwalking.*

Washington Post, March 7, 1994, Reeve Lindbergh, review of *Friends for Life*, p. C2.

Washington Post Book World, June 8, 1982, Deirdre M. Donahue, review of *Sleepwalking*; April 6, 2003, Kera Bolonik, review of *The Wife*, p. 6.

ONLINE

Barnes and Noble, http://www.barnesandnoble.com/ (November 18, 2004), "Meet the Authors: Meg Wolitzer."

Bookreporter.com, http://www.bookreporter.com/ (November 18, 2004), Heather Grimshaw, review of *The Wife.*

Brown Alumni Magazine Online, http://www.brownalumimagazine.com/ (September-October, 2003), Julia Bucci, review of *The Wife.*

Newsday Online, http://www.newsday.com/ (November 18, 2004), Dan Cryer, "Meg Wolitzer."

Random House, http://www.randomhouse.co.uk/ (November 18, 2004), "Author Interview: Meg Wolitzer."

Romantic Times, http://www.romantictimes.com/ (November 18, 2004), Jill M. Smith, review of *Friends for Life.**

Author/Artist Index

The following index gives the number of the volume in which an author/artist's biographical sketch appears: